MW01616719

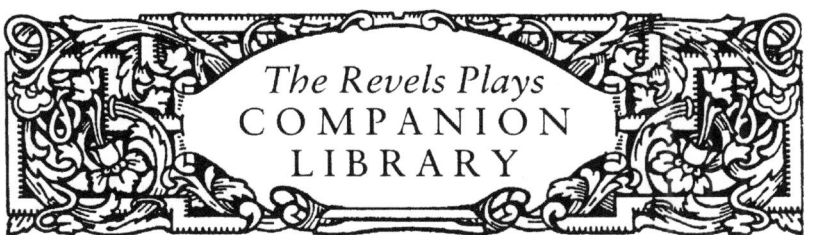

The Revels Plays
COMPANION
LIBRARY

SARAH DUSTAGHEER, PETER KIRWAN, DAVID MCINNIS and LUCY MUNRO
general editors

SUSAN BROCK, SUSAN CERASANO, PETER CORBIN, PAUL EDMONDSON,
E. A. J. HONIGMANN, GRACE IOPPOLO, J. R. MULRYNE,
ROBERT SMALLWOOD and MARTIN WHITE
former editors

For over fifty years *The Revels Plays* has provided for students of early modern English drama carefully edited texts of major and lesser-known plays of the period. *The Revels Plays Companion Library* aims to complement and expand upon the work of *The Revels Plays* through pioneering new research into the background, context, and afterlives of these plays and their authors.

The *Companion Library* aims to publish work that will enable students of early modern drama to examine the achievements of dramatists from a broader perspective, while supporting the work of editors through the development of contextual knowledge and new theoretical frameworks. The series includes volumes of a variety of kinds, from new editions of important primary documents to critical monographs and edited collections on authors and topics pertinent to *The Revels Plays*. Together, the two series offer a foundational base for new scholarship on early modern drama.

To buy or to find out more about the books currently available in this series, please go to: https://manchesteruniversitypress.co.uk/series/revels-plays-companion-library/

Queen Henrietta's Men and the Cockpit Repertory

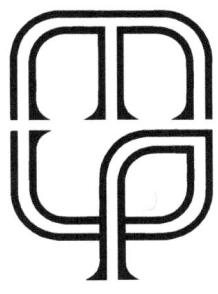

Manchester University Press

THE REVELS PLAYS COMPANION LIBRARY

Queen Henrietta's Men and the Cockpit Repertory

DRAMA ON THE DRURY LANE STAGE, 1626–36

Eleanor Collins

MANCHESTER UNIVERSITY PRESS

The right of Eleanor Collins to be identified as the author of this work has been asserted in accordance with the Copyright, Designs and Patents Act 1988.

Published by Manchester University Press
Oxford Road, Manchester, M13 9PL

www.manchesteruniversitypress.co.uk

British Library Cataloguing-in-Publication Data
A catalogue record for this book is available from the British Library

ISBN   978 0 7190 9086 8   hardback

First published 2025

The publisher has no responsibility for the persistence or accuracy of URLs for any external or third-party internet websites referred to in this book, and does not guarantee that any content on such websites is, or will remain, accurate or appropriate.

EU authorised representative for GPSR:
Easy Access System Europe, Mustamäe tee 50, 10621 Tallinn, Estonia
gpsr.requests@easproject.com

Typeset
by New Best-set Typesetters Ltd

CONTENTS

To Alex, Harry, and Zachary

Repertory, *n.*
Etymology: < classical Latin *repertōrium* inventory, catalogue (2nd or
3rd cent. A.D.) < *repert-*, past participial stem of *reperīre* to find by
looking, discover, to acquire, get, to find by inquiry, to devise, invent
(< *re-* re- *prefix* + *parere* to produce, bring forth
  Oxford English Dictionary, https://doi.org/10.1093/OED/9968435240

FIGURES

NOTES ON PRESENTATION

Throughout this book I have modernised the titles of plays and early modern publications for the reader's convenience. Since the original presentation of stage directions is key to the discussion in places, I have retained original spelling and punctuation in quotations from the plays themselves.

The dates of plays and their relation to the repertory are only mentioned where particularly relevant in discussion. Owing to the quantity of plays discussed in the book, and the complexities of many of the plays' relationships to the company and theatre, readers should refer to Appendix A for an overview of the relevant evidence for each play's connection to Queen Henrietta's Men. The appendix highlights any provisionality or uncertainty in terms of repertory attribution. Some early modern plays were later published under a title that differed from that under which they had previously been known or performed. With the exception of Shirley's *The Bird in a Cage*, now so well known under that title, all plays are referred to in discussion by the name under which they were performed.

Throughout this book, I refer to the Cockpit theatre as such, though it was also commonly known as the Phoenix following the rebuilding of the theatre in the wake of the 1617 Shrove Tuesday riots.

ACKNOWLEDGEMENTS

This book was written over many years and across many locations. It has been rewritten multiple times, once from the ground up. My debts are numerous and I am very grateful to all those who have assisted and encouraged along the way, and to those who remembered to ask me, in passing, about its progress. Its publication owes much to these reminders. I owe particular thanks to Kate McLuskie, who supervised the thesis from which the kernel of this book originates. Work on the thesis was funded by the AHRC and, without that generous assistance, would not have been possible. Friends and colleagues who provided invaluable comments on drafts of the work over the years include N. W. Bawcutt, Martin Butler, Sarah Dustagheer, Eva Griffith, Andy Gurr, William Ingram, Andy Kesson, Tom Lockwood, Christopher Matusiak, Lucy Munro, Richard Rowland, Julie Sanders, Erin Sullivan, and Martin Wiggins. Martin White critiqued the first draft in his role as (then) series editor, and Peter Kirwan and David McInnis have offered me support and guidance as current series editors while work on the book drew to a close. The academic debt that I owe to G. E. Bentley, Andy Gurr, N. W. Bawcutt, and Martin Wiggins is inestimable.

I would also like to thank the following friends and colleagues who provided support and thought-provoking conversation around various aspects of the work as it developed: Rebecca Bailey, Karen Britland, Richard Cave, Lizz Ketterer, Roslyn Knutson, Eleanor Lowe, Helen Ostovich, Will Sharpe, Emma Smith, and Adam Smyth. All errors are my own, and I look forward to being corrected by scholars of this and the next generations who harbour an enthusiasm for the dramatists of Queen Henrietta's Men and their plays.

In the course of my role as an editor I have been fortunate to work with many colleagues who have influenced and inspired my approach to academic work, both in terms of its writing and its publishing. These include, in particular, Peter Momtchiloff, Caroline Murray, Jacqueline Norton, Alison Powell, Rosemary Roberts, and Sarah Stanton. I have also been struck, on a daily basis, by the industry and commitment of the authors and editors with whom I work. They are too numerous to mention here but I wish to acknowledge the vibrant world of academic scholarship and publishing to which I have dedicated my professional life; it has proved a great inspiration. My thanks also go to Matthew Frost and Paul Clarke of MUP, who did not seem to mind how long this book was taking; and to Michelle Houston, Christian Lea, Siân Chapman, and Andrew Kirk for their work in bringing the book to publication.

Thank you to my parents, Irene and John, who supported my interest in literary studies and early modern drama from the beginning (and probably inculcated it in me at a young age). Also to my sisters, Anna and Thea, for unwavering friendship; my parents-in-law, Paul and Sarah, for all they do for our family; and Holly Lewsey, for so many years of laughter and conversation. Our cats, Monty and Bea, are much missed; they provided a source of great comfort and affection in the critical years over which the book started to come together.

Most of all, my thanks go to Alex Latter, for annotating numerous drafts, supporting me through prolonged periods of writing and revision, and demonstrating an unfailing belief in me and the book – a belief that was surely, sometimes, baffling even to him. This volume is dedicated to him and our two sons.

INTRODUCTION

The professional playing company known as Queen Henrietta's Men was one of the most important and influential in Caroline London. Between 1626 and 1636 the company performed at the Cockpit theatre, just behind Drury Lane, a theatre that was, until 1629, the newest of the indoor hall-playhouses. Over this time the company grew in stature and reputation to become the leading rival to the King's Men, performing a repertory – the collection of plays performed to entertain at the venue and at court – that was in direct competition with Shakespeare's plays, and offering something very different to the 'Shakespearean' norms around which much contemporary theatre history has been oriented. The drama that the company offered makes up one of the most substantial and diverse early modern repertories to survive in print, and ranges from a large number of under-explored and neglected plays to celebrated works written by dramatists now accepted in an early modern canon, including Thomas Heywood, James Shirley, and John Ford. Not only does the repertory of plays performed at the Cockpit account for a significant proportion of the surviving corpus of early modern drama written in the Caroline period, it also encompasses a selection of Elizabethan plays written in Philip Henslowe's day, alongside Jacobean revivals. The actor and theatre manager Christopher Beeston owned both the Cockpit theatre and its repertory, so that rather than the plays being attached to a particular company, they remained at the venue itself. This was a repertory that harnessed the richness of the theatrical past while drawing on and developing the latest fashions on the 1630s stage. In this way, it encapsulated the development of early modern drama – its unfolding catalogue of genres and diversity of styles – bringing it under one roof, and on to one stage.

Queen Henrietta's Men were managed by Christopher Beeston for the longest term at his Cockpit theatre. Throughout the years of their operation at the theatre the Cockpit repertory achieved its highest recognition and its greatest success, as evidenced by performances at court, allusions in contemporary printed material, and the volume of dramatic publications deriving from the company's tenure at the theatre. This book represents an effort to understand the ways in which Queen Henrietta's

Men accomplished these achievements in the competitive and changeable conditions of the period of their work, and to uncover some of the challenges that they faced. One of these challenges was the circumstances in which they inherited the repertory, as they did not oversee its composition from the outset, but took on a large part of it after the company's formation at the Cockpit. When Beeston first converted an old cockpit building into the new theatre in 1616, he subsequently worked to relocate Queen Anne's Men, the company he had been managing at the outdoor Red Bull theatre, to his new indoor venue – and a significant portion of the repertory they had been performing at the Red Bull came with them. This stock of plays was augmented by plays written under the tenancy of two further companies that performed at the theatre – Prince Charles's Men from 1619 to 1622, and Lady Elizabeth's from 1622 to 1625. The resultant corpus remained in the Cockpit for performance by Queen Henrietta's Men from 1626, but it had its own provenance and performance history before the new troupe came together there. This book is as much an investigation of the company's relationship to the Cockpit repertory, therefore, as it is an exploration of its contribution to it.

The inheritance of a repertory was one of the conditions that enabled the company's success, but the original transfer of plays from the Red Bull to the Cockpit has been construed as problematic and controversial in some critical accounts. This owes in part to interpretations of the riot that targeted (among other buildings in London) the newly converted theatre on 4 March 1617, just after the move of Queen Anne's Men, during which the Cockpit was assailed by 'lewde and loose persons, apprentices and others'.[1] The rioters were reported to have numbered between three and four thousand, some of whom 'wounded divers of the players, broke open their trunckes, & whatt apparrell, bookes, or other things they found, they burnt & cutt in peeces; & not content herewith, gott on the top of the house, & untiled it'.[2] Edward Sherbourne wrote that 'one prentise was slaine, being shott throughe the head with a pistoll, & many other of their fellowes were sore hurt', while John Chamberlain reported that Queen Anne's Men 'defended themselves as well as they could and slew three of them [the rioters] with shot and hurt divers'.[3]

The causes of the riot remain unclear, but the unrest has been interpreted in theatre history as a response to Beeston's transfer of the Red Bull repertory from the amphitheatre playhouse to his new indoor venue. Charles J. Sisson first suggested a direct causal relationship between the recent transfer and the riot when he stated, in a footnote, that the company's move constituted a 'desertion of the Red Bull' which, compounded by a lawsuit involving Beeston that became 'a matter of local notoriety', supplied grounds for resentful rioting at the company's new theatre.[4] Andrew

Gurr has since suggested that it was the relocation of a repertory that was responsible for the uprising, since the Cockpit's entry prices were higher and hence prohibitively expensive for the 'citizen' audiences of the Red Bull; the amphitheatre audience was 'presumably in protest at having their plays taken away'.[5] This is an appealing narrative in that it hinges on the premise that audiences cared about repertory, that plays made a difference to people's lives, and that the nature of plays available to audiences was a potentially inflammatory consideration in repertory management. But there are a number of considerations that undermine the riot's specificity to the repertory transfer, not least of which is the general dispersion of rioting around London on this date. Chamberlain writes that there were riots that day 'in divers places, as Finsburie feilds, about Wapping by St. Katherines, and in Lincolns Ynne fields, in which places beeing assembled in great numbers they fell to great disorders in pulling downe of houses'.[6] He goes on to describe how

> in Finsburie they brake the prison and let out all the prisoners, spoyled the house by untiling and breaking downe the roofe and all the windowes and at Wapping they pulled downe seven or eight houses and defaced five times as many, besides many other outrages as beating the sheriffe from his horse with stones.[7]

The work of cultural historians has also suggested, more generally, that disturbances of the peace rarely 'had as their object the attainment of specific, realistic goals', such as the return of a repertory to its original audience, in this particular instance.[8] The established theatre historical account does not fit with either the particular evidence, then, or the broader historiography of unrest in the capital.

The narrative of a repertory-induced riot is enduring, however, and its emphasis on reception-based readings of early modern drama and the importance of audience demand and preference provides an important context for this study. Critical engagement with the circumstances of the 1617 riot provides more than a chronicle of the Cockpit companies' fortunes as vested in the wood and brick of their playhouse, but has helped define the axes of audience and taste along which interpretation of early modern repertories is often coordinated – and which this book seeks to explore. For many years the understanding of amphitheatre and hall-playhouse drama was motivated by readings of the plays that linked their content and style to the social status, mental acuity, and cultural competencies of their audiences.[9] Known for its spectacular, 'tear-throat', 'drum-and-trumpet' plays, the Red Bull's reputation is often founded upon its provision of cheap entertainment for what has been understood as a plebeian and culturally negligible audience; the design of its plays is assumed to have sated the undiscerning appetites of 'ignorant asses' and 'Greasie-apron'-ed 'Fishwives'.[10] These are constructions that issued from the pens and print-houses of early modern writers and publishers themselves, but which have, in the past, been imported directly into criticism as factually accurate and historically 'true'.[11] It is a narrative that finds expression in readings of the 1617 riot which posit the boisterous Red Bull citizens as its agents; a core of fiercely local and loyal audience members who were willing to act upon their demands for a repertory over which they asserted ownership, its having originated in the playhouse which they frequented.[12]

In contrast, the Cockpit theatre has been diametrically opposed to the Red Bull in critical accounts. Its higher admission prices ensured a clientele with more disposable income. This, combined with the diminished size of the indoor theatres (thought to have curtailed the dramatic use of trumpets, drums and battle scenes), suggested to some critics a more sophisticated audience with refined tastes.[13] While it is now widely accepted that Shakespeare's Globe and Blackfriars plays moved regularly between the two venues,[14] this recognition has transferred less readily to the wider field of theatre history, due in part to the relative neglect of theatres and repertories beyond those associated with the King's Men. These questions of audience and taste, and the relationships that held between drama that originated in the amphitheatres and plays written newly for the Cockpit stage, provide central focal points of this study.

The interesting challenge that the Cockpit repertory has posed for criticism is that, according to the central tenets of repertory study, it embodies more than one corpus of plays. The methodology of repertory study holds that the relationship between a company's repertory and its conditions of production was shaping, and dynamic; and that, as Scott McMillin and Sally Beth Maclean argue, 'acting companies were respon-sible for the plays they performed and can be evaluated according to that responsibility'.[15] The emphasis on company and company productions can be traced back to the archival positivism of Sisson, in his accumula-tion of company-based evidence on an empirical basis, and of G. F. Reynolds, who explored the architectural features of the Red Bull in relation to the staging requirements of the extant repertory.[16] The focus given to the study of particular companies in more recent theatre history has been developed by the work of McMillin and Maclean on the first Queen's Men of the 1580s, Roslyn Knutson on the Lord Chamberlain's/King's Men, Mary Bly on the King's Revels, Lucy Munro on the Children of the Revels, Andrew Gurr on the Lord Chamberlain's/King's Men and the Admiral's Men, respectively, Tom Rutter – also on the Admiral's Men – and Eva Griffith on the Jacobean Queen's Men (Queen Anne's Men) at the Red Bull.[17] As these vital studies have shown, repertory-based approaches are able to liberate plays and company histories from author-centred studies, and resituate them according to an emphasis on the specific relationships between conditions of production and performance within a repertory system on the early modern stage. They share in common the central principle that companies, theatres, and repertories could all be reciprocally bound, defining of each other in some measure. When audience preference and demand enter the equation and are recognised as defining conditions of production, these factors too can play an important role in the analysis and interpretation of repertory – and in the case of the Red Bull, that relationship between audience and repertory has been expressed with unusual force and particularity. Extracting the Red Bull plays from the conditions that are thought to have defined them has proved difficult in past theatre-historical accounts, which is what has made the plays' transfer to the Cockpit appear so incongruous, if not somehow transgressive, as readings of the riot as a response to the move have shown.

Considerations of company identity and reputation are also tied into the debate, as is the definition of 'company' itself. McMillin and Maclean emphasise the importance in repertory study of identifying the 'special characteristics which gave [... a] company its identity', one of which was 'its sense of what constituted a worthwhile repertory of plays'.[18] The question of what makes a company is complicated, given that they were not fixed or stable entities. Personnel shifted, and many companies transferred between two or more theatres. Repertories themselves were constantly changeable, expanding with new acquisitions and contracting with the transfer or loss of plays. The idea that repertory has the capacity to be defining is important, and the extent to which company identity was tied to the plays that the company produced is fundamental to this study. But at the same time the notion of a repertory as dynamic is key to resolving the critical oppositions that have been invoked in accounts of the incorporation of characteristically 'Red Bull' fare into the repertory of Queen Henrietta's Men. Though repertory studies focused on other companies and theatres have treated revivals as an important part of company activity and repertory composition, historical accounts of the Red Bull and Cockpit repertories – including those presented by Bentley and Gurr – have, in the past, found irreconcilable differences between the dramas written for each venue. At least in part, this is because those accounts implicitly lean towards an idea of repertory as fixed, frozen in time, and inseparable from its original circumstances of production; Red Bull plays are thought to contain a core of meaning that inheres in them somehow, encoded in a way that only the original audience can access. These apparently divisive plays are thought to emblematise their origins and provenance in the most fundamental and resolute of ways. But repertories not only developed and

evolved over time; individual plays within them changed with each itera-
tion, in every performance. The responsiveness of repertory, its dependence
on context and the moment of enactment, meant that plays of *any* origin
might be reimagined and fundamentally altered on alternative stages. The
transfer of amphitheatre plays to the Cockpit was always going to induce
change, some form of metamorphosis in the drama.

Conceiving of plays that originated from the Red Bull as in some way
essentially and inextricably locked to that theatre, even following their
removal from it, also tends to assume that companies do not actively
engage or transform repertory. This issue concerns the degree to which
companies could shape an inherited repertory. As we know, Queen
Henrietta's Men were crucially bound to the legacies of their predecessors;
the troupe 'owned' some of the repertory in performance, but those plays
were not written *for* them, with the company in mind at the moment of
conception. Component parts of this same repertory had already enabled
the commercial success of previous companies at the Cockpit and at a
number of amphitheatres besides the Red Bull, and the stock of plays held
at the Cockpit in 1636 would also go on to comprise part of the repertory
of Beeston's Boys. These were plays with chameleon qualities, which seem
to have blended into a variety of different environments and contexts.
They threaten to undo the traditional binding of repertory to company,
and dissolve the lines along which theatre companies might seek to define
themselves – and along which a repertory study might operate.

In this book I suggest that it is precisely this potential for dislocation
between the inherited repertory and Queen Henrietta's Men that makes the
company and its collaborative activities a subject of such rich inquiry. The
inheritance of a repertory was both an advantage and a potential encum-
brance that the company recognised as such, and actively addressed in its
work. The collaborative labour of the dramatists and players of Queen
Henrietta's Men worked to transform a more passive form of ownership
into something active, creative, and dynamic, as the company members
strove to create a new aesthetic on their stage, which fully assimilated
and exploited the Cockpit's legacy in licensed plays. This was a strategy
that involved not only the revival but the reactivation of old drama, and
it was achieved in the writing of new plays to run in repertory beside
them, the revision of old drama, and in the realisation of its performance,
by the actors.

As I have noted, repertory studies shift critical focus away from originating individual authors, and towards patterns or characteristic features
that hold across a corpus of works that share in common their wider
conditions of production. The identification of those patterns or features
is crucial, for they establish the legitimacy of the approach, providing
evidence of the impact that belonging to a particular repertory could have

upon the design of its plays. But the account that follows suggests that, in important ways, it was the variety of the drama available at the Cockpit that distinguished the repertory, a corpus that was characterised by its range and diversity. The attempt to identify cohesion across a collection of plays as broad and eclectic as the repertory of Queen Henrietta's Men is by no means straightforward or even necessarily desirable, but this book offers an analysis of the ways in which the company found itself working towards that same end. It explores the company's attempts to establish a measure of coherence across the fare that it offered, both in terms of its aesthetics and theatrical presentation, and in terms of how the repertory related to cultural constructions of particular dramatic types – including revivals – as they developed over the 1630s.

*

This book is the first repertory study to focus on professional theatre in the Caroline period, and has been buoyed by a wave of critical interest in this later period of pre-Restoration drama. Contributions to this scholarly focus include Matthew Steggle's important monograph on Richard Brome, Adam Zucker and Alan B. Farmer's *Localizing Caroline Drama*, and a revival of interest in the drama of John Ford, James Shirley, Thomas Heywood, and Richard Brome, with the publication of major new scholarly editions of their works now in print and forthcoming.[19] The Caroline era was a period in which the professional theatre was relatively established, but was undergoing major changes in terms of the conditions under which drama was being produced, with the emergence of the courtier playwrights on to the scene. The appearance of new dramatists who were connected with the court influenced Caroline drama in terms of its content and themes, but it also led to changes in the way that professional drama was perceived or written about, and altered the criteria by which plays and dramatic traditions were evaluated – at least as construed in print. The 1630s is also a period characterised in current criticism by the cultural dominance of the hall-playhouses. It is important to recognise that the amphitheatre Red Bull and Fortune were still licensing new plays in this period, however. The marginalisation of the amphitheatres in accounts of Caroline drama has been unjust, and one of the aims of this study is to draw attention to the value and importance of amphitheatre-derived plays over this period. The work of Eva Griffith has made important claims in this respect, suggesting that Beeston retained his interest in the Red Bull for years after moving to the Cockpit – an indicator of the outdoor venue's continued worth, and that of the company performing there.[20] The phenomenon of adult companies performing in hall-playhouses was an established and important part of the theatrical landscape over this time, however, and the wider popularity of indoor playing spaces is evidenced further by the opening of another indoor theatre in 1629, Salisbury Court. Originally the home of performances by the King's Revels, which contained a higher proportion of boys than rival troupes at the time, the venue was used by adult troupes later in the period.

The Salisbury Court theatre is worth pausing over for a moment, since it became the home of another company called Queen Henrietta's Men over the Caroline period. In 1636/37 the relationship between company and theatre that the original Queen Henrietta's Men had forged during their tenure at the Cockpit was broken and the company dissolved; a new Queen's Men was formed. The new company was largely distinct from the former troupe in all but name. A few of the Cockpit's actors crossed to Salisbury Court, but the majority of the new company's personnel were independently recruited. The management, venue, and (largely) the repertory of the second Queen Henrietta's Men were separate – they formed, to the intents and purposes of this study, a distinct collaboration, and are not discussed here; to do so would require addressing a different set of repertory concerns, an alternative account of company management, and scrutiny of a different corpus of plays. Though interesting connections have been identified between the two companies, the current study concentrates solely upon the Cockpit company as it was managed at that theatre by Christopher Beeston, and the plays it performed there.[21]

It is this repertory that has also benefited from a succession of theatrical revivals over the last decade or so, invigorated in part by the opening of the Sam Wanamaker Playhouse at the Globe. Both the SWP and the Royal Shakespeare Company committed to a series of Jacobean and Caroline revivals during this period, making a range of hitherto unseen drama available on the public stage. Revivals of plays from the Cockpit repertory have included *'Tis Pity She's a Whore*, *The Knight of the Burning Pestle*, and *The Changeling* at the SWP, while the RSC produced *The Witch of Edmonton* in 2014, and productions of *The Jew of Malta* and Ford's *Love's Sacrifice* in 2015. This awakened interest in plays performed at the Cockpit repertory renders a fuller exploration of the work of Queen Henrietta's Men at the theatre timely, if not already overdue, and has enriched and enhanced the discussion of the repertory in performance where appropriate.

Experience of the plays in modern performance provides a unique (and historically precarious) category of evidence, but the account that follows is facilitated, most importantly, by a strong evidence base in terms of the quantity of extant printed plays known to have been performed in the repertory. These have survived in print at a very high rate: of a corpus of just over seventy known plays, only one is lost. An unknown and unknowable number of untraceable plays must be acknowledged, however, since as it stands this seems to be an extraordinarily high ratio of extant to lost plays.[22] David McInnis and Matthew Steggle give due warning of the 'unjustified inferences' that may arise from ignorance of any body of lost plays, since '[what] strikes us as dominant or frequent may in fact be an over-represented aberration'.[23] Proportions aside, the number of Cockpit plays to survive in print is likely to owe in part to periodisation, since it was towards the later period of this era of theatre (c. 1629–40) that a 'second boom' in the printing of plays occurred, seeing 'the highest edition totals of the entire early modern period' in play publication.[24] The work of Zachary Lesser, Alan B. Farmer, Douglas Brooks, and Lukas Erne has emphasised the role of printers and publishers as collaborative agents, whose intervention both propelled strategies of repertory on the stage and operated within the sphere of an emerging market for reader-ships.[25] By this time, plays were being appropriated by industries beyond the theatre, and repertories could be put to use beyond their theatrical origination. These factors did not only apply to new plays, but prompted the reissue and in some cases the first issue of older revivals. The body of stock left over from predecessors at the Cockpit underwent a revival that ensured not only their retention upon the stage, but also, in some cases, their publication. In this sense, the role of print in shaping the historical reconstruction of a repertory – let alone enabling a measure of access to it – is fundamental.

Besides the play-texts themselves lie even more contingent sources: the transcripts of Henry Herbert's office-book, which ostensibly present a large quantity of detail about the licensing (and dating) of plays in the period. They also present details about Herbert's interactions with company personnel, the companies' visits to court, and the reception of their plays both by a royal audience and by Herbert himself. The 'office-book' rep-resents a historical archive as singularly crucial and unique to the Caroline period as Henslowe's diary is to the Elizabethan era of playing, but unfor-tunately it is lost. The only access we have to its contents is through a series of transcripts, for which no means of verification survives after the original papers disappeared in around 1818.[26] The transcripts have a complicated provenance, and N. W. Bawcutt's invaluable edition should be consulted by anyone interested to learn more. Bawcutt suggests that Edmond Malone, the principal transcriber, might have recorded as little as a sixth of the complete records from 1625 to 1637.[27] This period coincides almost exactly with the career of the first incarnation of Queen Henrietta's Men. Following the publication of extracts in 1790, 1797, 1799, and 1818, Craven Ord then gained access to the manuscripts and transcribed a large number of entertainment licences.[28] Ord's transcript changed hands at least twice, and when Jacob Henry Burn came to own the transcript he copied those play-licences transcribed by Ord into a notebook that he was compiling on the office of the Master of the Revels, and also glued in a few selected cuttings from Ord.[29]

When Burn died, his papers were redistributed, but the Ord transcript was later identified around 1937 as dispersed among the scrapbook collection of J. O. Halliwell-Phillipps. There are many tens of scrapbooks in all; those containing extracts from the Ord manuscript are all held now in the Folger and in the library of Edinburgh University. Each is compiled according to the organising principle of a chosen name or grouping: 'The Fortune', 'Burbage', 'Plague and Lent', and 'Noble Companies', to name a few. Aside from the Ord transcripts, the scrapbooks contain newspaper clippings, excised quarto title-pages and cast-lists, scenes cut out from modern editions, scraps of paper inscribed with original signatures, hand-drawn sketches of family trees, and scraps of biography. Each entry is either glued in place or pinned with a needle, and annotated according to the perspective from which Halliwell-Phillipps was approaching the evidence – from a 'Fortune Playhouse' angle, for instance, or with an interest in a specific stage direction. The scrapbooks preserve both the most physical and crude manifestation of the selective process of sifting historical data, and some of the only surviving transcripts that have become crucial to our construction of the Caroline theatre.

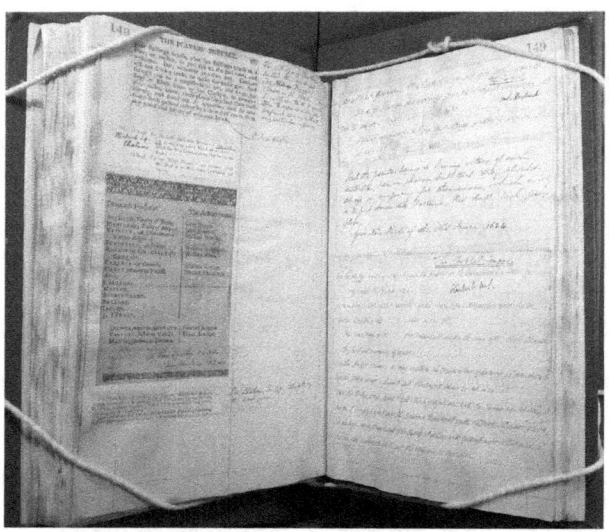

1   Scrapbooks of J. O. Halliwell-Phillipps, catalogue record W.b.156, pp. 148–9, Folger Shakespeare Library

This study tries to remain alert to the problems inherent in the transcripts we have left to work with; at the same time, they are a useful and
motivating reminder of the process of narrative building that underpins
theatre history. Halliwell-Phillipps adopted a number of organising principles in the assembly of his scrapbooks, focal points around which to
assemble evidence and read company history. Edmond Malone used a
similar approach when he came to transcribe entries from the office-book,
but made the King's Men the object of his attention, loyal to his particular
interest in Shakespeare and an academic compulsion that he termed
'Shakspearomania'.[30] When he transcribed Herbert's entries with a selective emphasis on that company and prior to the loss of the original office-
book, his scholarly approach became a self-fulfilling prophecy, a story in
which the King's Men dominated.

This level of scrutiny, the searching of the records for signs of
Shakespeare's influence – the thread that binds up the story – recalls the
etymology of repertory, from the Latin *reperire*: to 'find by looking, discover'. It is the 'Shakspearomaniac' tendencies of an established trajectory
of theatre history that have found, repeatedly, evidence in the King's Men's
repertory for their artistic excellence and dominance; evidence in the archives
for their status as a paradigmatic company model – a beacon of professional theatre in the early modern period. One of this book's most fundamental aims is to explore the extent to which the history of Queen
Henrietta's Men represents a different mode of operation to that provided
by the practices of the King's Men. In terms of their relationship to the
court, their business model, and the dramatic standard they came to represent over the Caroline period, Queen Henrietta's Men diverged in strategy
from their main competitors. Underlying the account is the recognition
that what is found may always be what has been looked for, always a
construction, a presentation, or a performance.

*

The book is divided into two parts: the first explores the circumstances
of production which underpinned company operation, and the second
turns its attention to a more detailed exploration of the plays themselves,
and the repertory in performance.

Chapter 1 examines the formation, composition, and commercial operation of Queen Henrietta's Men, and establishes the particular circumstances
at the Cockpit under which the actors, management, and dramatists worked.
This chapter explores in particular the role of Christopher Beeston as
manager of the company, and the ways in which he provided for it –
especially in terms of the provision of playbooks and props. The chapter
outlines the shape of the company and introduces its key personnel, as

well as establishing the ways in which both actors and playwrights were managed. The discussion extends to an analysis of the means by which Beeston acquired new drama for Queen Henrietta's Men, examining the historical precedents for contractual bindings between dramatist and playwright, and identifying the wider patterns of the nature of dramatists' employment over this period. The discussion establishes the relative autonomy of the Cockpit dramatists and the players of Queen Henrietta's Men, and reassesses the extent of Beeston's control over the company. Critical accounts have presented the impresario manager as tyrannical and ruthless, but his dealings from 1625/26 onwards do not support this reading. The company that emerges from this account is more collaborative, its agents more autonomous, than previous histories of the company have allowed. The formation of Queen Henrietta's Men appears much riskier; Beeston's authority more provisional.

Chapter 2 moves on to address the connections between Queen Henrietta's Men and the court, and the extent to which the company's relationship with its namesake patron might have influenced the repertory. The court's role in 1630s drama has been central and defining in criticism, and Queen Henrietta Maria's performances and theatrical patronage have inspired a rich variety of scholarship on the connections between professional theatre and courtly preoccupations and fashions over this time. The chapter provides an account of the company's visits to court, and considers the performance conditions and staging requirements of the plays that it took there. It goes on to address the influence that courtly tastes might have had upon the repertory, and identifies a specific period around 1633 during which Queen Henrietta's Men made a concerted effort to attract royal attention, staging a new play by the courtier Thomas Killigrew alongside drama that appealed to the queen's interests, including Heywood's *Love's Mistress*. The chapter provides an overview of the material rewards, and challenges, that performance at court required, and a sense of how far the Cockpit dramatists might have been motivated by the prospect of royal favour and the provision of courtly entertainment. It also explores the considerable influence that Henry Herbert had on repertory composition and the company's career, both at court and on the commercial stage.

The next chapter moves from a consideration of material circumstances and commercial imperatives to analyse the reception of the Cockpit repertory in the period, as far as it can be recovered, and the cultural contexts in which the company's drama was performed. It engages in particular with constructions of audience taste and the theatrical currency of different traditions of drama as they were configured and recorded in early modern print, including in the prologues and prefatory materials of the plays themselves. The constructions of audience adopted in these texts are key to our understanding of the reception of early modern drama and permeate criticism today, but little sustained analysis of their development and widespread appropriation has taken place. This account draws on a wide range of evidence from the period to construct a cultural history of theatrical taste, mapping its development over the period. It concludes with an account of the 'second war of the theatres', in which Thomas Carew denigrated the Cockpit repertory by associating it specifically with the 'adulterate' stage of the Red Bull. The chapter argues that the reception of revivals and drama that was construed as old-fashioned and rustic was a specific concern with which Queen Henrietta's Men found themselves directly engaged – and which was exacerbated by the emergence of the courtier playwrights in the 1630s. This context would come to influence the ways in which the company chose to position, perform, and develop the repertory.

Chapter 4 opens the second half of the book, which focuses on the repertory in performance. It explores the staging of the repertory, and draws on historical evidence and performance-based approaches to explore how Queen Henrietta's Men might have realised the repertory in play. The drawings of an indoor theatre by John Webb, held in Worcester College, Oxford, were once thought to be Inigo Jones's drawings of the Cockpit, and were read as evidence of its physical structure and shape; but their relationship to Beeston's venue has since been cast into grave doubt.[31] While the chapter may go some way towards providing a sketch of the material features of the theatre, its main focus is on providing an overview of the company's collaborative efforts in shaping the repertory's aesthetic and adapting dramatic traditions for the indoor stage. In particular, it examines the interplay between Queen Henrietta's Men's spectacular revivals – including *The Bloody Banquet*, Heywood's *Ages* plays, and *The Rape of Lucrece* – and new plays for the company. The discussion pays special attention to the challenges and opportunities that the transfer of amphitheatre drama into the indoor hall-playhouse provided for the company, and considers the physical requirements of the drama as suggested by the printed play-texts. It also draws on the research and experience that has come out of performances in the Sam Wanamaker Playhouse to consider the effect of moving the revivals indoors to the intimate, enclosed, candlelit space of the hall-playhouse, examining the shifts in theatrical effect and meaning that such a relocation might have had. Addressing staging requirements including duelling, dancing, the presentation of ghosts and gods, and the use of light and darkness on the stage, the chapter provides new dramatic contexts in the 1630s for the performance of a diverse body of Elizabethan, Jacobean, and Caroline drama. A rich account of the content of the repertory is provided, with a fresh recognition of the possibilities for theatrical experience in the 1630s indoor playhouse that fits with the evidence for revivals.

The final two chapters move to an analysis of the ways in which Thomas Heywood and James Shirley shaped the repertory and approached their roles as dramatists for the company. These chapters may be more traditionally author-focused than some repertory studies have previously allowed, but I suggest that the contribution of these particular dramatists to the repertory is both distinctive and conspicuous.[32] Both Heywood and Shirley went to remarkable lengths to write their drama with the particular requirements and skills of the company in mind; as such, their plays were always collaborative productions and, cumulatively, became essential to the success and cohesion of the repertory. The chapter on Thomas Heywood uncovers his encounters with the plays he had written for the Red Bull stage in revival, decades later at the Cockpit. This chapter builds on the analysis of staging and revivals undertaken in Chapter 4 to explore Heywood's role in creating new dramatic currency, and new aesthetic contexts, for his old plays. It explores revision and serialisation, the company's investment in the development of old traditions onstage, and the themes and arguments of *Love's Mistress*. This play was written for the company in 1634, and commits an entire narrative framework to working through the assumption that rambunctious, amphitheatre drama was suitable only for the dull senses of poor citizens. *Love's Mistress* has been traditionally interpreted through its courtly connections, but here it is relocated to its repertory context, in an argument which suggests that the play's defining and driving purpose is the performance of a strenuous renegotiation of aesthetic taste. The play recalibrates audience preference and expectations in line with the more traditional elements of the Cockpit repertory, with its 'ignorant' pleasures of spectacle, clowns, 'noyse and shows'. The discussion illuminates the cultural work that *Love's Mistress* performed for the repertory to which it belonged, and argues that its cultural agenda was directly related to its performance at the Cockpit.

The last chapter examines the role that James Shirley, principal dramatist for Queen Henrietta's Men between 1626 and 1634, played in repertory composition. A professional dramatist, Shirley developed his own courtly connections in the 1630s and was described as a Valet to the Queen's Chamber in 1634. This chapter evaluates Shirley's two roles as a Queen's Man – as a servant to Henrietta Maria, and as a company dramatist for her namesake company. It unpicks how these roles have been conflated in readings of the repertory, and goes on to explore his playful and (at times) irreverent approach to the repertory, particularly with respect to the appropriation of archaic source material, experimentation with theatrical convention, and a sustained engagement with the process of storytelling and the demands of performance. The chapter gives particular emphasis to Shirley's dramatic adaptation of Sidney's *Arcadia* and to a repertory-based interpretation of *The Bird in a Cage*, a play that is often read as a defence of Henrietta Maria's theatrical performances at court. It suggests that while the court's influences can be usefully identified in Shirley's writing, his plays need not be limited or defined by them, and it underscores Shirley's role with respect to consolidating and developing the repertory in new directions, while repurposing the literary and theatrical past, and remaining alert to the demands and challenges of the theatre profession.

The picture that emerges of Queen Henrietta's Men is one of a company of professionals at the height of their creative potential, working flexibly, energetically, and collaboratively within the vibrant, competitive, and changeable landscape of 1630s theatre, and engaging self-reflexively with the depth and breadth of their theatrical heritage while looking ahead, all the time, to the next performance, the newest addition to the repertory, and the shifting artistic and professional contexts in which their future productions would be received. Attention to Beeston's company, and to what motivated them in terms of both the money and the art that they made, sheds new light on assumptions that have long governed the telling of theatre history and which have tended to revolve around Shakespeare-led accounts of success, industry, and creative accomplishment. It also provides important methodological insights into repertory studies as a broader endeavour, when we think of plays as portable, changeable, inherently adaptable works capable both of becoming unfixed from their origins and their connections with either company or venue, and of becoming newly fixed to, or imbricated in, distinct theatrical contexts.

This book aims to give a detailed account of what Queen Henrietta's Men offered to their audiences and competitors, and also a sense of what they can offer to the study of theatre history more broadly. It illustrates the rewards of attention to this later period of early modern drama, in terms of the appreciation of these lively years of playwriting against the dramatic contexts that came before the 1630s; in terms of evaluating the claims and premises of theatre history as a discipline; and in terms of how we might conceive of company and repertory histories as new research continues in the years and decades ahead.

NOTES

1 'A letter to the Lord Major and Aldermen of London, and Commissioners of Oyer and Terminer in the citty of London and countye of Midlesex', 5 March 1617,

transcribed in *Acts of the Privy Council of England, 1616–1617* (London: His Majesty's Stationery Office, 1927), p. 175.

2 Letter of Edward Sherbourne, 8 March 1617, transcribed by J. O. Halliwell-Phillipps in the *Fortune* scrapbook (now held at the Folger Library), and reproduced by G. E. Bentley in *The Jacobean and Caroline Stage*, 7 vols (Oxford: Clarendon Press, 1941–68), VI, p. 54.

3 Letter of Edward Sherbourne, p. 54; letter of John Chamberlain to Dudley Carleton, 8 March 1617, transcribed in *The Letters of John Chamberlain*, ed. Norman Egbert McClure, 2 vols (Philadelphia: The American Philosophical Society, 1939), II, pp. 59–60.

4 Charles J. Sisson, 'The Red Bull Company and the Importunate Widow', *Shakespeare Survey*, VII (1954), 57–68 (p. 68).

5 Andrew Gurr, *The Shakespearean Stage, 1574–1642*, 4th edn (Cambridge: Cambridge University Press, 2009), p. 24; see also Andrew Gurr, *Playgoing in Shakespeare's London*, 3rd edn (Cambridge: Cambridge University Press, 2004), p. 204.

6 Letter of John Chamberlain, p. 59.

7 Letter of John Chamberlain, p. 60. See also Eleanor Collins, 'Repertory and Riot: The Relocation of Plays from the Red Bull to the Cockpit Stage', *Early Theatre*, 13.2 (2010), 132–49, for a more detailed historical contextualisation of the riot.

8 Steve Rappaport, *Worlds Within Worlds: Structures of Life in Sixteenth-Century London* (Cambridge: Cambridge University Press, 1989): 'throughout the sixteenth century London lacked [...] a pattern of pervasive instability' (p. 11); he also suggests that 'the disorderly behaviour of young men in sixteenth century-London was hardly ever organised or purposeful, at least not consciously' (pp. 11, 18).

9 See, for instance, Bentley's reasoning with respect to the provenance of *The Seven Champions of Christendom*, a 'naive, and formless piece' characteristic of the Red Bull (*Jacobean and Caroline Stage*, IV, p. 712); Arthur Melville Clark's description of *The Rape of Lucrece* as 'a popular presentation of a classical plot for the Red Bull audience' (*Thomas Heywood, Playwright and Miscellanist* [Oxford: Blackwell, 1931], p. 220); and F. S. Boas's framing of the songs in that same play as a 'reprehensible concession to the taste of the audience at the Red Bull' (*Thomas Heywood* [London: Williams and Norgate, 1950], p. 55).

10 John Webster, *The White Devil* (London, 1612), A2r; Thomas Dekker, *If This Be Not a Good Play, the Devil Is In It* (London, 1612), A4r.

11 See note 9 above, and, for an example of how elements of the narrative have persisted in subtler and much more nuanced formulations, Mark Bayer's connection of 'moments of spectacle' and the magnification of 'the role of lower-class characters' and concerns with a 'less educated' Red Bull audience ('Staging Foxe at the Fortune and the Red Bull', *Renaissance and Reformation*, 27 [2003], 61–94 [p. 70]). Richard Rowland takes issue with the broader tendency in both criticism and teaching to classify particular kinds of drama according to terms received from past decades, noting that today's students are 'still regaled repeatedly with terms like "low comedy" and "citizen fare", terms which were coined in the first half of the twentieth century, and which had no more historical validity or meaning then than they do now' (*Thomas Heywood's Theatre, 1599–1639: Locations, Translations, and Conflict* [Farnham: Ashgate, 2010], p. 4).

12 See Edmund Gayton, *Pleasant Notes upon Don Quixot* (London, 1654), p. 271, for a similar construction published in 1654: here, an amphitheatre audience riot in the playhouse if 'the popular humour' for plays was not 'satisfied'.

13 See Andrew Gurr on the preference for 'witplay' over 'swordplay' in the indoor playhouses ('Singing through the Chatter: Ford and Contemporary Theatrical Fashion', in

John Ford: Critical Re-visions, ed. Michael Neill [Cambridge: Cambridge University Press, 1988], pp. 81–96 [p. 84]). He also argues that '[c]itizens and working-class playgoers' of the Caroline era 'had their own repertoire', which was 'predominantly masculine and heroic' (*Playgoing*, p. 92), but the fourth edition of *The Shakespearean Stage* removed emphasis from these lines of argument; see p. 142; and p. 173 n.3, n.4 of this book. In a broader context, Evelyn Tribble has observed that Ben Jonson's prioritisation of poetry has resulted in the demotion, in critical accounts today, of spectacle and action, which have been considered 'concessions to popular taste' (*Early Modern Actors and Shakespeare's Theatre* [London: Bloomsbury, 2017], p. 150).

14 See Sarah Dustagheer, *Shakespeare's Two Playhouses: Repertory and Theatre Space at the Globe and the Blackfriars, 1599–1613* (Cambridge: Cambridge University Press, 2017), for the 'combined [spatial] practices' that the King's Men adopted as they moved between the Globe and Blackfriars, 'with individual plays which combined practices from both playhouses to produce performances with valuable and distinct spatial resonances at the Globe and Blackfriars, respectively' (p. 3).

15 Scott McMillin and Sally Beth Maclean, *The Queen's Men and their Plays* (Cambridge: Cambridge University Press, 1998), p. xii.

16 C. J. Sisson, *The Boar's Head Theatre: An Inn-yard Theatre of the Elizabethan Age* (London: Routledge and Kegan Paul, 1972); G. F. Reynolds, *The Staging of Elizabethan Plays at the Red Bull Theater, 1605–1625* (New York: Modern Language Association of America, 1940).

17 McMillin and Maclean, *The Queen's Men*; Roslyn L. Knutson, *The Repertory of Shakespeare's Company, 1594–1613* (Fayetteville: University of Arkansas Press, 1991); Mary Bly, *Queer Virgins and Virgin Queans on the Early Modern Stage* (Oxford: Oxford University Press, 2000); Lucy Munro, *Children of the Queen's Revels: A Jacobean Theatre Repertory* (Cambridge: Cambridge University Press, 2005); Andrew Gurr, *The Shakespeare Company, 1594–1642* (Cambridge: Cambridge University Press, 2004); Andrew Gurr, *Shakespeare's Opposites: The Admiral's Company, 1594–1625* (Cambridge: Cambridge University Press, 2009); Eva Griffith, *A Jacobean Company and its Playhouse: The Queen's Servants at the Red Bull Theatre (c. 1605–1619)* (Cambridge: Cambridge University Press, 2013).

18 McMillin and Maclean, *The Queen's Men*, p. xii.

19 Matthew Steggle, *Richard Brome: Place and Politics on the Caroline Stage* (Manchester: Manchester University Press, 2004); Adam Zucker and Alan B. Farmer (eds), *Localizing Caroline Drama: Politics and Economics of the Early Modern Stage, 1625–1642* (Basingstoke: Palgrave Macmillan, 2006). The Ford, Shirley, Heywood, and Brome editions are published by and forthcoming from Oxford University Press.

20 Griffith, *A Jacobean Company and its Playhouse*, pp. 69–70; and see p. 32 of this book.

21 See Martin Butler's discussion of the circumstances under which Beeston 'seize[d] the initiative which in 1630 had been his rivals' distinctive selling point', creating a young company at the Cockpit after Queen Henrietta's Men were disbanded, and leaving Richard Heton at Salisbury Court to form 'a revived Queen's Men, on the standard adult model'. While the two Queen Henrietta's Men companies were separate, the demise and the creation of the other were not isolated events. Martin Butler, 'Adult and Boy Playing Companies 1625–1642', in *The Oxford Handbook of Early Modern Theatre*, ed. Richard Dutton (Oxford: Oxford University Press, 2011), pp. 104–19 (p. 113); and Martin Butler, 'Exeunt Fighting: Poets, Players, and Impresarios at the Caroline Hall Theaters', in *Localizing Caroline Drama: Politics and Economics of the Early Modern Stage, 1625–1642*, ed. Adam Zucker and Alan B. Farmer (Basingstoke: Palgrave Macmillan, 2006), pp. 97–128. Lucy Munro

has also noted a connection between the two companies in terms of the theatrical patronage offered by the queen, who appears to have been 'supporting the new companies at both the Cockpit and the Salisbury Court' at this time ('The Queen and the Cockpit: Henrietta Maria's Theatrical Patronage Revisited', *Shakespeare Bulletin*, 37.1 [2019], 25–45).

22 Between 1567 and 1642, David McInnis and Matthew Steggle write, 'it is now clear that in the commercial context, identifiable lost plays are significantly more numerous than extant ones' (*Lost Plays in Shakespeare's England* [Basingstoke: Palgrave Macmillan, 2014], p. 2).

23 McInnis and Steggle, *Lost Plays*, p. 3.

24 Alan B. Farmer and Zachary Lesser, 'Canons and Classics: Publishing Drama in Caroline England', in *Localizing Caroline Drama: Politics and Economics of the Early Modern Stage, 1625–1642*, ed. Adam Zucker and Alan B. Farmer (Basingstoke: Palgrave Macmillan, 2006), pp. 17–41 (p. 20).

25 Alan B. Farmer and Zachary Lesser, 'Vile Arts: The Marketing of English Printed Drama, 1512–1660', *Research Opportunities in Renaissance Drama*, 39 (2000), 77–165; Zachary Lesser, *Renaissance Drama and the Politics of Publication: Readings in the English Book Trade* (Cambridge: Cambridge University Press, 2004); Lukas Erne, *Shakespeare and the Book Trade* (Cambridge: Cambridge University Press, 2013); Douglas A. Brooks, *From Playhouse to Printing House: Drama and Authorship in Early Modern England* (Cambridge: Cambridge University Press, 2000).

26 N. W. Bawcutt (ed.), *The Control and Censorship of Caroline Drama: The Records of Sir Henry Herbert, Master of the Revels 1623–73* (Oxford: Clarendon Press, 1996), pp. 13–21.

27 Bawcutt (ed.), *Control and Censorship*, p. 21.

28 Malone published extracts in 1790, George Chalmers in 1797 and 1799, and Rebecca Warner in 1818; Bawcutt (ed.), *Control and Censorship*, pp. 17–18.

29 Bawcutt (ed.), *Control and Censorship*, p. 19.

30 Peter Martin, *Edmond Malone, Shakespearean Scholar: A Literary Biography* (Cambridge: Cambridge University Press, 1995), p. 38; *Reports of the Historical Manuscripts Commission*, XII, Part 10 (London: Her Majesty's Stationery Office, 1891), p. 343.

31 See Jon Greenfield and Peter McCurdy, 'Practical Evidence for a Reimagined Indoor Jacobean Theatre', in *Moving Shakespeare Indoors: Performance and Repertoire in the Jacobean Playhouse*, ed. Andrew Gurr and Farah Karim-Cooper (Cambridge: Cambridge University Press, 2014), pp. 32–64 (pp. 32–7); Oliver Jones, 'Documentary Evidence for an Indoor Jacobean Theatre', in ibid., pp. 65–78 (p. 71).

32 Roslyn L. Knutson notes a similar value in exploring the work of Thomas Middleton in relation to the 'commercial dynamic of the adult companies'. She investigates the ways in which his professional career 'challenges the scholarly truism that the so-called elite venues and their dramatists were aesthetically and financially superior to the so-called citizen playhouses'. Roslyn L. Knutson, 'The Adult Companies and the Dynamics of Commerce', in *Thomas Middleton in Context*, ed. Suzanne Gossett (Cambridge: Cambridge University Press, 2011), pp. 168–76 (p. 168).

PART I
Material and Cultural Circumstance

THE COMPANY, THE THEATRE, AND THE DRAMATISTS: CHRISTOPHER BEESTON AND THE FORMATION OF QUEEN HENRIETTA'S MEN

The career of Queen Henrietta's Men began and ended in times of plague. The playhouses are likely to have been closed from around May of 1625, in response to London's rising death toll. In July the Lord Chamberlain affirmed that Henry Herbert, the Master of the Revels, was 'not to suffer any Players to play in any Part of *England*' at this time.[1] This closure was symptomatic of the potentially limitless disruption that plague continued to cause to theatrical business in the 1630s, for though the profession was well established by now, precautions taken to restrict the spread of the contagion remained a serious obstacle to playing and a threat to commercial success. Furthermore, the 'Time of this Infection' followed hard on the heels of James I's death, which is likely to have prompted closure from late March of that year.[2] As G. E. Bentley observed, it is unlikely that the theatres reopened after James's funeral, since the number of deaths from plague was rising steadily over this time.[3]

But for the actor and theatre manager Christopher Beeston, the long closure that took place over at least six months of this year offered the opportunity for consolidation, reorganisation, and renewal. Beeston was a veteran of the theatre profession by this time; his experience on the stage is likely to have begun with the Chamberlain's Men, probably under the apprenticeship of Augustine Phillips, with whom he appears in the cast-list of Jonson's *Every Man in His Humour*.[4] He joined the Earl of Worcester's Men in 1602, then at the Rose Theatre, before becoming a prominent figure in Queen Anne's Men from 1604, who were based at the Boar's Head and Curtain playhouses before moving to the Red Bull in Clerkenwell. Beeston had first-hand experience of working in a number of theatrical venues, a long history in the profession, and all of the networks and knowledge that came along with it. Even so, his enthusiasm for a return to normality following the theatre closure in 1625 proved to be misjudged; on 6 December 1625 a court order prohibited the proceedings of 'the players of the howse at the Cockpitt, beinge next to his Majesties Courte at Whitehall', since (as Beeston must have known) 'the drawinge of people togeather to places was a great meanes of spreadinge and continewinge the infeccioun'.[5] If these players were the new Queen

Henrietta's Men, it seems that Beeston could hardly wait to launch the company on London.[6]

The first surviving piece of evidence for the troupe from the transcripts of Herbert's office-book entries is recorded by Edmond Malone: a licence for a new play, James Shirley's *The Maid's Revenge*, which was granted by the Revels Office on 9 February 1626. The transcript fails to specify either the company or the theatre to which Shirley's play was allowed, but the play's first-edition title-page (1639) affirms that it enjoyed 'good Applause at the private house in Drury Lane, by her Majesties Servants'.[7] The plague closure had prompted reform behind the doors of the Drury Lane playhouse, amid the theatrical inactivity that it otherwise enforced; the Cockpit's previous occupants – Lady Elizabeth's Men – do not appear again in records of performance relating to the theatre. With the accession of Charles I and his queen Henrietta Maria to the English throne, a new Queen's Men stepped on to the scene of early modern theatrical London.

The accession of 1625 was certainly an 'auspicious' moment for 'the launching of a company under the patronage of the new Queen', as Bentley noted, but the relation between the two events of Henrietta Maria's accession and Beeston's formation of a new company seems based on historical contingency.[8] As far as the evidence shows, Beeston does not appear to have been responding to any kind of royal wish or instruction when he organised his troupe. This is quite unlike the circumstances that surrounded the formation of the second Caroline company of Queen Henrietta's Men in 1636/37 at Salisbury Court, and the creation of Beeston's Boys, or Their Majesties Servants, at the same time. In the first instance, Richard Heton (the manager at Salisbury Court) wrote in 1639 that following the plague closure of 1636–37, 'had not my lo: of Dorsett taken care to make up a new Company for the Queene, she had not had any at all'.[9] The Earl of Dorset was a member of the queen's household, a loquacious supporter of 'his majesty's dear consort, our royal queen, and my gracious mistress'; his active involvement in the formation of the new queen's company suggests that there might be a political dimension to account for here.[10] The transcripts of Henry Herbert's revels entries also suggest that the second Queen Henrietta's Men might have borne something more of a resemblance to the state-organised Queen's Men of 1583, a company that had been formed by Herbert's predecessor, Edward Tilney.[11] Malone's transcript of an entry by Herbert dated 23 February 1637 stated that Herbert had 'disposed of' key members of Beeston's original Queen Henrietta's Men 'to Salisbury Court, and joynd them with the best of that company'.[12] The transfer of three leading actors to the Salisbury Court troupe under the direction of Herbert suggests a concerted and deliberate effort to form the basis of a successful company; a degree of state intervention that seems lacking in the formation of Beeston's 1625/26 enterprise.

The formation of Beeston's young company in 1637 also appears engineered in comparison with the first Queen Henrietta's Men – or at least that was Edmond Malone's interpretation of events. Malone's transcript of Herbert's entry states that 'Mr. Beeston was commanded to make a company of boyes, and began to play at the Cockpitt with them the same day'.[13] This record appears on 23 February with an announcement declaring the reopening of the theatres, though Beeston's Boys had already played at court on 7 and 14 February 1637.[14] Beeston was then paid on 10 May 1637 for two performances 'Acted by the new Company' at court.[15] It is unclear whether the payment relates to the February performances, but it seems that Beeston's Boys had been in rehearsal before the playhouses reopened in February 1637, having closed the previous May because of the plague. The new company, formed on 'command', debuted at court before its launch into the commercial marketplace. The circumstances might indicate a qualitatively different kind of relationship with the court to the one experienced by Queen Henrietta's Men, for whom there is no recorded evidence of immediate requirement at court; and, for the first few years after their formation, there is no known evidence of a connection between Queen Henrietta's Men and their namesake patron.[16] At the same time, royal involvement in the formation of Beeston's Boys and the Salisbury Court Queen Henrietta's Men might be suggestive of a pattern, or a tendency of the queen to support companies with a connection to her name, and could add support to the suggestion that Beeston created the company under the direction of the new monarch and her court, or to attract her attention.

Without such an explanation, the rationale behind Beeston's actions at this time is far from self-evident. Beeston's previous company, Lady Elizabeth's Men, had been successful at the Cockpit. The performances the company gave in Drury Lane of plays written by the leading dramatists of the time, including Middleton, Dekker, Shirley, and Ford, made sufficient profit for it to donate a generous sum of money to the building of a new church in its local parish, St Giles-in-the-Fields.[17] They also appear to have been relatively popular at court, and were invited to perform there at least five times during their tenancy at Beeston's theatre.[18] 'Tenancy' does seem to be an accurate description of the company's claims to the theatre, for Beeston appears to have had complete control over the use of the Cockpit playhouse. As far as the historical records can show, the company left the venue quietly, as did the Prince's Men before it. Neither troupe left a paper trail (that is known) in the court records of injustices felt or contractual wranglings. The plague closure itself and the

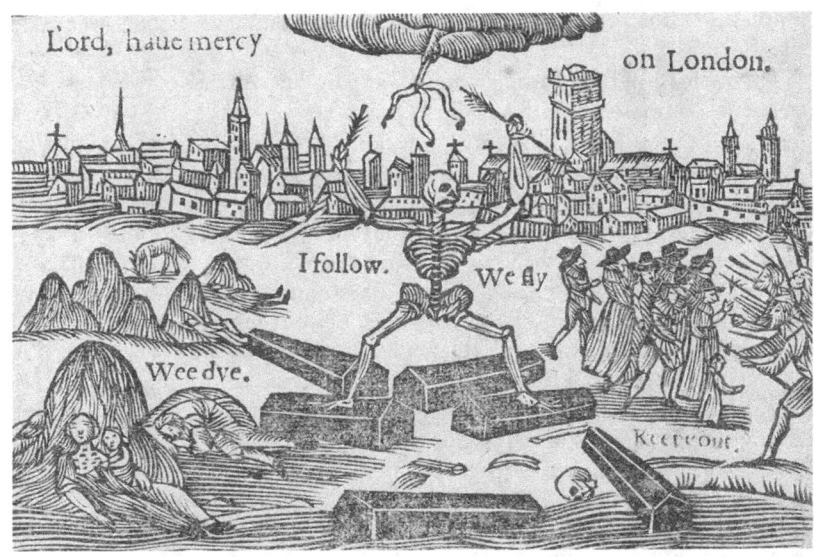

2   Title-page illustration from Thomas Dekker, *A Rod for Run-awayes* (London, 1625). Bodleian Libraries, University of Oxford, 2025. Weston Mal. 601 (1)

loss of profits over this period alone do not seem likely to have provided reason to break up a company, though this is a factor that might have contributed to Beeston's decision. London was in a dire situation. The plague was more virulent than it had ever been; over 26,000 plague burials in the city of London and its liberties alone were recorded in the space of that year, and the infection was responsible for over 4,000 deaths a week at its peak in August; this outbreak was known as 'the Great Plague' until it was outstripped by the death toll of the 1665 epidemic.[19]

Yet despite the grim realities of enduring through such an outbreak, the commercial impact on Beeston and Lady Elizabeth's Men was determined largely by the length of closure. Though Beeston's finances were probably on a firmer footing by 1630, following another five years of profitable business, Queen Henrietta's Men survived the seven-month plague closure between 17 April and late November 1630 without recorded incident.[20] Furthermore, the creation of a new troupe would only prove advantageous once the theatres had reopened; in the meantime, new troupe or old, the whole operation was indefinitely stalled. Why didn't Beeston choose to carry on with his winning formula of Lady Elizabeth's Men at the Cockpit? Or, if opportunistic rebranding were the issue at stake, rename the existing company the 'Queen's Men' and apply for a new patent? Why would Beeston choose to bring together a largely new troupe of actors, investing in freshly recruited colleagues, at this difficult and uncertain time? From the point of view of theatrical production and the marketable aesthetic of drama at the Cockpit, why would he risk untried theatrical groupings between actors, and the unknown effects of a brand new dynamic on the Drury Lane stage?

No answer to these questions has ever been satisfactorily formulated, and Beeston's motivations for creating Queen Henrietta's Men have become confused and exaggerated by a tendency in theatre history to project a variety of personality traits and characteristics on to the impresario. As will emerge over the course of this chapter, such a practice is not entirely unfounded. But it has governed the interpretation of the origins of Queen Henrietta's Men in ways that are unhelpful. In this particular instance, Beeston's decision to break his previous commitment to Lady Elizabeth's Men is most often ascribed to a brand of caprice that has become specifically associated with him, portrayed as he is as one of the most shrewd, manipulative impresario managers of the Caroline period. He has been described as having 'always kept a velvet glove on his iron hand', and his managerial model has been contrasted with the democratic strategy employed by the sharers of the King's Men and with the management of Richard Heton, who has been seen as more autocratic in his style of management.[21] In opposition to the idealised workings of Shakespeare's company, Beeston's decisions are cast as governed by the strict pursuit of capital gain. His relation to a number of companies over the 1620s has led to the view that the changeovers at the Cockpit were prompted by a kind of routine restlessness – a pattern of wilful making and breaking of companies that might evidence, on the one hand, an unsympathetic, profit-driven persona, and on the other an easily bored businessman who 'saw his opportunity' on the queen's accession and took it, in the grip of growing tedium and frustration throughout the 'plague-enforced idleness'.[22] The former is the more pervasive characterisation, for a number of reasons relating to his dealings with former companies at the Red Bull and the Cockpit; these unfold below. For now, it is fair to conclude that the formation of Queen Henrietta's Men is not known to have been causally dependent upon the new queen's accession. We can also surmise that, in the lack of all other evidence, Beeston's entrepreneuralism – without reaching further afield to make claims about his personality – fits conveniently with the 'facts' as we know them.

Of greater importance to the formation and establishment of the company than circumstantial opportunism and an official nomenclature were the practical conditions of playing – not least, the availability of a playhouse itself. In this regard, Beeston had a lot to offer. He had converted the Cockpit from a cock-fighting ring in 1616, after leasing the former animal-baiting venue, its cock-houses and sheds, adjoining tenement, and a 'little Garden' from the grocer John Best, at a rate of £45 per annum for a term of thirty-one years.[23] The transformation of the site did not go as smoothly as Beeston might have hoped. While the theatre was constructed on existing foundations, Beeston's attempt to erect what was described as a 'base tenement' next to it and alongside the King's Passage was reprimanded by the Privy Council. In this pursuit, Beeston had failed to heed 'his Majestie's proclamacions', which forbade the sinking of new foundations. He was commanded to pull it down not once but twice, after he began to reconstruct the partially dismantled building the following year; the second reprimand was accompanied by a stern threat of imprisonment.[24] Repairing his 'spoyled', 'defaced' new theatre and its 'untiled' roof following the Shrovetide riots must have been both disheartening and expensive for Beeston, and this took three months to complete.[25]

Beeston's commitment of money and time to the project, however, gave him a distinctive edge over the market, as a manager. He was the owner of a brand new indoor playhouse in the fashionable West End, two minutes away from the burgeoning Covent Garden and within walking distance of Whitehall and the Inns of Court. Not only that, but his construction of the theatre must have been informed by the knowledge and understanding of theatre and performance venues that he had gained as an actor. Some of the physical features of the Cockpit stage are discussed alongside the staging requirements of the plays in Chapter 4, but for now it is worth remembering that Beeston's Cockpit was a playhouse built by a player. Within the constraints of the Cockpit's original site, Beeston would have known how much space was needed in the tiring-house to achieve certain effects; how much room was required in corridors and walkways through which actors might need to pass each other in full costume. It is likely that he had an opinion about what kind of relationship between the main stage and the area 'above' was desirable; and he would certainly have been able to account adequately, during construction and the organisation of the building and its site, for the storage requirements of the physical bulk of props and costumes. Beeston had an intimate knowledge of the most practical, material obstacles and challenges that faced the daily operation of a working theatre. As the owner of the building, and a manager who, as unfolds below, had an unusual amount of control over both the physical playhouse and the accoutrements of playing, it was in his interests to pre-empt or diminish those challenges where he could – just as it was in his interests to ensure the smooth daily running of the theatre by building good relations between the dramatists and players who worked there, and with the authorities who governed the theatre profession.

SHARES AND SHAREHOLDING

What Beeston does not appear to have offered Queen Henrietta's Men, or any of the companies that had come before, was the opportunity to purchase shares in the playhouse. The lease of the buildings was made out in 1616 to Beeston alone, as was its renewal in 1633. Playhouse shares offered players, and also external speculators, the opportunity to invest and hold a proportional interest in the material fabric of the playhouse itself. Allowing company members to purchase playhouse shares might, then, have been one way of alleviating the financial burden of the payment of the lease and the conversion or building of the playhouse for Beeston, as a strategy of managing the investment required to set up and maintain permanent venues. The Burbage brothers had relied upon the financial support of company members when the Globe was erected in 1599, for instance – and at the time, this constituted an innovation in the development of company shareholding. Edward Alleyn – owner of the Fortune playhouse – attempted to echo this model after the Fortune burned down in 1621, with an arrangement that spread the cost of construction between some of the company members, and a larger number of speculators unconnected with the theatre profession.[26] Beeston had also experienced a system of playhouse sharing while at the Red Bull – a circumstance that Eva Griffith has argued ultimately led to considerable difficulties for the company, and the weakening of its financial independence.[27] Lessons learned and a keen vision for the future running of the Cockpit might have combined in Beeston's decision not to offer playhouse shares in his new venue. He seems neither to have needed, nor desired, the collective financial support of Queen Anne's Men – not even after disaster befell the Cockpit in the riot of 1617.

Queen Anne's Men may not have held playhouse shares, but it is possible that they might have held *company* shares, an investment that was quite different in kind, though players might hold both playhouse and company shares if granted the opportunity and bestowed of the means. Whereas a playhouse share constituted something akin to the purchase of property, the ownership of a company share entailed an investment in the running costs of the company and the purchase of properties, playbooks, and costumes, and – in addition – something 'less tangible'. As Andrew Gurr explains, they were usually 'part of the collective goodwill that made the company work successfully', and they also repaid the sharer to some degree, as a company share entitled its owner to a share of the company's profits.[28] If playhouse shares were not available, there is evidence to suggest that company shares continued to hold some kind of value at the Cockpit, though the precise details of the arrangement are unclear. There must have been some kind of company sharing system in place during the Prince's Men's occupation of the Cockpit, as upon 'the remove of some of the sharers' from the Cockpit they are reported to have taken a play away with them.[29] But this was a company that Beeston hosted rather than created, and established company procedures might have proved difficult or impossible to dismantle within Beeston's doors. Beeston did operate some kind of company sharing system as manager for Beeston's Boys. When he died, his will stated that he stood 'possessed of fower of the six shares in the Company for the King and Queenes service att the Cockpitt in Drury lane', and he bequeathed two of those to his wife, declaring that the other two should be 'delivered vpp for the advancem^t of the said Company'.[30] Even if the available two shares not taken by Beeston were subdivided, Beeston's responsibilities to this later company were significant. At least in monetary terms, he claimed the majority until his death.

In some respects Beeston's strategy was consonant with wider changes and developments that took place within the theatrical system of sharing over the 1620s. Over this time the market in theatrical shares saw, as K. E. McLuskie and Rebecca Rogers have argued, the erosion of 'a neat correlation between communal effort and individual gain' within company dynamics, as 'fixed London venues increased the stakes' in theatrical ventures, and shares in playhouses became prohibitively expensive for the players.[31] Whereas the earlier model of shareholding focused on company shares and represented 'a combined interest in time, skill, and capital', Susan Cerasano interprets the reformed priorities of householder- or playhouse-sharers as increasingly rooted in concerns of land and property, in a system that threatened to overturn the traditional values and benefits of collective collaboration and company participation.[32] Shareholders in playhouses now reserved the right to bequeath theatrical shares to relatives with no immediate connection to or interest in the playing profession. This undermined the theatrical sharing system's resemblance to a guild system, and privileged the individual investor rather than collective investment made by a group of players who ostensibly shared the same interests.[33] And the potentially conflicting interests of non-theatrical sharers and the players of the company, who McLuskie and Rogers argue inevitably 'worked much harder for their share of the profits', was an aspect of company management from which problems could arise, as the King's

Men's shareholder's dispute of 1635 suggests.[34] Systems of shareholding were undergoing revision, which was to unsettle and disadvantage players across the profession in the satisfaction of evolving commercial priorities and imperatives.

Beeston's case is a little different, of course, since he took sole responsibility for the costs associated with the playhouse himself, and seems to have retained the majority share in the company. The company was thus less of a collaborative enterprise than it might otherwise have been – and this gave the players less long-term security, but it also burdened Beeston with the risk, and it meant that his interests were very much tied to their prosperity. He was part of the theatrical community in an important way, with ties and relationships within the profession, and an understanding of the lives and careers of actors; when he died, his company shares were passed to his family, also part of London's theatrical community. While the players did not have access to a sharing system that might have been available to them elsewhere, or in earlier years, and while the payoffs of longer-term investment were not forthcoming, the shorter term attraction of a financially stable, fully funded base is likely to have offered some recompense. The sharing situation at the Cockpit might have disadvantaged the players, in comparative terms, but it did not present an obstacle large enough to preclude their employment there, and the ongoing investment of their time, energy, and individual careers under Beeston's management.

'APPARELL, BOOKS [AND] OTHER THINGS'

Playbooks

While the level of control that Beeston maintained over the Cockpit has contributed to his characterisation as unsympathetic and ruthless, his career spent working in the theatre industry meant that he had a lot more to offer Queen Henrietta's Men than an empty theatre – not only in terms of knowledge, but also in material assets. Beeston's careful acquisition of playbooks for the Cockpit's repertory gave the troupe the headstart of which they, more than any former Cockpit company, were in need. All of the companies previously managed by Beeston were already established and had performed together immediately prior to their tenancy at the Cockpit – Queen Anne's Men and Prince Charles's Men at the Red Bull, and Lady Elizabeth's Men as a touring company. They already had working repertories and access to the resources needed to perform them. In this respect, as with their relation to the Cockpit playhouse, the players who formed Queen Henrietta's Men were more dependent than had been typical on the provision of their manager. Not only did Beeston exercise sole control over the theatre; he also came to own the majority of the playbooks which crossed its threshold. For both the company and Beeston, the launch of Queen Henrietta's Men might have felt like a very new and distinctive kind of venture – an extraordinary departure from familiar practice.

The evidence for Beeston's control over the repertory is remarkably clear. Following Christopher Beeston's death in 1638, his son William took over management of the Cockpit. In 1639 William Beeston petitioned the Lord Chamberlain to protect a long list of plays for the performance of Beeston's Boys at the Cockpit alone. The edict that the Lord Chamberlain issued in response provided formal confirmation that the plays 'doe all & euery of them properly & of right belong to the sayd House, and consequently that they are all in his propriety'.[35] The document provides a list of plays which are likely to have been considered the theatre's most valuable dramatic assets (or otherwise, those that rival companies had expressed an interest in performing); plays that other companies were forbidden to 'intermedle wth or Act'. And it not only demonstrates that Beeston passed the repertory on to his son as 'property', but reveals the extent to which he retained plays formerly owned by visiting companies to the theatre – remnants of the repertories of all the Cockpit companies appear in the list. This includes Heywood's *The Rape of Lucrece*, which was written for Queen Anne's Men at the Red Bull, and a number of plays written for Lady Elizabeth's Men during their occupancy of the Cockpit in the early 1620s. The 1633 title-page of William Rowley's *All's Lost by Lust*, for example, claims performance by Lady Elizabeth's Men and then Queen Henrietta's Men at the Cockpit. This play is likely to have arrived at the Cockpit with Prince Charles's Men, for the dramatis personae printed in the edition suggests that Rowley himself performed in it, and he is known to have been linked with that company on other occasions; the play also appeared in a Revels document listing other plays performed by the Prince's Men.[36] The fact that the majority of the plays listed in the Lord Chamberlain's edict were retained from earlier repertories attests to the value that revivals continued to hold in the Caroline period.

Tracing the provenance of these plays establishes a relatively secure repertory route by which plays travelled with Queen Anne's Men to the Cockpit to remain there after the company broke in 1619; other troupes contributed their own plays to the repertory, and left behind new drama that they had premiered under Beeston's management. The migratory pattern of plays draws attention, again, to the extent to which repertory requires thinking of in terms of process, rather than as a static end-product – a tendency that has been encouraged by the fixity of the printed texts, with their title-page claims to performance in particular places, by certain companies. Gurr has observed that '[t]he printed texts of playscripts work against that feature of a play in performance as a transient event or occasion'[37] – and this observation applies equally to reconstructions of repertory. The printed texts provide only a snapshot, or freeze frame, of the theatrical process that repertory studies attempt to interpret, by allowing us to isolate a corpus of plays and locate them within a specific context. But as the migration of plays from the Red Bull to the Cockpit shows, repertory was in flux, and travelled across categories that typically remain fixed in our framing of theatre history: those of venue and company.

In this case, Beeston's retention of play-texts, in what appears to have been a privately steered theatrical project, suggests that Queen Henrietta's Men did not 'own' their repertory beyond the sense of possession that might be conferred by performance. The repertory – in its unembodied, formal sense: a collection of licensed play-texts – belonged to the theatre, or rather the theatre-owner, and not the company. Queen Henrietta's Men might be described as caretakers of the repertory, which is not to say that they did not embellish, augment, and indeed bring to life the corpus in important, unique, and lasting ways. But their use of the Cockpit repertory in practical terms was impermanent. They inherited it temporarily. Legally, and in the most fundamental terms, these plays made up part of the catalogue of Beeston's professional acquisitions and material assets.

Even so, Beeston knew all too well how unstable the processes of repertory formation could be, and had experienced at first hand the fraught, potentially indeterminate nature of ownership claims on plays. In the first instance, not all of the plays performed by Queen Anne's Men at the Red Bull necessarily made it to the Cockpit. According to John Chamberlain, a number of playbooks were lost in the 1617 riot, burned or, as Edward Sherbourne might suggest, 'cutt in peeces'.[38] At around the same time as Queen Anne's Men were transferring to the Cockpit, the company also appears to have lost some of its playbooks to a former colleague, Robert Leigh, when he left the troupe. Leigh promised to return to the company any '^cloaths^ bookes of playes, & other goodes belonging therunto, as he had then, or were trusted in his handes or Custody' in return for a fee.[39] Queen Anne's Men managed to pay most of the fee in agreed instalments, but Leigh then seems to have had a change of heart. According to the ensuing lawsuit, he detained 'diuers bookes, apparell & other goodes' belonging to the company – as well as seven (or more) 'young men' whom they had trained – in order to start up his own splinter company.[40] Perhaps the impact of such material loss, tallied at equivalent to £100 by the players plus another £200 in damages, goes some way to explaining the level of control that Beeston enforced over the inventory he would later acquire. Beeston could be generous in the sharing of theatrical assets with colleagues to whom he was bound in kin, though – notably Robert Browne, his brother-in-law. Christopher Matusiak has noted how

Browne travelled to Europe performing versions of plays associated with Queen Anne's Men, and suggests that Beeston might have procured plays for his London-based company through Browne and his connections.[41]

Furthermore, as Eva Griffith's work has established, Beeston retained a professional interest in the Red Bull into the 1630s, in the form of a share in the building.[42] He also had an interest in the Curtain estate, though not (as far as is known) in the actual Curtain theatre itself at which Queen Anne's Men had licence to play, and, as Griffith has discovered, might have been seeking to extend his theatrical reach by maintaining an interest in inn-yard venues.[43] She suggests that Beeston might have 'shuffled people' between theatres to which he had 'access' – amphitheatres and the hall-playhouse – since the destinations of the companies that Beeston worked with at the Cockpit prior to Queen Henrietta's Men 'were always Beeston-associated playhouses'.[44] As she notes, the move away from the indoor playhouse 'can no longer be interpreted as a simple demotion and/or rejection [... it] was a demotion of a kind, but not of a simple kind'.[45] Perhaps some of his plays went back and forth too, in a sharing of repertory that was not bound by company or venue; a repertory that could be 'demoted' or 'promoted' at different theatres in a similar way to those moving, shuffled companies. This would provide a clear explanation for the title-page of Kirke's *The Seven Champions of Christendom*, published in 1638 and composed between 1625 and 1634 during Queen Henrietta's Men's time at the Cockpit. The title-page claims performance at both the Red Bull and the Cockpit; this formulation is more common for plays written prior to 1616–17 which were transferred to the Cockpit and published following revival there, but not for those written after this time, once Beeston had started using the indoor playhouse. It might be that the play was more properly shared between the hall and amphitheatre playhouses, written with both venues in mind or designed to move from one venue to the other.[46]

This scenario also makes better sense of the removal of *The Escapes of Jupiter* from the Cockpit in 1623. The transcript of Herbert's revels account entry says that this 'olde' play, which had already been performed 'in the Kings house', was 'taken from the Cockpitt upon the remove of some of the sharers' – apparently Herbert allowed the removal because 'It was not complained of by the company of the Cockpitt': 'the Cockpitt gave way'.[47] It seems likely that Prince Charles's Men took the play with them when they were moved from the Cockpit to the Curtain, to make way for Lady Elizabeth's Men. But Beeston's continued involvement in the amphitheatres might suggest that he did not, in fact, relinquish the play in a straightforward sense – rather, his allowance of its removal, a form of repertory control in itself, enabled the play's fresh revival at a different venue in which he might have held some kind of interest.[48] In this sense, plays might have migrated away from the Cockpit to be performed elsewhere – much as they did when they were taken on tour or to court – in patterns of circulation which resist the understanding of repertory as tied to a particular theatre, and to a more permanent sense of company ownership. On occasion, Beeston allowed plays to leave his circle of influence altogether; the title-page of Nabbes' *Hannibal and Scipio* boasted performance by Queen Henrietta's Men at the Cockpit; it also featured a cast-list naming actors of the company. But by 1636 it had moved to Salisbury Court where it was performed by the Prince's Servants; according to Malone, Herbert received the benefit of its second day 'as a satisfaction for a debt due' by Richard Gunnell, the manager of that theatre.[49]

Most strikingly, the level of control that Beeston might have exercised over the repertory extended beyond material ownership into the realm of artistic intervention and dramatic design. In January 1632 a transcript made by Malone testifies that Herbert licensed, or 'allowed', an 'ould play, new written or forbisht by Mr. Biston'.[50] The identity of the play is unknown, the extent of the revisions impossible to verify, but the evidence suggests that either Christopher or his son William Beeston revised passages of a play in their possession, revamping (or 'refurbishing') it for the Cockpit stage. This might suggest Christopher Beeston's continued interest in the experience of theatrical production itself, and an active dedication to the provision of a certain kind of fare at the theatre, or otherwise that of William – an actor, heir to Beeston's theatrical legacy, and (self-proclaimedly) 'bred up in the art of stage playing, and [...] skilled in that science'.[51] It seems that one or other of the men laboured here to fulfil what he must have perceived as certain dramatic criteria; the 'Biston' to whom Malone's transcript refers had a shaping interest in the content of the repertory, and his agency took an artistic, 'editorial' nature, deliberately directed towards a particular aesthetic achievement or effect.

Properties and possessions

Christopher Beeston also controlled and contributed to the aesthetics of the Cockpit productions on a more fundamental, material level, as Matusiak has observed, for it is likely that he owned the large majority of the properties and costumes required to stage plays at his theatre. Beeston's professional role at the Red Bull had involved procuring such items for the company – he was described by the players at that theatre as responsible for 'the buyeing & Defraying of the charges of the furniture & apparrell [...] & other necessaries', a task 'of greatest chardge & trust' that could only 'fall vpon a thriueing man & one that was of abilitie &

meanes'.[52] Under legal duress he denied the primary role that he had in furnishing the company with apparel, but as Matusiak suggests, this was a task he had undertaken as an actor with Worcester's Men under Henslowe's management at the Rose theatre, providing a 'manes gowne of Branshed velluet / & A dublet' and, a few months' later, a 'Jerken' in 1602.[53] He also continued to purchase costumes for Queen Anne's Men at least as late as 1617, as just over twenty years later he was taken to court, along with two of his colleagues, for debts incurred in the purchase of hats from Richard Holden.[54]

The Red Bull inventory transferred to the Cockpit with Queen Anne's Men, even if it did not all survive; as with the playbooks, John Chamberlain's letter refers to the rioters in 1617 'cutting the players apparell all in pieces, and all other theyre furniture'.[55] Some of the surviving props and costumes, and those that must have been purchased after the riot to replenish lost stock, appear to have remained at the Cockpit to form the basis of future companies' inventories. In proceedings of a lawsuit between John Smith and Beeston initiated in 1619, John King, a hired man of Queen Anne's Men, claimed that 'at the sep*araci*on of the sd Company the sayd Beeston did take and Carry Away all the apparrell that was then amongst the sd Company and Converted them to his owne vse / and since disposed of them to other Companyes at his pleasure'.[56] It is unclear to what activity 'his owne vse' refers, though Matusiak has made a convincing case for Beeston's involvement in a black market in second-hand clothes.[57] '[D]isposing' of costumes 'to other Companyes' might suggest that he sold the items for cash, as well as holding back, for himself, those specialist props and costumes required to perform the repertory his Cockpit companies would come to perform.

During the same lawsuit, Beeston was charged again with dishonesty and double-dealing; this time it was the players of Queen Anne's Men themselves levelling the accusations, when they claimed that Beeston had been embezzling surplus funds left over from the money with which he purchased properties and apparel for the Red Bull-based company. The claims came to light through Smith's demands for payments owed by the company for 'stuff*es*' purchased between 1612 and 1616, which had not been satisfied.[58] Smith reported that the company claimed the debt had already been settled by Beeston and his colleagues, who said they had made the payments either to himself or to his servant, Thomas Chambers. But Chambers was Smith's 'onlie witnes' of the delivery of goods and the debt that was owed, and Smith went on to claim that Beeston and the actors, 'combyning themselves', had sent Chambers 'beyond the Seas or into some vnknowne & remote place' to prevent him giving evidence against them. Yet Smith's initial impression of the company's united front was radically overturned; he reported that they had fallen at 'variance' and 'strife amongst themselves'.[59] Ellis Worth, Richard Perkins, and John Cumber – all of the Red Bull at this time – then claimed that Beeston had 'Deducted & Defaulked divers greate somes of money outt of the collec-cions & gatheringes aforesaid & hath wth the said moneyes much enritched himself', providing 'a false accompte of fower hundred poundes'.[60] For his part, Beeston denied that he was Smith's main contact as the company's main purchaser of props and costumes, suggesting that 'sometymes one, and sometymes another of the said Company Did provide Clothes and other necessaries for the setting forth of the actors of that Company', and he denied owing Smith anything.[61]

This £400 has been the basis of much scrutiny and speculation concerning the building costs of Beeston's Cockpit; the sum was, as many have pointed out, enough money to begin as ambitious a project as the construction of a new theatre. If this were the case, Queen Henrietta's Men were bound to Queen Anne's Men through more than the inheritance of a number of plays – the bricks and mortar of the playhouse in which they performed were procured from Red Bull profits. Beeston's venue, which gave the new company such an advantage, has become deeply implicated by the narrative of debt, embezzlement, and underhand manipulation that surrounds him. A lawsuit of 1623, involving Ellis Worth of the Red Bull and Susan Baskervile, the widow of the former manager of the Red Bull, Thomas Greene, provides an account of Beeston as unscrupulous and unremittingly tactical, and has generated a pervasive distrust of the manager and his motives.[62] The discovery of a lawsuit in which Beeston stood accused of rape in 1602 reinforced suspicions that lingered around his character and reputation.[63] Without diminishing the seriousness of this charge, this chapter limits itself to a consideration of Beeston's professional role as a theatre manager rather than providing a more general account of his historical character or conduct. When considering Beeston's behaviour, we should acknowledge the responsibilities he had, for the attitudes of the impresario managers might have reflected the changed conditions of playing into the 1630s, and arose from the very real risk that they had taken through their own personal investment in the profession. Beeston's degree of control and ownership, including his guardianship of the plays, props, and costumes borrowed by the companies he nurtured, might have emerged in prudent response to the pressures he faced.

What the lawsuits do tell us about Beeston's capacity as the manager of Queen Henrietta's Men is how experienced he was; they also indicate that, at least at one time, he was popular among his colleagues. Thomas

Heywood related his managerial acumen in the Worth vs. Baskervile lawsuit, stating that 'both before and synce the decesse of Thomas Greene [... the company members] did repose their mayne Trust and Confidence in [Beeston], for and concerning the Managing of their Affayres'.[64] Whether Beeston betrayed that trust in full or not, the loss that Queen Anne's Men suffered was to the advantage of the new Queen Henrietta's Men. With few start-up costs and the inheritance of an amalgamated repertory of proven commercial viability, Queen Henrietta's Men were never to be delayed by a lack of performance material and the means by which to stage it. In this sense, the largely predetermined repertory of the new company, accompanied by a full wardrobe and a stock of props, was non-negotiable in terms of both content and aesthetics – at least initially. After two decades' experience working in the theatres, and eight years' management of the Cockpit behind him, Beeston had all the necessary material assets in place to ensure his new company's success. It was the actors and dramatists who were tasked with taking that investment forwards.

MANAGING THE ACTORS

Beeston recruited the actors who would make up Queen Henrietta's Men from various origins, drawing together a troupe with a range of experience and aptitudes between them. Some of the actors he had known for years – some stayed with Queen Henrietta's Men for the length of the company's career, and remained at the Cockpit with Beeston's Boys from 1637. Some of them moved around between several companies over this time; a few went on to have more successful careers following the breaking of Queen Henrietta's Men. In several cases, meaningful, lasting relationships were formed between company personnel, and one of the actors married into Beeston's family. Others emerge in the records from nowhere, with no trace of prior theatrical experience behind them. They appear a few times in cast-lists, and then fade into obscurity. There is limited evidence on which to draw when establishing the company make-up, but it is possible to develop a sense of the shape of the company from the few cast-lists and records that survive, and establish the core of actors who held the larger responsibilities. What becomes particularly clear is that Beeston did not manage the actors themselves in as authoritative a fashion as has been supposed. While Beeston may have owned the material possessions in his theatre outright, his dealings in human resources were far more conditional.

A closer look at the recruitment of the company foregrounds the extent to which Beeston depended on the good will and trust of his actors, as

much as they upon his assets. Few of Queen Henrietta's Men had performed at the Cockpit previously, and so they lacked the expertise that
Beeston's former acting colleagues had gained at the venue. Only Anthony
Turner and William Sherlock transferred from Lady Elizabeth's Men at
the Cockpit to the venue's new troupe, while John Blaney, William Robbins
(or Robinson), and Richard Perkins joined the company from Queen
Anne's Men (who were by then known as the Revels company) at the Red
Bull. With the exception of Blaney, these men have more prominence in
the records than many of their colleagues. Beeston entrusted the two men
he had worked with most recently at the Cockpit with duties related to
the running of the theatre and company. Sherlock occupied the tenement
adjoining the Cockpit in 1617, and presumably acted as some kind of
keeper for Beeston's property at this time and perhaps in the years following.[65] He was also one of the more prominent actors in the company;
the cast-lists that survive suggest that he was called on to play roles
including the treacherous Brand in *King John and Matilda* – a performance
he executed 'excellently well' according to the edition's cast-list – Ruffman
in *The Fair Maid of the West*, and Lodam, 'a fat Gentle-man', in Shirley's
The Wedding.[66] Turner's roles were smaller – though Bentley points out
that three of his known parts were old men, he was also cast (presumably
for comic effect) in the role of a kitchen maid in *The Fair Maid of the
West*. But in addition he played some kind of administrative, but financial,
role for Beeston in company operations. A transcript from Herbert's records
made by Craven Ord suggests that he visited the Revels Office in 1631,
when Turner was entrusted with the money required to repay Herbert for
a cask of claret given to the Treasurer of the Chamber on behalf of Queen
Henrietta's Men.[67]

When it came to acting parts, it was Beeston's colleagues from the Red
Bull who took centre stage and became talked-of performers in his new
venture. William Robbins was known for playing comic parts; he was
referred to as a 'Comedian', and was also described in the 1640s as one
of '[t]hose of principal Note at the *Cockpit*'.[68] He played the parts of
eunuchs in both *The Renegado* and *The Fair Maid of the West*, and
Rawbone, the exaggeratedly 'thin' comic counterpoint to Sherlock's cor-
pulent Lodam, in *The Wedding*. Richard Perkins had also gained years
of acting experience at the Red Bull, and was congratulated for his role
in Webster's *The White Devil*; Webster wrote that 'the worth of his action
did Crowne both the beginning and end' of the play.[69] He also played the
part of Barabas in the 1630s revival of Marlowe's *The Jew of Malta* by
Queen Henrietta's Men, as well as a wide variety of roles and character
types in other plays of the company's for which cast-lists are available.
The fact that he left to join Beeston's new troupe and abandoned the

successful King's Men, the most dominant company of that period in critical accounts, has been read as evidence of Beeston's formidable powers of persuasion; for what other reason would Perkins forsake the King's Men and their celebrated repertory?[70] At the same time, Beeston's recruitment of Perkins has been considered to be a tactical coup, and, more widely, likened to a 'private cull' of one of the market's leading players; a variation on the state-sponsored intervention of 1583, in which the Master of the Revels directed the formation of the first Queen's Men, and of 1594, when the official duopoly held by the Lord Admiral's Men and Lord Chamberlain's Men was established.[71]

The execution of such a strategic enterprise would have required not only a level of systematic calculation that is unsupported by the evidence, but powers of coordination which outstripped Beeston's reach. Perkins, Sherlock, and Turner were slow to join Queen Henrietta's Men, and were not in place as actors on the company's opening. As Bentley suggests, their absence from the early cast-list of *The Renegado*, licensed to Lady Elizabeth's Men but performed by Queen Henrietta's Men at the Cockpit, cannot be explained by 'an oversight, nor the performance of small unassigned roles, nor the omission of suitable parts from the play'.[72] These established actors appear to have joined the company slightly later, and their delayed entry indicates the existence of personal or professional bonds to be negotiated in company transfers, rather than a decisive and authoritarian selection on Beeston's part – particularly, perhaps, on the part of Perkins. The apparent postponement of Turner's and Sherlock's company membership is less accountable, but the possibility that there might have been hesitation among actors to subscribe immediately to the player-manager's new project has never been seriously entertained. It might also account for the conspicuously few other known players to have become involved in the new queen's company; Beeston had already displaced three companies from his new venue within a decade, while legal accusations from one of them, Queen Anne's Men, were only a few years old.

The fact that some of the actors in the newly formed Queen Henrietta's Men do not appear in theatrical annals prior to 1629 further suggests that Beeston's efforts to assemble a company were somewhat provisional, and not as finely orchestrated as has been thought.[73] These players included John Dobson and William Reignolds, who appear in one or two cast-lists and are not heard of again. Edward Shakerley, who was at the Cockpit in 1623, is hard to trace from 1625; his absence in the records after this time felt so pronounced to Bentley that he conjectured that the actor might have died thereafter.[74] The boy players associated with the company included John Page, Hugh Clark (Beeston's nephew),[75] Edward Rogers, and Theophilius Bird. These young actors are likely to have had some experience of performing onstage before taking on roles such as the tavern-maid heroine Bess in *The Fair Maid of the West* and the strong female parts in *The Renegado*, but whether they were connected with any company prior to their work with Queen Henrietta's Men remains unclear. The relative anonymity of most of the men and boys indicates that the company was 'new' to London theatre audiences in the most fundamental of ways. This provides a staunch challenge to Bentley's curious assumption that Beeston's primary motivation for the formation of a new company was the drawing 'from the two companies in which he was interested' (Queen Anne's Men and Lady Elizabeth's Men) 'to form a third'.[76] The launch of the new company, lacking Perkins, Sherlock, and Turner at the outset, seems instead to have been decidedly risky for Beeston. A fully furnished playhouse and prop store might have enabled commercial success, but it was upon this set of largely unknown actors, novices among them, that Beeston depended for his return.

Beeston would continue to depend on the actors for as long as the company operated, a professional reliance that, technically at least, afforded players a position of power within the economy of the theatre business. His predecessors and contemporaries in company management recognised this, and sought to ensure the continued loyalty of company members through contractual bonds that demanded unconditional allegiance. The bonds that Philip Henslowe enforced in 1597/98, demanding the loyalty of actors to his company, are an early example of a system of prescribed assurances and agreements that developed with the risks associated with playhouse ownership. After Richard Jones and Thomas Downton left the Admiral's Men in 1597 to play for Pembroke's Men at Francis Langley's Swan theatre, the ensuing scandal over *The Isle of Dogs* necessitated their prompt return to Henslowe at the Rose, who consequently enforced bonds from his company members.[77] Langley had similarly imposed bonds and sureties upon five of Pembroke's Men at their opening of one hundred pounds per actor, ensuring their employment for twelve months.[78] These bonds appear to have set a precedent for future company procedure, as in 1624 Richard Gunnell also arranged a contractual agreement with his players at the Fortune, who obliged 'themselves to the said Mr. Gunnell to stay and play there' at his theatre.[79] When Richard Heton managed the second Queen Henrietta's Men at Salisbury Court, he attempted to ensure that the company 'enter[ed] into Articles wth me to continew there for 7 yeares, upon the same condicons they haue had for a yeare and halfe last past, and such as refuse to be removed, and others placed in their roomes'.[80]

There is no evidence to suggest that Beeston placed such stringent demands on the players in his employment, however. Heton appears to have been under considerable duress at the time of issuing his 'Instructions' to the new Queen Henrietta's Men. He mentions that some of the company had 'many tymes threatned' to leave Salisbury Court.[81] Heton suspected that they 'wold make use of o^r house but untill they could p'vyde another upon better termes', complained that the actors, unbound by a formal agreement, were 'at libertie' among themselves, and reported 'many differences and disturbances' between the actors and the housekeepers.[82] The manager was plagued by 'generall discontents' within his company, which included an active attempt on the part of his actors to bring about a working scenario that more closely represented their past experience at the Cockpit, or – more decisively – to leave Salisbury Court altogether for the Cockpit; he wrote that 'some of' the actors – possibly those who had just transferred from Beeston's company of Queen Henrietta's Men – 'have treated upon Condicons for the Cockpit playhouse'.[83] This evidence implies that Beeston ran his company in a way that was mutually beneficial for all parties involved, under conditions that were held up to Heton as a desirable model for future arrangements, in contrast with the strict bonds that he planned to impose. The relative freedom that the actors experienced at the Cockpit is presented negatively by Heton as responsible for the breaking up of the company in 1636: 'When her M^{ts} servants were at the Cockpitt, beinge all at liberty, they disperst themselves to severall Companies.'[84] At Salisbury Court, the actors were accused indirectly of 'exact[ing] [...] new imposicons upon the housekeepers at their pleasure'.[85] Perhaps, under Beeston's roof, the actors were granted considerably more latitude and agency than Heton felt appropriate. If that was the case, it was a strategy that worked; very few of Beeston's company members left Queen Henrietta's Men once they had joined. The departures of William Wilbraham, John Young, and the clown Timothy Reade, who had all left to perform at Salisbury Court by 1634, implies that they were free to do so if they wished.

The bonds of allegiance that were formed within the company also suggest another factor underlying its apparent unity and stability, one that was based on more solid, meaningful, and permanent grounds than those provided by inhibiting legalities. Many of Queen Henrietta's Men formed lasting relationships and connections with each other during the period of their work in the company. Richard Perkins had known Beeston since his time at the Red Bull, and was one of the actors, named alongside Beeston, in an order made in 1622 to repair the highways outside the theatre.[86] As we have seen, a few years prior to this he had testified against Beeston in the Smith vs. Beeston lawsuit. But in the 1630s Perkins was called to court alongside him, to answer for debts incurred by the purchase of hats. Though legal wrangling might have tested the relationship, Perkins was accustomed to supporting his manager in legal and practical terms, and an element of the personal presumably contributed to the lasting association between the men. Perkins had been performing Heywood's plays on and off for three decades, and his friendship with Michael Bowyer and John Sumner is evidenced more precisely. Bowyer left a large sum of money to Perkins upon his death: £50 or 5s a week for life.[87] If James Wright's testimony can be trusted, it seems that Sumner and Perkins retired together and, in the last years of their life, 'kept House together at *Clerkenwel*, and were there Buried [...] some Years before the Restauration'.[88] William Allen – who played the part of Massinger's renegado, and Mullisheg in Heywood's *Fair Maid of the West* – was charged with Beeston's wife for repeated instances of recusancy between 1614 and 1616.[89] Theophilius Bird married directly into the Beeston family during his time at the Cockpit; Beeston refers to his daughter Anne, in his will, as Theophilius's wife.[90] William Robbins married Cisley Browne, Beeston's sister-in-law, in 1622.[91] The bonds of allegiance cultivated at the Cockpit suggest that relationships held the company in place as much as any contract could.

The importance of actors' agency is also borne out by the patterns in which actors moved together across companies – for they often appear to have moved in pairs or units, suggesting that strong interpersonal relations could underlie professional choices. When Wilbraham and Young left the Cockpit for Salisbury Court, it is likely that they went together. When Henry Herbert 'disposed' of Perkins, Sumner, Sherlock, and Turner to Salisbury Court in 1637, he chose to transfer a unified team of actors who had both worked together for years and claimed the kinds of strong personal and professional ties that could provide a measure of stability in times of upheaval and unrest. Many of the actors of Queen Henrietta's Men stayed on at the Cockpit to perform in Beeston's boy company, but we need not assume that their loyalty was based on contractual obligation. Biography-centred research in theatre history (particularly the work of William Ingram and David Kathman) continues to demonstrate the importance of individual commitments and preferences among players and theatrical personnel, in addition to those of their managers. It is important not to discount or deny the players' autonomous, interpersonal networks, networks that could equal those established by the managerial figures who loom out of theatre history at us – Henslowe, Heton, Langley. Beeston seems to have taken on control of the properties, plays, and finances of the company in a way that positions him at the forefront of the records – it is he who receives money for court payments and participates in the majority of transactions with the Master of the Revels. But he operated within a professional industry that required the good will and resources of players in relationships that were respected and formalised to some degree, but which were not necessarily unconditional or legally binding. In this respect, Beeston's position seems far more negotiable than has previously been allowed; his efforts to maintain not only a repertory, but also a corresponding and complementary company to act it, required more skill and personal investment than he is typically credited with.

MANAGING THE PLAYWRIGHTS

The procurement of new plays for the company was a continuing priority and concern for Beeston. What was the nature of his relationship with the dramatists whose work shaped and embodied the repertory, in its rawest terms, and as it developed over the 1630s? The issue of playwright management is crucial to the understanding of repertory study, determining as it does the process by which competitive repertories were produced and accumulated, the degree of control that 'impresario' managers had over the repertories that their companies performed, and the autonomy of their immediate originators, the playwrights. It is a particularly interesting question to ask in relation to Queen Henrietta's Men, as Beeston's practice in this regard has been thought to parallel those of his contemporaries, Richard Gunnell and Richard Heton. On 20 July 1635 the dramatist Richard Brome agreed to a contract with the King's Revels company, then under the leadership of Richard Gunnell, and bound his services as a playwright exclusively to the Salisbury Court theatre. Brome had committed himself 'for the terme of three years [...] with his best Arte and Industrye [to] write eve*r*ye yeare three plays and deliu^er them to the Companye of players theere Acteinge for the tyme beinge'.[92] At the same time, he had agreed not to provide 'any playe or any *p*te of a playe to anye other players or playe howse'. Brome's payment for such services was to amount to fifteen shillings a week, plus an extra day's profit for every new play. The implications that contractual work of this kind had for the production of repertories was significant. Under these conditions, playwrights became associated exclusively with companies, to which the extent of their obligation was formally defined. Contract-holding managers like Gunnell exerted a regulatory control over the repertory, its rate of consolidation, and the origination of its plays.[93]

The contractual model provided by Brome's contract has become representative, in theatre-historical accounts, of standard theatrical practice in the period. The assumption of contractual bindings is most commonly made in relation to James Shirley, as a consequence of his steady production of plays for Queen Henrietta's Men. Shirley has been described in terms of one of Beeston's 'acquisitions', the Cockpit's 'resident writer'.[94] Bentley found Shirley's production of 'an average two plays a year' for

Queen Henrietta's Men consistent with contractually regimented behaviour, which resulted in the conclusion that 'Evidently [...] Shirley was under contract to the company or the manager of the Phoenix [the Cockpit], as Richard Brome is known to have been at Salisbury Court.'[95] But the assumption that Beeston bound the Cockpit dramatists by contract rests upon the extrapolation of the terms of Brome's contract to the wider profession, and the perception of Beeston's propensity for manipulative behaviour. Casting Beeston in this role is also related to the wider tendency to consider Caroline drama as limited, weakened, somehow subdued, in which context impresario managers bent the wills of their hired playwrights under the banner of financial gain – a narrative that stands in contrast to the 'democratic' practices of the King's Men, who, in this received account, crafted their repertory in harmonious collaboration.[96] But how typical was Brome's contract, and how far can it be applied to playwright–manager relations at this time and the operations of Queen Henrietta's Men? The remainder of this discussion attempts to extricate what is actually known about Brome's contract, in the context of legal precedents and the specific circumstances of the agreement, from what has been assumed. In doing so it repositions the relevance of Brome's contract to the interpretation of Beeston's managerial practice and the repertory strategy of Queen Henrietta's Men. As with the actors at the Cockpit, there is no evidence that Beeston enforced longstanding contractual obligations among dramatists. The sense of an archetypal impresario seems, once more, to exist more firmly in inherited narratives than in the records and the historical evidence itself.

The first indication that Brome's contract might not constitute normal practice in the theatre profession is that Brome found himself in a situation that was untenable; he broke the terms of the contract repeatedly. The terms and conditions of the agreement are recorded in a requests proceedings bill of complaint filed on 12 February 1640 by the company then renting the Salisbury Court to which Brome was contracted: the new, second Queen Henrietta's Men. They claimed that Brome had failed to deliver four of his nine promised plays by 1638, and that he had, in addition, sold 'one of the playes which hee made [...] in the said tyme vnto Christopher Beeston gent and William Beeston' at the Cockpit.[97] Heton attempted to bind Brome by a second contract in 1638 – an agreement that was, as Bradley Ryner has pointed out, not signed by Brome, and tilted in favour of Heton and his Salisbury Court players; this second contractual effort on Heton's part was in a sense a response to the failures of the first, a negotiation that Ryner rightly argues 'should invite scepticism that either party could have seen it as a tenable framework for a continued relationship', so severe were the repercussions for Brome's failure to meet its terms.[98] Under the terms of the 1638 contract it was proposed that Brome's salary would rise to twenty shillings a week, but three plays annually were required for a term of seven years, on top of the plays already owed. Though the contract was left unsigned, Heton claimed that Brome had agreed to honour the new arrangement – though once again Brome was not able to meet its terms, and by the end of the year he was accused of being in arrears by one new play. The Heton complaint records that, by this time, Brome had 'wholly applie[d] himself vnto the said Beeston and the Companie of players Acteinge att the playhowse of the Phoenixe [or Cockpit] in Drury Lane'.[99] For his part, Brome denied the charge, and argued instead that the company had turned down two new plays written for Heton – one around September of 1638, and another before Easter 1639.

The only other formal contract known at the time of writing was made between Lawrence and John Dutton, Thomas Goffe, and the playwright Rowland Broughton, and this agreement was also unsustainable. A lawsuit of 26 January 1573 records that Broughton failed to produce the *eighteen* plays that he had promised to deliver at deadlines spaced over a period of two and a half years.[100] Although Broughton's case was extreme, such measured demands had proved an unsuccessful mode of theatrical production sixty years prior to Brome's agreement. Beyond this, there is little precedent for contracts that bound playwrights in this way, although Roslyn Knutson has drawn attention to two contracts documented in Henslowe's papers.[101] The first of these was made on 28 February 1599: an agreement between Henslowe (on behalf of the Admiral's Men) and Henry Porter. Henslowe's loan to Porter of forty shillings 'in earneste of' a play is recorded here, and also the agreement that 'for the Resayte of that money' Porter gave Henslowe 'his faythfulle promysse that I shold haue alle the boockes wch he writte ether him sellfe or wth any other'.[102] These circumstances suggest that Henslowe claimed the right to all of Porter's plays, including those that he wrote collaboratively with other dramatists, but it does not specify a rate of production or impose delivery deadlines. Indeed, a 'faythfulle promysse' was deemed sufficiently binding. Henry Chettle might also have been bound to Henslowe in a similar manner, since on 25 March 1602 Henslowe lent the sum of £3 to Thomas Downton and Edward Alleyn to pay Henry Chettle, who would 'writte for them' an unspecified number of plays (the entry is unfinished).[103] This arrangement is more typical of the way in which Henslowe commissioned plays for the Admiral's Men during this time, however, rather than a more formalised and exclusive contractual binding.[104]

These examples suggest that although dramatists often made agreements with managers concerning the destination and ownership of their plays, formalised contracts in the sense that are suggested by Brome's court depositions were unusual. Heton failed to safeguard the contractual documents, both the original contract and the unsigned draft of the second agreement, which might indicate that such formal bindings were not a common priority in the theatrical profession. He complained that the 'Artickles and writeinges' of the contractual agreements between himself and Brome had been 'casually lost & mislayed or are Cõme to the hands of the said Brome', leaving him with no material basis for legal prosecution.[105] C. J. Sisson observed a similar uncertainty when it came to dealing with binding contractual agreements issued by playhouse managers, writing with respect to Langley's bonds of 1600 that the court seemed 'reluctant to deal with contracts of this nature, either because of their intangible quality, or because they were beneath the dignity of the Court, or for both reasons'.[106]

It is also important to note the conditions under which contractual bindings arose. When Henslowe enforced bonds from his actors in 1597, he had just experienced the players' expression of their own autonomy at its most extreme, in their abandonment of his playhouse. Langley initiated contracts among the actors at the Swan at the outset of a new theatrical investment; the bonds with which Gunnell tied Palsgrave's Men were enforced during perpetual financial struggle following the fire at the Fortune.[107] With respect to the arrangements made between Henslowe and Porter, Knutson has suggested that this might have been prompted by the imminent arrival of new competition, when the Chamberlain's Men moved to the nearby Maid Lane.[108] The specific circumstances in which Brome's contract was formed were also highly unusual.[109] As far as is known, Heton did not possess the wealth of experience upon which Beeston could draw when it came to making managerial judgements and decisions in the theatre business. As we have seen in the discussion of actors' contracts above, his continued attempt to formalise relations and tighten his governance through written conditions was company-wide; maintaining contractual relations with Brome was just part of the process. When the contract was first formulated, the Salisbury Court company was 'in the Infancie of theire setting vpp'.[110] These were times of financial and professional stress. Contracts provided what must have looked like an indemnity plan to managers for whom the stakes had risen, a safe method of ensuring the production of new plays, and the prosperity that could come with this, over periods of disruption and uncertainty; however, that does not make them generally representative.

Furthermore, while systems of bonds and contracts among players continued to hold currency over the decades, Henslowe's 1597 bonds suggest that contracts were not usually used in the management of playwrights.

Henslowe contracted Thomas Heywood, who was writing plays for the Lord Admiral's Men at the time, in the capacity of a player rather than a dramatist, and Ben Jonson also seems to have been free from a binding contract.[111] There is evidence that playwrights understood themselves to be at liberty to identify the best buyer for plays, even after making promises or receiving part payment from another buyer, as Robert Daborne's behaviour while working on *The Arraignment of London* seems to suggest.[112] Such elasticity in 'contractual' arrangements, perceived or otherwise, might go some way to explaining the disconnect between Heton's expectations and those of Brome, who claimed that he was 'vnwilling to vndertake [...] more then hee *could well performe*' at the time of committing to the terms of the 1635 contract, but nevertheless signed on the line.[113] As Ann Haaker noted, the Salisbury Court players had assured him that the annual stipulation of three plays was a guarantee of dedication rather than the quantitative obligation that it appears to be; if loyal, he need not produce more plays than he 'could or should bee able well and conveyniently to doe or perform*e*'.[114]

More generally, the behaviour of professional dramatists over the wider period suggests that contractual obligation, as it is understood in the Brome–Heton case, is an inappropriate description of established methods of production. John Fletcher wrote for various companies until 1616, and Jonson, Heywood, and Dekker all tended to work periodically for a set of established employers while branching out into new relationships and securing relatively short-term associations with a variety of companies. Ford also invested in a network of companies for which he might work.[115] The demands of particular managers in terms of new plays, and the commitments of other dramatists, might also have affected the opportunities available for playwrights. Shirley appears to have been at his least active for Queen Henrietta's Men in the years prior to 1630, when he was writing around one play every eighteen months for the Cockpit. This period coincides with the time during which Heywood and Ford were writing most for the Cockpit stage. During his work for Queen Henrietta's Men, Shirley also wrote *The Changes* for the King's Revels at Salisbury Court and might have revised *Love's Pilgrimage* for the King's Men in 1635, inserting into it a scene from Jonson's *The New Inn*.[116] This latter instance is recorded by Malone in one of his transcripts from Herbert's office-book, but has been largely ignored as it coincides with the period in which Shirley was assumed to have been writing, exclusively, for Queen Henrietta's Men.

If Shirley had revised plays for the King's Men at the same time that he wrote plays for Queen Henrietta's Men, it would resemble a kind of behaviour that was more representative of typical relations between dramatists and companies. He would return to work for the King's Men again after 1640. Perhaps it would be helpful to think of his relationship with the King's Men as more continuous and ongoing than has been recognised, rather than as interrupted by an isolated period of time during which his services were strictly commandeered by their rivals at the Cockpit. Patterns of employment across the profession suggest that the autonomy of playwrights was an important factor in the building of repertories; the results of that autonomy could also become definitive in the formation of early modern canons, bringing about collaboratively authored plays which have received much critical attention.[117] Beeston's commitment to contractual relations is indeterminate, but importantly so, in this context.

Beeston took an active role in commissioning plays on an individual basis, however; Brome sought employment from the manager and his son during the plague closure of 1636; William Beeston lent him £6 on the basis that he 'Compose and write a play for the Cockpitt Company'.[118] As Matusiak notes, this suggests that the Beestons remained intimately involved with the process of repertory-building at its most basic level, and 'directly negotiated for new scripts on behalf of the Cockpit's actors'.[119] So Christopher Beeston's determination of the repertory, aided by the agency and skills of his son, encompassed not only the provision of revivals, which in at least one case had been rewritten or revised by one of them, but decisions about which dramatists to accept work from – and, as Chapter 2 explores, influence over the content of that work. The potential for Beeston's aesthetic influence over the shape of the repertory is, therefore, appreciable; at the very least, he was invested in the repertory's content in a hands-on and engaged way, as the revision of an old revival shows. This was a quality that playwrights might have found appealing in a manager, if not challenging.

The fact that Brome felt he could seek effective employment from Beeston – relief from the financial hardship brought on by plague – is further evidence of Beeston's respectable and fair dealings with the front line of his theatrical personnel at this time. Heton felt that the Beestons had been manipulative in this; they had promised to be Brome's 'good freinde and to give him more salarye' than he himself had offered.[120] But the policies that Beeston implemented at the Cockpit during the late 1620s and the 1630s seem to have been, for both actors and playwrights, preferable to some of the alternatives offered elsewhere. As the next section sets out, Beeston worked hard to maintain a trustworthy reputation and promote good will in his dealings on behalf of the company with Henry Herbert, the Master of the Revels. His involvement in the licensing of plays, and the role he played as a mediating figure between dramatists and the authorities, gives a more concrete indication of the ways in which Beeston was accustomed to easing professional relationships and minimising conflict to the mutual benefit of all involved.

MANAGING THE AUTHORITIES

The relationship between company manager and the Master of the Revels was crucial to company success. Transcripts from Herbert's records of the Revels Office suggest that Beeston was well aware of this, and that negotiating that relationship could take up a considerable amount of resources in time and energy. This was an aspect of management for which Beeston took primary responsibility; the transcribed records to which we have access suggest that Beeston met most often with Herbert, and acted as his point of contact with the company. Many of the transcripts fail to name any company member; as has been noted in the Introduction, such features of the transcripts might reflect the directed interests and preoccupations of those scholars who wrote out and often paraphrased Herbert's original entries.[121] What we see in terms of Beeston's representation of the company to the Revels Office might be a result of skewed evidence, then – but we know at least that he played a key role in transactions with the licensing authorities. In August 1633 Herbert 'Received of Biston' a fee of £3 for *Hymen's Holiday*, and a further £1 for 'some alterations in it' – perhaps, as with the other 'ould play' Herbert licensed for the Cockpit, those alterations and revisions were made by Christopher or William. This payment was made face-to-face, at a meeting arranged 'at the ould exchange'.[122] In other cases, the lines of communication seem a little less direct; when the king commanded that a troupe of visiting players be permitted to use the Cockpit as a venue over Lent in 1634, Herbert apparently 'signifyed' this information 'to Mr. Beeston the same day'.[123] The command might have been conveyed by messenger, but Beeston was the sole recipient; instructions were carried straight to him rather than going through an intermediary. He chose to remain at the centre of his operation.

At no time was this more important than when one of the dramatists he had employed overstepped the mark and provoked Herbert's condemnation, in the Master of the Revels' role as state censor. When Shirley's *The Ball* attracted the wrong kind of attention in its satirical impersonation of courtiers, Beeston pre-empted Herbert's intention to forbid its performance by promising the play's correction, and assuring future vigilance against similar occurrences.[124] His treatment of the situation was conducted with appropriate gravity; a company asset was at stake, as well as a professional reputation. Malone's transcript of Herbert's entry suggests that Beeston transferred final responsibility to the play's author, offering that he 'would not suffer [the offence] to be done by the poett any more, who deserves to be punisht'.[125] The sincerity of Beeston's sentiment as represented by Malone has been doubted, treated as an empty promise or another attempt to defer responsibility. G. E. Bentley viewed the assurance with suspicion, as further proof of Beeston's shrewd and artful manipulation of those with whom he dealt on a professional level: 'It was not every manager who could so soothe away the indignation of the Master of the Revels and promise his company back into favour.'[126] Though Beeston blamed Shirley for the fault, his promise to take responsibility for the dramatist's punishment can be read as another expression of control over the repertory.[127]

Furthermore, the relationship between Beeston and Herbert appears to have gone beyond the strictly professional. His gift of 'a payre of gloves, that cost him at least twenty shillings' to Herbert's wife on the same occasion that he made the payments relating to *Hymen's Holiday* is suggestive of a carefully managed relationship – one that depended on a personal, more intimate, level of investment.[128] Queen Henrietta's Men also appear to have given Herbert a 'play share' at one point, which might have constituted a share in Beeston's profits at a certain time.[129] The benefits of such a relationship might work both ways. Beeston worked hard to smooth relations and give his company the best chance possible in the face of the strictures of state censorship and the potentially ruinous consequences of royal dictates. But at the same time, the Master of the Revels depended upon the continued success of the theatre for his livelihood and the legitimacy of his royal appointment, and required the respect of the players to ensure this.[130] On occasion, Herbert made his own allowance and gesture of good will in order to secure these relations with Beeston, as is evidenced by the entry in which Turner repaid Herbert for the case of wine that he had sent on behalf of the company.

This is one of the relatively rare occasions on which we glimpse one of Beeston's players interacting with Herbert, but there might have been other such instances when company members represented Beeston, or visited Herbert on company business. One of Malone's transcripts seems to imply that Herbert expected a visit from Shirley after licensing *The Young Admiral*, and that Shirley might read from the office-book itself: 'When Mr. Sherley hath read this approbation, I know it will encourage him to pursue this beneficial and cleanly way of poetry.'[131] The relationship between Herbert and Shirley is certainly of note, and prompts further discussion later in this book.[132] Over the years various members of Queen

Henrietta's Men must have had face-to-face dealings with the Master of the Revels, members whose names have dropped out of the transcripts and disappeared from the record. The immediacy of the kind of contact that Beeston and nominated actors had with Herbert enabled all involved to reach compromises on censorship, the demands of court performance, and the administrative tasks of company operation, which were reciprocally advantageous; in this, Beeston and Herbert cooperated and were collaborative.

This is not to suggest that Beeston's relationship with Herbert was manipulative, or that this approach was indicative of underhand dealing. Herbert maintained similar relationships based on mutual assurance and trust with other companies, in his willingness to license unexamined plays on the assurance of the players.[133] It is likely that any London-based company manager knew that striking a respectfully friendly relationship with Herbert might permit them to take the odd liberty, provided they did not jeopardise the Master's professional role, and that they limited social commentary to within the 'acceptable band of loyal opinion' that Herbert sought to enforce.[134] According to this model, Beeston's negotiations with Herbert need not represent disreputable plays for favour or bribes, but are characteristic of the normal operation and priorities of the Office's system of management and licensing. In the case of Queen Henrietta's Men, Beeston's relationship with Herbert proved important to the company, rescuing dramatists from 'punishment'. As is explored in Chapter 2, in a fuller discussion of Herbert's interest and involvement in the company, the relationship could impact on repertory formation, dramatic content, and the aesthetic focus of particular plays, or groups of plays within a repertory. But it was not necessarily inappropriate or coercive. Beeston worked to establish a trustworthy and reliable reputation with Herbert, within a gift economy, one in which small loans, favours, and personal assurances continued to retain currency.

THE COMPANY ON TOUR

The last part of this chapter discusses the evidence for an important part of company life from which critical accounts have typically excluded Queen Henrietta's Men. Since the first permanent playing structures were erected in London, touring had been a crucial facet of professional business for players based in the city. As the *Records of Early English Drama* (*REED*) project has emphasised, managers and companies were doing more with their repertories than London-based records can witness. There is ample evidence that established, London-based companies were regularly abroad in the English countryside, even after the profession began to ground itself more firmly within the social structure and topography of London and to obtain security in the city.[135] Instead of playing before the same audience base each day, touring companies could (in theory) rehearse only one play and carry it from town to town, assuming no overlap in patrons. For any repertory company, touring represented a means of exploiting the commodity of the play to its maximum potential, and in doing so engage in one of the most fundamental principles of early modern professional theatre and repertory strategy: that of making old plays new, or newly popular. But until relatively recently, touring has been traditionally construed as a means of easing trauma or commercial crisis, such as the breaking of a company or loss of a patron.[136] And Beeston in particular has been considered averse to leaving London, focused intently on his Drury Lane playhouse and the allure of the royal court.[137] But Beeston had already travelled on tour with Queen Anne's Men in the 1610s, and there was at least one touring Queen's Men active in the 1630s. Did Beeston's managerial influence over company operations extend beyond the running of the Cockpit on Drury Lane, and out across the countryside towards East Anglia and the Midlands?

A company called the Queen's Men appears twice in provincial town records of the Caroline era. In June 1633 the Mayor's Court Books of Norwich document that 'Elias Gost and his Company of the Quenes players haueinge shewed to mr Maior their patent were desired to forbeare And had Twenty Shillinges as a gratuity given to him.'[138] Dismissals of this kind were not uncommon in this period, especially in Norwich, a town that appears to have grown increasingly inhospitable to travelling companies.[139] Significantly, dismissal might indicate an unscheduled visit, and the probability of widespread touring rather than a specific, planned appointment. It is reasonable to infer that during the same period the Queen's Men played at other provincial venues. The company's second appearance is documented in November 1636, this time in Coventry, and this time in performance. The Chamberlain's and Warden's Account Book records a payment of twenty-five shillings for a play by 'the Queenes players at the parlor'.[140] By this time, the theatres in London had closed; when they reopened, Beeston's Boys would have replaced Queen Henrietta's Men at the Cockpit. The record might constitute evidence of the company's effort to reap rewards from their playing beyond the city during its prohibitive sickness. The 1633 tour, on the other hand, does not correspond with any documented plague closure or recorded event in the career of the company, although the incident in 1635, when the king deprived Queen Henrietta's Men of their commercial base by offering their Cockpit playhouse to a visiting French troupe, suggests that professional companies could never wholly rely upon their permanent and even privately owned playhouses.[141]

So few details survive concerning the touring Queen's Men that the relationship of the company to Beeston's enterprise is very difficult to ascertain. What is interesting about the presence of a Queen's Men on tour in the 1630s is the question that it foregrounds in terms of the nature and definition of company, for the touring Queen's Men of the 1630s might not have borne any relation to Beeston's London company. Evidence which might suggest that we need to decouple the Cockpit's Queen Henrietta's Men from the company recorded in the provinces begins with the identification of Elias Guest – or Ellis Guest, as he is more commonly known – the recipient of the Norwich dismissal gratuity. Guest was presumably a leading company member of the touring Queen's Men as they were assembled at Norwich, or was at least in some way representational, but he is not once associated with Queen Henrietta's Men at the Cockpit – or with any professional, London-based troupe. Alone, this amounts to little; though cast-lists and the official company patent provide relatively accurate details of company composition at given moments, the practicalities of touring and of general circumstances in company operation might have necessitated irregularities in membership. Itinerant actors such as Guest appear to have changed company allegiance relatively freely, and performed in a number of troupes. And companies on tour were far more flexible than their London-based incarnations, which could be in themselves relatively transient. According to necessity, they gained and lost members as they travelled, divided, and sometimes joined with other companies to give joint performances or tours.[142] It is conceivable that Guest, as an experienced travelling actor, could have joined the London-based company on its tours – though perhaps surprising that he would receive payment on its behalf.

Equally, it is possible that there was a provincial company travelling under the name of Queen Henrietta's Men. Guest might have been the entrepreneurial leader of such a troupe, capitalising upon the name of Beeston's troupe. Lady Elizabeth's Men appear to have had a provincial counterpart, which played under the same name in parallel to the London company.[143] The companies were entirely independent, in terms of membership and repertory, and Ellis Guest was also connected to this earlier provincial 'duplicate'.[144] Another possibility is that Guest's duplicate company was fraudulent, and that he was appropriating the queen's name unlawfully to further an impostor company. The actor Martin Slater, whom Guest toured with later in the 1620s, was apprehended for doing just this with Thomas Swinnerton in 1616 after duplicating a patent for a Queen Anne's company and separating 'themselves from their said Company'.[145]

A further possibility is that the touring Queen's Men were unrelated to Queen Henrietta Maria in any sense at all. The assumption that a company's name must refer to the current ruling queen, which is the only basis for the connection of the 1630s troupe to Henrietta Maria, is a dangerous one. After Queen Elizabeth's death, there are at least two records in the provinces of a company playing in her name, both of which are connected to Martin Slater, bearer of fraudulent patents. Bentley suggested that this company attribution was 'an obvious mistake, perhaps of a clerk whose memories of the days of Good Queen Bess were too strong for him'.[146] But reaching for administrative error, induced in this narrative by fond nostalgia, only glosses over what appears to be one of the most interesting features of provincial travelling. A company travelled under the auspices of the late Queen Anne after her death, journeying into the country sometime during 1619/20; it played in Coventry in 1620, represented there by Daniel Swinnerton.[147] Daniel Swinnerton's real identity has been the subject of much debate, as a Thomas Swinnerton is found in the 1603/4 patent for Queen Anne's company; Thomas also owned a share in the Red Bull playhouse, was named in the patent for Queen Anne's Men in 1604, and led a touring Queen's Men from 1616 until long after Anne's death. Thomas also applied for and was granted a patent for playing with Ellis Guest in March of 1624/5.[148] Were Guest and Swinnerton, whoever he was, playing together in this period under the auspices of the deceased Queen Anne? In this case, the nomenclature of the Queen's Players functions as a general title – a signifier empty of specificity, perhaps deliberately.

This is not necessarily a negative conclusion, a retreat from circumstances in which company output could be more clearly defined with respect to political purpose and patronage. Rather, it might be seen as characteristic of drama in the Caroline period, after so many years of development, so much cross-repertory movement, and two instances of regime change. But the shadowy presence of the touring Queen's Men at the peripheries of the records, the edge of the narrative, also indicates the lack of control over nomenclature and identity that managers such as Beeston might have experienced, knowingly or otherwise.

CONCLUSION

This chapter has examined the conditions of formation and the operations of Queen Henrietta's Men, from analysis of what is known about the company's economic circumstances, company composition, and the management of playwrights, to broader questions of control over company characteristics and identity. Attention to the origins of the company has led to a reassessment of the level and range of Beeston's authority as a theatrical manager. Beeston's process of recruitment – which seems to have been more prolonged than previously recognised, and less strategic than imagined – suggests that the company was newer in terms of its personnel, more of a novelty on the London theatrical scene, than might have been thought. Recognition of the autonomy of players, playwrights, and other theatrical personnel removes the control of company and identity from the locus of authority presumed by the impresario model, and permits the collaborative input of agents other than Beeston in the career of Queen Henrietta's Men and the management of their repertory. The importance of Henry Herbert's connection to Beeston, and Herbert's support of Shirley, underscores the extent to which commercial success might remain reliant on professional relationships that veered into the personal, and were conditional, sensitive by nature, governed by a diplomacy that need not entail deviance. It is particularly interesting that the elements of provisionality identified in this account can be diagnosed not in Beeston's formal arrangements – in relation to leaseholds, shareholding, and the ownership of possessions; all of these legalities, and the question of ownership over material assets, seem to have remained firmly within his control. They are seen, instead, in the human relationships that underpinned the business, the complex and subtle negotiations that Beeston seems to have readily acknowledged were not to be so neatly defined nor so easily contained. Rather than view these relationships as peripheral to Beeston's business in theatre, marginal in comparison with the commercial risk associated with impresarial playhouse ownership, they are recognised here as at the operation's centre, its heart. The picture that emerges of Queen Henrietta's Men seems more provisional, and more uncertain, than has been allowed – the company has a new beginning.

A surprising part of that new beginning is the kind of role that Beeston should be credited with in the creation and development of Queen Henrietta's Men. The design of the theatre, the revivals his companies produced, the costumes that dressed the actors, and the properties that dressed the productions – all of these were in Beeston's hands. His active role in the commissioning of plays and managing relations with the playwrights he employed, alongside the possibility that he might have had a hand in revising old plays for production, shows that his control over the aesthetics of the repertory also extended to design and content. In this way, he was intimately involved with the style of the repertory and its realisation as it was embodied in performance, as well as its management and the uses to which it was pressed. The next chapter goes on to explore one of the most high-profile and conspicuous of these uses, in the plays' performances at court before the royal audiences that gathered at Whitehall, Richmond, and Hampton Court.

NOTES

1 N. W. Bawcutt (ed.), *The Control and Censorship of Caroline Drama: The Records of Sir Henry Herbert, Master of the Revels 1623–73* (Oxford: Clarendon Press, 1996), p. 162; see also Leeds Barroll, *Politics, Plague, and Shakespeare's Theater: The Stuart Years* (Ithaca, NY: Cornell University Press, 1991), pp. 99–100.
2 Bawcutt (ed.), *Control and Censorship*, p. 162.
3 For more details on the playhouse closures of this year, and the ambiguity of the dating, see also G. E. Bentley, *The Jacobean and Caroline Stage*, 7 vols (Oxford: Oxford Clarendon Press, 1941–68), II, pp. 654–7.
4 Bentley, *Jacobean and Caroline Stage*, II, p. 363.
5 Bentley, *Jacobean and Caroline Stage*, II, p. 656.
6 Other theatre managers and companies clearly had the same idea, since shortly afterwards the Lord Mayor and Council reported 'comon stageplaies about the Citty'. Bentley, *Jacobean and Caroline Stage*, II, p. 656.
7 Bawcutt (ed.), *Control and Censorship*, p. 162; James Shirley, *The Maid's Revenge* (London, 1639).
8 Bentley, *Jacobean and Caroline Stage*, I, p. 219.
9 Transcribed by Peter Cunningham in *Shakespeare Society's Papers*, 4 vols (London: Shakespeare Society, 1844–49), IV, p. 96.
10 See reports of Dorset's defence of Henrietta Maria following the publication of William Prynne's *Histriomastix* in *A Complete Collection of State Trials and Proceedings for High Treason and Other Crimes and Misdemeanours from the Earliest Period to the Year 1783*, compiled by T. B. Howell, 33 vols (London, 1816–28), III (1816), pp. 582–4; and see also George L. Craik, Charles MacFarlane, and Hans Claude Hamilton, *The Pictorial History of England*, 8 vols (London, 1838–49), III (1840), p. 155.
11 See Scott McMillin and Sally Beth Maclean, *The Queen's Men and their Plays* (Cambridge: Cambridge University Press, 1998), pp. 10–17, for a historical and political overview of the 1583 formation of the Queen's Men.
12 Bawcutt (ed.), *Control and Censorship*, p. 201.
13 Bawcutt (ed.), *Control and Censorship*, p. 201.
14 Bentley, *Jacobean and Caroline Stage*, I, pp. 324–6; Bawcutt (ed.), *Control and Censorship*, p. 200.
15 Bentley, *Jacobean and Caroline Stage*, I, p. 327.
16 The question of how far the company was under the patronage of Queen Henrietta is explored in detail in Chapter 2.
17 Bentley, *Jacobean and Caroline Stage*, I, p. 184.
18 See licences given in Bawcutt (ed.), *Control and Censorship*, pp. 146, 147, 148, 159, 160.
19 Bentley, *Jacobean and Caroline Stage*, I, p. 186; Paul Slack, *The Impact of Plague in Tudor and Stuart England* (Oxford: Oxford University Press, 1985), p. 151; Patrick Morrah, *Restoration England* (London: Constable, 1979), p. 202.

20 Bawcutt (ed.), *Control and Censorship*, pp. 170–1.

21 Andrew Gurr, *The Shakespearian Playing Companies* (Oxford: Clarendon Press, 1996), p. 432; for descriptions of Heton as 'hard-nosed' and 'strong-minded', see p. 431.

22 Bentley, *Jacobean and Caroline Stage*, I, p. 218; and G. E. Bentley, 'The Theatres and the Actors', in *The Revels History of Drama in English, Volume IV: 1613–1660*, ed. Philip Edwards (London: Methuen, 1981), pp. 69–124 (p. 100).

23 TNA C2, Ch. I, H 28/26, transcribed in Bentley, *Jacobean and Caroline Stage*, VI, p. 48. The lease was renewed again in 1633.

24 *Acts of the Privy Council of England (1613–26)*, 8 vols (London, 1921–34), 1616/7, pp. 15, 334.

25 Letter of Edward Sherbourne, dated 8 March 1617, copied out by J. O. Halliwell-Phillipps in the *Fortune* scrapbook (now held at the Folger Library), and transcribed again by Bentley in *Jacobean and Caroline Stage*, VI, p. 54; John Stow, *Annales, or a Generall Chronicle of England, continued and augmented by Edmund Howes* (London: Richard Meighen, 1631), p. 1026b; letter from John Chamberlain to Sir Dudley Carleton, in *The Letters of John Chamberlain*, ed. Norman Egbert McClure, 2 vols (Philadelphia: The American Philosophical Society, 1939), II, pp. 59–60; Bentley, *Jacobean and Caroline Stage*, VI, p. 56.

26 Susan Cerasano, The "Business" of Shareholding, the Fortune Playhouses, and Francis Grace's Will', *Medieval and Renaissance Drama in England*, II (1985), 231–51 (pp. 245–56).

27 Eva Griffith, *A Jacobean Company and its Playhouse: The Queen's Servants at the Red Bull Theatre (c. 1605–1619)* (Cambridge: Cambridge University Press, 2013), pp. 227–35.

28 Gurr, *Shakespearian Playing Companies*, p. 97. See also Andrew Gurr, *The Shakespeare Company, 1594–1642* (Cambridge: Cambridge University Press, 2004), pp. 85–9.

29 See below, pp. 32–3; Bawcutt (ed.), *Control and Censorship*, p. 143.

30 See Bentley, *Jacobean and Caroline Stage*, II, pp. 631–3 for a transcript of Beeston's will.

31 K. E. McLuskie and Rebecca Rogers, 'Who Invested in Early Modern Theatre?', *Research Opportunities in Renaissance Drama*, XLI (2002), 29–61 (p. 44).

32 Cerasano, 'The "Business" of Shareholding', p. 242.

33 Cerasano points out, however, that the resultant 'corporation' of sharers was 'impervious to external governmental control, unlike any trade guild' ('The "Business" of Shareholding', pp. 235, 238).

34 McLuskie and Rogers, 'Who Invested in Early Modern Theatre?', p. 42.

35 See Bentley, *Jacobean and Caroline Stage*, I, pp. 330–1.

36 Bentley, *Jacobean and Caroline Stage*, V, pp. 1019–20.

37 Gurr, *Shakespearian Playing Companies*, p. 15.

38 Letter of Edward Sherbourne, transcribed in Bentley, *Jacobean and Caroline Stage*, VI, p. 54.

39 See Glynne Wickham, Herbert Berry, and William Ingram (eds), *English Professional Theatre, 1530–1660* (Cambridge: Cambridge University Press, 2000), pp. 239–41 for the full transcript; the transcript quoted here is from Griffith, *A Jacobean Company and its Playhouse*, p. 174, from the original document held in the National Archives (C2/JASI/P16/14).

40 Transcribed by Griffith, *A Jacobean Company and its Playhouse*, p. 175, from C2/JASI/P16/14.

41 Christopher M. Matusiak, 'The Beestons and the Art of Theatrical Management in Seventeenth-Century London', unpublished PhD thesis, University of Toronto, 2009, pp. 45–6, n. 51.

42 Griffith, *A Jacobean Company and its Playhouse*, pp. 69–70.

43 Wickham et al. (eds), *English Professional Theatre*, pp. 405–6; Griffith, *A Jacobean Company and its Playhouse*, pp. 90, 240–1, 261.

44 Eva Griffith, 'Christopher Beeston: His Property and Properties', in *The Oxford Handbook of Early Modern Theatre*, ed. Richard Dutton (Oxford: Oxford University Press, 2011), pp. 607–22 (p. 619).

45 Griffith, 'Christopher Beeston', p. 619.

46 See Martin Wiggins, in association with Catherine Richardson, *British Drama, 1533–1642: A Catalogue* (Oxford: Oxford University Press, 2011–), #2432, for the dating of the play.

47 Bawcutt (ed.), *Control and Censorship*, p. 143.

48 As above, Beeston did not have a share (that we know of) in the Curtain theatre but was invested in the Curtain estate; Griffith, *A Jacobean Company and its Playhouse*, p. 90.

49 Bawcutt (ed.), *Control and Censorship*, p. 199.

50 Bawcutt (ed.), *Control and Censorship*, p. 174.

51 Quoted by Bentley, *Jacobean and Caroline Stage*, II, p. 370.

52 C. W. Wallace, 'Three London Theatres of Shakespeare's Time', *Nebraska University Studies*, IX (1909), 287–342 (pp. 321–2).

53 R. A. Foakes (ed.), *Henslowe's Diary*, 2nd edn (Cambridge: Cambridge University Press, 2002), pp. 215, 219; see Matusiak, 'The Beestons and the Art of Theatrical Management', p. 36.

54 See Griffith, *A Jacobean Company and its Playhouse*, pp. 237–8.

55 Letter from John Chamberlain to Sir Dudley Carleton, in *The Letters of John Chamberlain*, pp. 59–60.

56 Wallace, 'Three London Theatres', p. 334. For John King's relation to Queen Anne's Men, see Griffith, *A Jacobean Company and its Playhouse*, p. 201.

57 Matusiak, 'The Beestons and the Art of Theatrical Management', pp. 46–54.

58 Wallace, 'Three London Theatres', p. 318.

59 Wallace, 'Three London Theatres', pp. 319, 322.

60 Wallace, 'Three London Theatres', p. 322.

61 Wallace, 'Three London Theatres', p. 326.

62 For a fully comprehensive account of the lawsuit and its proceedings, see Griffith, *A Jacobean Company and its Playhouse*, pp. 225–41; see also C. J. Sisson, 'The Red Bull Company and the Importunate Widow', *Shakespeare Survey*, 7 (1954), 57–68. Bentley observed, more generally of Beeston's enterprises, that '[i]t is rather suspicious that the old company should always have left in reduced circumstances, [and] that the new company should apparently prosper' (*Jacobean and Caroline Stage*, II, p. 364).

63 See Wickham et al. (eds), *English Professional Theatre*, p. 175, and Duncan Salkeld, 'Literary Traces in Bridewell and Bethlem, 1602–1624', *The Review of English Studies*, 56 (2005), 379–85 (pp. 381–2).

64 Sisson, 'The Red Bull Company', p. 64.

65 Bentley, *Jacobean and Caroline Stage*, II, p. 572.

66 Robert Davenport, *King John and Matilda* (London, 1655), Thomas Heywood, *The Fair Maid of the West*, Part I (London, 1631), and James Shirley, *The Wedding* (London, 1629).

67 Bawcutt (ed.), *Control and Censorship*, p. 173.
68 James Wright, *Historia Histrionica* (London, 1699), p. 4; Bentley, *Jacobean and Caroline Stage*, II, p. 549.
69 John Webster, *The White Devil* (London, 1612), M2v.
70 Bentley, *Jacobean and Caroline Stage*, II, p. 526.
71 Gurr, *Shakespearian Playing Companies*, pp. 376, 419.
72 Bentley, *Jacobean and Caroline Stage*, I, p. 221.
73 In 1629 the quarto edition of Shirley's *The Wedding* was published. Thought to have been first performed between 1626 and 1629, the play's attendant cast-list provides the first trace in records connected to the theatre of many of the players.
74 Bentley, *Jacobean and Caroline Stage*, II, p. 561.
75 Matusiak, 'The Beestons and the Art of Theatrical Management', pp. 85–6.
76 Bentley, *Jacobean and Caroline Stage*, I, p. 220. Curious because Bentley recognised himself that the 'large number of hitherto unknown actors' associated with the company made this 'very hazardous'.
77 Foakes (ed.), *Henslowe's Diary*, pp. 238–41.
78 E. K. Chambers, *The Elizabethan Stage*, 4 vols (Oxford: Clarendon Press, 1923), II, p. 131.
79 Bentley, *Jacobean and Caroline Stage*, VI, p. 158.
80 'Heton's Papers', originally published by Peter Cunningham, *Shakespeare Society Papers*, 4 vols (London, 1844–49), pp. 95–100 (pp. 95–6).
81 'Heton's Papers', p. 96.
82 'Heton's Papers', pp. 96, 97.
83 'Heton's Papers', pp. 97, 96.
84 'Heton's Papers', p. 96.
85 'Heton's Papers', p. 96.
86 'Middlesex Sessions Rolls: 1622', in *Middlesex County Records: Volume 2, 1603–25*, ed. John Cordy Jeaffreson (London, 1887), pp. 164–73; *British History Online*, http://www.british-history.ac.uk/middx-county-records/vol2/pp164-173 (accessed 21 March 2017).
87 Bentley, *Jacobean and Caroline Stage*, II, p. 387.
88 Wright, *Historia Histrionica*, p. 10.
89 Bentley, *Jacobean and Caroline Stage*, II, p. 345.
90 See Bentley's transcript of the will: *Jacobean and Caroline Stage*, II, pp. 631–3.
91 Bentley, *Jacobean and Caroline Stage*, II, p. 548; see Matusiak, 'The Beestons and the Art of Theatrical Management', pp. 30–40 for the full description of events.
92 For a full transcript of the depositions and detailed discussion, see Ann Haaker, 'The Plague, the Theatre, and the Poet', *Renaissance Drama*, n.s. 1 (1968), 283–306 (p. 297).
93 I have written extensively elsewhere about Brome's contract, and what follows is a brief summary drawing on the material presented in Eleanor Collins, 'Richard Brome's Contract and the Relationship of Dramatist to Company in the Early Modern Period', *Early Theatre*, 10 (2007), 116–28, and 'Richard Brome and the Salisbury Court Contract', *Richard Brome Online*, https://www.dhi.ac.uk/brome/viewEssay.jsp?file=EC_SALISBURY (accessed 29 April 2025). See also Bradley D. Ryner, 'Narratives of Value in Richard Brome's Dispute with the Salisbury Court', *Early Theatre*, 23.2 (2020), 79–94, for more, and a few corrections.
94 Gurr, *Shakespearian Playing Companies*, p. 419.
95 Bentley, *Jacobean and Caroline Stage*, I, p. 227.
96 See Gurr, *Shakespearian Playing Companies*, pp. 8–9.

97 Haaker, 'The Plague', p. 298.
98 Ryner, 'Narratives of Value', pp. 85, 82.
99 Haaker, 'The Plague', pp. 299–300.
100 Mark R. Benbow, 'Dutton and Goffe versus Broughton: A Disputed Contract for Plays in the 1570s', *REED Newsletter*, 6.2 (1981), 3–9.
101 Roslyn L. Knutson, *Playing Companies and Commerce in Shakespeare's Time* (Cambridge: Cambridge University Press, 2001), p. 55.
102 Foakes (ed.), *Henslowe's Diary*, p. 105.
103 Foakes (ed.), *Henslowe's Diary*, p. 199.
104 See Chambers, *Elizabethan Stage*, II, pp. 160–2.
105 Haaker, 'The Plague', p. 300.
106 C. J. Sisson, 'Notes on Early Stuart Stage History', *The Modern Language Review*, 37 (1942), 25–36 (p. 34).
107 Bentley, *Jacobean and Caroline Stage*, VI, p. 158.
108 Knutson, *Playing Companies and Commerce*, p. 55.
109 Collins, 'Richard Brome and the Salisbury Court Contract'.
110 Haaker, 'The Plague', p. 301.
111 Chambers, *Elizabethan Stage*, II, p. 153. Jonson was writing for Henslowe when he returned from prison in 1598, but new plays of his were also performed by the Chamberlain's Men (*c*. 1597–98), the Children of the Queen's Revels (*c*. 1597–1609), and from 1603 he was writing for the King's (previously Chamberlain's) Men, before selling *Bartholomew Fair* to Lady Elizabeth's Men at Henslowe's Hope theatre.
112 Henslowe had commissioned the play, but Daborne suggested that, nevertheless, he might sell it on to the King's Men. Knutson, *Playing Companies and Commerce*, p. 55.
113 Haaker, 'The Plague', p. 301.
114 Haaker, 'The Plague', p. 302. See also Martin Butler, 'Exeunt Fighting: Poets, Players, and Impresarios at the Caroline Hall Theaters', in *Localizing Caroline Drama: Politics and Economics of the Early Modern Stage, 1625–1642*, ed. Adam Zucker and Alan B. Farmer (Basingstoke: Palgrave Macmillan, 2006), pp. 97–128: Butler argues that 'Heton's managerialism, distinctive though it looks, was not an a priori ambition or a predetermined ethos but an attitude that crystallized haphazardly in response to changing circumstances, his plans being provoked as much by short-term necessity as by strategic foresight' (p. 100).
115 Collins, 'Richard Brome's Contract', pp. 121–2.
116 Bawcutt (ed.), *Control and Censorship*, p. 194.
117 For instance, the *Late Lancashire Witches* had become a canonical repertory piece (of a kind) for the King's Men at the Globe theatre, but was written collaboratively by Heywood and Brome, both of whom wrote ordinarily, and relatively regularly at this time, for the Cockpit. For examples of critical interest in this play, see Herbert Berry, 'The Globe Bewitched and *El Hombre Fiel*', *Medieval and Renaissance Drama in England*, 1 (1984), 211–30; Heather Hirschfeld, 'Collaborating Across Generations: Thomas Heywood, Richard Brome, and the Production of *The Late Lancashire Witches*', *Journal of Medieval and Early Modern Studies*, 30 (2000), 339–74; and Kathleen E. McLuskie, 'Politics and Aesthetic Pleasure in 1630s Theater', in *Localizing Caroline Drama: Politics and Economics of the Early Modern Stage, 1625–1642*, ed. Adam Zucker and Alan B. Farmer (Basingstoke: Palgrave Macmillan, 2006), pp. 43–68.
118 Haaker, 'The Plague', p. 303.

119 Matusiak, 'The Beestons and the Art of Theatrical Management', pp. 90–1.
120 Haaker, 'The Plague', p. 299.
121 Bawcutt (ed.), *Control and Censorship*, p. 21. See also Eleanor Collins, 'Ghosts in the Archive: Edmond Malone, Craven Ord, and the Missing Texts of Henry Herbert's "office-book"', *Critical Quarterly*, 55 (2013), 30–41.
122 Bawcutt (ed.), *Control and Censorship*, p. 181. The 'Biston' of this exchange and those below has always, as far as I am aware, been assumed to relate to Christopher Beeston, who is in control of and responsible for the company, managing the theatre's operations and Shirley. Malone seems to clarify that it is 'Christopher Beeston' in an interpolation in his transcript of the entry relating to *The Ball*, but whether this is his own assumption is unclear. I am grateful to Christopher Matusiak for raising the question of identity with respect to the two Beestons. Christopher Beeston *is* named in livery allowances (as are Richard Perkins, Anthony Turner, and William Allen) and in entries for payment after court performances, however, though it is worth noting this particular ambiguity in the office-book transcripts. See also p. 33 for another instance in which the particular identity of the Beeston is unclear.
123 Bawcutt (ed.), *Control and Censorship*, p. 191.
124 Bawcutt (ed.), *Control and Censorship*, p. 177.
125 Bawcutt (ed.), *Control and Censorship*, p. 177.
126 Bentley, *Jacobean and Caroline Stage*, I, p. 229.
127 For the possible effects of this manoeuvre on the relationship between Herbert and Shirley, see pp. 237–8.
128 Bawcutt (ed.), *Control and Censorship*, p. 181.
129 Bentley, *Jacobean and Caroline Stage*, VI, p. 64. This 'play share' appears to have then been granted by Herbert to William Blagrave 'for one hundred pounds'. In a related manner, Bentley suggested that the £3 payment Beeston made to Herbert for *Hymen's Holiday* might have derived from a benefit performance of the play, in which the company gifted to Herbert the profits from one of its performances – so Herbert might have made direct financial gains based on the performances of at least two of the company's plays (Bentley, *Jacobean and Caroline Stage*, V, p. 1024).
130 See Richard Dutton, *Mastering the Revels: The Regulation and Censorship of English Renaissance Drama* (London: Macmillan, 1991), pp. 51–4, in relation to Tilney's role as Master of the Revels.
131 Bawcutt (ed.), *Control and Censorship*, p. 180.
132 See pp. 76–8, pp. 237–8.
133 With respect to the King's Men, for instance; see Bawcutt's discussion, *Control and Censorship*, p. 58.
134 Dutton, *Mastering the Revels*, p. 72.
135 Gurr, *Shakespearian Playing Companies*, pp. 4–5.
136 Bentley writes of Lady Elizabeth's Men that 'serious losses reduced the company to a provincial status' (*Jacobean and Caroline Stage*, I, p. 177); see also McMillin and Maclean, *The Queen's Men*, p. 55.
137 Gurr, *Shakespearian Playing Companies*, p. 423, for Beeston's 'prejudice against travelling'.
138 *Records of Early English Drama [REED], Norwich*, ed. David Galloway (Toronto: University of Toronto Press, 1984), p. 210.
139 *REED, Norwich*, pp. xxxii–xxxiii.
140 *REED, Coventry*, ed. R. W. Ingram (Toronto: University of Toronto Press, 1981), p. 439.

141 Bawcutt (ed.), *Control and Censorship*, pp. 191–2.
142 McMillin and Maclean, *The Queen's Men*, pp. 62–3.
143 Bentley, *Jacobean and Caroline Stage*, I, p. 182.
144 Gurr, *Shakespearian Playing Companies*, p. 51; Bentley, *Jacobean and Caroline Stage*, II, p. 453; Gurr also notes the 'multiple use of the king's name' in provincial activity during the 1620s and 1630s, which suggests that more than two companies were travelling under the same name at any one time (*The Shakespeare Company*, p. 67).
145 Bentley, *Jacobean and Caroline Stage*, II, p. 574.
146 Bentley, *Jacobean and Caroline Stage*, II, p. 574.
147 *REED, Coventry*, p. 410.
148 Bentley, *Jacobean and Caroline Stage*, II, p. 589. 'Arthuret Grimes' was also granted the patent, as a joint holder.

2

QUEEN HENRIETTA'S MEN AT COURT:
PERFORMANCE AND PATRONAGE

Packing up and sorting costumes; journeys laden with theatrical props. Stately halls with high ceilings, hung with tapestries. European ambassadors in their glistering finery, and the king and queen enthroned, waiting for the play to begin. Players rubbing shoulders with princes.

The centrality of court performance to theatre history has been key to critical approaches to early modern drama for many decades, and proves enduring not only because of such romanticised visions of opulence and glamour, but also because it places the theatre companies within the political hub of the realm, at the centre of power structures built around the monarchy, and before the richest, and perhaps most cosmopolitan, audiences that England had to offer. As a powerful source of wealth and influence, the monarchy had offered theatre companies both patronage and protection for decades. Such royal 'fostering' of drama has lent credence to the construct of a special relationship between theatre and the court, which Martin Butler most persuasively unpicked in *Theatre and Crisis*; he worked to discredit the connection between the 1642 closure of a theatre industry thought to be increasingly decadent and escapist, on the one hand, and failing confidence in the court, on the other, that had been proposed by mid-twentieth-century critics including Clifford Leech. The narrative that drama of this period represented 'Cavalier' and Puritan divisions across the 1630s derived in part, as Butler observed, from the publication of loyalist propagandist verses with plays in the 1640s, after the theatres had closed; but Butler argued forcefully against the 'deeprooted convictions about the inevitability of the decline of Caroline drama' that had, at that time, become reflected in modern criticism. He presented a series of readings of 1630s plays which emphasised the extent to which dramatists offered provocative explorations of the political and moral ambiguities of the time in which they lived, and argued that, contrary to the dominant critical view, their works engaged in vital explorations of 'un- and anti-courtly sentiment'.[1]

The perception of court performance as an accolade, rather than as an indicator of political allegiance with the court, is now more widespread. Evidence of invitations to court is seen to confer a particular brand of authority on the company in question, and a kind of aesthetic value on the plays performed there.[2] Again, this critical position derives in part from the celebration of court performance in early modern printed sources; though John Astington confirms that the relationships which often held between theatre companies and patrons were 'oblique', he also notes that 'performance at court was a sign of favour and prominence, frequently touted on the title-pages of published plays'.[3] Frequency of court performances and theatrical service at court has continued to function in critical accounts as a measure of success – for Andrew Gurr, the King's Men enjoyed 'unquestioned pre-eminence' from 1609 to 1642, relishing a security that 'was as complete as was their pre-eminence at court'; they stayed 'in position, continuing to cater loyally to the king and queen at court and at the Blackfriars'.[4]

Critical emphasis on court performance might have arisen, in part, as a result of the increased visibility of companies that appeared at court in the extant Revels accounts. This might be especially true of the King's Men, who dominate both the records of court performance and most buildings-based, theatre-historical accounts. In terms of quantitative data, the King's Men's visits to court have generated more traces in the archive, clearer paper trails. Instead of the blanks and silences in the records relating to the north London amphitheatres at this time, positive signs of activity, engagement, and commerce survive. But as skewed as the remaining evidence might be – in particular the transcripts of Herbert's Revels office papers over this period – the terms of celebrity in which court performances have been described are difficult to shake. Writing before Butler, G. E. Bentley had claimed that the triple court performance of Thomas Heywood's *Love's Mistress* 'attained [… for Queen Henrietta's Men] a distinction generally reserved for the more famous King's Men'; and Arthur Melville Clark commented that this represented a 'dizzy' height in Heywood's career.[5] This sentiment continued to be echoed in critical accounts which appeared much later, though. For Raymond C. Shady, the play's performance was a 'triumphant conclusion', recognising Heywood's position as a 'poet of royal favor'; for Gurr, its production was linked to the company's '[gain] in status while their patron's profile as a lover of plays strengthened'.[6]

Queen Henrietta's Men performed at least seventy-three times at court between 1629 and 1636.[7] It was the only company to come close to the number of court performances given by the King's Men over this time, and – if the records give an accurate indication of company activity over these years – it came close to outstripping the King's Men more than once, in terms of quantitative contribution to court entertainment. Two of the company's most widely known plays – Heywood's *Love's Mistress* and Shirley's *The Bird in a Cage* – owe much of their critical recognition to courtly connections. The company's involvement in the provision of royal entertainments required an appreciable professional commitment on its part which, according to historical precedent, was befitting of a troupe which bore the queen's title. In 1583 Queen Elizabeth's Master of the Revels, Edmund Tilney, oversaw the formation of the Queen's Men on his patron's behalf, and decreed that the company would be free to perform in public as preparation for royal performances; it could thus 'conveniently satisfie [her] recreation'.[8] The players were licensed 'to use and practice stage plaies, whereby they might be the better enabled and prepared to shew such plaies before her Majestie'.[9] But by 1603 the clause emphasising 'practice' had been dropped from the King's Men's patent of that year, which recognised that the players were required not only for the king's pleasure, but 'aswell for the recreation of our lovinge Subjectes'.[10] By the time the Duke of York's Men received their licence in 1610 its wording had changed to acknowledge the increasingly commercial aspects of theatre; the patent now permitted the company to play not only 'to their best comõdite', as previous patents had allowed, but also to their best 'advantage'.[11] No patent for Queen Henrietta's Men is known to survive, and Gurr suggests that by the Caroline era the use of royal patents to legitimise playing had been discontinued for the most part.[12] But notionally, and in name at least, Henrietta Maria was a figurehead for the company, and Beeston's choice of company identity worked to exploit an association between the Cockpit and a royal patron who was known for her love of drama.

Henrietta Maria's strong and involved interest in the theatre was most visible in her performances at court, which included Walter Montagu's play *The Shepherd's Paradise* and William Davenant's masque *Salmacida Spolia*, and unlike her predecessor Queen Anne, she took speaking parts for herself. In this respect Henrietta Maria was a groundbreaking advocate of female performance and a radical innovator of established theatrical tradition in England, and her role as a patron and performer of drama has become increasingly clear, and been carefully observed, in recent criticism.[13] Drawing on influences from French and European theatre, and promoting her own set of ideologies and cultural agendas, Henrietta Maria established a following of literary young men at court – many of them poets and playwrights themselves, such as William Davenant, Lodowick Carlell, and Thomas Killigrew. These 'courtier playwrights' began to compose drama for the professional stages which drew on, explored, flattered, and sometimes critiqued the queen's political, religious, and social ideals. Rebecca A. Bailey has written in detail on the extent to which Shirley and Davenant both tailored their drama, in sensitive and nuanced ways, to acknowledge the politics of Henrietta Maria's masque performances, to accommodate her tastes, and to address her Roman Catholic beliefs.[14] The contribution that Shirley and the courtier playwrights made to the repertories of the indoor theatres over the 1630s was significant, and Henrietta Maria's influence effected changes of an appreciable scale in English drama.[15] As a patron, the queen afforded rich opportunities, both monetary and cultural.

Yet it is still unclear how far the relationship influenced Queen Henrietta's Men, and in what that relationship consisted. Until recently there has been scant evidence of Henrietta Maria's engagement with the company, and Beeston's enterprise seemed largely independent of the court. But neglected documents are now coming to light that cast doubt on how far Queen Henrietta's Men were unbound by political and economic dependency on royal patronage, as once seemed to be the case – and it is possible, indeed likely, that previously unknown or neglected documents and archival materials will continue to emerge that will alter the told history of this company and others.[16] To some extent, this becomes an account of historical priorities again – but interestingly so. Evidence relating to Shakespeare's company might have been given pre-eminence, survives in greater abundance as a consequence, or is more widely exposed, viewed, catalogued, and cited; and as a result, the Chamberlain's/King's Men have come to provide the model on which our understanding of the workings of theatre history are often based. In contrast, evidence relating to the activities of Queen Henrietta's Men seems to have been relegated somewhat, buried in the archives, and so the story has become skewed; again, this applies not only to specific accounts of Beeston's company, but to the relationship between companies and the wider theatrical landscape.

This chapter works towards providing an account of the kinds of connections between court and theatre that held for Queen Henrietta's Men, based on the available evidence. It also explores the impact that their extraordinary patron might have had upon the repertory's content and composition, before turning to a consideration of the role that Henry Herbert, Master of the Revels, played with respect to shaping the repertory and bringing the company to the court's attention. It has long been apparent that critical perceptions of the company's success at court have depended upon Herbert, through the surviving transcripts of his office-book. The catalogue of plays performed by the company, the evaluative record of which plays were 'likt', and Herbert's effusive commentary on Shirley's *The Young Admiral* have all governed the kind of story that would be told about Queen Henrietta's Men and the company's relation to the court. But the impact that Herbert had upon shaping the career of Beeston's company has not yet been fully understood. Herbert's relationship with Queen Henrietta's Men went beyond a shared interest in the thriving of the theatre profession. The level of his interest in Queen Henrietta's Men extended to an influence over the composition and aesthetics of the repertory, in what looks like an attempt to promote the company at court as a serious alternative to the King's Men.

EVIDENCE AND CHRONOLOGY

The first records of court performance by Queen Henrietta's Men appear in the Treasury Accounts for 1629–30, which record a warrant for payment following the company's performance of ten plays at court between October and February.[17] In the years between the company's formation and this Christmas season, surviving accounts suggest that the King's Men had dominated the scene at court. It is possible that Queen Henrietta's Men had performed at court before 1629–30, for earlier in June of 1629 the company had received livery allowances for 'three yardes of Bastard skarlet a peece' and 'thre yardes and a halfe of Crimson Veluet for Capes' to wear on special state occasions.[18] The Treasury Accounts do not detail *which* plays were performed by the company in 1629–30. Shirley's *The Faithful Servant* might have been one of them, licensed during this court season on 3 November 1629, but there is no hard evidence. The subject matter of this play might have either recommended it for court performance or precluded it, since it addresses the theme of vexed betrothals, one of them an arranged marriage for political ends. This theme might have strayed too near the marital discord that followed Charles and Henrietta's betrothal and subsequent marriage in the first years of Charles's rule.[19] Though the thwarted relationships in Shirley's play are resolved, the play was topical in ways that might prove controversial if not well received.

Their performances presumably recommended the company for further attendance at court, as the following year Henry Herbert invited the troupe back again – this time to perform (at least) three plays in September–October of 1630, probably in Hampton Court's Great Hall, and then a further thirteen over the Christmas season of that year.[20] A bill for plays performed at court by the King's Men in 1630 survives, and provides a list of the plays they presented 'for the Kinge'.[21] So although we cannot identify any of the plays that Queen Henrietta's Men performed over that Christmas, we know that they appeared interspersed in a court season that included Shakespeare's *A Midsummer Night's Dream*, Jonson's *Volpone*, and Webster's *The Duchess of Malfi*. Such context provides clear evidence that over these seasons Herbert was commissioning old revivals for enjoyment at court alongside new fare, and across various genres; at least eleven of the twenty-one recorded King's Men court performances that took place in that season were of plays written over a decade prior to 1630;

four of them from the 1590s or very early 1600s. Once again, Beeston would have found that his strategic retention of plays from the previous Cockpit companies gave his new troupe a competitive edge. The company's professional playhouse repertory, and the selection that it took to court, depended on a familiar stock of plays.

Queen Henrietta's Men continued to perform regularly at court for the next couple of years – as the Accounts witness, their presence almost matched that of the King's Men over the early 1630s. Interestingly, the recorded performances for the companies correspond in closely related peaks and troughs between 1629 and 1632–33; there is a striking and distinctive relationship between the two sets of figures. It does not appear to have been the case that a set quota on demands for plays existed from year to year, which meant that an increase in performance by one company need not have pre-empted opportunities for another. Over these years, the court's demands on the King's Men and Queen Henrietta's Men – as far as they are evidenced by the historical documents to hand – waxed and waned in tandem.

In November 1633 Queen Henrietta's Men performed Shirley's *The Young Admiral* at court, just over four months after its premiere on the London stage. Herbert had been particularly impressed by this offering, writing (what appears to be) an unusually fulsome entry which Edmond Malone transcribed. This transcript suggests that the play had given Herbert 'much delight and satisfaction in the readinge', while he hoped that it 'may serve for a patterne to other poetts'.[22] After this date there is a marked increase in the number of office-book transcripts which relate to Queen Henrietta's Men and record the name of the play that was performed, including the entry which records how Shirley's play was performed on the king's birthday, and 'likt' by both monarchs.[23] It is impossible to know how far the increase in entries relating to Queen Henrietta's Men reflects the original contents of the office-book, and the actual activity of the company. It might owe to Edmond Malone's new or renewed interest in the company following Herbert's endorsement, though this assumes that Malone took a strictly chronological, perhaps unnaturally linear, route through the office-book while transcribing the entries. Another alternative is that it was Herbert's interest that was piqued, and that this was reflected in the level of detail provided in his entries. And another is that Queen Henrietta's Men really did become more prominent after this date, establishing their presence in the market (and in the archive). These possibilities are not mutually exclusive.

The success of *The Young Admiral* was followed by the performance of (the now lost) *Hymen's Holiday* at Whitehall on 16 December – an 'ould play' by William Rowley which had been revived at the Cockpit in the summer of that year; Beeston had paid the Revels office to license 'some alterations' to its contents.[24] Queen Henrietta's Men performed two further unnamed plays at Whitehall between November and March during the Christmas period, and, on 14 January 1634, Jonson's *A Tale of a Tub* – an offering which turned out to be misjudged, since it was 'not likte'.[25] Herbert might have had good reason to believe that this play would go down well. He had already taken pains to purge the play of offence, having ensured that 'Vitru Hoop's parte [was] wholly strucke out, and the motion of the tubb', by command of the Lord Chamberlain, after Inigo Jones perceived in those aspects of the play 'a personal injury unto him'.[26] Perhaps Herbert had trusted the company to self-censor to an extent, following his warning to Beeston over Shirley's *The Ball* (licensed and performed in 1632), in which there were 'divers personated so naturally, both of lords and others of the court, that I took it ill'.[27] The company's next two recorded plays at court received notable acclaim, though. Fletcher's *The Night-Walkers*, revised (or 'corrected') by Shirley and licensed within four days of *A Tale of a Tub*, was performed on 30 January 1634 before the king and queen, and 'Likt as a merry play'.[28] And Shirley's new play at court that season, *The Gamester*, was received as 'the best play' the king had seen 'for seven years'.[29]

It was the following season of Christmas 1634–35, with royal performances of Heywood's *Love's Mistress*, that would outstrip the company's prior popularity at court. The work's 1636 title-page proudly states that the play was presented three times 'before their two Excellent MAJESTIES, within the space of eight dayes'.[30] Heywood's prologue to the performance that took place on the king's birthday suggests that one of these occasions was on 19 November at Denmark House, and the prologue to the second court performance states that this took place 'the same Week'.[31] Any evidence of Herbert's comments on the play is lost, if it ever existed. Not even a transcript of the licence survives. But the play was clearly popular with the king and queen. Queen Henrietta's Men performed at least seven more plays that Christmas season at Whitehall, and at least nine more the following year – including a revival of Beaumont's *Knight of the Burning Pestle* at St James's Palace, which was to be the company's last recorded court performance.

Over these years Queen Henrietta's Men established themselves as a chief constituent in the provision of royal entertainment. Other plays in the repertory which were performed at court include Robert Davenport's *King John and Matilda*, published as late as 1655, which claims multiple court performances by Queen Henrietta's Men in its printed cast-list: a catalogue of 'The Names of the Persons in the Play, And of the Actors that first Acted it on the Stage, and often before their *Majesties*'.[32] The

1633 quarto of Marlowe's *The Jew of Malta* advertises court performance by her Majesty's Servants on its title-page, and contains an epilogue written for the occasion by Heywood, who claims, in a dedication, to have 'vsher'd it unto the Court, and presented it to the Cock-pit'.[33] The 1635 edition of Joseph Rutter's *The Shepherds' Holiday* also memorialises performance by Queen Henrietta's Men before their Majesties, while the production of Heywood's *The Fair Maid of the West*, Part I and Part II at court in the 1630s is indicated by its title-pages, and a prologue and epilogue which were published separately in *Pleasant Dialogues and Dramas*.[34] John Ford and Thomas Dekker's play *The Sun's Darling* and Henry Glapthorne's *Love's Trial, or The Hollander* advertise performance at court, and at the Cockpit in Drury Lane by 'their' Majesties' Servants – Beeston's later boy company. It is possible that they were taken to court by Beeston's Queen Henrietta's Men before the company broke; *The Sun's Darling* is the most likely candidate, licensed as it was in 1624 for their predecessors at the Cockpit. It is also possible that John Ford's *'Tis Pity She's a Whore* might have been performed at court by Queen Henrietta's Men, though evidence to support this is less conclusive.[35]

VENUES AND STAGING

The plays that Queen Henrietta's Men took to court were performed in a variety of different spaces, which required a degree of flexibility on the part of the company. The venues in which they performed included Hampton Court – probably in the Great Hall which can be visited today – located downriver, to the south-west in Richmond; the Presence Chamber at St James's Palace in Westminster; Somerset House on the north bank of the river, just south of the Strand (the queen's residence, renamed by Queen Anne as Denmark House); and the Cockpit-in-Court, a purpose-built playhouse in Whitehall. The Hall at Hampton Court was one of the largest performance spaces at court – a stone structure measuring 106 by 40 feet, lit from all sides and one end by high windows, and crowned with an ornate, hammer-beam roof. When set up for entertainments, a wooden stage was erected at one end of the hall and a screen used to create a backstage area for the actors.[36] Temporary seating was supplied for the audience, while the royal state in which the king and queen are likely to have been seated was positioned at one end of the room.[37] In contrast, the playing space at St James's Palace was much smaller; the Presence Chamber, in use from 1633–34, was not a hall, but, as John Astington argues, a second-storey room measuring about 20 by 40 feet – a much more intimate venue.[38] There were a number of rooms available for use as performance venues in Somerset House: the Hall measured 60 by 31 feet, while Henrietta Maria also used the Presence Chamber and the Privy Chamber to present a 'scenic stage', 'motions', and 'dancing' around 1634 – small rooms similar to the Presence Chamber at St James's Palace. Astington suggests that while larger venues were available, there seems to have been a fashion for 'miniature' shows of elaborate display; it 'may have been one kind of court fashion accompanying the more usual royal taste for grand and expansive effects'.[39]

The queen also made special commissions for venues, enclosing the courtyard at Somerset House to create the inventive Paved Court theatre for Walter Montagu's *The Shepherd's Paradise* in 1632/33. The Cockpit-in-Court was the most fixed of the court venues though, specially repurposed by Inigo Jones into a permanent theatre at Whitehall in 1629. The space had functioned as a cockpit ring during Henry VIII's reign; it was small and octagonal, and plans drawn up by John Webb show that the stage and tiring-house took up almost half of the space of the theatre.[40] Banks of seats curved around the auditorium to face the stage; in this way, as Astington observes, the venue was similar 'in size and character', if not with respect to dimensions, to London's indoor playhouses.[41] Glynne Wickham suggested that there was an 'intimate relationship' between the converted Cockpit-in-Court and Beeston's Cockpit, supposing that it would have been 'natural' for Inigo Jones and Charles I to turn to Beeston's 'example'.[42] Though Beeston rebuilt his theatre following the Shrovetide riot in 1617, Wickham suggests that Beeston would not have been able to cause 'serious damage to the fabric of the original buildings', which 'might [have made …] him liable to the forfeit of his lease' of the property.[43] Beeston's theatre also seems to have shared in common with the octagonal court venue a broadly circular, or spherical, layout.[44]

The fundamental conditions of performance for Queen Henrietta's Men at court might have varied considerably given the different characteristics of the venues in which they were invited to perform. Adjustments might have been required to accommodate fluctuating audience sizes, in terms of acting style and the methods through which actors might choose to engage their audience. In the most basic terms, the troupe would have had to recalibrate the scale of their physical movements to the size of the stage, filling the larger spaces of Hampton Court and confining themselves to tighter blocking on the stage in the Presence Chamber of St James's Palace. A few of the plays taken to court by Queen Henrietta's Men specify group dancing of some description: the revels in *King John and Matilda*, for instance; the spectacular dance of Vulcan and the cyclopes in *Love's Mistress*; and the maypole dance in *The Sun's Darling*.[45] Astington notes that the size of the venue did not necessarily determine which kinds of plays were performed there: 'large chambers could contain small stage platforms, and [...] famous companies presented sweeping historical drama in intimate palace chambers'.[46] But in each of these particular instances, Queen Henrietta's Men would have worked to fit their play to the stage, however cramped or downscaled the morris might have become, or however many extra beats of music it took the masquers to cross the larger spaces at Hampton Court.[47]

The material conditions of each venue not only affected the company's execution of the plays' staging, but the way in which these plays were experienced by an audience: the style of spectacle, the degree of intimacy in the venue, and the physical proximity of the royal audience to the unfolding action. The acoustics of the venues would differ depending on the size of the room, height of the ceiling, material construction, and whether or not sound-absorbent tapestries remained during performances or were dismantled.[48] The plays of Queen Henrietta's Men that were performed at court employ a range of musical instruments, from distinctive, reedy hautboys to the sad music of flutes in *King John and Matilda*. But the choice of instruments and level of musical accompaniment would have been determined partly by the circumstance of venue. How the company sounded the 'alarm' in *The Fair Maid of the West*, Part I, produced the 'loud music' in *King John and Matilda*, and created the sound effects for the 'storm' that takes place in *The Young Admiral* – a play performed in the small space of the Presence Chamber at St James's Palace – would have depended on the size of the room and the way that sound carried within it. The performance of songs might also have been affected. Too loud an instrument in the Cockpit-in-Court might have deafened; too soft a tune in Hampton Court could go unheard.

The location of the musicians also played its part here, for their positioning would have influenced acoustic effect and clarity. If space allowed, they might have been seated in a gallery above the stage – in the permanent gallery shown in the plans for the Cockpit-in-Court, or in an upper level of the stage constructed specially for court performance in the other venues.[49] Though Astington suggests that temporary, two-storey tiring-houses would have been constructed for performances in the Presence Chamber at St James's Palace, there might not have been the space to accommodate musicians within this limited area.[50] If this were the case, it is reasonable to imagine that musicians would have had to be positioned either offstage and out of view of the action – making cues and any kind of deliberate synchronisation with the action difficult – or somewhere in the space of the room ordinarily reserved for the audience.

Lighting is also an important consideration. Depending on the time of day and year, controlling the level of lighting in the larger halls might have proved more challenging in comparison with the smaller, galleried space of the Cockpit in Drury Lane. In the Presence Chamber at St James's, the room could be lit with 'branches' (or chandeliers), as were used in the professional indoor playhouses, and also by candles held in sconces attached to the walls; the branches and sconces, otherwise known as 'wallers', appear to have been installed specially for each performance.[51] The Cockpit-in-Court would have offered the players different ways to experiment with light, however, if they were rehearsing or performing during the day. As Astington has described, the Cockpit-in-Court featured a large window in the centre of the roof, above the middle of the stage, and so 'the building was focussed on a central point'.[52] Renovations to the venue seem to have included the installation of a star-spangled calico ceiling that would block out the light from this window, while some of the venue's other windows were boarded over and painted to resemble glass, and others still were shuttered.[53] As Martin White suggests, even though performances at the venue often took place after dark, 'there was still a desire to reduce the daylight entering, so emphasizing the impact of the artificial light'.[54] Even if it was not possible to dim the Cockpit-in-Court to pitch blackness, White's research on lighting emphasises that 'the impact of artificial lighting in the playhouse lies precisely in the relationship between the darkness and the light', and he elaborates that brightly lit areas of the stage, illuminated by an abundance of candles and torches, create the illusion of a deeper darkness once they are removed, though the stage might remain visible.[55]

Many of the plays that were (or might have been) taken to court by Queen Henrietta's Men call for the use of lanterns and torches to light the way, but two make particular use of varying levels of illumination. In 'Tis Pity She's a Whore, Grimaldi enters carrying 'a Darke-lanthorne' and, in a moment of confusion, under cover of darkness, stabs Bergetto, who calls for 'lights, lights, ho lights'.[56] While similar scenes had been staged for decades in the broad daylight of the amphitheatres, the level of control that a purpose-built indoor theatre such as the Cockpit-in-Court offered would have proven highly effective in narrative and visual terms. In another case, Fletcher's The Night-Walkers, a number of scenes would have benefited from the sense of intrigue and mystery imparted by dim candlelight. This play's late-night scenes set in a bedevilled house and a 'haunted' churchyard had the potential to be highly entertaining in an intimate theatre.[57] Economics had its part to play here too, since the contrast between dark and light can be achieved most dramatically when candles and lights are not in short supply. As White observes, the companies would have worked to reduce the cost of candles when playing in their own houses, but at court the constraints of finance might give way to art.[58]

On the whole, the plays performed at court do not have many staging requirements that would have presented difficulties in their transfer to a new venue. Many of them specify discoveries, which presumably took place in a doorway from the backstage area to the stage, or even, depending on the play's other requirements and the size of the room, a temporary structure erected onstage (the upper platform of which would also double as an area 'above'). Discoveries could be enacted either by pulling aside a curtain – such as the arras or hangings through which Valerio is stabbed in *The Duke's Mistress* – or by opening a door to reveal a small tableau, often depicting one of the play's characters in the interior of a house.[59] In *The Gamester*, the stage direction '*Enter Hazard, Acre-lesse, Little-stocke, Sell-away, as in a Taverne*' might suggest discovery in a tavern-like setting, but could otherwise be an attempt to specify the behaviour of the actors, who are being directed (somewhat obscurely) to 'behave as you would do if you were in a tavern'.[60] The dumb shows in *The Fair Maid of the West* might have been discovered, though this is not specified in stage directions. More certain instances include the chair of state that is discovered in *King John and Matilda* (D2v), and the discovery of Cupid '*sleeping on a bed*' in *Love's Mistress* (F2r). Giovanni and Annabella also enter '*lying on a bed*' in *'Tis Pity She's a Whore*, and the play contains two discoveries of a study.[61] In *The Jew of Malta*, Barabas is discovered '*in his Counting-house, with heapes of gold before him*', and the fatal cauldron into which he falls at the close of the play is also 'discovered'.[62]

The Jew of Malta is also one of the only plays taken to court by Queen Henrietta's Men to require a performance space 'above' the stage, as necessary to the action. While *'Tis Pity She's a Whore*, *The Gamester*, *King John and Matilda*, *The Fair Maid of the West*, Part I, *The Young Admiral*, and *A Tale of a Tub* all specify an 'above', a performance space over the stage often proves dispensable, since the desired effect (usually of distance) can be created by positioning characters on different parts of the stage. The case is a little different in *King John and Matilda*. It is unclear whether the direction for a group of Lords to '*Exeunt from the walls*' (meant to represent battlements here, I3v) suggests that they should descend onstage, in full sight of the audience. But in this case the separation between the king and his once-rebellious barons on different levels makes better sense of the action, in which the 'above' is physically representative of a locale (the fortified castle under siege). This is also true of the 'window' from which Barabas's daughter Jessica '*Throwes downe*' gold and jewels in *The Jew of Malta* (D2v), but it is in the theatrical representation of Barabas's death that the requirement for a performance space 'above' becomes crucial to the staging. The diabolical contraption that he hammers at, '*very busie*', in the 'dainty Gallery' above, is designed to open some kind of trap or 'fall asunder', dropping him into the boiling cauldron in the discovery space below (Kr, Kv). The title-page of *The Jew of Malta* states that it was performed at Whitehall, and while it does not specify the Cockpit-in-Court this is likely, its being the custom-built court playhouse of the Caroline era. The theatre did have an area 'above', a reasonably sized window which could have accommodated the action, but the temporary stages in the larger court venues would also have had some kind of provision for an area above.[63]

Descents from the heavens or a similar area were another matter, and could only have been staged, ordinarily, in the Cockpit-in-Court, which had descent machinery installed into its starry ceiling, covered by a retractable cloth.[64] Some kind of representation of a sun appears in *The Sun's Darling* (a 'Moral Masque') – the 'Sun' speaks of descending and appears 'above'.[65] If a descent in another of the court performance spaces was deemed a spectacle worthy of investment, the Revels Office and Inigo Jones, Surveyor of the Works, became involved, and built the set and machinery for the occasion. This appears to have been the case with Heywood's *Love's Mistress*, the only other play to feature descents – a special case that is discussed in more detail below.[66] But for the most part, a level of adaptation and improvisation in staging plays would have been the norm when companies travelled to court, and foreknowledge of the chosen venue and familiarity with each of them would have been an advantage.

AESTHETICS AND AMBITIONS: BIDS FOR FAVOUR, 1633–36

Was there anything particularly distinctive or characteristic about the plays that Henry Herbert chose for performance at court – not in terms of physical staging requirements, but with respect to style and narrative content? In earlier eras, the Master of the Revels' professional responsibility included overseeing and arranging all court performances; the companies therefore relied heavily upon his facilitating role at court, and the Revels Office controlled, and was accountable for, all drama presented there. But by the 1630s, evidence suggests that the role of the Master of the Revels as a supplier of courtly performances had been diminished – he arranged and helped to prepare plays for performance at court, but no longer took responsibility for the production of the plays, in terms of arranging costumes and properties for the actors, for instance.[67] W. R. Streitberger has described the extent to which the Master was 'transform[ed] [...] from the absolute monarch of the entertainment industry in the Elizabethan [era], to something of a contractor by the end of the Caroline period'.[68] Yet despite this reduced role in the production of drama at court, Herbert's endorsement was still an important concern of the companies and their managers; in the later 1620s the accountant of the Revels Office recorded expenditure for the wages and entertainment of Herbert, 'for Rehersalls, and making choice of playes, and Comodyes, and reforminge them amounting in all to iiij dayes'.[69]

Herbert continued to wield some power in the 'choice' of plays that he made, then – a selection process which might have entailed Herbert's attendance at a 'preview' performance, such as the ones attended by Edmund Tilney in his lodgings prior to the 1579–80 court revels season.[70] But a consequence of the gradual change in responsibilities of the Revels Office meant that Herbert's role centred more specifically on the licensing of plays for performance, rather than on the practical aspects of court production. This gave him an intimacy with the newest drama being written for the Caroline stage, the distinctive characteristics of its writers, and the repertory styles and preferences of each of the professional companies. While the mechanisms by which the companies accessed court were changing, Herbert sought to develop his role in new ways and positioned himself as an authority on the content and style of the drama. When he praised Shirley's *The Young Admiral*, Malone's transcript of his original account suggests that Herbert not only applauded its lack of 'oaths, prophaness, or obsceanes' but also set out something of an aesthetic agenda, commenting on the state of the art as it was then, and pointing the way forwards. It appears to have been his hope that other dramatists would follow Shirley's example, 'not only for the bettring of manners and language, but for the improvement of the quality, which hath received some brushings of late'. The entry continues:

> When Mr. Sherley hath read this approbation, I know it will encourage him to pursue this beneficial and cleanly way of poetry, and when other poetts heare and see his good success, I am confident they will imitate the original for their own credit, and make such copies in this harmless way, as shall speak them masters in their art, at the first sight, to all judicious spectators.[71]

Herbert's estimate of the level of influence he could wield over the drama was high. The transcript ends with what seems to be an aside from Herbert: 'I have entered this allowance, for direction to my successor, and for example to all poetts, that shall write after the date hereof.' But such aspirations were not necessarily unrealistic. The revisions and demands for change that were made by the Master of the Revels could affect the text in ways that can reasonably be described as creatively interventionist – he had the potential to be, in a very real sense, a collaborator on each play that he censored. Richard Dutton's work on Tilney suggests that this would have constituted a continuation of Tilney's practice as Master, who 'did not simply hire in from the actors' repertoire, as if it were "off the shelf", but intervened to make their shows as appropriate as possible for the court'.[72] If the professional companies prioritised royal favour and court entertainment highly enough, then winning Herbert's approval through the production of 'cleanly', 'harmless' art, as *The Young Admiral* had, might prove fruitful. And as his praise for Shirley shows, Herbert's attitudes to contemporary drama and the process by which he developed his ideas about its virtues and vices might be influenced by the dramatists around him, and their creative output. Theatrical personnel might have been alert to the opportunities here in terms of establishing an intellectual rapport with Herbert, for more than once Herbert received gifts or compensation from companies in the form of books; one of those gifts came from Beeston as a new year's present.[73]

Herbert's authority in the office and his appreciation for certain standards of drama might also have developed alongside the king's own interests in dramatic writing and censorship. In January 1634 Malone's transcript of one of Herbert's entries reveals how 'the kinge was pleasd to call mee into his withdrawinge chamber to the window, wher he went over all that I had croste in Davenants play-book [...] in the greater part [he] allowed of my reformations'.[74] A degree of tension emerged from the supervision, which was brought on by a complaint by Endymion Porter, one of the King's Men. The transcript describes how the king did not count '*faith, death, slight*' for oaths, 'to which I doe humbly submit as my masters judgment; but under favour conceive them to be oaths, and enter them here, to declare my opinion and submission'.[75] Davenant's play, *The Wits*, was performed at court before the king and queen a few weeks later; Malone's office-book transcript suggests that it was 'Well likt. It had a various fate on the stage, and at court, though the kinge commended the language, but dislikt the plott and characters.'[76] The meta-commentary that Herbert offers here and elsewhere – his preoccupation with whether and why it was 'likt' or not, at court but also beyond – positions him as the 'judicious spectator' he gestured towards when speaking of *The Young Admiral*. In these Revels transcripts, we find evidence of Herbert refining his relation to Caroline drama, and articulating a new degree of control over it.

Nowhere is this demonstrated more clearly than when Herbert 'gave' Queen Henrietta's Men plays to perform in their repertory, or imparted ideas for plotlines that he felt confident would go down well at court. This happened at least twice in the history of the company. *The Gamester* was written by Shirley and licensed in 1633, but it was made, as Herbert describes, 'out of a plot of the king's, given him by mee'.[77] This revelation shows the extent to which Herbert was able to transmit (and, in doing so, mediate) royal tastes to Queen Henrietta's Men, in a way that appears to promise them (or at least make very likely) a court performance – and a successful one. This was a clear case of demand from the court driving supply, and introduced an additional collaborative dimension to Beeston's repertory design. Herbert's gift of the plot to the company might well have been interpreted by Beeston as encouragement from the court, certainly as encouragement from Herbert himself.

The other instance in which Herbert provided performance material to Queen Henrietta's Men is revealed in the licence entry transcribed by Malone for *Hymen's Holiday* – one of the plays that then transferred to court for performance there. Herbert (or Malone) records the fee from Beeston for alterations to the drama, 'being a play given unto him for my use'.[78] The meaning of 'gave' (sold, rented, or lent?) and 'for my use' is unclear, but it is generally thought that it implies that Herbert somehow owned the manuscript, and charged Beeston either for the purchase of it (as well as the alterations) or the temporary rights to performance.[79] Herbert appears to have offered, in himself and through the Revels office, a means for the migration of plays, acting as a channel or conduit in the process of repertory composition. Beeston had been on the wrong end of this arrangement before, in 1623, when Lady Elizabeth's Men had attempted to perform Henry Shirley's *The Martyred Soldier*; in response to the company's decision to 'stet' Herbert's corrections, Herbert decided to 'keep the booke', and later sold the play to Richard Gunnell at the Fortune.[80] But as the entry for *Hymen's Holiday* shows, Beeston also stood to benefit from Herbert's interventions into repertory composition.

In this respect Herbert assumed a particular role in the relationship between Queen Henrietta's Men and the court – one that seems, at times, to overreach his strictly professional duty. Indeed, during his time as Master of the Revels, Herbert's influence with respect to the ownership of plays more widely, across the London theatres, was notable in terms of the deliberate interventions he made in particular repertories. A few transcripts survive which suggest that Herbert was interested not just in the core duty of licensing plays when he came to office in 1623, but in licensing plays *to specific venues*, indicating that he was involved at a wider level with controlling or contributing to the repertories of particular theatres and, by extension, the reputations of the companies performing in them. When the sharers removed *The Escapes of Jupiter* from the Cockpit, Herbert 'allowed' of it, but he almost did not grant permission – and he seems to have been conflicted about the decision, if the transcript can be trusted: 'It was not complained of by the company of the Cockpitt and that moved mee likewise to allowe of itt. / I had not allowed of itt but that the Cockpitt gave way.'[81] As noted above, his decision to keep *The Martyred Soldier* when Beeston's company did not heed his revisions to the play meant that he was in a position to license it elsewhere later that month.[82] The movement of playbooks was a clear concern of Herbert's, and the kinds of intervention that he could make in a repertory were known to him.

With respect to Herbert's two contributions to the play-stock of Queen Henrietta's Men, these interventions do seem to resemble a deliberate repertory strategy on Herbert's part, since they worked to move the repertory in a particular direction, towards two of the most fashionable strands of drama of that period. *The Gamester*, as a mannered comedy, took its place alongside Shirley's *Hyde Park* and was accompanied, two years later, by *The Lady of Pleasure*. Though *Hymen's Holiday* is lost, its name suggests that it was a pastoral, and if that were the case, this old revival drew on a new trend for pastoral and romance, promoted at court by Queen Henrietta Maria. It was a genre for which Henrietta Maria had developed an appreciation at an early age at the French court, and the queen had expressed her enthusiasm for the form with the staging of *Artenice*, a French scenic pastoral, at the English court shortly after Charles I's accession.[83] Montagu's *The Shepherd's Paradise*, in which she performed in January 1633, was also an exemplar of the genre. If *Hymen's Holiday* fell into this category, it appears that both plays given, in one way or another, by Herbert to Beeston would appeal to predilections that Herbert would have identified with the court. But how far did Beeston and Queen Henrietta's Men concern themselves with catering to such tastes, beyond Herbert's interventions?

There is some evidence to suggest that, around 1633–34, Queen Henrietta's Men did make a concerted effort to attract attention from the court and their namesake patron. By this time in their career they had been performing to Cockpit audiences for at least seven years, and had been giving court performances for at least three. The commercial success of the venture was confirmed, and the inherited fare of the Cockpit proved to be a valuable asset. This was a period in which Beeston might have been expected to branch out, or to exploit the company's foothold in the professional market for plays. And in a series of carefully chosen acquisitions, clustered together within the space of two years, that appears to be what he attempted.

In January 1633 James Shirley's play *The Beauties*, or *The Bird in a Cage*, was licensed for the company – a play that is discussed at greater length later in this book.[84] This play explicitly engaged with ideas of performance and theatrical skill, and in doing so staged female performance, thus contributing to the debate that Henrietta Maria's performances provoked, repeatedly, throughout her reign. The drama features a play within a play, instigated and performed by Princess Eugenia and her ladies, and might have been provocative given the bafflement and surprise registered at court over Henrietta Maria's performances, which were deliberately challenging and political in themselves.[85] But Shirley's play was made particularly topical in light of the recent scandal that William Prynne's attack on female performance had caused, in his anti-theatrical text *Histriomastix: The Player's Scourge, or Actor's Tragedy*, published in late 1632. Prynne's allusion to women actors as 'notorious whores' is unlikely to have been aimed at Henrietta Maria, for *Histriomastix* had been in preparation for almost a decade by the time of publication.[86] But the queen was in rehearsal for Montagu's *The Shepherd's Paradise* at the time. Prynne was arrested and awaiting trial when *The Bird in a Cage* was published in 1633. The printed playbook carried a pointed satirical attack on the imprisoned polemicist: in the prefatory material, Shirley congratulated Prynne on his 'happy *Retirement*'.[87] This mocking dedication works to align *The Bird in a Cage* with the queen's interests and, combined with the decision to publish the play so quickly, seems a clear, and clearly topical, manoeuvre.

There is no evidence that *The Bird in a Cage* was performed at court, but in so far as the play was advertised and made available through publication, this play-text contributed to a focus on royal interests. In August of the same year the company revived *Hymen's Holiday* – the play 'given' to Beeston by Herbert and then performed at court. For Beeston, the purchase or rent of performance rights for an old play – even including the Master of the Revels' fee for alterations – proved a cheap, low-risk alternative to the commissioning of a brand new play in what constituted for Queen Henrietta's Men an almost unknown, barely proven genre.[88] It seems, from Malone's transcript, that two fees were paid – £1 for alterations, and £3 for the rent, purchase, use, or licence of *Hymen's Holiday*. In the 1590s Henslowe routinely paid playwrights £6 for a new play, while in 1636 William Beeston loaned Brome a £6 advance for a commission, before the licence fee had been taken into consideration; this revival was a cut-price alternative.[89]

If *Hymen's Holiday* was a way of testing the waters of court favour with an 'ould' but newly popularised style of play, Beeston appears to have been encouraged by the results. The following year, Queen Henrietta's Men produced Heywood's *Love's Mistress*. The play's success at court is unlikely to have been coincidental, for Heywood went out of his way to present it as a drama specifically tailored to the queen's tastes. It was subtitled 'The Queen's Masque', which appears either to position the play as a crossover of kinds, from commercial drama into the arena of courtly entertainment, or to make a claim for the play and its suitability for royal consumption, given its performance on the king's birthday as a gift from the queen.[90] Either way, this naming strategy indicates a desire on the part of the company to promote its new play – by description and publicly in print – as a courtly entertainment of a kind, and under the banner of the company's royal patron. The play incorporates masque elements in the form of spectacle and scenes reminiscent of antimasques, and also in the prologue, in which Cupid 'descend[s] in a Cloud' from the heavens to address the audience. Such staging decisions appropriated dramaturgical elements common to old amphitheatre drama but also at this time (somewhat paradoxically) associated with the spectacular visual nature of the masque form. And like a masque, there are aspects of the play that appear to have been designed especially to flatter the interests of the royal patron: Heywood's satirical dig at Prynne, which emerges in the play's narrative, affirmed the company's support of the queen once more.

Heywood recycled and adapted parts of an old Admiral's Men's play called *Cupid and Psyche* (1600), now lost, in order to establish *Love's Mistress* as in dialogue with the new styles now popular at court. This is accomplished by the inclusion of elements of pastoral and romance within a narrative framework centred on classical mythology.[91] The play's focus on the story of Cupid and Psyche related a tale that had become close to the hearts of Henrietta Maria and Charles. As Jane Kingsley-Smith has commented, this was 'one of the central myths by which Charles and Henrietta Maria constructed the public image of their marriage', from before their union was ever consecrated.[92] In 1637 Shakerley Marmion presented a poem, *The Legend of Cupid and Psyche*, to Charles's nephew, and by 1639 an oil painting of the subject had been commissioned from Anthony van Dyck to decorate the Queen's House at Greenwich.[93]

The play's exploration of ideals associated with the construction of platonic love which Henrietta Maria promoted at court signal attention to the queen's cultural and political preoccupations. The doctrine of platonic love was centred, as Lesel Dawson describes, on love as 'ideal, chaste, and spiritual, rather than disorderly and pathological'.[94] It emphasised female beauty and purity as virtues that would imbue women with a natural authority – a 'politicization of love', in which worship and obedience were inspired in the male beholder.[95] As Dawson outlines, 'the emphasis within Neoplatonic philosophy upon the need to avoid sexual intercourse meant that women were able to extend the time of their courtship, the liminal period during which they exercised control over their suitors'.[96] Through the commissioning of works of art and performances, Henrietta Maria wielded this neoplatonic ideology in order to gain authority and the servitude of courtiers. A partly mythologised scenario arose in which she was figured as the radiant centre of the court, surrounded by her circle of courtier-suitors, all devoted to her in a strictly platonic, metaphysical sense. Furthermore, Karen Britland has illustrated how Henrietta Maria was encouraged, even as she journeyed to England, to press the association of light with spiritual purity to use in a 'conversionary' Catholic 'mission', in which the trope of 'religious illumination' emerged as a dominant metaphor.[97]

In this context, Heywood's references to pure, spiritual love in *Love's Mistress* appear neither neutral nor incidental. In a scene in which Apuleius explains the moral of the main action to Midas, explicating its lessons to the audience and introducing explicitly religious undertones to the interpretation of the classical courtship of Cupid and Psyche, Apuleius emphasises Psyche's links with the 'Virgin', 'Immortall' soul, admired by all: 'All love faire *Psiche*, all cast amorous eyes / On the soules beautie' (Dv–D2r).[98] He goes on to draw a distinction between 'good' and 'ill' desire – 'true' desire, which 'Doates on the Soules sweete beauty', the keeper of a 'chast bed' and 'Celestiall pleasur', as opposed to 'untemperate lust' which 'inflame[s] the soule' (D2r). While Psyche is loved by all – a consequence of her spiritual excellence – her only match is heaven, Apuleius explains, embodied here by Cupid, on to whose classical persona a religious iconography is overlaid. When Midas asks why Psyche took 'such paines' to 'get a husband', Apuleius continues to moralise:

> This shewes how many strong adversities,
> Crosses, Pricks, Thornes, and stings of conscience,
> Would throw the ambitious soule affecting heaven,
> Into dispaire, and fainting diffidence,
> [...] the Soule must flie
> Through thousand letts, to seek eternitie (D2r)

Apuleius' exposition relates the classical plot of Cupid and Psyche within a context recognised by both the court and London audiences as distinctive of Henrietta Maria's favoured ideologies, with its focus on sexual purity, dedication to spiritual beauty, and emphasis on religious devotion.

At the same time, Heywood's choice of source material acknowledged and exploited Henrietta Maria's familiarity with, and fondness for, classical mythology; her masque *Chloridia* also featured Greek and Roman gods, and the dramatic realisation of *Love's Mistress* might have echoed certain elements of the explicitly courtly spectacle within which the queen actively participated. Elements of pastoral were also included, with the incorporation of Arcadian swains and shepherds. In important respects, *Love's Mistress* was clearly designed to connect with the dominant courtly tastes of the 1630s, building on the success of *Hymen's Holiday*. And the company did not abandon its emphasis on this fashionable genre, for several of its other plays performed at court exemplify similar themes or tropes. Joseph Rutter's *The Shepherds' Holiday*, 'A Pastorall Tragi-Comædie', was performed around the same period (between 1629 and 1635), and is set in Arcady. It features a cast containing a substantial number of shepherds, including a runaway princess disguised as a shepherd and a 'chorus' of shepherds. The play bespeaks a preoccupation with the difference between corporeal and true, spiritual love, and includes a scene in which the shepherds don classical costumes and 'properties' to perform in a masque. Shirley's *The Arcadia* was also first performed by the company in the early to mid-1630s, an adaptation of Sidney's work of the same name and a play which self-consciously reflected on courtly behaviours and fashions.[99] *The Sun's Darling*, another spectacular piece which might have been performed at court by Queen Henrietta's Men, crosses over more explicitly into the genre of the masque. A self-consciously 'courtly' repertory asset, its allegorical characters embody the seasons and the virtues, and include a personification of Time and the god Cupid (perhaps the costume for the part would have been shared for the same role with the same character in *Love's Mistress*; the parts may have been played by the same actor).

These repertory acquisitions by Queen Henrietta's Men look like a deliberate attempt on the company's part to appeal to the queen's tastes and satisfy the aesthetic criteria of a royal audience.[100] By appealing to courtly fashions, professional companies could seek to increase the likelihood of their attendance at court, and might become more explicitly entrepreneurial in the advertisement of their plays to the court, through subtitles which positioned their plays as masques, for instance. Lucy Munro has also recognised the extent to which the title-pages and paratexts of the company's plays, in addition to prologues and epilogues in Heywood's *Pleasant Dialogues and Dramas*, 'position Queen Henrietta Maria's Men as the subjects of royal patronage'.[101] And Beeston also appears to have employed another repertory strategy at around this time, to the same ends – a strategy that was quite remarkable to Queen Henrietta's Men, and which introduced a new degree of interdependency between the company and the court. At some point between 1632 and 1635, Thomas Killigrew's play *The Prisoners* was performed by Queen Henrietta's Men on the Cockpit stage; and another of his plays, *Claracilla*, was written for performance around 1636, possibly for Queen Henrietta's Men at the Cockpit, though it was not licensed until 1639 and ended up with another company.[102] Both of these plays were tragicomedies, based on French narrative sources. They drew heavily on themes of platonic love, figuring their romantic heroines, Cecilia and Claracilla, as spiritual beauties who evoke awe and admiration in all they encounter, and encourage temperance and chastity in the advances of their suitors. The subject matter treated by Killigrew's plays is clearly suggestive of the continued investment in the themes that Heywood had started to explore in *Love's Mistress*. But what is also notable about the performance of *The Prisoners* on the Cockpit stage is the company's choice of dramatist. Thomas Killigrew was a courtier playwright rather than a professional; he appears to have written largely to gain favour at court and promote his literary reputation with Henrietta Maria, and did not share the same economic dependency upon the theatre as did Shirley and Heywood. He is also the only courtier playwright known to have written for Queen Henrietta's Men, making Beeston's decision to stage such fare on the Cockpit stage somewhat anomalous. This looks like a new strategy for the company, which depended on the employment of fashionable new producers of drama writing from within the court itself.

This was a strategy that had already proved successful by the King's Men, for courtier playwrights had been writing for the Blackfriars stage since the late 1620s. Davenant was the most prolific – though his status did not approach that of a courtier until the later 1630s, his close connections with aristocratic patrons of drama and the courtier poets positioned him as a writer from 'within' the circles of courtly influence.[103] His plays *The Cruel Brother* and *The Just Italian* had premiered with the King's Men in 1627 and 1629. In 1634 the King's Men performed *Love and Honour*, which was closely followed at court by his masque, *The Temple of Love* – a work which exhibited exceptionally strong links to Henrietta Maria's doctrine of platonic love, and in which the queen performed herself. Lodowick Carlell's *The Deserving Favourite* was also performed at the Blackfriars by 1629, before his two parts of *Arviragus and Philicia* in 1635–36. These plays would be followed in the later 1630s and early 1640s by Davenant's later works, plays by John Suckling, at least one by William Cavendish, Earl of Newcastle, and (possibly) at least one lost play by Thomas Carew.[104]

Between them, the courtiers contributed a sizeable corpus of work to Caroline drama, and their broad focus on the fashionable genre of tragicomedy, with attention to ideals of platonic love and female agency, had a significant influence on the output of the professional stage. This is evidenced not only by *Love's Mistress*, but also by plays including Ford's *The Lover's Melancholy* (1628) and Massinger's *The Emperor of the East* (1631) and *The Bashful Lover* (1636).[105] Many of the plays produced by courtiers also appear to have garnered the royal favour that they sought. *Love and Honour* and the second part of *Arviragus and Philicia* were seen at court, and the title-page of *The Deserving Favourite* also claims court performance. According to Malone's transcript from Herbert's office-book, Queen Henrietta Maria visited the Blackfriars herself in April 1634 to see a performance of Carlell's *The Spartan Ladies*.[106] Of the plays performed by Queen Henrietta's Men at court, several emphasise, in different ways, new attention to female agency and heroism. A notable example is Heywood's *Fair Maid of the West*, Part II, which updates the earlier, Jacobean Part I with a renewed focus on its female protagonists' heroism.[107]

There is no record of court performance of *The Prisoners*, but Killigrew must have thought it worthwhile to write *Claracilla* following the first play's London premiere, even though it would not be licensed in time for performance by Queen Henrietta's Men at the Cockpit. But in staging their first 'courtier' play at the Cockpit, Queen Henrietta's Men were participating in the newest – and perhaps most conspicuous – trend in repertory composition. In comparison to the repertories of the Blackfriars and Salisbury Court, the absence of more plays written by courtier poets seems striking. But Beeston's commissioning of Killigrew's work between 1632 and 1636 looks likely to have been part of a wider tactic designed to position the company's theatrical activities in full view of the court. As one of the queen's circle of courtiers, Killigrew was ideally placed to secure royal attention. At the very least, Beeston might have hoped to follow up the company's success with *Love's Mistress* with another play focused on the themes of platonic love.[108] How far the attempt to draw patronage from the court was orchestrated entirely by Beeston might also be debated, given that Shirley and Killigrew, at least, had motivations beyond the welfare of Queen Henrietta's Men for pleasing royal tastes: individual preferment at court, for one.[109] But the design of the repertory between 1633 and 1636 suggests a directed, and managed, effort to bring the repertory into line with the latest literary fashions – fashions which also permeated the commercial repertory, but which were closely connected with the queen. Beeston's dramatic acquisitions over this time strongly imply that royal favour was a motivating factor at this particular time in the company's history.

TRAVAILE, EXPENSE, AND LOST AFTERNOONS

It is unclear how far this effort rewarded Queen Henrietta's Men. The investment Beeston made in the development of the Cockpit repertory between 1633 and 1636 would have entertained the theatre's regular London audiences, and it seems likely to have strengthened the relationship between court and company. But there is a dearth in the records relating to court performances by Queen Henrietta's Men in the 1633–34 season; for the first time since 1629, the relative fortunes of the King's

Men and Queen Henrietta's Men at court appear to have significantly diverged. In that year there survive records of well over thirty court performances by the King's Men, while extant evidence suggests that the employment of Queen Henrietta's Men at court might have dropped to only seven performances in the season. Evidence for the following year suggests a similar discrepancy in royal demand for the two companies, despite the repeat performances of *Love's Mistress*. If the historical record represents anything like what was actually happening in relation to court performances at this time, this tailing-off in royal appointments, and the widening gap in terms of court attendance between Queen Henrietta's Men and their main competitors, must have occurred at an alarming rate for Beeston. And despite Beeston's confidence in Killigrew's *The Prisoners*, some doubt does linger over its success as a repertory piece for a commercial audience; it was not recorded in the list of plays protected by William Beeston for the successor company in 1639.

If the popularity of Queen Henrietta's Men wavered within royal circles, or their attendance there declined for another reason, what kind of impact would diminishing rewards at court have had on the company? The idea that court performances generated 'extra' profits for the companies has, in some cases, reinforced the sense that companies were to some extent financially dependent upon the royal institution as part of a professional strategy.[110] But court performances themselves might have played a relatively marginal role in the finances of Queen Henrietta's Men, and might even have damaged the daily turnover of profit rather than enhancing it. Richard Dutton has drawn attention to the important point that though dealings with the Master of the Revels (Tilney, in the period of which Dutton writes) may have required the outlay of fees to the Revels Office, and though companies may have made more money within the walls of their own playhouses than at court, it should not be forgotten that without Tilney, 'they might well not have a livelihood at all, certainly not one as privileged as they had'.[111] The court's historical role in protecting the players, and enabling them to earn money in permanent venues, underpinned the companies' operations. Nevertheless, attendance at court could adversely affect the routine trade of companies, and this was a consideration for any theatre company – so much so that the need for monetary compensation was formally recognised by the Lord Chamberlain in 1630. An entry in the records of the Lord Chamberlain's office claims that the King's Men were granted 'the like somme of Twenty poundes for one other Play which was Acted in the day time at Whitehall, by meanes whereof the Players lost the benefitt of their House for that day'.[112] The fee that companies received from court was not always an additional windfall in trade, but a substitute for everyday business, and, as J. Leeds Barroll points out, it had not increased with inflation since Elizabeth's era.[113]

The inadequacy of the standard £10 per court performance is revealed quite frequently by extra payments by the Lord Chamberlain's office to cover expenses. A payment of £170 for sixteen plays performed by Queen Henrietta's Men in 1630–31 breaks down as 'aboue the ordinary Allowance of 10^li for euery play) 10^li more in consideration of their Charge in Attending at Hampton Court'.[114] As expenses paid to the King's Men show, this 'charge' might include 'the trauaile & expences of the whole Company in dyet & Lodgeing'.[115] On 13 December 1636 the King's Men were also issued with £20 a week from the king's 'princely bounty', which was to compensate for the players' obligation 'to assemble their company and keep themselves together near the Court'.[116] These are not one-off payments comparable to compensations during times of plague, but active attempts to cover a shortfall in profits, offset expenses, and recognise inconvenience to the company. Money was paid not only to cover the players' loss of profits from commercial performance, but also to compensate for time spent in preparation for court performance, as the King's Men found in 1632 when a rehearsal at the Cockpit-in-Court meant that they 'lost their afternoone at the [play]House'.[117]

It is unclear how much in profit Queen Henrietta's Men would have made from a typical day's performance, so comparison of a day's takings with a fee paid for court performance is difficult. Standard entry to the Blackfriars, which was similar in social catchment and proportion to Queen Henrietta's Cockpit theatre, was from three to six pence, while seats in the boxes alongside the stage cost two shillings and six pence.[118] It appears, however, that the Cockpit was a slightly smaller theatre than the Blackfriars, and presumably its audience capacity was reduced as a result.[119] The wider context of payments for court performances should be taken into account, however, since for a professional theatre company to either recoup lost profits or claim a rewarding fee, timely payment for services rendered must have been a consideration. But there could be considerable delay between a court performance and its payment. According to the Chamber Accounts, the interim period between performance and payment for Queen Henrietta's Men was anything from three months to a year, though it could have been longer – a payment to the Children of the Revels for three plays performed in 1631 was not issued until three years later.[120] As such, money generated from court performance was not immediately accessible revenue: the security it offered was unreliable, and the cash rewards of court performance could be indefinitely deferred. Means of financial support offered by the court during plague closures, when royal patrons continued to see plays at court, did not constitute a source of instant payment which might remedy immediate financial strife, then. This is a commercial scenario that stands in direct opposition to the alternative of touring.[121]

Exacerbating the situation further, the time lag in payment meant that while Beeston might have received delayed payments, the original members of Queen Henrietta's Men might never have seen the benefit of then. In May 1637 Beeston received payment for nine plays performed at court by Queen Henrietta's Men in 1635, even though that company had since dispersed over the plague closure. The money was received with payment for two plays performed there by Beeston's new boy company, to which he had been sworn governor three months earlier.[122] This meant that court performance did not always guarantee the return of a company's collaborative efforts. It could also cost the company upfront, in the form of gratuities paid to the Master of the Revels. In 1623 Edward Shakerly paid Herbert on behalf of Lady Elizabeth's Men at the Cockpit: he brought Herbert £2 as a gratuity 'with a note of Playes for Christmas'.[123] After Christopher Beeston's time at the Cockpit, his son appears to have paid Herbert '60[li] per ann besids vsuall Fees & allowances for Court Plaies' during the first year of Restoration theatre.[124] Though no similar records survive relating to Queen Henrietta's Men, the fact that fees and allowances were considered 'usual', suggests that this extra outlay for the companies may have been a standard arrangement.

Invitation to court also involved preparation in practical terms, physical labour, and the risk of damage to assets in their transportation from Drury Lane to the court theatres. Whereas once the Office of the Revels had made provision for the properties and costumes for all plays performed at court, by the 1630s the professional companies were expected to provide their own, so that, as Wiggins states, 'plays seem to have become ready-made commodities bought in from the acting companies'.[125] Many of the properties distinctive to the plays performed by Queen Henrietta's Men at court are very small and easily portable – such hand-held, easily pocketed items as the magic, poisoned mirror in *The Shepherds' Holiday*, the remarkable jewel and the hour-glass in *The Fair Maid of the West*. But several of the plays call for larger items – most commonly beds, banqueting tables, coffins, and altars. There are traces in the Revels accounts which suggest that a few props were supplied to the companies by George Wilson, Groom and Purveyor of the Office of the Revels, who claims several times in the accounts 'for divers pperties vsed about the Players', or similar.[126] Perhaps larger, general or multi-purpose items could have been provided at court (hampers or chests, for instance), but on the whole it seems that the company was responsible for furnishing its own productions with the assets it would use in public performances. *Love's Mistress* was unusual, given its requirements for flying machinery, scenery, and the 'excellent Inventions' with which Inigo Jones, Surveyor of the Works, furnished the production. Scenery was painted specially – Heywood describes how Jones 'gave such an extraordinary Luster' to the play, 'upon every occasion changing the stage, to the admiration of all the Spectators' (A2r).[127] But for the most part, the Office of the Works – the department that busied itself with maintaining the structure of the venues and modifying them for performance – simply readied the halls of the court venues for performance by 'Setting vpp rayles, and Degrees in the hall for playes' – temporary seating for the audiences – organising the lighting for the performances, and, if necessary, constructing any other basic, material structures: the 'diverse Instrumentes for performinge of the Acte there'.[128] This minimal approach to assistance given to the professional players was also adopted by the Revels Office, the surviving accounts of which record little else in the way of provision beyond fuel, bellows, and fire-lighting paraphernalia to heat the Cockpit-in-Court during rehearsals and perform- mances, and other admittedly crucial necessities: 'Chamberpotts for the Play:ʳˢ'.[129]

In addition to properties, Queen Henrietta's Men would have been required to transport a stock of costumes to the courtly venues. The wardrobe of a company was a considerable asset, and the rich materials and fabrics used could be very expensive – as costly to companies, if not more so, than the purchase of play-texts.[130] *Love's Mistress* calls for the entry of Cerberus at one point, among the mythical gods and monstrous creatures of its cast – the silver-winged Zephyrus, Apollo, with his 'yellow tresses' that shine 'Like curled flames' (B3r), Vulcan, and four cyclopes. The Revels Office might have helped supply some of these fantastical costumes, though no evidence for this survives. But other plays call for sartorial extravagance on a similar scale: embodiments of the Seasons in *The Sun's Darling*, the 'Masquers' with 'properties' in *The Shepherds' Holiday*, and the two Furies with 'black tapers' in *The Night-Walkers*. The Revels accounts document the costuming of the 'Venusses or Amorouse Ladies' in a masque presented in 1554, and describe 'clothe of gold embrodred vpon Crymesen Satten', 'white Clothe of Silver purple velvett pinked rewe with Silver threedes', and 'yellowe clothe of gold cutte compasse wise garded with clothe of golde chevered with blacke velvett'.[131] Similarly, for a 'Maske of Ladies with lightes being vj vertues', the haberdasher was paid for 'sylver paper for the Maskers sleeves', the silkwoman for 'Buttons and flowers for Maskers heddes', the upholsterer for 'pendentes of burnished golde for the Maskers garmentes', and another supplier for 'perles sett vpon silver bonelace for the Ladys Maskers heades'.[132] The costumes paid for by the Revels Office for royal masques would have been especially sumptuous given the royal funding that went into them, but descriptions such as these show how much attention to detail could go into apparelling theatrical performances, and how precious – and fragile – the costumes would have been.

While expenses such as boat hire to transport the companies' properties and costumes about London and to Greenwich continued to be covered by the Revels Office, the potential damage to which the company's physical assets were subjected was an unavoidable feature of transporting plays whole.[133] As John Astington notes, 'The constant handling the Revels gear sustained would have consequences for its durability', and repairs to costumes and properties were a recurrent and ongoing expense that the Revels Office was required to cover.[134] The same would have applied to Queen Henrietta's Men and the other professional companies when they assumed responsibility for providing the costumes for their own court performances; transportation and the storage of the company's material assets in temporary facilities was not only an inconvenience but also a risk.

The perceived benefits of court performance did not always match the material reality, then, even if the extant records of court performance do not offer anything like an accurate picture of events over the 1630s. But other forms of reward were available through contact with the court. Archival evidence relating to the King's Men reveals the practical advantages of active royal patronage, in terms of both protection and support. On 6 May 1633 the king issued a proclamation that aimed to remedy the 'late decease, infirmity & sicknes of diuerse principall Actors of his Ma^tes Company of Players' that 'hath much decayed & weakened them', by permitting them to 'choose, receaue & take into [...] [their] Company any such Actor or Actors belonging to any of the lycensed Companyes w^thin & about the Citty of London'.[135] It is not known whether the King's Men acted upon this proclamation.[136] But the order raises important issues concerning the power of the court to overturn the everyday operations of commercial companies. G. E. Bentley refers to the order as 'unique in the theatrical annals of the time', but a similar scenario had arisen in 1583, when the best players from the London companies were uprooted from their troupes and joined together to form Queen Elizabeth's Men.[137] Nevertheless, this gesture of support towards the King's Men was radical, and would have had potentially disastrous consequences for the remainder of London's professional theatre.[138] The intervention had the potential to skew the independence and development of the other, implicitly lesser, companies, and underscored the king's active interest in the fortunes of his namesake company.

The queen's interest in her own theatrical company is evidenced by a document in the National Archives recently brought to critical attention by Lucy Munro, which records a payment of 100 marks from Henrietta Maria to Beeston in his capacity as manager of Queen Henrietta's Men in 1630. This clearly indicates what Munro describes as a significant level of engagement with the company on the part of Henrietta Maria, corroborating a tangible connection between the queen and her namesake company over this period.[139] Henrietta Maria's investment in the theatrical culture of London more generally is also evidenced by her visits to the public theatres at this time: to the Blackfriars between 1632 and 1638, and at least once to the Cockpit, to see *Love's Mistress*, as the play's prefatory material attests.[140] She gifted clothes and costumes from 'her owne pastoral' to the King's Men in 1633, which were used in a performance at Denmark House of Fletcher's *The Faithful Shepherdess*.[141] A monarch's support could also benefit companies in times of adversity, as the King's Men found in 1630 when they received £100 from the king's 'free guift and bountie' during a plague closure.[142] The queen supported Beeston's young company in this way; in a document brought to light by Karen Britland, it emerged that Henrietta Maria gave Beeston £30 in 1637, 'in consideration of his charges and pains in breeding and keeping' the company during 'the time of the sickness', following the plague closure in which the original Queen Henrietta's Men folded.[143] As Munro notes, the 1630 payment to Queen Henrietta's Men was also granted during a plague closure, and in light of these instances, which give insight into the specific nature of the relationships of patronage that held over the 1630s, it might be that other similar payments to Beeston have now been lost from the records; indeed, Munro reads the 1630 payment as 'part of a longer series of patronage interactions'.[144]

Another indication that Beeston's company was bound, formally or otherwise, into a relationship with the court came in 1635, when the king offered the Cockpit to a visiting French troupe, who occupied the professional theatre at specific times and used its performance space to their own advantage. Malone's transcript of Herbert's account suggests that Beeston 'obeyd readily' the king's demands, and that the French company 'had the benefitt of playinge on the sermon daies, and gott two hundred pounds at least; besides many rich clothes were given them'.[145] Further benefits bestowed upon the visiting French players included the Lord Chamberlain's licence 'to act playes at a new house in Drury-lane', the street in which the Cockpit was located, and to build a new playhouse.[146] The Frenchmen were apparently 'commended unto' Herbert 'by the queene'. Queen Henrietta's Men had lost the space in which they would ordinarily rehearse over the Lent closure, and were obliged to accept (or 'obey') the terms of this inconvenience. The French company 'had freely to themselves the whole weeke before the weeke before Easter' at the Cockpit.[147]

For many years the nature of Henrietta Maria's relationship with Beeston's troupe seemed minimal, virtually non-existent in comparison with evidence relating to the network of patronage that other companies enjoyed – most notably the King's Men. The company's relative independence from the court seemed distinctive. But with the emergence of new evidence, the understanding of Henrietta Maria's investment in her namesake company will continue to develop and reveal new insights into the workings of Beeston's operation, and the fuller extent to which the queen's priorities influenced the drama on the Drury Lane stage. As Munro suggests, the company was 'a more court-orientated company at this time' than has previously been thought.[148]

CONCLUSION

There is little doubt that Christopher Beeston negotiated the company's relationship with the court to the troupe's best advantage, developing the repertory in ways that would appeal to a gift-giving namesake patron and offering the company's commercial base when required for actors visiting from Henrietta Maria's homeland. Though the rewards of court performance were not as bountiful as might be expected, they warranted and encouraged other forms of patronage in the nature of gratuities and payments. If sacrifices had to be made by the company in terms of the loss of its house or an afternoon's lost profits, then either it was commercially robust enough to withstand these effects or Beeston found eventual reimbursement in another form. This need not have been in strictly fiscal terms, and in this account of the relationship between Queen Henrietta's Men and the court it becomes clear that reward was not always calculable. Examining the financial returns of court performance provides an important perspective on the company's commitments in business terms, bringing consideration of the practical realities of court performance to the fore and revealing those realities in relation to the priorities of a commercial company.[149] By the same token it is worth considering that from the perspective of the court, the players provided a luxury 'commodity', part of the fulfilment of royal expectation and a basic requirement of hospitality.[150] But the relationship was often more complicated than a straightforward service rendered, a fee paid, and not so easily quantified. Not all of the capital gained from an association with the court could be accounted for in the books, and it was not always recorded or documented, traceable in the archive, even as new evidence charting the transactions that underpinned these relationships is in the process of being rediscovered.

The company's connections with the court and with courtly interests have emerged, throughout this chapter, as twofold: through the dramatists' attention to the preoccupations and ideologies promoted by Queen Henrietta Maria and the forms of direct patronage with which she provided the company; and through avenues of both access to court and repertory-building provided by Henry Herbert. Through his licensing responsibilities and his role as an occasional purveyor of plays or dramatic content, Herbert can be seen as a key intermediary between the company and its royal patron, not only arranging its appointments at court as part of his official duties but making active interventions into the repertory that were likely to promote the company's popularity and status as providers of royal entertainment. In this way, Herbert collaborated with Queen Henrietta's Men in order to make them more visible to Henrietta Maria and the courtly circles within which she moved, and, therefore, he can be viewed as responsible in part for facilitating the examples of direct patronage that the queen bestowed on the company in the form of payouts during plague closures.

In terms of less direct forms of patronage, Herbert's contribution to shaping the repertory and supporting the company through its commercial pursuits was an important associated benefit of the company's attendance at the court. The dramatic material with which he provided the company – *Hymen's Holiday* and the plot of *The Gamester* – worked to promote Queen Henrietta's Men before the court by staging genres and narratives that would appeal to royal audiences, but it also contributed to the fare available to the company's everyday patrons at the Cockpit. Herbert's contributions to the repertory therefore provided financial returns, manifest in the coins that changed hands at the theatre doors, and they also contributed to the form and content of the commercial repertory presented to the wider 1630s audience, including those 'judicious spectators' who Herbert imagined would uphold his own judgements as an arbiter of taste. These same idealised spectators, and the discourses that governed constructions of audience and taste in the period more widely, are the subject of the next chapter, which turns to the company's work in negotiating attitudes towards new and revived drama in London's lively print market and playgoing populace, far beyond the bounds of the court.

NOTES

1 Martin Butler, *Theatre and Crisis, 1632–1642* (Cambridge: Cambridge University Press, 1984), pp. 2–11, 8, 23, 5.

2 Andrew Gurr, *The Shakespearean Stage, 1574–1642*, 4th edn (Cambridge: Cambridge University Press, 2009), p. 34: 'To be summoned was an acknowledgement of status. Only the best of the companies performing in London were ever called for. So in a sense playing at Court was the ultimate goal of all the players.'

3 John H. Astington, *English Court Theatre, 1558–1642* (Cambridge: Cambridge University Press, 1999), pp. 7, 6.

4 Andrew Gurr, *The Shakespearian Playing Companies* (Oxford: Clarendon Press, 1996), pp. 366, 154, 422. Gurr also connects the rise of Queen Henrietta's Men to court performance: ten performances over the winter season of 1629–30 'compared with twelve by the King's Men, who up to then had given as much entertainment to the Court as all the other companies put together' (*Shakespearean Stage*, p. 81).

5 G. E. Bentley, *The Jacobean and Caroline Stage*, 7 vols (Oxford: Clarendon Press, 1941–68), I, pp. 233; Arthur Melville Clark, *Thomas Heywood: Playwright and Miscellanist* (Oxford: Blackwell, 1931), p. 131.

6 Raymond C. Shady, 'The Stage History of Heywood's *Love's Mistress*', *Theatre Survey*, 18 (1997), 86–95 (pp. 86, 87); Gurr, *Shakespearian Playing Companies*, p. 422.

7 See Appendix B.

8 Gurr, *Shakespearian Playing Companies*, pp. 198–201; see *Malone Society Collections*, I.1 for a transcript of Sir Francis Walsingham's letter to the Lord Mayor of the City: Malone Society Reprints (Oxford: Oxford University Press, 1907), p. 67.

9 *Acts of the Privy Council*, ed. J. R. Dasent, 32 vols (London: Her Majesty's Stationery Office, 1890–1907), XXVIII, p. 327.

10 Andrew Gurr, *The Shakespeare Company, 1594–1642* (Cambridge: Cambridge University Press, 2004), pp. 167–8.

11 *Malone Society Collections, I.3*, Malone Society Reprints (Oxford: Oxford University Press, 1910), pp. 272–3.

12 Gurr, *Shakespearian Playing Companies*, p. 417.

13 For Queen Henrietta Maria's role as performer, see Melinda J. Gough, '"Not as Myself": The Queen's Voice in *Tempe Restored*', *Modern Philology*, 101 (2003), 48–67; and Melinda J. Gough, 'Courtly *Comédiantes*: Henrietta Maria and Amateur Women's Stage Plays in France and England', in *Women Players in Early Modern England, 1500–1660: Beyond the All-Male Stage*, ed. Pamela Allen Brown and Peter Parolin (Aldershot: Ashgate, 2005), pp. 193–215. For discussion of Queen Henrietta's role as patron, and the Cockpit's 'specific connection to the Queen's patronage', see *Three Seventeenth-Century Plays on Women and Performance*, ed. Hero Chalmers, Julie Sanders, and Sophie Tomlinson (Manchester: Manchester University Press, 2006), p. 25. See also Astington, *English Court Theatre*, p. 217, for Queen Henrietta Maria's enthusiasm for drama, and the extent to which Charles I's 'support for players, writers, and theatrical activity of many kinds combined with the similar interests of his wife to produce an unprecedentedly rich cultural ambience at the court'. Karen Britland's *Drama at the Courts of Queen Henrietta Maria* (Cambridge: Cambridge University Press, 2006) offers an extensive and insightful analysis of Henrietta Maria's cultural patronage of drama, beyond professional theatre.

14 Rebecca A. Bailey, *Staging the Old Faith: Queen Henrietta Maria and the Theatre of Caroline England, 1625–1642* (Manchester: Manchester University Press, 2009).

15 On one aspect of that contribution, see Eleanor Collins, 'Changing Fashions: Tragicomedy, Romance, and the Heroic Woman in the 1630s Hall-Playhouses', in *Moving Shakespeare Indoors: Performance and Repertoire in the Jacobean Playhouse*, ed. Andrew Gurr and Farah Karim-Cooper (Cambridge: Cambridge University Press, 2014), pp. 217–36.

16 See pp. 89–90.

17 For documentary evidence of all court performances, and citations of the source material, see Appendix B.

18 *Malone Society Collections, II.3*, Malone Society Reprints (Oxford: Oxford University Press, 1931), p. 350.

19 See, for instance, Martin Wiggins's comment on the plot: 'the Duke redirects his amorous attentions to Cleona, who is Savoy-born and so poses none of the problems of language and obedience associated with a foreign wife'. Martin Wiggins, in association with Catherine Richardson, *British Drama 1533–1642: A Catalogue* (Oxford: Oxford University Press, 2011–), #2287.

20 Astington, *English Court Theatre*, p. 258.

21 'Playes for the Kinge this present yeare of o^r Lord God. 1630', transcribed in Bentley, *Jacobean and Caroline Stage*, I, pp. 27–8.

22 N. W. Bawcutt (ed.), *The Control and Censorship of Caroline Drama: The Records of Sir Henry Herbert, Master of the Revels 1623–73* (Oxford: Clarendon Press, 1996), p. 180.

23 Bawcutt (ed.), *Control and Censorship*, p. 184.

24 Bawcutt (ed.), *Control and Censorship*, p. 181.

25 Bawcutt (ed.), *Control and Censorship*, p. 186; Astington, English Court Theatre, p. 261.

26 Bawcutt (ed.), *Control and Censorship*, p. 179.

27 Bawcutt (ed.), *Control and Censorship*, p. 177; see pp. 48–9; p. 237 in this book.

28 Bawcutt (ed.), *Control and Censorship*, pp. 179, 187.

29 Bawcutt (ed.), *Control and Censorship*, p. 187.

30 Thomas Heywood, *Love's Mistress* (London, 1636), title-page.

31 Heywood, *Love's Mistress*, A3r, A4r.

32 Robert Davenport, *King John and Matilda* (London, 1655), title-page verso.

33 Christopher Marlowe, *The Rich Jew of Malta* (London, 1633), A3r.

34 Thomas Heywood, 'A Prologue to the Play of Queene Elizabeth as it was last revived at the Cock-pit', in *Pleasant Dialogues and Dramas* (London, 1637), pp. 248–89.

35 Martin Wiggins has suggested that we might infer a context of court performance from the dedication of the play to the Earl of Peterborough in the printed playtext of 1633: *'Tis Pity She's a Whore*, ed. Martin Wiggins, New Mermaids (London: A. & C. Black, 2003), p. 9.

36 Astington, *English Court Theatre*, pp. 44, 46, 64. For accounts of stages being set up by the Office of the Works prior to performances of both masques and plays in the 1630s, see *Malone Society Collections, X*, Malone Society Reprints (Oxford: Oxford University Press, 1975), p. 43.

37 Astington, *English Court Theatre*, p. 48.

38 Astington, *English Court Theatre*, p. 67.

39 Astington, *English Court Theatre*, p. 70.

40 John Webb, the plans of the Cockpit-in-Court, *c.* 1660, held at Worcester College, Oxford. The document is reproduced in Astington, *English Court Theatre*, p. 54.

41 Astington, *English Court Theatre*, p. 123.

42 Glynne Wickham, *Early English Stages, Volume Two, Part II: 1576–1600* (London: Routledge, 1972), p. 78.

43 Wickham, *Early English Stages, Volume Two, Part II*, p. 89.

44 Oliver Jones, 'Documentary Evidence for an Indoor Jacobean Theatre', in *Moving Shakespeare Indoors: Performance and Repertoire in the Jacobean Playhouse*, ed. Andrew Gurr and Farah Karim-Cooper (Cambridge: Cambridge University Press, 2014), pp. 65–78 (p. 72).

45 Dancing of one form or another is also specified in *'Tis Pity She's a Whore*, *The Duke's Mistress*, *The Shepherds' Holiday*, and *The Knight of the Burning Pestle*. See Chapter 4 for a discussion of the kind of evidence provided by stage directions, which also applies here.

46 Astington, *English Court Theatre*, p. 88.

47 The number of actors onstage in these scenes might certainly have been reduced, and across the cast as a whole. Simon Palfrey and Tiffany Stern have suggested that the doubling of actors in parts of plays performed at court may have been encouraged, as 'performers at court were under some obligation not to fill the palace with too many people': *Shakespeare in Parts* (Oxford: Oxford University Press, 2007), p. 55. The basic and inevitable expense incurred by transportation of props and costumes, and hospitality might well have contributed to this practice of moderation; see pp. 88–9 in this book.

48 Astington, *English Court Theatre*, pp. 51, 64.

49 John H. Astington, 'Court Theatre', in *The Oxford Handbook of Early Modern Theatre*, ed. Richard Dutton (Oxford: Oxford University Press, 2011), pp. 307–22 (pp. 318–19).

50 Astington, *English Court Theatre*, p. 208.

51 Astington, *English Court Theatre*, p. 208; Martin White, '"When Torchlight made an Artificial Noon": Light and Darkness in the Indoor Jacobean Theatre', in *Moving Shakespeare Indoors: Performance and Repertoire in the Jacobean Playhouse*, ed. Andrew Gurr and Farah Karim-Cooper (Cambridge: Cambridge University Press, 2014), pp. 115–36 (pp. 123–4).

52 Astington, *English Court Theatre*, pp. 53–5.

53 White, '"When Torchlight made an Artificial Noon"', p. 122.

54 White, '"When Torchlight made an Artificial Noon"', p. 122.

55 Martin White, *Renaissance Drama in Action* (London: Routledge, 1998), pp. 149–50.

56 John Ford, *'Tis Pity She's a Whore* (London, 1633), F4v.

57 See discussion on pp. 167–9.

58 White, '"When Torchlight made an Artificial Noon"', pp. 122–3.

59 James Shirley, *The Duke's Mistress* (London, 1638), Ir.

60 James Shirley, *The Gamester* (London, 1637), C3r.

61 Ford, *'Tis Pity She's a Whore*, I4r, C4v, F3v. For Giovanni and Annabella's entry on the bed, see White, *Renaissance Drama in Action*, pp. 175–6.

62 Marlowe, *The Rich Jew of Malta*, Bv, K2r.

63 John H. Astington, 'Court Theatre', in *The Oxford Handbook of Early Modern Theatre*, ed. Richard Dutton (Oxford: Oxford University Press, 2011), pp. 307–22 (pp. 318–19).

64 Astington, *English Court Theatre*, p. 54.

65 John Ford and Thomas Dekker, *The Sun's Darling* (London, 1656), B3v.

66 See pp. 80–2.

67 For an account of these changes, see Astington, *English Court Theatre*, pp. 8–17.

68 W. R. Streitberger, in *Malone Society Collections*, XIII, Malone Society Reprints (Oxford: Oxford University Press, 1986), p. xxiii.

69 *MSC, XIII*, p. 99.

70 See Wiggins, *British Drama*, #676–#682.

71 Bawcutt (ed.), *Control and Censorship*, p. 180.

72 Richard Dutton, *Shakespeare, Court Dramatist* (Oxford: Oxford University Press, 2016), p. 46.

73 Bawcutt (ed.), *Control and Censorship*, p. 149; see also p. 160, for Herbert's receipt of a copy of *The Arcadia* (presumably) in 1625. At some point Herbert would turn theory into practice by writing his own play, *The Emperor Otho*, though there is no clear evidence that it was performed (Dutton, *Shakespeare, Court Dramatist*, p. 59). Dutton suggests that Herbert might have expected it to be performed, since he kept a careful tally of lines.
74 Bawcutt (ed.), *Control and Censorship*, p. 186.
75 Bawcutt (ed.), *Control and Censorship*, p. 186.
76 Bawcutt (ed.), *Control and Censorship*, p. 187.
77 Bawcutt (ed.), *Control and Censorship*, p. 187.
78 Bawcutt (ed.), *Control and Censorship*, p. 181.
79 See David Nicol's entry on variant readings by G. E. Bentley and Tiffany Stern in the Lost Plays Database, http://www.lostplays.org/index.php/Hymen%27s_Holiday_or_Cupid%27s_Vagaries (accessed 28 July 2017).
80 Bawcutt (ed.), *Control and Censorship*, pp. 143, 144. As Bawcutt says, Gunnell was in need of plays after many of those in the repertory of Palsgrave's Men were destroyed in the fire at the Fortune. He must have taken the play with him to Salisbury Court, where it was performed by Heton's Queen Henrietta's Men, under whose auspices the play appears to have been published in 1638.
81 Bawcutt (ed.), *Control and Censorship*, p. 143.
82 Bawcutt (ed.), *Control and Censorship*, pp. 143, 144.
83 See Karen Britland's chapter on *Artenice* for an illuminating discussion of this new 'French fashion' in drama at court (*Drama at the Courts of Queen Henrietta Maria*, pp. 35–52).
84 See Chapter 6, pp. 223–35.
85 See Gough, 'Courtly *Comédiantes*', pp. 202–8.
86 William Prynne, *Histriomastix: The Player's Scourge, or Actor's Tragedy* (London, 1632) (the title-page date given of 1633 is erroneous).
87 James Shirley, *The Bird in a Cage* (London, 1633), A2r.
88 The chronology here depends on the date of composition of *The Arcadia*; see pp. 212–13.
89 Gurr, *Shakespearian Playing Companies*, p. 102; Ann Haaker, 'The Plague, the Theatre, and the Poet', *Renaissance Drama*, n.s. 1 (1968), 283–306 (p. 303).
90 I am grateful to Martin Wiggins for drawing the latter possibility to my attention in personal correspondence.
91 Wiggins, *British Drama*, #1247.
92 Jane Kingsley-Smith, *Cupid in Early Modern Literature and Culture* (Cambridge: Cambridge University Press, 2010), p. 173.
93 Richard Rowland, *Thomas Heywood's Theatre, 1599–1639: Locations, Translations, and Conflict* (Farnham: Ashgate, 2010), p. 292; Kingsley-Smith, *Cupid*, p. 73.
94 Lesel Dawson, '"New Sects of Love": Neoplatonism and Constructions of Gender in Davenant's *The Temple of Love* and *The Platonick Lovers*', *Early Modern Literary Studies*, 8.1 (2002), para 4, http://extra.shu.ac.uk/emls/08-1/dawsnew.htm (accessed 28 July 2017).
95 Butler, *Theatre and Crisis*, p. 35.
96 Dawson, '"New Sects of Love"', para 2.
97 Britland, *Drama at the Courts of Queen Henrietta Maria*, pp. 8–9.
98 See also Kingsley-Smith, *Cupid*, pp. 172–3, on the ways in which Heywood 'platonizes Cupid' within a wider cultural history of Cupid's representations in early modern literature.

99 See pp. 214–19.

100 Perhaps the play with the closest affinities to *Love's Mistress* is Glapthorne's *Argalus and Parthenia*, though this may not have been performed until Beeston's Boys were underway at the Cockpit. Based on Sidney's *Arcadia*, it features references to classical mythology, platonic love, and models of courtship. The main action is framed by the antics of a group of shepherds who pass judgement on the action as it unfolds. Like Midas and Apuleius, they function as a kind of anti-masque, disrupting the main action and entertaining the audience with dancing (though they also entertain the protagonists of the central narrative). Glapthorne seems here to adapt and repurpose the formal underpinnings of Heywood's play, and the two plays would sit alongside each other in the repertory of Beeston's Boys.

101 Lucy Munro, 'The Queen and the Cockpit: Henrietta Maria's Theatrical Patronage Revisited', *Shakespeare Bulletin*, 37.1 (2019), 25–45.

102 Either Heton's Queen Henrietta's Men at Salisbury Court, or Beeston's Boys at the Cockpit; Wiggins, *British Drama*, #2529.

103 Ira Clark, *Professional Playwrights: Massinger, Ford, Shirley, and Brome* (Lexington: University of Kentucky Press, 1992), pp. 3–5. See also Deborah C. Payne, 'Patronage and the Dramatic Marketplace under Charles I and II', *Yearbook of English Studies*, 21 (1991), 137–52, on Davenant's status and its fashioning.

104 William Cavendish wrote *The Country Captain* for the King's Men before 1641, and, possibly, *The Variety* around the same time; Bentley, *Jacobean and Caroline Stage*, III, pp. 149–51; for Carew's lost play, see Bentley, *Jacobean and Caroline Stage*, III, pp. 110–11.

105 See Collins, 'Changing Fashions', for more details.

106 Bawcutt (ed.), *Control and Censorship*, p. 188.

107 See pp. 187–91.

108 For more on these themes, and for suggestions that Killigrew's plays did not exclusively endorse Queen Henrietta Maria, see Eleanor Collins, 'From Court to Cockpit: *The Prisoners* and *Claricilla* in Repertory', in *Thomas Killigrew and the Seventeenth-Century English Stage: New Perspectives*, ed. Philip Major (Farnham: Ashgate, 2013), pp. 21–44. The criticism of platonic love that I observe in this chapter is by no means specific to Killigrew; see Dawson, '"New Sects of Love"'.

109 Shirley dedicated a significant number of plays to courtly patrons, and became Valet to the Chamber of Queen Henrietta Maria by 1634; for more on this, see p. 212; p. 239 n.18. But note also Rebecca A. Bailey's nuanced account of Shirley's 'self-positioning', which suggests that 'Shirley's genuine religious principles led to his court niche rather than a realisation of the advantages of being "servant to Henrietta Maria"' (*Staging the Old Faith*, p. 58).

110 Astington, *English Court Theatre*, p. 116.

111 Dutton, *Shakespeare: Court Dramatist*, pp. 13–16, 25.

112 *MSC, II.3*, p. 355.

113 J. Leeds Barroll, *Politics, Plague, and Shakespeare's Theater: The Stuart Years* (Ithaca, NY: Cornell University Press, 1991), p. 69.

114 *MSC, II.3*, p. 355.

115 *MSC, II.3*, p. 354.

116 Bentley, *Jacobean and Caroline Stage*, I, p. 53.

117 *MSC, II.3*, p. 360.

118 Andrew Gurr, *Playgoing in Shakespeare's London*, 3rd edn (Cambridge: Cambridge University Press, 2004), p. 27.

119 The building in which Beeston's Cockpit was housed is thought to have been 40 feet square, while the Blackfriars' internal measurements were given in 1609 as 66 x 46 feet (Jones, 'Documentary Evidence', pp. 71, 67). Sarah Dustagheer estimates that the Blackfriars seated around 600 people ('To Glisten in a Playhouse: Cosmetic Beauty Indoors', in *Moving Shakespeare Indoors: Performance and Repertoire in the Jacobean Playhouse*, ed. Andrew Gurr and Farah Karim-Cooper [Cambridge: Cambridge University Press, 2014], pp. 184–200 [p. 184]).

120 *Malone Society Collections, VI*, Malone Society Reprints (Oxford: Oxford University Press, 1962), p. 84.

121 Scott McMillin and Sally-Beth Maclean, *The Queen's Men and their Plays* (Cambridge: Cambridge University Press, 1998), pp. 39, 175–88. Due to the nature of touring, payments to companies were dispensed within days of performance, before the company left the town or vicinity, offering prompt financial reward.

122 *MSC, II.3*, p. 383.

123 Bawcutt (ed.), *Control and Censorship*, p. 146.

124 Bawcutt (ed.), *Control and Censorship*, p. 242.

125 See Wiggins's note on the dating of *The Three Sisters of Mantua*, British Drama, #652; this change was effected from the late 1580s.

126 See, for instance, *MSC, XIII*, pp. 130, 133.

127 For a summary of the scenery that has been identified to date, see Wiggins, *British Drama*, #2451.

128 For lighting, and also the expense this could incur at court, see White, '"When Torchlight made an Artificial Noon"', pp. 120, 123–4; *MSC, X*, pp. 37, 39.

129 *MSC, XIII*, pp. 106, 111, 117, 124.

130 Gurr, *Shakespearian Playing Companies*, p. 103.

131 *Documents Relating to the Office of the Revels in the Time of Queen Elizabeth*, ed. Albert Feuillerat (Louvain, 1908), p. 22.

132 Feuillerat (ed.), *Documents*, pp. 206–11.

133 See, for instance, *MSC, XIII*, p. 135 for the necessity of boat hire.

134 Astington, *English Court Theatre*, p. 12.

135 *MSC, II.3*, p. 361.

136 For Bentley's discussion of the matter, see *Jacobean and Caroline Stage*, I, pp. 34–6.

137 Bentley, *Jacobean and Caroline Stage*, I, p. 35; McMillin and Maclean, *The Queen's Men*, pp. 1–2.

138 For obvious reasons, but see also McMillin and Maclean, *The Queen's Men*, pp. 12–32, who suggest that the effect of the first Queen's Men, which was assembled from extant playing troupes in the Elizabethan period, was limiting to the profession in that it attempted to harness drama as an instrument of state machinery, and 'control' the profession by reducing the number of companies that could act in the playhouses. J. Leeds Barroll has suggested that the formation of Queen Elizabeth's Men operated as a mechanism designed to contain the growth of playing ('Drama and the Court', in *The Revels History of Drama in English, Volume III: 1576–1613*, ed. Clifford Leech et al. [London: Methuen, 1975], pp. 1–27); he argues that the Queen's Men constituted 'a possibly restrictive monopoly' that may 'have retarded the development of the drama in England' (p. 25). Andrew Gurr's article 'Three Reluctant Patrons and Early Shakespeare', *Shakespeare Quarterly*, 44 (1993), 159–74, provides a compelling account and exploration of the implications of the events of 1583 for other companies and patrons.

139 Munro, 'The Queen and the Cockpit', p. 26.

140 Bawcutt (ed.), *Control and Censorship*, pp. 174, 188; Bentley, *Jacobean and Caroline Stage*, I, pp. 39, 48.
141 Bentley, *Jacobean and Caroline Stage*, I, p. 39.
142 Bentley, *Jacobean and Caroline Stage*, I, p. 27.
143 National Library of Wales, Wynnstay 181, fol. 15v, quoted in Martin Butler, 'Exeunt Fighting: Poets, Players, and Impresarios at the Caroline Hall Theaters', in *Localizing Caroline Drama: Politics and Economics of the Early Modern Stage, 1625–1642*, ed. Adam Zucker and Alan B. Farmer (Basingstoke: Palgrave Macmillan, 2006), pp. 97–128 (p. 126).
144 Munro, 'Queen and Cockpit', pp. 27, 31.
145 Bawcutt (ed.), *Control and Censorship*, pp. 191–2.
146 Bawcutt (ed.), *Control and Censorship*, p. 193.
147 Bawcutt (ed.), *Control and Censorship*, p. 192.
148 Munro, 'Queen and Cockpit', p. 27.
149 See also Martin Butler's article 'Royal Slaves? The Stuart Court and the Theatres', *Renaissance Drama Newsletter*, Supplement 2 (1984), 1–23, which addresses the tendency in current criticism to 'underestimat[e] the autonomy centred on the professional stage by its commercial structures' through focus on the court, and particularly his discussion of the 'rich, varied' drama that flourished in the professional theatres beyond the narrow strictures of court entertainment (pp. 18–21).
150 See Astington's construction of the court, its demands, and the nature of what was demanded from the playing companies; the court is construed here as highly institutionalised, consumerist, and concerned to promote cultural 'magnificence' before its guests (*English Court Theatre*, pp. 1–7).

3

'AN OULD PLAY REVIVED AT THEIR HOUSE': THEATRICAL TASTE AND THE CULTURAL STATUS OF REVIVALS IN CAROLINE LONDON

The material conditions that underpinned a company's success play a central part in an account of Queen Henrietta's Men: playbooks, venues, the rewards of a relationship with the court. But there also existed other conditions and circumstances which are less immediately tangible but which impacted in important ways on the company's popularity, its identity and reputation. One of these circumstances was audience taste, and articulations about the value and desirability of certain kinds of plays that were circulating in the 1630s. As this chapter explores, constructions of theatrical taste and the currency of different traditions of drama as they were revived and played out on the Caroline stage had a vital role in the building of company identity and commercial success. Although this was a determining condition of production over which Beeston and Queen Henrietta's Men had less direct control, the changing professional landscape of the 1630s required them to negotiate it with increasing urgency. Shifts and developments of a social and cultural nature were as much a part of the historical circumstances that influenced the activities of Queen Henrietta's Men and the consolidation of the repertory as those practical conditions that had brought about the company's formation, and that had supported it over its years of playing.

Ideas of theatrical taste and dramatic value were a concern and a preoccupation of all playing companies, in London and beyond. But for Queen Henrietta's Men, the discourse that governed constructions of audience reception in the printed accounts that survive proved more than an intermittent distraction or a generalised undertone to their operation. Instead, the company found itself inextricably bound up in the debate, as the reception of both old fare and drama that originated in the amphitheatres was portrayed in increasingly derogatory terms. While the drama that Queen Henrietta's Men had inherited from Beeston and his former Red Bull company contributed to the speed with which the company could gain a foothold in the market, this inheritance turned out to have both positive and negative repercussions, as writers of verse, dramatists, printers, publishers, and chroniclers of the time all worked to contest its value and deride its defenders throughout the later Jacobean and Caroline periods.

Changing attitudes to old favourites and once-popular traditions had consequences for the company's continued stability as a commercial enterprise,
and its aesthetic credibility and standing as an indoor playhouse in a
thriving and competitive market.[1] With the material inheritance of Red
Bull plays came a loaded cultural legacy.

   This chapter engages with constructions of audience taste, expectations,
and demand, and the particular relation that this discourse came to bear
on amphitheatre revivals on the Cockpit stage; it offers a sense of the
climate in which the company operated and was required to develop its
repertory. The discussion takes in a range of sources to provide an account
of the expression of theatrical taste in the seventeenth century as it survives
in print, mapping its development from the early 1600s through to the
1630s and beyond, in retrospective anecdotes, into the Restoration. Its
focus on the particular tropes and ideas operating in the period, within
a chronology of theatrical taste as it was variously construed or concocted
by printed texts, offers a new perspective on the commercial position of
Queen Henrietta's Men within the marketplace. Importantly, the discussion is not concerned with evidence relating to documented instances of
playgoing: questions of who went where, when, and how they might
actually have behaved once in situ. Though recent work on audience
behaviour and experience has made an important contribution to our
understanding of London playgoing, those lines of enquiry privilege different priorities.[2] What is under scrutiny here is not what happened, but
what was communicated; the words and terms by which writers, playwrights, and publishers chose to describe playgoers and theatrical taste
to the audiences they were addressing (whether in print or on stage); what
was reported or recorded in the period, and the particular constructions
which became embedded in the language and business of the theatre
profession as it developed, and as it came to be remembered.

   The concept and practice of reportage, in the sense of relating events
in the style or context of a particular genre, is apt in this case. The
accounts cited in this chapter were concerned with articulating subjective agendas rather than anything approaching 'objective' documentation.
While this condition presents an obstacle to any interpretative strategy that
is invested in uncovering a positivist truth, it adds crucial context to the
texts under discussion. A large proportion of these texts consist in prefatory material to the plays: prologues, commendatory verses, notes to the
reader, and other similarly paratextual matter. These texts were designed
to mediate the response of an audience or reader, and they were shaped
and informed by a variety of factors, including the competitive strategies
of early modern publishers and the conventions of the print market; the
particular dramatic, literary, and social concerns of individuals in the print

and theatre professions; and the commercial dynamics of the repertory system.

Scholarship on all of these areas has seen significant advances in recent years, as critical appreciation of paratextual material has benefited from detailed research into textual provenance and material conditions of production, and as fresh critical approaches in theatre history have developed. These approaches look beyond the dramatist to other originating agents, and as such they have nuanced and helpfully complicated Gérard Genette's understanding of the literary and bibliographic role of paratextual material. Douglas Bruster and Robert Weimann recognise the special and particular nature of prologues in particular, characterising them as 'interactive, liminal, boundary-breaking entities that negotiated charged thresholds between and among, variously, playwrights, actors, characters, audience members, playworlds, and the world outside the playhouse'.[3] Tiffany Stern's work has shown further that prologues were detachable from the plays to which they were once thought to 'belong' in a more permanent sense; they were sold, copied, circulated, and read independently, and could be multi-purpose in the sense that they might become associated with more than one play.[4] Stern has also drawn attention to the prologue's very specific function, which was to introduce a new play on its very first performance. The 'temporary' nature of these texts and the sense in which they belonged to 'the opening day only' renders this category of evidence particularly interesting, for although prologues were not necessarily anchored to a particular play, they were tied to a very precise moment in a play's life and in a working repertory. They had, therefore, a tightly defined function: to win the audience's approval and, through that approval, secure further performance, the benefits of which would be passed to the dramatist.[5]

More recently, the work of Helen Smith and Louise Wilson on early modern paratextual material has noted the extent to which these particular and somehow privileged interventions 'operate in multiple directions' and are situated 'as a place which both frames and inhabits the text'.[6] Brian Schneider has explored, at monograph length, the opportunities afforded by this special status in relation to prologues, detailing the extent to which prologues between 1580 and 1660 exhibit 'extraordinary experimentation' on the part of their authors. He notes the conflicts and contradictions that seem inherent to this genre. Examining the relationships between prologues and epilogues of the period, he writes that these framing texts 'celebrate the self-referentiality' in the drama they accompany, 'and are themselves full of such referencing; they attempt to anatomize the audiences of the period, but cannot conclude what is the perfect audience [...] they become increasingly important elements in the theatrical experience, and yet are constantly resisted and criticized by many of the playwrights themselves'.[7] These features do not render the study of framing texts trying or frustrating, though; it is the framing text's status as somehow both insider and outsider that makes it so rewarding, as all of these critics argue. This critical stance was given further material acknowledgement when Thomas L. Berger and Sonia Massai published a two-volume reference work anthologising many early modern paratexts, in recognition of the critical value of studying paratextual materials 'as a key body of texts in their own right', constituting a 'repository of information about all aspects of the production, reception and transmission of dramatic literature in the period'.[8]

The survival of many prologues in printed plays of the period has facilitated their collective use as the kind of knowledge-rich repository towards which Berger and Massai gesture, since the medium of print has offered prologues a kind of fixity and relative stability to which these ephemeral, peripheral, and fraught texts might not otherwise lay claim – and it is this interplay between print and performance that any analysis of this category of evidence must bear in mind. While prologues derived from the theatre and, in the most literal of ways, the *business* of playing, Stern's work also suggests that their presence in printed editions might have played a similarly specific role in encoding the text as a 'new' play in print – a strategy that drew on the close connection between newly performed plays and a spoken prologue. The publication of a play with prologues and epilogues might have therefore 'implied that the text was young' (new or newly revived).[9]

But publishers also intervened in the presentation of texts in a myriad of other ways. In some cases these interventions in a text's framing were direct and candid, such as in the printer's address to the reader that appears in the preliminary pages of *The Two Merry Milkmaids*: this text is followed by a prologue for the stage, but takes some of the prologue's work on itself in its appeal to the reader to 'Receiue it well'.[10] But other strategies are coming to light, much more understated and encoded, by which those who controlled the printed page could articulate meaning and address the reader. This was a process designed to shape audiences and consumers more than describe them, for publishers were actively involved in creating markets for the plays that they chose to print. Key to a publisher's print strategy was the extent to which audiences and readers overlapped or were fashioned as distinct in the presentation and marketing of a printed edition. Marta Straznicky's analysis of the Red Bull repertory in print suggests, for example, that its publishers were 'largely responsible for the construction of an identifiable repertory', what is now thought to be characteristically Red Bull fare; her work suggests that the printed editions were 'intended to serve as replicas of the stage play' for interested members of the Red Bull audience, rather than as 'displacements of it', or a reconfiguration of the drama for a separate reading market.[11]

While the Red Bull publishers might have catered to a literary market of Clerkenwell playgoers, Zachary Lesser's analysis of Walter Burre's publishing strategy suggests that other publishers were invested in a cultural programme of publication which depended on distancing plays from performance and their original audiences. Burre's selection of plays for publication that emphasise 'the importance of wit as a sign of gentility', and his use of particular presentational strategies in their printing, suggest to Lesser the importance of examining 'a publisher's work with a view toward identifying cultural divisions' across playgoing and reading publics.[12] More recently, Eoin Price has explored the use of the labels 'private' and 'public' to describe playhouses in the seventeenth century – terminology that is used particularly on title-pages, the space of which 'was valuable in many respects', powerful for 'a number of agents [who] would have had an interest in occupying it with words and images', including publishers, printers, booksellers, theatre owners and managers, and dramatists.[13] In the framing of plays, Price argues, these terms became 'an important part of the politicised culture of Renaissance playmaking, playgoing, play printing, and play reading', and he shows how the use and value of the designation 'private' developed as the reputation and number of indoor playhouses grew.[14]

The interventions and influences of publishers could be subtle and unannounced, then, and it is increasingly clear that features of printed texts that might once have seemed incidental – the layout of text on the page, and the inclusion or omission of certain kinds of prefatory material – were part of specific strategies that were developed and mobilised in order to package plays in print, and that evolved over time. As Berger and Massai note more generally, experimentation with 'different features of the dramatic paratext suggest the extent to which these types of texts, their purpose and their place within the physical make-up of a printed playbook were still perceived as fluid'.[15] The degree to which the prologues, addresses to readers, title-pages, and other accoutrements of printed plays were actively involved in shaping constructions of audience and taste, engaged in processes of instigation that remained in flux, rather than documentation, is a fundamental feature of the evidence. The prologues and texts discussed in this chapter, originating from within and around the profession, took on work similar to the title-pages' fostering of ideas of public and private playgoing, committed as they were to promoting particular conceptions of playgoers that were, themselves, emerging and sometimes contested.

For these reasons, this account resists treating the ideas and associations that arise from the evidence as a reflection of the kinds of relationship that actually held between audience types, taste, and particular theatres or dramatic traditions. This is a tendency that theatre history has too willingly admitted in the past. As John Astington notes, the reputations of the Red Bull and Fortune have been defined by the 'legends' that have attached to the two theatres, their repertories, and audiences; he observes that 'disparagement of the large outdoor theatres had become a cultural fashion' by the 1640s.[16] This is a useful summary, since the kind of habitual stereotyping that emerges from reading the prologues of the period together continues to define accounts of the Red Bull in particular, and the myths that attach to it. The configurations of taste that are received from these sources continue to undergird the familiar juxtaposition of the high poetry of the 'refined' indoor playhouses with the hurly-burly, war-filled stages of the amphitheatres. Theatre history inherited a certain prejudice against the (perceived) tastes of the 'citizen' audiences for empty spectacle, gore, and formless plots, in contrast with the wit and artistry attributed to the indoor playhouses, which catered to the preferences of wealthier audiences.[17] This binary rests in part, and is conveniently upheld, by the physical structures of the two types of playhouse: the amphitheatres held larger crowds and so provided cheaper entry; it has been thought that the larger stage enabled more boisterous display; opening to the sky above, the older playhouses might support otherwise objectionable levels of noise: drums, alarums, the crack of gunpowder and dazzle of fireworks.[18] Assumptions about audience taste became retroactively inscribed into the buildings themselves, as the correlation between venue, audience composition, and repertory has become rooted in the way that we think about the early modern theatre, but as Astington notes, this is not grounded in much 'respectable historical detail'.[19] When attention to that detail is given, these narratives often fail to hold up, as other scholars have also noted.[20] But despite work that seeks to recover and rehabilitate the reputations of the north London amphitheatres, their fare, and the alleged tastes of their audiences, the perceived division between amphitheatre and indoor playhouses has proved pervasive in accounts of the amphitheatres, and has only relatively recently undergone revision.[21]

The present account endeavours to remain alert to the extent to which the descriptions of playgoers that emerge from the artifice of the prologues, verses, and anecdotes are as full of satire, humour, and hyperbole as the plays themselves, and do not necessarily offer the kind of assurances and evidence for which they are often mined. These are accounts of playgoers and preferences that are idealised, exaggerated, perhaps wholly if not partly fictionalised; they are active attempts at origination, rather than passive reflections. It is difficult to distinguish unwitting, casual comment from wilful fabrication, but each of the traces of evidence discussed below contributes to a narrative on playgoing and taste that was both circulating in print and uttered in the spaces of the theatres throughout the decades leading up to the 1630s. Taste and audience preferences were, and are, irreducibly individual, personal, and entirely subjective, and demands for particular fashions were also inconstant, changeable, and (by definition) in flux. As this chapter will outline, the constructions of audience taste that remain compete with and contradict each other, repeatedly shift focus and switch tactics, and appear to become increasingly fraught into the 1630s.

The chapter begins with an exploration of the delineation of audience types that the literature forges and gradually develops, and then traces the ways in which stereotypical portrayals of particular patrons and the ways in which they engaged with drama became associated with specific playhouses and sites of performance. The discussion then moves towards an analysis of how ideas of audience taste developed and became linked to generalisations about certain dramatic traditions and repertories. It examines ideas of qualification in audiences, addressing notions of which kinds of audience members were ideally situated to judge plays, and shows how the writers involved in promoting particular ideas about audiences, repertories, and taste had established a trajectory of theatre and dramatic tradition by the 1630s against which to ground their own narratives. Most importantly for this book, the chapter evaluates the particular position of Queen Henrietta's Men within the debate, focusing on an analysis of the cultural context of revivals into the 1630s, and the exchange of verses in 1629 between Thomas Carew and the courtier poets of the Blackfriars on the one hand, and the dramatists of the Cockpit on the other. This exchange, and the response of writers connected to Queen Henrietta's Men, suggests that emergent narratives which sought to establish a link between older dramatic traditions and undiscerning audience members became a concern that the company felt the need to answer and address.

PENNY STINKARDS, SILKEN GULLS, AND THE 'MANY-HEADED BENCH'

The depiction of unsavoury playgoers in early modern London recurs throughout the official documents and formal Acts and Orders relating to early modern theatre. The Lord Mayor's letter to Lord Burghley, written on 3 November 1594, cast aspersions on 'the qualitie of such as frequent the sayed playes' and described the playhouses as meeting places 'for all vagrant persons & maisterles men that hang about the Citie, theeues, horsestealers, whoremoongers, coozeners, connycatching persones, practizers of treason, & such other lyke'.[22] The depiction of playgoers as morally questionable wastrels had already been in circulation for years: in 1574 an Act of the Common Council had complained about 'the inordynate hauntyinge of greate multitudes of people, speciallye youthe, to playes, enterludes, and shewes', citing 'vnthriftye waste of the moneye of the poore and fond persons, sondrye robberies by pyckinge and Cuttinge of purses, vtteringe of popular busye and sedycious matters, and manie other Corruptions of youthe and other enormyties' as some of the problems the theatres brought.[23] Concerns about the spread of plague are an important context here, both in terms of the spread of disease among the city's populace but also with respect to the fear that playing would attract the wrath of God and even outside of plague time would bring further visitations of sickness.[24] Attention to other contexts on the level of the individuals behind regulating orders and the specific circumstances surrounding them is also significant, as Ian Archer has shown in work that rightly questions the assumption that city authorities were united in an enduring opposition to the theatre, and challenges the sense of 'monolithic' hostility towards the companies.[25] Nevertheless, some of the orders that issued from the City carried with them a legal gravitas that threatened not only to tar the reputation of London's playgoers, but actively deprive them of their chosen pastime.

The language of the 1574 Act reflects the particular concerns of the individuals behind its composition, but it is possible that it circulated far more widely in print. Mark Jenner has examined the extent to which the City adopted print as a means of communicating official pronouncements, and observes that the City's expenditure on printing grew markedly between the 1580s and 1630s.[26] These printed orders and bills grew to become an important part of the textual landscape of the city, as Jenner suggests that they might have had a wider distribution than many pamphlets circulated in the period, were read out at meetings, and in some cases were posted in the streets and in markets.[27] The 1612 Order suppressing jigs at the end of plays, made in Middlesex's General Session of the Peace in October 1612, might have been communicated more directly to those within the theatre profession in the course of its introduction and enforcement. This was an Order that passed comment on the 'divers cutt-purses and other lewde and ill disposed persons' who gathered at the Fortune 'in greate multitudes' at the end of every play.[28] But it would be a mistake, as Jenner suggests, to posit too much of a separation between 'rulers and ruled'; he emphasises the 'social depth of early modern governance', and suggests that 'large numbers of adult male householders [...] were called upon to act as constables, scavengers, or other public officials'.[29] As such, the language and terms adopted at official meetings of local governance were not necessarily sequestered from more widespread discourse, and might find expression in everyday contexts.[30]

Official pronouncements might, then, offer much more than a glimpse of the particular phrasing chosen in civic contexts in the attempt to control events at the theatres. Instead, the representation that they offered of citizens in and around the theatres is likely to have percolated into the lives and consciousness of many Londoners. Moreover, printed Acts would have been posted about London in a similar manner to the way that playbills were attached to posts, walls, and doors around the city, advertising the fare of the professional theatres.[31] Tiffany Stern has suggested that royal and legal proclamations were posted in spaces that were more prominent than the places occupied by playbills, so that playbills 'were situated in apposition to the formal, sanctioned, authorised space of the printed legal bill'.[32] In this way, the two kinds of text were in a kind of dialogue with each other, and possibly – if Acts relating to control of the theatres were printed and posted – in tension. At the same time, advertisements for drama and official proclamations concerning the audiences of that drama might have been found in close proximity to each other on the streets, and formed part of the experience of traversing, and reading, the city for an increasingly literate population.[33]

The printed pamphlets that proliferated in London and beyond also offered depictions of playgoers that would have been widely read and circulated.[34] The writers of these works, some of them dramatists too, offer a degree of literary flair and crafted exaggeration, and the images that they conjure of audiences draw on imaginative and often sensational metaphors. Thomas Middleton's *Father Hubbard's Tale*, a prose pamphlet published in 1604, refers to the 'dull Audience of Stinkards sitting in the Penny-Galleries of a Theater, and yawning vpon the Players': an image that might suggest a visual link between open-mouthed spectators nestled in the galleries, and demanding but witless fledglings, scraggly birds waiting to be fed.[35] Thomas Dekker also dwells on the unpleasant olfactory qualities of some of his audiences, and provides a number of grotesquely entertaining references to them prior to 1610. In *The Seven Deadly Sins of London* he speaks of the playhouses which 'smoakt everye after noone with Stinkards, who were so glewed together in crowdes with the Steames of strong breath, that when they came foorth, their faces lookt as if they had been per boylde'.[36] The 'basest stinkard in London, whose breath is stronger then Garlicke, and able to poyson all the 12. penny roomes' makes a pungent entrance in *The Raven's Almanac* (1609), and the malodorous reek of the 'garlike mouthd stinkards' also appears as a trope in *The Gull's Hornbook*.[37] Such evocative portraits offer a certain humour and theatricality to depictions of the early Jacobean theatre audience. The stinkards who poison the '12. penny roomes' suggest that unpleasant smells were not exclusively associated with the parts of the theatre to which the cheapest tickets offered access, though the characterisation of a 'Greasie-apron[ed]' crowd full of roaring fishwives in a prologue published with one of Dekker's Red Bull plays in 1612 identified the amphitheatre audience with grimy street hawkers.[38]

The general identification of audience members who frequented the amphitheatres with those at the lower end of the social scale endured and then set in throughout the period. Such typified spectators included the 'Prentizes, and Apell wyfes' who in 1632 Alexander Gill claimed visited the Fortune playhouse – John Tatham echoed this language in 1640 when he compared the noise made by the Fortune audience to the din of '*Rables, Apple-wives* and Chimney-boyes'.[39] But it was not just the cheaper entry fee of the amphitheatres that encouraged playwrights to characterise a playgoing public in this way; one of Ben Jonson's characters also associates the cheaper seats of the indoor playhouses with 'sinfull sixe-penny Mechanicks' in the Induction to *The Magnetic Lady* at the Blackfriars, performed in 1632. These morally questionable characters were to be found 'in the oblique caves and wedges of your [play]house', obscured in shadow.[40] This reference re-establishes the link between tradesmen and low-priced playhouse entry more generally, and passes moral judgement on those poor of pocket, lurking in the darkened recesses of the theatre.

Alongside characterisations of distasteful or deprived audience members provided by playwrights there also appeared accounts of similarly down-at-heel, desperate, or disreputable playgoers in ballads and epigrams, which circulated in oral and print form. In 1598 Everard Guilpin's satire observed the Curtain's proximity to a 'house of sinne', and alludes to patrons shared by both the amphitheatre and the local stews or brothels.[41] The poet John Taylor referenced beggars enjoying the fare of the playhouses in a tongue-in-cheek pamphlet published in 1621, while in an anonymous ballad of around 1625 a naive young tourist from Cornwall, having spent most of his money, manages to muster the entry fee to the Red Bull's yard and ends up the victim of thieves: 'pressing forth among the folke' he lost his 'purse [...] hat and cloke'.[42]

The imaginative pleasure taken in such characterisations of playgoing also extended to the stereotyped portraits of audience members at the other end of the social spectrum: the elite gallants, those of 'Plush and Velvet-outsides!'[43] These patrons were also subject to ridicule in a way that was inextricably bound to social standing. As Master Damplay negotiates for a play in the 'Poetique Shop' which stocks 'all the variety the Stage will afford for the present' in Jonson's Induction to *The Magnetic*

Lady, he figures the audience members on behalf of whom he shops (implicitly the audience of the Blackfriars, where the play was performed) as 'the better, and braver sort [... who] stick your house round like so many eminences'; but the shop's boy corrects him, joking that the eminence of those sort relates to 'clothes, not understandings'.[44] Everard Guilpin teases the 'braue gallant youth' who 'sits o're the stage' in the Lord's Rooms, 'new printed to this fangled age', dressed in 'a hat scarce pipkin high' and 'dagge cases' for boots.[45] In 1612 an address 'To the Knowing Reader' was printed to introduce Robert Daborne's *A Christian Turned Turk* to its new audience in print, an audience that does not, presumably, include the 'silken gulls' and 'ignorant Cittizens' who throw 'contempt' upon excellent 'Poesy'.[46] The foolish, fond young gallant of Francis Lenton's satire *The Young Gallant's Whirligig* – a patron of the Cockpit, Blackfriars (the 'Torchy Fryers'), and the Globe who is headed for financial ruin – is garbed in spangled silk and satin.[47] Dekker's choice of words is characteristically biting: in his *Seven Deadly Sins* he jokes that 'Sloth himselfe will come, and sit in the two-pennie galleries amongst the Gentlemen' playgoers.[48] These vain, posturing, ostentatious, and idle audience members are portrayed in very different terms from their poorer counterparts, but are similarly sent up and portrayed as undesirable spectators: lazy and fashion-conscious, with more money than sense.

The caricatures of playgoers peddled by writers of the period are, for the most part, exactly that: attempts to reduce the playgoing populace to familiar, conventionalised types, within a knowable and navigable market.[49] Other prologues of the period might indicate why this could be desirable, for the appropriation of easily recognisable stereotypes drew focus away from the daunting task of satisfying the unpredictable and essentially unknowable desires of audiences. The prologue to Henry Glapthorne's *The Lady's Privilege* wonders: 'How shall we then / Please the so various appetites of men. / It starts our Authors confidence' – and this anxiety is echoed in the prologue printed with Middleton's *No Wit, No Help Like a Woman's*: 'How is't possible to suffice / So many Ears, so many Eyes?'[50] The prologue printed with Shirley's *The Duke's Mistress* indicates the capricious tastes of the audience in similar manner – 'This likes a story, that a cunning plot / This wit, that lines, here one, he know's not what'.[51]

While audiences were made up of individuals and might be rationalised into types, they could be united in their capacity for displeasure – and this capacity was deliberately invoked in the performance of the prologue, which was provocative and instigative in nature. In performance, prologues were spoken by an actor dressed in a black cloak, similar to a scholar's gown, with a wreath of laurels around his head signifying poetic accomplishment.[52] While the Prologue as character spoke on behalf of the dramatist, soliciting the audience's approval in order that he might earn his pay from benefit day, Stern suggests that this performance was part of a 'reauthoring process', in which the Prologue 'offers the play in the most positive way possible, standing wreathed in laurels won for the success of other plays (by other playwrights) and remembered fondly by the audience for the last new play "he" introduced'.[53] Prologues were separated, in this sense, from the authorial voice of the dramatist, and furthermore might not have been written by the dramatist of the ensuing play but by another dramatist altogether; they were 'thus the least playwright-related bits of the text'.[54] But the role that they played was crucially bound up in the space of the theatre, and also the workings of a repertory company more broadly. Invested with the authority that his position and costuming gave him, the Prologue worked to encourage a critical response from the audience, reminding them of their responsibility to their own 'various appetites'.

This was an active, generative process, and the act of judging was inscribed into the theatrical event of first performance, since, as Stern has noted, audiences would often pay higher entry prices to see a new play.[55] Prologues were designed to prompt the audience's feedback as much as limit or contain it. Not only was this a necessary part of testing a play's commercial value and its suitability for inclusion in a repertory, but, as Simon Smith argues, passing censure on a play was part of the theatrical pleasure that audiences took in visiting the playhouses, for 'pleasure and judgement [were not ...] alternative modes of response, but simultaneous aspects of playhouse experience'.[56] There was, he argues, not just an acknowledgement but an expectation that audiences could enjoy theatre while 'remaining critically engaged', and that in the early modern playhouse drama 'was expected to delight and to provoke censure in equal measure'.[57] While prologues played an important role at first performances, a culture of playgoing in which critical judgement formed part of the pleasure of the theatrical event was more widespread. The *'many Ears'* and *'Eyes'* gathered together in the playhouse were more of an immediate preoccupation for companies and dramatists at first performances, but they were an intractable feature of the theatrical landscape far beyond that moment, and one that might be celebrated.

For dramatists whose plays had failed, and their conciliatory friends, the anticipation of approval gave way to expressions in which a worryingly homogeneous audience featured, united in opprobrium. Jonson referred to Fletcher's audience in the printed edition of *The Faithful Shepherdess* as the '*many headed* Bench'; in commendatory verses for the same play, Beaumont refers to the '*thousand men* [who] *in judgement sit*'.[58] These two instances were designed to apologise for the play, in retrospect, for its disappointment on the stage. In 1606 one of John Day's characters attributed audience dissatisfaction to a kind of rancorous incomprehension, remarking in the induction to *The Isle of Gulls* that 'Neither quicke mirth, inuective, nor high state, / Can content all: such is the boundlesse hate / Of a confused Audience.'[59] Drayton describes a theatre audience as 'thick-brayn'd', while Middleton and Dekker's 'yawning' spectators seem both bored and insatiable at once.[60] These were generalised caricatures, but the familiar constructions of the penny stinkard and the silken gull endured, resurfacing in contexts that dwelt on one outcome that the culture of judgement might have in the playhouse: the potential for theatre to confer equal authority on all its customers, regardless of the price they had paid to secure entry.[61] Dekker wrote in *The Gull's Hornbook* that:

> your Stinkard has the selfe same libertie to be there in his Tobacco-fumes, which your sweet Courtier hath: and that your Car-man and Tinker claime as strong a voice in their suffrage, and sit to give judgement on the plaies life and death, as well as the prowdest Momus among the tribe of *Critick*.[62]

In his commendatory verse for *The Faithful Shepherdess*, Jonson had also imagined a censuring audience that comprised knights, captains, and richly accoutred ladies, alongside the '*shops* Foreman, *or some such* brave spark, / *That may judge for his* six-pence'.[63] These expressions gesture towards a scenario in which wealth and status might not necessarily confer greater judging privileges when divergent audiences were brought together in one theatre, one shared space.

But Dekker's words should be read in the context of the satirical handbook in which they appear, a self-consciously unreliable text offering the gulls of London knowing and dubious instruction intended to reveal their simple absurdity. This was a text prefaced by the disclaimer that 'if it lead you right, thanke me: if astray, men will beare with your errors, because you are *Guls*'.[64] Among other judgements about the theatre, the *Hornbook* advises the gull to '[spread] your body on the stage [... and be] a Justice in examining of plaies'; to 'laugh alowd in the middest of the most serious and saddest scene of the most terriblest Tragedy'; and, if the dramatist has offended, 'rise with a skreud and discontented face from your stoole to be gone: no matter whether the Scenes be good or no'.[65] And though Jonson recognised that audiences comprised a wide range of types, he went on to engage in an ongoing debate concerning the legitimacy of different approaches to judging drama. As the following discussion explores, the notion that all audiences might be equal was to be rebuffed and resisted

– in the realm of print and the discourses of taste that dominated it, if not in the theatres themselves.

In 1612 John Webster's *The White Devil* was printed by Nicholas Okes for Thomas Archer. This was another play that had failed on account of the audience's censure, and the framing text that prefaces the printed play is imbricated in a strategy that serves both to distance it from, and link it to, that disappointment. While Webster praises the 'action of the play' and Richard Perkins's performance at the Red Bull in the play's epilogue, the note 'To the Reader' works to blame its failure on the stage on a combination of seasonal despondency and the inadequacies of its audience. This note suggests that the Red Bull audience lacked 'a full and vnderstanding Auditory', and compares them to 'ignorant asses'.[66] Webster has confidence that the printed play will be received well, since 'Nec Rhoncos metues, maligniorums': his book will not fear the sneers of the malicious.[67] His grievance over the play's reception manages to achieve something close to a conflation between the material conditions of performance, at '*so dull a time of Winter*' in '*so open and blacke a Theater*' (A2r), and the dim wits of the audience. He claims that had he produced '*the most sententious Tragedy that euer was written*', the '*breath that comes*' from the '*vncapable multitude, is able to poison it*' (A2v).

Webster's address to his reader is concerned with establishing his work as an accomplishment of note: he deploys classical allusion, quotes Latin repeatedly, and congratulates his fellow dramatists, acknowledging the '*labor'd and vnderstanding workes of Maister* Johnson [Jonson]' (A2v). But though hopes for reputational (and commercial) rescue lay in the play's printing and its presentation before a literary reading audience, Webster's praise seems to foreground the idealised 'vnderstanding Auditory' of listening playgoers nonetheless, while his reference to the sneers of the malicious and the breath of the multitude evokes means of physical articulation, and the expressions and functions of the mouth. The emphasis on the oral (and what becomes, in utterance, the aural) might be traced back to Webster's source in Martial's *Epigrams*, in which the 'little book' must please the learned who, if he 'shall receive you to his heart', might 'repeat you with his lips'. The condemned book, on the other hand, might be subject to material and textual mutilation, sent to the market stall, where its 'back' might be 'scribbled upon by [meat-sellers'] boys', those tradesmen most viscerally involved in the preparation and sale of inanimate flesh.[68]

Webster's address foregrounds the vexed and often contradictory relation between the physicality of performance/vocalisation and real-time reception in the playhouse, and the 'literary' acts of publication. The emphasis he pays to corporeal expression and articulation – twisted mouths, lips, and exhalations – attests to the enduring and immediate impact of live performance, even as the printed text attempts to remove the play from that mode of reception and from its amphitheatre origins. But the address also establishes a complaint about the mental capacity and uninformed tastes of the Red Bull audience in particular, a group of patrons implicitly linked here to the *'vncapable multitude'*, who do not possess the requisite skills for the enjoyment of such a play. It is, in particular, Webster's reference to that *'vnderstanding Auditory'* that draws attention to a certain preoccupation in printed prologues and paratextual material of this time with particular ways of approaching, apprehending, and judging theatre. Webster represented his audience as lacking the faculty to listen to and understand his words, and by praising Ben Jonson, the author of *'vnderstanding workes'*, he invoked an ongoing debate over the preferred modes of consuming drama.

Over the course of his career, Jonson drew a number of times on the idea of the desirable audience that judged and perceived through listening.[69] In the context of a court masque it was flattery to contrast the 'quicke eares' of a courtly audience with the 'sluggish ones of *Porters*, and *Mechanicks*, that must be bor'd through, at euery act, with *narrations*',[70] but Jonson's recourse to the value of an attentive, aurally attuned audience is a recurrent theme in the texts that frame his plays. The epilogue to his *Every Man Out of his Humour* claims, for instance, that the play was not designed 'For euery vulgar Pallat, but prepar'd / To banket [banquet] pure and apprehensiue eares', where the reference to palates links bodily consumption and the tastes of the common to undiscerning appetite.[71] Both Jonson and Webster portray some audiences as deficient as a result of the way in which they engaged with the drama, what they brought to it, and what they might have expected from it. They also suggest that engagement with plays through the understanding and auditory was linked to status and intellection – Jonson does so explicitly, in his socially inflected comparison between court wits and slow porters, while Webster's reference to his ignorant audience was directed at the same amphitheatre audience linked in that year to the playgoers imagined in the prologue to Dekker's play at the Red Bull: the yard full of fishwives, patrons dropping pennies from greasy aprons. They roar for plays 'whose *Rudenes*, *Indians* would abhorre'.[72]

Accounts of the Red Bull audience demonstrate this evolving connection between audience types, taste, and means of engagement with the most clarity, and also draw attention to the ways in which particular theatrical venues and their reputations were drawn into the narrative that Webster came to endorse in print in 1612. The theatre began to develop a reputation for staging comic relief in 1578, when it was reported in association with 'Comedies' and 'knauerie', as John Florio published in his English–Italian conversation book of that year.[73] Florio's comment is not particularly evaluative, but the link between comedy and amphitheatre drama more widely was reiterated in 1610 by John Heath, when he wrote of Momus's study of London drama as a means to perfect his own dramatic performance. Hoping to '*act the fooles part*' with '*exquisite*' precision, Momus looks for professional instruction to the actors of the amphitheatres: the Globe, Fortune, and Curtain.[74] By 1613, four years after the King's Men started playing in the Blackfriars playhouse, the connection between the amphitheatres, foolery, and nonsense had been underscored once more. William Turner's *A Dish of Lenten Stuff* refers to 'the fat foole of the Curtin, / and the leane foole of the Bull', and the rambunctious nature of drama at the Red Bull is also emphasised: the Globe and Swan 'Will teach you idle trickes of loue, / but the Bull will play the man'.[75] The tone becomes more critical in George Wither's description of the poetry of the Red Bull and Curtain as 'broken stuffe'; substandard but also with the suggestion of being worn down, exhausted, defunct.[76] Thomas Tomkis's description of Trincalo the Clown who visits the Red Bull and Fortune in order to memorise compliments for his mistress, and 'learne all the words I speake and understand not', does little to dispel the myth of an amphitheatre audience with diminished sense or ingenuity; here, the clown fails to understand what he speaks, as well as what he hears. Articulations of the 'stinckards' attending the Fortune amphitheatre emerged again in 1616, when these playgoers were described as hissing at plays 'without a cause', while applauding 'baudy jeast[s]'.[77]

Webster's characterisation of the (implicitly) sneering but incapable Red Bull audience built on years of representations of an amphitheatre type, then, but as time went on a more pointed differentiation emerged between the audiences of the amphitheatres in juxtaposition with those of the hall-playhouses. This distinction appropriated the crude but ingrained stereotypes of the penny stinkard and the silken gull, but drew on the provocative discourse about the ways in which drama should be enjoyed, experienced, and understood. Increasingly, the lower strata of amphitheatre audiences were figured not only as misunderstanding and ignorant, but as desirous of drama full of shows, dances, armed combat, and fireworks – fare that rewarded not the ears, but the eyes. The prologue to Thomas Heywood's *The Brazen Age* (1613) alludes to the growing association between unlearned audiences and their construed desire for visual delight, for instance, distinguishing between the 'learnd' and the 'vnlettered' Red Bull patrons.[78] Of the latter, the prologue requests that they 'attend' the play rather 'then judge' it, 'for more then sight / We seeke to please'. This prologue gestures towards the riches of experience that playgoers can expect to access if they search for satisfaction beyond the visual and privilege instead the 'understanding eare', and predates Jonson's professed hope in the prologue to *The Staple of News* that 'you were come to heare, not see a Play'. Here, two conflicting modes of consumption stood at odds, for though the company must entertain the audience 'in the way of showes' and satisfy the immediate appetite for the visual, Jonson would 'haue you wise, / Much rather by your eares, then by your eyes', and privilege reflective understanding.[79]

The prologue to *The Two Merry Milkmaids*, a Red Bull play published in 1620, recognised the received connection between amphitheatre audiences and a taste for spectacle even as it worked to complicate such a straightforward identification. It entreats the audience 'To expect no noyse of Guns, Trumpets, nor Drum, / Nor Sword and Targuet; but to heare Sence and Words', and in doing so draws attention to the familiar narrative that amphitheatre audiences came to be entertained by the spectacle of martial conquest and the thrill of battle scenes. The prologue goes on to hope that 'for your owne good, you in the Yard / Will lend your Eares, attentiuely'. The prologue's author is conscious of the play's shortcomings in terms of what might be expected from amphitheatre drama; as the prologue acknowledges, the decision to omit the fireworks which would usually accompany Clowns and Conjurers in a play might prove a gross misjudgement.[80] In its attempt to resist and recast the established stereotype that had come to define its audience, this prologue paradoxically relies on the audience's easy familiarity with that same, resonant trope. It also demonstrates the ways in which the perceived tastes of an identifiable audience could be used to characterise the repertories of the theatres themselves, in a culturally loaded conflation of audience composition and demand, repertory, and venue.

The distinction between audiences pleased by the aural and by the visual – those '*So many Ears*' contrasting with '*so many Eyes*' – was recurrent in the prologues of early modern drama, as critics including Andrew Gurr and Brian Schneider have both explored at length.[81] While Gabriel Egan's work suggests that plays were thought of more often as 'visual rather than aural experiences in the literary and dramatic writing of the period',[82] the tension between these two modes of engagement continued to be exploited and exacerbated in prologues and other paratextual writing, and formed part of the wider context in which theatre was discussed in the period. Jonson's polarisation of the capacities of ideal and wanting audiences has been of particular influence in critical accounts, in part as a result of the ideas that Jonson promoted about his own learning and qualification, and his own readerly engagement with classical literature. Questions about whether hearing or seeing was to be privileged reached back to classical antiquity, and, as Joseph Wallace has shown, Jonson's engagement with debates over reception and judgement drew upon, and adapted, principles drawn from Aristotle's formulations of the capacities of the senses.[83] But Jonson is also something of a special case: his uneasy relationship with visual aspects of the theatre has been widely recognised, and the ways in which he set out his learning in addresses to audiences and readers might have been part of a broader, far more complex, ethical schema.[84] And while Jonson regularly articulated the distinction between seeing and hearing, it is important to recognise that these were ideas that were percolating more generally within the community of playgoing and beyond, as the prologue to *The Two Merry Milkmaids* suggests.[85] The use to which that prologue put those ideas in 1619, applying them specifically to the problem of ensuring a play's good favour at the Red Bull, was a negotiation of the tripartite associations between audiences, venues, and repertory that had grown up around the theatre over its years of operation – an attempt to recalibrate the reputation of the theatre, and to realign the Red Bull audience with the ideals of temperate, intellectual engagement.

James Shirley adopted a similar strategy in 1640, when he introduced a play of language and poetry before an audience at the Globe amphitheatre. Writing that *The Doubtful Heir* was not '*calculate*[d]' for '*this Meridian*', his prologue goes on to profess that the play contains '*No shews, no dance, and what you most delight in, / Grave understanders, here's no target fighting* [...] *No bawdery, nor no Ballets* [...] *No clown, no squibs, no Devill in't*'.[86] He likens the audience to mischievous squirrels, begs them not to '*crack the benches*', and solicits them to behave '*As you were now in the* Black-Fryers *pit, / And* [...] *not deaf us, with leud noise and tongues*'. Shirley's claim that the play was '*meant for your persons, not the place*' implies an explicitly causal link between audience behaviour and venue, in which the physical environs – '*the place*' – are somehow responsible for the bad behaviour of amphitheatre audiences. Such a claim underscores the rowdy reputation of the amphitheatres and suggests that the venues created or nurtured particular tendencies in their audiences; that audience reception was encoded, structurally and culturally, within the 'vast Stage' of the outdoor performance venue.[87]

This kind of cultural encoding is precisely the work that playwrights and writers had been involved in for decades, in their literary and dramatic depictions of audience members, their dramatic preferences, and the venues with which certain groups became associated. But it seems that by 1640 those ideas and associations had crystallised, and enabled conditions under which the venues themselves could be recognised as determinate of audience response, characterised by a set of overriding expectations that defied anything as nuanced as the recognition of various audience tastes among individual playgoers or sectors of the audience. Here, the link that Shirley posits between venue and audience reception is inextricable, and audience composition, as such, had much less to do with it: Shirley's play was, he claimed, *'meant for your persons'*. Shirley was able to articulate this complex abridgement of the relationship between venue, taste, and audience much more clearly than Webster had done in 1612; though Webster gestured in part towards the same idea when he lodged his complaint about the Red Bull, *'so open and blacke'*, the amphitheatre audience as he represented it still lacked the capacity to enjoy the play. As time went by, playwrights such as Shirley found themselves in a position to experiment with the associations available to them, forge new connections and contractions of the relationships between audiences and repertory, disrupt existing narratives, and find new ways to flatter and define their paying audiences. These were audiences that remained as demanding as ever: *'Squirrels that want Nuts'*, 'Pallat[s]' that need pleasing. In such accounts, playwriting remained a balancing act which demanded the dramatist 'calculate' his plays for particular venues, repertories, and appetites with great care; a situation which bore out to the extreme the maxim given in the printer's note to the reader of *The Two Merry Milkmaids*, almost twenty years before, that *'Every Writer must gouerne his Penne according to the Capacitie of the Stage he writes too, both in the Actor and the Auditor'* (A2r).

The subtleties of Shirley's prologue did little to diminish the increasing identification of amphitheatre fare with dull, plebeian audiences, delighted by spectacle and bloodshed, lacking the capacity to appreciate sophisticated poetry. The prologue reveals, however, the ways in which the engagement and preferences that amphitheatre audiences became associated with, in print and performance, became key terms at the centre of an ongoing commercial and aesthetic contest in which the market appeal of particular playhouses – and, ultimately, their historical legacies – were gradually determined. The emphasis on vociferous, spectacle-loving audiences who roared for fare at the amphitheatres served to define and create new markets in playgoing: Shirley's prologue recognises and draws attention to the choices now available between 'this place', the Blackfriars, and the range of other destinations in the landscape of London theatre. Those alternative venues were also surrounded by particular constructions of audience and experience. As early as 1600, 'good', desirable audiences had been linked to the smaller venues of the indoor theatres – one of John

Marston's dramatic characters remarked of St Paul's that he liked the 'good gentle Audience' who gathered there; in contrast with the theatres to which Dekker would later refer, in St Paul's 'A man shall not be choakte / With the stench of Garlicke, nor be pasted / To the barmy Jacket of a Beer-brewer'.[88] Marston had reason to praise the sweeter air of St Paul's and to flatter its audience: the play was performed in that venue. But such agenda-driven instances of publicity provide the basis of circulating ideas and configurations of audience.

The cumulative effect of this narrative, which linked particular audiences and behaviours with specific sites of performance, carried through to the decades following the closure of the theatres. In 1654 Edmund Gayton wrote of an audience associated with a range of amphitheatre plays (though some of those plays would go on to be revived in indoor playhouses). He noted that unless

> the popular humour [for plays was] satisfied [...] the Benches, the tiles, the laths, the stones, Oranges, Apples, Nuts, flew about most liberally, and as there were Mechanicks of all professions, who fell every one to his owne trade, and dissolved a house in an instant, and made a ruine of a stately Fabrick.[89]

This was a theatre packed over the holidays with 'Saylers, Water-men, Shoomakers, Butchers and Apprentices', and Gayton writes that it was 'good policy to amaze those violent spirits, with some tearing Tragædy full of fights and skirmishes'. Comenius wrote in 1659 of the 'common sort' standing in the playhouse yards, who 'clap the hands if any thing please them'; in 1671 Edward Howard wrote that he recalled the 'Red Bull writers, with their Drums, Trumpets, Battels, and Hero's'; and in 1699 James Wright retrospectively recorded that the Fortune and Red Bull 'were mostly frequented by Citizens, and the meaner sort of People'.[90] What had started out as a literary and commercial repertory tactic for playwrights and theatrical professionals in the Jacobean and Caroline eras had ossified into something approaching historical 'fact', while early modern portraits of audience types continue to have a distorting effect on literary criticism today.[91]

AGE AND ANTIQUITY: REVIVALS AND THE THEATRICAL PAST

The trajectory of theatre history to which Comenius, Wright, and Gayton all contributed has played an important role in the critical reception of 1630s drama. Though these writers offered reconstructions of a theatrical past, they drew upon formulations of a chronology of drama that were being actively shaped by the discourse surrounding audience composition and taste in the 1620s and 1630s, before the theatres closed. The desirability of new drama over old had been promoted by Marston around 1599 in *Jack Drum's Entertainment* at St Paul's, when the Prologue promised the audience no 'mouldy fopperies of stale Poetry' or 'drie mustie Fictions' (though in fact it is precisely 'Such mustie fopperies of antiquitie' that the company of St Paul's is criticised for later, in the dialogue of the play [A2v, H3v]). As time went on, and as histories and reputations attached to certain venues, the connection between the outdoor theatres and a particular, definitively older, type of drama advanced. In 1621 Peter Heylyn wrote of the 'musty phrases' of the Red Bull, contrasting the 'diets' and preferences of amphitheatre audiences with the royal tastes of the king.[92] John Melton's descriptions of *Dr Faustus* at the Fortune characterised amphitheatre drama as chaotic and exhilarating, with its 'shagge-hayr'd Deuills [who] runne roaring ouer the Stage with Squibs in their mouthes, while Drummers make Thunder in the Tyring-house, and the twelue-penny Hirelings make artificiall Lightning in their Heauens'.[93] Writing in 1620, it is unclear whether Melton is speaking nostalgically here of a past performance of the play or of a contemporary revival on the Fortune stage, but his description foreshadows Samuel Pepys's Restoration recollection of Thomas Killigrew and his

> way of getting to see plays when he was a boy. He would go to the Red Bull, and when the man cried to the boys, 'Who will go and be a devil, and he shall see the play for nothing?' then would he go in, and be a devil upon the stage, and so get to see plays.[94]

Pepys's anecdote reconstructs and romanticises a dramatic tradition of the past – a time when the entrepreneurial innovators of Restoration theatre were enthusiastic boys taking small roles in the amphitheatres.

The similarly nostalgic view that some Caroline writers took of earlier periods of drama also helped to establish a trajectory of theatre history which placed constructions of the dull, unsophisticated fare of the early years at the amphitheatres at one end, and the new, refined, more fully developed and intellectual poetic fare of the hall-playhouses at the other. In a prologue published in 1643, Davenant spoke of the theatre, full of '*Good easie judging soules, with what delight / They would expect a jigge or Target fight*'. The '*fore-fathers*' of the current audience, he suggests, were '*dull and humble-witted people*', '*homely Ancestors*'.[95] His tone of wistful condescension to earlier audiences both contrasts and chimes with the words of one of Brome's characters, whose tongue-in-cheek description of the late sixteenth-century stage describes the 'dayes of *Tarlton and Kempe, /* Before the stage was purg'd from barbarisme, / And brought to the perfection it now shines with.'[96] The Praeludium to Thomas Goffe's

The Careless Shepherdess, which might also have been written by Brome around the same time, participates in a similar construction of the theatrical past. This text rehearses the contrast between the wit of new poetry and the old spectacle of amphitheatre drama which was familiar to the speakers' 'Forefathers, whose dull intellect / Did nothing understand but fools and fighting'.[97] These descriptions define the writers for the newer indoor theatres in contrast to older amphitheatre fare, enabling Caroline dramatists to develop and refine their own sense of identity, which emerged partly in opposition to the theatrical past.

The creation of distinction between brands of theatre and different dramatic traditions would have been as important to those amphitheatres – the Fortune and Red Bull, for instance – as it was to writers such as Brome and Davenant. Publicity – even the kind that mocked and reviled its audience and drama – still worked to promote the amphitheatres; in its way, it confirmed the niche that they held in the market. Towards 1642, the identification and idea of a characteristic 'Red Bull' drama seems to have become a fixed landmark in the aesthetic landscape, as Jasper Mayne's allusion to the '*Red-Bull* wars' in 1638 suggests; such drama was cited as a direct counterpart to Jonson's dramatic style, which Mayne applauded for remaining free of gods and monsters too, in addition to spectacular violence.[98]

But negative and patronising associations attached to 'old' forms of drama, that same quality of 'mustiness' to which the Red Bull was linked, had important consequences for the status of revivals in the Caroline period. For the staging of revivals was itself a deliberate repertory strategy which worked to complicate and disrupt attempts to establish a definitive chronology of theatre history. By bringing old amphitheatre plays into the fashionable indoor theatres, Queen Henrietta's Men, alongside other companies that adopted the same strategy, repeatedly foregrounded the past in the present. In this way revivals might have become an expression of archaism in the repertory, in the sense of the term that Lucy Munro describes: 'the self-conscious incorporation' of particular 'styles that would have registered as outmoded or old-fashioned to [...] audiences or readers'.[99] As Munro suggests in her illuminating discussion of archaism in English literature, archaism 'violates chronology', 'unsettles relationships between past, present and future', and 'undermine[s] linear temporality'.[100] The temporality of art in this period was a complicated and nuanced negotiation, as Christopher S. Wood and Alexander Nagel have shown, in an argument that Munro develops in relation to the visual arts' more literary counterparts. Early modern playgoers were accustomed to the crossings of tradition and innovation in art and life, and to what Wood and Nagel describe as the plural temporality of art as it points 'away from' the moment of its creation to a prior, founding myth, and at the same time points 'forward to all its future recipients who will activate and reactivate it as a meaningful event'.[101] In this model, revivals on the early modern stage might gesture towards their temporal origin, but they were actively, literally engaged in addressing new audiences. The revival of archaic drama did not involve, then, a straightforward transferral of old styles into the present, which presupposes the neat division between the 'barbarism' of the old theatre and the shining new stage. Revivals contributed to a much more complex unsettling of origin, an experimental and provocative blurring of the bounds of tradition, innovation, and the anchorage of both of those concepts in time.

The narrative insisted on by some writers of the period, which sought to juxtapose new drama with the 'fools and fighting' favoured in decades past by 'dull' ancestors, stood in direct tension with the drama's capacity for plural temporality, and with contemporary theatrical practice that recognised that capacity. Patrons of the Cockpit and Blackfriars were regularly presented with old revivals. This became increasingly conspicuous into the 1630s, by which time drawing attention to the relative age or newness of a play had become a strategy designed to contribute directly to a sense of its value. Henry Herbert frequently noted the distinction between new and old plays, and this was an administrative requirement, as Herbert tended to charge a lower fee for the licensing of revivals.[102] Why this continued to be so is unclear, as in 1633 he clarified the need for stricter licensing practices in the allowing of revivals, since 'in former time the poetts tooke greater liberty than is allowed them by mee'.[103] Herbert's recognition that old plays might demand a different kind of attention and scrutiny in newer times gestures towards the wider commercial appeal of revivals that, though dated, familiar, favoured, or even famous, might be as surprising or innovative as new plays when reintroduced into a repertory. The practice of making old plays new in revival was an active strategy on the part of playing companies, one that was directly enabled through performance choices. Just as old plays could take on new political valences in different contexts, and 'greater libert[ies]' taken 'in former time' might cause offence at a later date, the aesthetic features of the plays might resonate in new ways within particular repertories. Established traditions or tropes could emerge as fresh once more on a different stage, or before a new audience, in the way that Munro recognises with respect to the 'recycling of old linguistic and stylistic conventions', which 'pull[s] the past into the present' but, more than that, explores the 'aesthetic and interpretative possibilities that the combination of old and new forms provides'.[104] In this sense, staging revivals always constituted an attempt – whether conscious or not – to revamp or overhaul the old, and breathe new life into drama that had been retired from earlier repertories.

The more active efforts of Queen Henrietta's Men to present revivals as new repertory pieces are visible in the revisions and reworkings of old plays; Shirley's 'corrections' to *The Night-Walkers* and the alterations that were made to *Hymen's Holiday* adjusted and modified plays that might otherwise have fallen into the category of perishing plays described in Goffe's Praeludium to *The Careless Shepherdess*: 'cold meats, (which are grown / Mouldy and stale)' (B3v) – unappetising leftovers, unfit for consumption. The evocation of appetite here alludes again to theatrical taste as somehow bodily, grossly corporeal, especially when linked to undesirable drama or its patrons: Shirley's description of the audience as starving squirrels and Middleton's yawning playgoers with their mouths agape reinforces the link. In other instances, references to the age of source material actively exploit the multiple temporalities of drama and literature. In Rutter's *The Shepherds' Holiday*, one of the characters about to be presented with a masque questions whether it tells 'the old storie' of Paris and Oenone, but is reassured that the tale, though dated, has been 'newly made, and fashion'd to my purpose'.[105] This classical story has been reinterpreted, in the context of Rutter's play, for a performance given in Arcadia, within a 'pastoral-tragicomedy' written for a 1630s audience. This layering of different chronologies and periods is hinted at again in the note to the reader at the end of Henry Shirley's *The Martyred Soldier*:

> That this play's old, 'tis true; but now if any
> Should for that cause despise it, we have many
> Reasons, both just and pregnant, to maintaine
> Antiquity ...[106]

The play itself is old, but the note works to justify this by gesturing to the inherent value of antiquity, calling to mind as it does so not only the quality of the play's age, but the period of historical antiquity (in the fifth century) in which the drama is set. The verse reverts to address the current theatrical context, comparing the fashion for plays with changing sartorial taste, suggesting (with a hesitant, rising inflection) that 'what's now out of date, who is't can tell, / But it may come in fashion, and sute well?'

Heywood's prologue to the court revival of *The Jew of Malta* also suggests a slightly uncomfortable awareness of the play's age, craving '*pardon*' for '*so boldly*' daring to present the play, '*writ many yeares agone, / And in that Age, thought second unto none*'.[107] This play contrasts with '*other Playes that now in fashion are*', where 'fashion' also gestures (in its now-obsolete usage) towards the act of making or the workmanship of crafting plays for particular audiences. The prologue underscores the relation of the play's stage history to its uncertain reception, but at the same time emphasises specifics of its theatrical past and legacy, applauding Edward Alleyn's original performance of the titular character in the later Elizabethan period. Richard Perkins, star actor of Queen Henrietta's Men, played the role of Barabas in the Caroline revival, and the prologue insists that it was not Perkins's '*ambition / To exceed, or equall*' Alleyn's famed performance; being '*More modest*' than such an aspiration would suggest, his wish was only '*To proue his best*' at '*The part he hath studied*' (A4r). Summoning the spectre of Alleyn to the stage, this prologue and the comparison it invites between two leading stars of different eras participates in an active reinvigoration of a performance tradition, a harking-back that is not, as Munro says of archaism more generally, 'reducible to nostalgia because it not only looks back to the past but also insists upon the present's ability to match past achievements and even [...] to outstrip them'.[108] Though the prologue frames Perkins's performance in the role as modest and bashful ('*at the vrgence of some friends*'), it does hint at the 'collusive and competitive' spirit of archaism that Munro perceives, a rivalry that was intergenerational, as companies recast and reimagined old plays, combining innovation in stage practice and a later era of actors with more traditional elements of repertory content.

The importance of generational difference has been explored in relation to stage performance in particular by Munro, who emphasises not only the gaps between generational tastes and styles but the continuities too; this circumstance means that older works might 'simultaneously repel and attract' the younger generation.[109] It is this dynamic that seems to be at work in Davenant's recollection of the last generation's '*Good easie judging soules*', Brome's reminiscence of the 'dayes of *Tarlton and Kempe*', and the reference to dull 'Forefathers' in the Praeludium to *The Careless Shepherdess*. These writers strive to distance themselves from what has come before, but by summoning such audiences and actors to the imagination they pay homage to the legitimacy and pleasure of a theatre now described as lost to the past.

The inclusion of archaic plays in the repertory came with its own set of challenges and opportunities; revivals encouraged comparison between the old and the new, and helped to provide the context within which the debate over theatrical taste and aesthetics was to take place. Negotiating the currency and appeal of old plays was an aspect of theatrical production that became increasingly visible in the 1620s and 1630s, with which every company had to engage. Alan B. Farmer and Zachary Lesser have shown that this was a matter of interest to printers and publishers in the Caroline period too, who deliberately drew attention to the age of old plays as they were published as old, favourite classics, in contrast with new plays also available in print.[110] By this time, whether a play was 'new' or 'old' was a defining feature in the established profession of the later Jacobean and Caroline period: a play's age and provenance helped to characterise it in the industry and in both theatrical and print markets. As the final section of this chapter shows, the relationship between old and new fare became a particularly pressing issue for Queen Henrietta's Men, given the specific provenance of many of the company's Red Bull revivals. The widening distance between new hall-playhouse and old amphitheatre drama that emerged in printed accounts was to have lasting consequences for Queen Henrietta's Men at the Cockpit theatre, as Beeston's company found itself mired in the task of reconciling an amphitheatre-based repertory in the face of a developing and prevailing discourse that denigrated that repertory, and that sought to devalue the currency of the professional playwrights with which it was associated.

MECHANICK PLAYWRIGHTS, ROARING WHIFFLERS: THE COCKPIT AND ITS REPUTATION

The connection between the Cockpit and the Red Bull was noted by Leonard Digges in his commendatory verse for one of Shakespeare's Folios. Though unpublished until 1640, Andrew Gurr dates the verse to 1623, and John Freehafer to 1632 or just before, for the publication of Shakespeare's second folio in that year.[111] Digges addresses the 'upstart Writers' of 'this Age', urging

> [I]f you needs must write, if poverty
> So pinch, that otherwise you starve and die,
> On Gods name may the Bull or Cockpit have
> Your lame blancke Verse, to keepe you from the grave.[112]

It seems significant that this criticism appeared in a print Folio, a form of publication that claimed a particular cultural prestige linked to authorial and literary ambitions and that worked, in the cases of Shakespeare and Jonson, to create distance from the plays' theatrical origins. This criticism of the Red Bull alone, and the implied bankruptcy of its verse, was echoed in 1638 by R. Bride-oake, who wrote, in a prefatory verse to the publication of Thomas Randolph's poems, of drama conceived in the addled brains of drunk thieves, the 'sneaking Tribe' of those who 'drinke and write by fits', and whose plays are put on by the Red Bull '(more was the pitty)'. Explicitly linking intellectual profit (or lack thereof) with the poor audience of the Red Bull, Bride-oake reflects on the 'emptinesse, both in the Braine and Purse' of such dramatists, and suggests that the Red Bull and its writers were poor in both wealth and talent – a judgement that casts its own aspersions on consumers of that drama, the patrons of the playhouse.[113]

What is unusual about Digges's criticism, however, is that in contrasting Shakespeare's work for the Blackfriars with the quality of writing found at the Red Bull and the Cockpit, he binds together the amphitheatre with Beeston's new enterprise at the indoor theatre in derogatory terms. This strategy disrupts the narrative which places new, hall-playhouse drama in opposition to amphitheatre drama and its perceived deficiencies, and elevates Shakespeare's drama in contrast to both the substandard fare of the Red Bull and the rival indoor theatre that had appropriated some of its repertory. What links the old amphitheatre and Beeston's new enterprise, in Digges's words, are dramatists forced to write out of hunger and need, bent on maximising their profits at the expense of artistic integrity, and the 'lame' drama that both theatres share in common.

Digges was not the only writer to draw unfavourable comparisons between the Red Bull and the Cockpit with the aim of promoting drama at the Blackfriars. Thomas Carew's commendatory verse, published in 1630 in the prefatory material to Davenant's *The Just Italian*, articulates a similar connection. He offered a defence of Davenant's Blackfriars play by comparing it to the aesthetic standard of Queen Henrietta's Men at the Cockpit, and telescopes relations between the quality of the Red Bull and the Cockpit audience and their capacity for discernment through a lamentation about the ignorant 'Rabble'. Carew shuns the audience that will:

> [...] *still slight*
> *All that exceeds Red Bull, and Cockepit flight.*
> *These are the men in crowded heapes that throng*
> *To that adulterate stage, where not a tong*
> *Of th'untun'd Kennell, can a line repeat*
> *Of serious sense: but like lips, meet like meat* [...][114]

The insult to the Cockpit in particular operates through the conflation of the Red Bull and Cockpit repertories and audiences: Beeston's indoor playhouse, which had appropriated the drama of the Red Bull, now draws to its door those same '*crowded heapes*' typically associated with the amphitheatres. But instead of critiquing the repertories on the basis of the so-called antiquated spectacle and 'lame verse' that they contained, Carew relocates difference and undesirability to performance technique and style. The tongues of rival actors at the Red Bull and the Cockpit '*meet like meat*'; they are thick and senseless, while this reference to the physical means of articulation recalls once more the 'sneers' and poisonous breath of Webster's '*vncapable*' multitude. The '*Kennell*' – which can be glossed either as a mob or pack of actors, or the dog-house containing them – renders an '*untun'd*' and discordant noise on the '*adulterate stage*', in clear contrast to the Blackfriars' '*true brood*' of actors, who tend towards '*naturall unstrayn'd Action*'. Carew's argument brings to the fore the importance of acting style in repertory, and – linking it now to repertory content – compares the King's Men's rehearsal of '*The tearser Beaumonts or great Johnsons* [Jonson's] *verse*' to Beeston's fare. The broad emphasis remains with the presentational effect and characteristics of the Red Bull and Cockpit repertory: the scene, its '*noyse*', and attendant rabble.

The imaginative link that both Digges and Carew drew between the Red Bull and the Cockpit might have been only that, since both writers were concerned with applauding or defending the King's Men and its writers. Both of these verses belong to a tradition of prefatory apparatus which sought to create value in the work that was to follow, and congratulate or console the author. The extent to which Carew could subscribe to and appropriate the aesthetic criteria and terms of evaluative judgement of the theatre demonstrates how entrenched the connections between performance venue, audience composition, and repertory style had become by 1630. Yet the very real, material links between the Red Bull and the Cockpit – shared play-texts, shared money, an element of shared aesthetics through costuming, properties, and repertory content – suggest that the comparisons that Carew and Digges drew between the two theatres was based on more substantial grounds. The association between the theatres was a recognition of the provenance of the Cockpit repertory in its most fundamental terms, and an exposure of the origins of Beeston's company that was designed to be unflattering.

For theatre historians, the publication of Carew's verse first constituted evidence of the popularity of Queen Henrietta's Men, but it is now read more commonly as a slur against the troupe, with lasting critical appeal.[115] Carew's comments have provided an important and defining moment in accounts of the company, appearing in print midway through the company's career. They suggest that the amphitheatre origins of the Cockpit repertory remained conspicuous in the theatrical marketplace, a subject of scorn within the profession, into the last five years of the company's life. But as the remainder of this book will argue, Carew's verse should not be seen as the conclusion or culmination of these debates, memorable though it is. Rather, it presents a snapshot of the negotiation over repertory, audience composition, and venue that was developing over the decades preceding – the dynamic and animated backstory to the operation of

Queen Henrietta's Men, which informed the way the dramatists and actors worked, and tells us about the cultural context in which they performed and the kinds of repertory decisions they made.

The immediate response to Carew's verse gives some insight into the situation in which Queen Henrietta's Men found themselves in 1630. Though Carew was a relatively high-profile figure in courtly, literate circles, he was not directly involved with the theatre profession; an Oxbridge graduate and courtier, he became a gentleman of the privy chamber in April 1630, and was promoted shortly afterwards to the role of sewer-in-ordinary of the king.[116] His poetry, although largely unpublished during his lifetime, circulated widely in manuscript among the aristocracy, but he did not have the same kind of connection with the theatre that his fellow poets Davenant and Suckling clearly did. Carew's verse provided a traditional conciliatory function, therefore, but the comments that he offered on the current state of drama launched his critical judgements into the realm of a profession to which, from the perspective of the professional playwrights at least, he did not properly belong. They were to make an important contribution to the direction that the debate over Red Bull and Cockpit drama would take. Philip Massinger was among the first to offer a response to Carew's verse and defend the reputation of the Cockpit and its dramatists. Massinger wrote primarily for the King's Men at this time, but had written several plays for Beeston prior to that, which remained in the Cockpit repertory. He wrote on behalf of Queen Henrietta's Men in a manuscript prologue to *The Maid of Honour*. Peter Beal has argued that the prologue was written by Massinger for a revival of the play on the Cockpit stage shortly after the publication of Carew's verse, but Martin Wiggins believes the play was written newly for Queen Henrietta's Men.[117] Massinger asserted the resilience of the company ('wee') against Carew's 'single Calumny, / publish[d] to our Disgrace', and justified his response by stating that 'by beeing silent', Queen Henrietta's Men might be seen to 'confesse' to 'such a Guiltinesse / as wee are taxt with'.[118]

The circulation of Massinger's prologue seems to have prompted a direct response from an anonymous author in support of Carew and the courtier playwrights. The author draws heavily on social distinction in order to denigrate the professional dramatists, comparing Massinger to a 'Mechanicke play=wright', a 'rude Carpenter or Mason' who lays 'his axe or trowell in the ballance' against 'Euclidès learned pen'.[119] Such a construction recalls the 'rude mechanicals' of Shakespeare's *A Midsummer Night's Dream* – a play that remained in performance in the repertory of the King's Men, and that was performed before the court in October 1630.[120] Summoning the farcical troupe of craftsmen to mind, Carew's

champion casts Massinger into the low, dull role of a perfunctory tradesman, and might hint at a comparison between the Cockpit actors and the
bumbling, ridiculous amateur actors of Shakespeare's play. The anonymous
writer compares Carew's 'naturall straines' with Massinger's 'flat / dull
dialogues fraught wth insipit chatt', and he contrasts again the overtly
'Mercenary' work of the commercial theatres with the 'loose raptures'
produced by the privileged courtier. The socially inflected bias that the
writer deploys is clear – he claims that professional playwrights excuse
their shortcomings as a result of their small income: the 'salary of a hirelinge'. The author laments the 'roaringe whifflers' that 'keepe the stage',
claiming that the professionals are cheapened in their 'poore [...] trade'.
The point is tritely underscored in the penultimate few lines: 'Y^e difference
/ twixt yo^u [Carew] & him [Massinger] will well bee vnderstood / whil'st
yo^u for pleasure sing, he sweats for food'.

The commendatory verses published in James Shirley's *The Faithful
Servant* (published as *The Grateful Servant*) also contributed to the debate,
and they appear to have been a concerted effort to affirm the Cockpit
repertory's legitimacy, and control its reputation in light of Carew's criticism. Most of the verses comment directly on Carew's slight, and they
direct their energies towards a hyperbolised defence of Shirley and the
poetry that he wrote for the Cockpit stage. Thomas Randolph claims that
on the Cockpit stage he 'heare[s] the muses birds with full delight / Sing
where the birds of mars were wont to fight'.[121] Yet at the same time, the
statement recognises and embraces the connection between the two theatres, and acknowledges the Cockpit's inheritance of Red Bull repertory
pieces: those warring 'birds of mars' made up part of the cultural and
theatrical history of the theatre. Perhaps most conspicuously, the cumulative effect of these verses, taken together, works to place Shirley at the
centre of the debate over the legitimacy of the Cockpit repertory. Aesthetic
responsibility was directed towards Shirley, and he became somehow representative of Queen Henrietta's Men in this exchange – central to the
debate over distinctions in repertory, and to the health of the professional
theatre at this time. The publication of *The Faithful Servant* fixed into
print the tensions between Carew and the professional playwrights, while
the response of the Cockpit dramatists and Queen Henrietta's Men reads
as a deliberate strategy to undo the harm that Carew's claims might have
caused, while rather conspicuously calling attention to them. It has also
signalled for critics the seriousness of the debate, which has become known
as the beginning of 'a second war of the theatres': a dialogue over the
aesthetics of drama.[122]

More was at stake than the reputations of individual venues, however.
The emergence of courtier playwrights, including Davenant, had important

consequences for the Cockpit company in particular, and the professional industry more generally. As has been discussed in Chapter 2, Beeston eventually attempted to capitalise on the fare provided by courtier dramatists with the commissioning of at least one of Thomas Killigrew's plays in the mid-1630s. But the intervention of the courtiers in the theatrical market prompted a radical shift in the operations of theatre from the supply side. Their emergence represented a scenario in which former audience members actively participated in dramatic composition, and shaped plays according to priorities that differed from those of the established writers of commercial repertories. It invited the creation of repertory under new terms, according to new prerogatives. And it starkly refigured and reanimated differentiating factors of social status and taste which had been developing from the 1600s – the cultural stereotypes that had evolved from the opposition between the penny stinkard and the silken gull.

The distinction that Carew's anonymous champion made between the courtiers, free from financial strife and able to devote themselves to the pursuit of 'great art', and the penny-pinching professionals echoes Digges's critique of the Red Bull and Cockpit dramatists. According to Massinger, observers such as Carew and his defender were not strictly qualified to pass judgement on the current state of drama: 'Why is hee / The Poets Tribu[n]e, and authority / Conferr'd on him to free or to condemne / all what is writt or spoke by other men?'[123] For Massinger, at least, such condemnation and critical ire was an encroachment on the ground of professional theatre, whether it was voiced in person or articulated in print: a violation against 'mee & mine'. But rumours of the redundancy of the professional playwrights were aired again in the Praeludium to Thomas Goffe's *The Careless Shepherdess*.[124] Here, it is hinted that the professionals' 'trade / Must needs go down' in the face of competition from 'The Court, and Inns of Court', which 'Of late bring forth more wit, then all the Tavernes'. Thrift, the fictional playgoer of the piece, announces: 'I do not think but I shall shortly see / One Poet sue to keep the door, another / To be prompter, a third to snuff the candles', in an echo of the reference to Massinger's 'hirelinge' worth.[125]

Devaluation and demotion threatened, in provocative depictions that emphasised the lowly status of professional writing and the comparative inferiority of commercial drama. Old, audience-based distinctions were being revived in new, challenging contexts that now directly implicated the social rank of the playwrights, as well as their audiences. And in the broader terms of repertory strategy, a new critical binary was invoked between the old, quaint, and tired familiarity of the Red Bull fare and its reuse on the Cockpit stage, and the new direction of the fashionable courtier playwrights primarily associated with the Blackfriars.

CONCLUSION

As this chapter has explored, the inheritance of the Red Bull plays – so crucial to the initial momentum of Beeston's Cockpit companies – became increasingly conspicuous, carrying a stigma that was cumulative in nature, and in some ways retrospective. The pressures brought to bear by the courtier playwrights exacerbated extant tensions between tradition and innovation in drama. Carew's verses and the response they elicited offer a glimpse into the changing conditions of production in Caroline London: a situation that was in flux, but that must inform readings of the company and the context in which the repertory is interpreted. As this discussion of the relationships between stereotyped audience members, theatrical venues, and repertories has shown, the repertory that Queen Henrietta's Men inherited both demanded and defied control by its dramatists, as a site of growing controversy within a marketplace expanding in breadth in the 1630s, and deepening in intensity. It became the professional duty and the artistic challenge of the dramatists connected with Queen Henrietta's Men to pre-empt and minimise charges of aesthetic illegitimacy that derived from audience-based distinctions, as the company continued to bring drama that was being associated with amphitheatre audiences to the patrons of its hall-playhouse. The ways in which the dramatists writing for Beeston became engaged in both an imaginative process of reinvention in the adaptation of old plays and traditions, and a negotiation of the aesthetic terms which helped define them, is the subject of the remainder of this book.

NOTES

1 This was a market that was also visibly expanding into the 1630s, with the opening of the Salisbury Court theatre in 1629.
2 See, for instance, the work of Penelope Woods, who argues that the reconstructed Globe 'can be used as a tool, a hypothetical mapping exercise, to think about the ways in which performance space produces certain kinds of audiences and audience responses'. Penelope Woods, 'Shakespeare's Globe Audiences: Old and New', in *The Cambridge Guide to the Worlds of Shakespeare, Vol. 2: 'The World's Shakespeare, 1660 to the Present'*, ed. Bruce R. Smith and Katherine Rowe (Cambridge: Cambridge University Press, 2016), pp. 1538–44. More broadly, Lori Humphrey Newcomb's introduction in the same volume, and Richard Preiss's essay, both provide valuable considerations of the issues at stake when considering early modern audiences and approaches to reconstructing them.
3 Douglas Bruster and Robert Weimann, *Prologues to Shakespeare's Theatre: Performance and Liminality in Early Modern Drama* (Abingdon: Routledge, 2004), p. 2.
4 Tiffany Stern, 'A Small Beer-Health to his Second Day: Playwrights, Prologues, and First Performances in the Early Modern Theater', *Studies in Philology*, 101

(2004), 172–99 (pp. 179–80); Tiffany Stern, *Documents of Performance in Early Modern England* (Cambridge: Cambridge University Press, 2009), pp. 97–103, 111.

5 Stern, 'A Small Beer-Health', pp. 172, 175.

6 Helen Smith and Louise Wilson (eds), *Renaissance Paratexts* (Cambridge: Cambridge University Press, 2011), pp. 4, 5.

7 Brian Schneider, *The Framing Text in Early Modern English Drama: 'Whining' Prologues and 'Armed' Epilogues* (Abingdon: Routledge, 2011), pp. 155–6.

8 Thomas L. Berger and Sonia Massai (eds), *Paratexts in English Printed Drama to 1642* (Cambridge: Cambridge University Press, 2014), pp. xii, xi.

9 Stern, *Documents of Performance*, p. 102.

10 J. C., *The Two Merry Milkmaids* (London, 1620), A2r.

11 Marta Straznicky, 'The Red Bull Repertory in Print, 1604–60', *Early Theatre*, 9.2 (2006), 144–56 (pp. 146, 151).

12 Zachary Lesser, 'Walter Burre's *The Knight of the Burning Pestle*', *English Literary Renaissance*, 29 (1999), 22–43 (pp. 32, 40).

13 Eoin Price, *'Public' and 'Private' Playhouses in Renaissance England: The Politics of Publication* (Basingstoke: Palgrave Macmillan, 2015), p. 33.

14 Price, *'Public' and 'Private' Playhouses*, p. 73.

15 Berger and Massai (eds), *Paratexts*, p. xiii.

16 John Astington, 'Playing the Man: Acting at the Red Bull and the Fortune', *Early Theatre*, 9.2 (2006), 130–43 (pp. 141, 130).

17 Bentley's work exhibits many examples of such an inheritance, describing the post-1625 theatre as a 'dual institution: one theatre for the court, the gentry, and the literate, another theatre for the vulgar masses', and differentiating between the plays written for each on the basis of their perceived commitment to poetry, on the one hand, and spectacle on the other. G. E. Bentley, *Shakespeare and His Theatre* (Lincoln, NE: University of Nebraska Press, 1964), pp. 106, 111. See also Andrew Gurr, *Playgoing in Shakespeare's London*, 3rd edn (Cambridge: Cambridge University Press, 2004), p. 196, for a continuance of the sense that plays were 'more and more designed for citizens' in the northern amphitheatres predating 1625, following the opening of the Blackfriars in 1609.

18 Andrew Gurr, 'Singing through the Chatter: Ford and Contemporary Theatrical Fashion', in *John Ford: Critical Re-visions*, ed. Michael Neill (Cambridge: Cambridge University Press, 1988), pp. 81–96 (p. 84); Andrew Gurr, *The Shakespearean Stage, 1574–1642*, 3rd edn (Cambridge: Cambridge University Press, 1992), p. 15.

19 Astington, 'Playing the Man', p. 131.

20 Roslyn L. Knutson, 'The Adult Companies and the Dynamics of Commerce', in *Thomas Middleton in Context*, ed. Suzanne Gossett (Cambridge: Cambridge University Press, 2011), pp. 168–76.

21 Astington, 'Playing the Man', and all of the essays in the same special issue of *Early Theatre*; and see p. 142; and p. 173 n.3, n.4 of this book. for Andrew Gurr's partial reworking of his own argument in the fourth edition of *The Shakespearean Stage*. Siobhan Keenan also notes Gurr's evolving narrative in *Acting Companies and their Plays in Shakespeare's London* (London: Bloomsbury, 2014), p. 132, and draws attention to the overlap of hall and amphitheatre repertories in the 1630s (p. 142). Eva Griffith notes that critics have 'loved' to see the Red Bull, its audience, repertory, and company 'within a certain mindset', and that the theatre was 'always an exciting and excitable place', but that the plays contained 'intellectual challenge' alongside spectacle. Eva Griffith, *A Jacobean Company and its Playhouse: The*

Queen's Servants at the Red Bull Theatre (c. 1605–1619) (Cambridge: Cambridge University Press, 2013), pp. 16, 19.

22 Letter from the Lord Mayor to Lord Burghley, 3 November 1594, transcribed by E. K. Chambers, *The Elizabethan Stage*, 4 vols (Oxford: Oxford University Press, 1923), IV, p. 317.

23 Other problems included 'soundrye slaughters and mayheminges of the Quenes Subiectes […] by ruines of Skaffoldes, fframes, and Stagies, and by engynes, weapons, and powder used in plaies'. Act of Common Council of London, 6 December 1574. Transcribed by Chambers, *Elizabethan Stage*, IV, pp. 273–4.

24 See Ian Archer, 'The City of London and the Theatre', in *The Oxford Handbook of Early Modern Theatre*, ed. Richard Dutton (Oxford: Oxford University Press, 2011), pp. 396–412 (pp. 404–5).

25 Archer, 'The City of London and the Theatre', p. 411.

26 Mark Jenner, 'London', in *The Oxford History of Popular Print Culture, Volume 1: Cheap Print in Britain and Ireland to 1660*, ed. Joad Raymond (Oxford: Oxford University Press, 2011), pp. 294–307 (p. 301).

27 Jenner, 'London', pp. 304, 301.

28 Chambers, *Elizabethan Stage*, IV, pp. 340–1.

29 Jenner, 'London', p. 305.

30 In the same way that, as Jenner observes, 'A printed precept circulated to such officers was not, therefore, being published to an especially socially exclusive coterie' ('London', p. 305).

31 Stern, *Documents of Performance*, pp. 36–62.

32 Stern, *Documents of Performance*, p. 54.

33 On literacy rates in London, and the calculation and 'counting' of literacy, see Heidi Brayman Hackel, 'Popular Literacy and Society', in *The Oxford History of Popular Print Culture, Volume 1: Cheap Print in Britain and Ireland to 1660*, ed. Joad Raymond (Oxford: Oxford University Press, 2011), pp. 88–100, esp. pp. 92–7.

34 See Jason Peacey, 'Pamphlets', in *The Oxford History of Popular Print Culture, Volume 1: Cheap Print in Britain and Ireland to 1660*, ed. Joad Raymond (Oxford: Oxford University Press, 2011), pp. 453–70.

35 Thomas Middleton, *Father Hubbard's Tale* (London, 1604), B4r.

36 Thomas Dekker, *The Seven Deadly Sins of London* (London, 1606), p. 27.

37 Thomas Dekker, *The Raven's Almanac* (London, 1609), C1v; Thomas Dekker, *The Gull's Hornbook* (London, 1609), p. 2.

38 Thomas Dekker, *If This Be Not a Good Play, the Devil Is In It* (London, 1612), A4r.

39 Alexander Gill, in *Ben Jonson, The Critical Heritage*, ed. D. H. Craig (Abingdon: Routledge, 2010), p. 165; John Tatham, 'A Prologue spoken upon removing of the late Fortune Players to the Bull', in *The Fancies Theater* (London, 1640), ²H2v–²H3.

40 Ben Jonson, *The Magnetic Lady*, in *The Works of Ben Jonson* (London, 1640–41), Induction.

41 Everard Guilpin, *Skialetheia* (London, 1598), B8v.

42 John Taylor, *The Praise, Antiquity, and Commodity of Beggery, Beggers and Begging* (London, 1621); Anon., reproduced in G. E. Bentley, *The Jacobean and Caroline Stage*, 7 vols (Oxford: Oxford University Press, 1941–68), VI, p. 240.

43 Jonson, *The Magnetic Lady*, Induction.

44 Jonson, *The Magnetic Lady*, Induction.

45 Guilpin, *Skialetheia*, B4r–v.
46 Robert Daborne, *A Christian Turned Turk* (London, 1612), A3r.
47 Francis Lenton, *The Young Gallant's Whirligig* (London, 1629), C3r–4v.
48 Dekker, *The Seven Deadly Sins of London*, E2r.
49 For more on this suggestion, see Kate McLuskie, 'Figuring the Consumer for Early Modern Drama', in *Rematerialising Shakespeare: Authority and Representation on the Early Modern Stage*, ed. Bryan Reynolds and William N. West (Basingstoke: Palgrave Macmillan, 2005), pp. 186–206, who writes that 'theatre writers [...] had to manage their audience discursively. They did so by constructing categories out of social types and intellectual dispositions [...] the consumer came to be constructed by the product even though the rhetoric of liberty suggested the opposite' (p. 195).
50 Henry Glapthorne, *The Lady's Privilege* (London, 1640), A3v; Thomas Middleton, *No Wit, No Help Like a Woman's* (London, 1657), A2r.
51 James Shirley, *The Duke's Mistress* (London, 1638), A2r.
52 Stern, 'A Small-Beer Health', p. 182.
53 Stern, 'A Small-Beer Health', pp. 183, 182.
54 Stern, 'A Small-Beer Health', p. 183.
55 Stern, 'A Small-Beer Health', pp. 187–8.
56 Simon Smith, 'Acting Amiss: Towards a History of Actorly Craft and Playhouse Judgement', *Shakespeare Quarterly*, 70 (2017), 188–99 (p. 190).
57 Smith, 'Acting Amiss', p. 190.
58 Ben Jonson, in Francis Beaumont and John Fletcher, *Fifty Comedies and Tragedies* (London, 1679), p. 233.
59 John Day, *The Isle of Gulls* (London, 1606), A3v.
60 Michael Drayton, 'The Sacrifice to Apollo', in *Poems* (London, 1606), p. 290; Middleton, *Father Hubbard's Tale*, C1v; Dekker, *News from Hell* (London, 1606), B1v.
61 See also Kate McLuskie's analysis of Goffe's Praeludium, which 'complicates assumptions about any simple connection between social standing, wealth and artistic judgement' ('Figuring the Consumer', p. 189).
62 Dekker, *The Gull's Hornbook*, E2v.
63 Ben Jonson, in Beaumont and Fletcher, *Fifty Comedies and Tragedies*, p. 233.
64 Dekker, *The Gull's Hornbook*, A3r.
65 Dekker, *The Gull's Hornbook*, E3r, E3v, E4r.
66 John Webster, *The White Devil* (London, 1612), A2r.
67 Latin translation from John Webster, *The Duchess of Malfi and Other Plays*, ed. René Weis (Oxford: Oxford University Press, 1996), p. 365.
68 Martial, *Epigrams*, Bohn's Classical Library (London: George Bell & Sons, 1987), Book IV, 86. The emphasis of the epigram may vary in English translations, however; James Doelman notes of early modern selected translations that the endeavour was particularly difficult given the epigram's dependence on wordplay and the challenges posed by fitting material to English meter and rhyme. James Doelman, *The Epigram in England, 1590–1640* (Manchester: Manchester University Press, 2017), p. 17.
69 Gurr, *Playgoing*, pp. 95–124.
70 Ben Jonson, *The Masque of Queens* (London, 1609), B2v.
71 Ben Jonson, *Every Man Out of His Humour* (London, 1600), R2v.
72 Dekker, *If This Be Not a Good Play*, A4r–v.
73 John Florio, *Florio, His First Fruits* (London, 1578), fol. 1.
74 John Heath, *Two Centuries of Epigrams* (London, 1610), E3r–v.

75 William Turner, *A Dish of Lenten Stuff*, reproduced in *A Pepysian Garland*, ed. Hyder E. Rollins (Cambridge, MA: Harvard University Press, 1992), p. 35.
76 George Wither, *Abuses Stript and Whipt* (London, 1613), D3v.
77 William Fennor, *Fennors Descriptions, or a True Relation of Certaine and Diuers Speeches* (London, 1616), B2v.
78 Thomas Heywood, *The Brazen Age* (London, 1613), L3v. *The Brazen Age* is particularly spectacular in nature, which might also explain the epilogue's preoccupation with seeing and hearing here.
79 Ben Jonson, *The Staple of News* (London, 1631), p. 5.
80 J. C., *The Two Merry Milkmaids*, A2v.
81 Schneider, *The Framing Text*, pp. 71–91; Gurr, *Playgoing*, pp. 102–16.
82 Gabriel Egan, 'Hearing or Seeing a Play? Evidence of Early Modern Theatrical Terminology', https://www.dora.dmu.ac.uk/bitstream/handle/2086/7053/GEgan_Hearing_or_Saying_2001.pdf?sequence=1 (accessed 4 September 2023).
83 Joseph Wallace, 'Wandering Eyes: Jonson's *Catiline* and the Problem of Sight', *Renaissance Drama*, 41 (2013), 85–106, esp. pp. 90–2.
84 Jonson, *The Masque of Queens*, B2v. See, for instance, Michael O'Connell, *The Idolatrous Eye: Iconoclasm and Theater in Early Modern England* (New York: Oxford University Press, 2000), pp. 125, 143, who suggests that Jonson's attitudes towards visual spectacle were furthermore bound up in wider cultural debates concerning spectacle and the image following the Reformation. See Sean Keilen, 'Jonson', in *The Oxford History of Classical Reception in English Literature, Volume 2: 1558–1660*, ed. Patrick Cheney and Philip Hardie (Oxford: Oxford University Press, 2015), pp. 621–40, for Jonson's engagement with classical literature.
85 Similarly, classical ideas and literature also had a wider resonance than is sometimes assumed. Aristotle's *Poetics* and the ideas attached to it were circulating more widely in the sixteenth and seventeenth centuries than has been thought, and these ideas are likely to have been familiar to a wider circle of readers, too – those who were not classically trained or educated, in the same way that Simon Smith has drawn attention to the ways in which classical principles concerning the judgement of acting can be identified as part of a 'wider cultural movement', a 'culture of judgement not limited to former students of Cicero'. For the availability of the *Poetics* in sixteenth-century England, see Micah Lazarus, 'Aristotelian Criticism in Sixteenth-Century England', in *Oxford Handbooks Online* (Oxford: Oxford University Press, 2016), DOI: 10.1093/oxfordhb/9780199935338.013.148; Smith, 'Acting Amiss', pp. 196–7.
86 James Shirley, *The Doubtful Heir* (London, 1653), A3r.
87 See also Schneider, who writes that Shirley suggests that 'the balance between the auditory and visual requirements of the spectators may be a factor of the theatre in which the play is performed' (*The Framing Text*, p. 88).
88 John Marston, *Jack Drum's Entertainment* (London, 1601), H3v.
89 Edmund Gayton, *Pleasant Notes Upon Don Quixot* (London, 1654), p. 271.
90 Comenius, *Orbis Sensualium Pictus* (London, 1659), p. 265; Edward Howard, *The Six Days' Adventure* (London, 1671), A4v; James Wright, *Historia Histrionica* (London, 1699), p. 5.
91 Simon Smith's description of Jonson's approach to audience characterisation as 'polemical' reaches to the heart of the matter, for, as Smith argues, it encouraged a lasting critical tradition that distinguishes between 'judicious criticism and unthinking pleasure as distinct modes of engagement' ('Acting Amiss', p. 190).

See also Jenny Sager's work on the drama of Robert Greene, which responds to the critical tendency to distinguish between the unthinking marvel of low culture and the visionary wonder of Shakespeare, and which argues that 'sensory delight and intellectual contemplation are not mutually exclusive, they are inextricably linked'. Jenny Sager, *The Aesthetics of Spectacle in Early Modern Drama and Modern Cinema: Robert Greene's Theatre of Attractions* (Basingstoke: Palgrave Macmillan, 2013), p. 29.

92 Peter Heylyn, in Bentley, *Jacobean and Caroline Stage*, VI, p. 135.

93 John Melton, *Astrologaster* (London, 1620), p. 31.

94 *Diary and Correspondence of Samuel Pepys, the Diary deciphered by J. Smith, with a Life and Notes by Richard Lord Braybrooke*, 6 vols, 4th edn (London, 1875–79), I, p. 344, entry of 30 October 1662.

95 William Davenant, *The Unfortunate Lovers* (London, 1643), A3r–v.

96 Richard Brome, *The Antipodes* (London, 1640), D3v.

97 Praeludium to Thomas Goffe, *The Careless Shepherdess* (London, 1656), B3r.

98 Jasper Mayne, in *Jonsonus Virbius* (London, 1638), E4r.

99 Lucy Munro, *Archaic Style in English Literature, 1590–1674* (Cambridge: Cambridge University Press, 2013), p. 3. Munro is here describing the incorporation of styles into two of Spenser's texts, but the same principle holds when a repertory is treated as an artistic work or whole, and if we recognise that the acts of repertory-building and of performance involve a comparable level of agency and artistic influence to authorship.

100 Munro, *Archaic Style*, pp. 18, 5, 17.

101 Christopher S. Wood and Alexander Nagel, *Anachronic Renaissance* (New York: Zone Books, 2010), p. 9.

102 Sometimes no fee was required; see N. W. Bawcutt (ed.), *The Control and Censorship of Caroline Drama: The Records of Sir Henry Herbert, Master of the Revels 1623–73* (Oxford: Clarendon Press, 1996), pp. 45–6.

103 Bawcutt (ed.), *Control and Censorship*, pp. 182–3.

104 Munro, *Archaic Style*, p. 18.

105 Joseph Rutter, *The Shepherds' Holiday* (London, 1635), D7v.

106 Henry Shirley, *The Martyred Soldier* (London, 1638), K2v.

107 Thomas Heywood, in Christopher Marlowe, *The Rich Jew of Malta* (London, 1633), A4r.

108 Munro, *Archaic Style*, p. 21.

109 Munro, *Archaic Style*, pp. 138–9.

110 They observe that 'while there had always been old plays, in the Caroline period what had earlier been a mere fact of chronology had now become an important division among *two kinds* of playbook – both in the functioning of the market and in the minds of stationers and, so they imagined, of their customers'. Alan B. Farmer and Zachary Lesser, 'Canons and Classics: Publishing Drama in Caroline England', in *Localizing Caroline Drama: Politics and Economics of the Early Modern English Stage, 1625–1642*, ed. Adam Zucker and Alan B. Farmer (Basingstoke: Palgrave Macmillan, 2006), pp. 17–42 (p. 30).

111 Gurr, *Playgoing*, pp. 280–1; John Freehafer, 'Leonard Digges, Ben Jonson, and the Beginning of Shakespeare Idolatry', *Shakespeare Quarterly*, 21 (1970), 63–75. Digges died in 1635.

112 Commendatory verses in William Shakespeare, *Poems* (London, 1640).

113 R. Bride-oake, 'Upon Mr. Randolph's Poem, collected and published after his death', in *Poems, with the Muses Looking Glass and Amyntas* (London, 1638), **r.

114 Thomas Carew, in William Davenant, *The Just Italian* (London, 1630), A3v–A4r.

115 Bentley read the purpose of the verse as, primarily, a comment on the full houses of the Cockpit and Red Bull, though he did note that referencing the two theatres together 'may well be just an attempt to belittle the Cockpit by associating it with the notoriously vulgar Red Bull' (*Jacobean and Caroline Stage*, I, p. 225). Andrew Gurr developed this interpretation, suggesting that 'Carew lumped the Cockpit and Red Bull tastes together, in a complaint clearly designed to be offensive to the Cockpit' (*Playgoing*, p. 208). Eoin Price also suggests that the plays, players, and playwrights shared in common between the Cockpit and Red Bull 'gave ammunition to its critics [and so ...] the Cockpit was regularly denigrated as an unsophisticated theatre with a plebeian clientele'. Eoin Price, 'The Cockpit', in *The Map of Early Modern London*, ed. Janelle Jenstad (Victoria, BC: University of Victoria), http://mapoflondon.uvic.ca/COCK5.htm (accessed 4 September 2023).

116 Scott Nixon, 'Thomas Carew', *Oxford Dictionary of National Biography*, www.oxforddnb.com/view/10.1093/ref:odnb/9780198614128.001.0001/odnb-9780198614128-e-4639 (accessed 19 February 2018).

117 Peter Beal, 'Massinger at Bay: Unpublished Verses in a War of the Theatres', *The Yearbook of English Studies*, 10 (1980), 190–203 (p. 191). Martin Wiggins, in association with Catherine Richardson, *British Drama, 1533–1642: A Catalogue* (Oxford: Oxford University Press, 2011–), #2291.

118 Beal, 'Massinger at Bay', p. 192.

119 The full transcript is to be found in Beal, 'Massinger at Bay', p. 194. All subsequent quotations are from Beal's transcript.

120 Wiggins, *British Drama*, #1012

121 Thomas Randolph, in James Shirley, *The Grateful Servant* (London, 1630), A3r.

122 Peter Beal named the 'literary quarrel' a 'War of the Theatres' in the title of his article and wrote of the 'opening shots [...] fired' by Carew ('Massinger at Bay', p. 190). For Matthew Steggle, this exchange constitutes the early stages of the second war, defined as 'a series of verbal skirmishes between those who believed that drama was a species of literary activity [the courtiers], and those who thought that it required no such apology [the professionals]'. Matthew Steggle, *Wars of the Theatres: The Poetics of Personation in the Age of Jonson* (Victoria, BC: University of Victoria Department of English, 1998), p. 124.

123 Massinger writes in response to those verses written in defence of Carew following the circulation of the prologue to *The Maid of Honour*. Beal, 'Massinger at Bay', p. 197.

124 See Kate McLuskie's analysis of the Praeludium, in which she traces the 'tensions between received artistic values and the realities of commercial theatre production' prevalent in this text ('Figuring the Consumer', p. 199).

125 'Praeludium' to *The Careless Shepherdess*, B3v.

PART II

The Repertory in Play

4
STAGING THE COCKPIT REPERTORY

Queen Henrietta's Men would not have remained in business with Beeston at the Cockpit for a decade had they not offered their patrons a vibrant and varied programme of plays in performance. The company's live engagements with its audiences were crucial to business: in the most basic sense, they brought money into the playhouse, but they also provided a means by which Queen Henrietta's Men could address and engage with constructions of the Cockpit repertory in performance, and manage the ways in which that repertory was experienced, described, and identified. In the imaginations and writings of some contemporary dramatists and poets, the repertory was linked to the Red Bull, the stereotypes of its undesirable and undiscerning patrons, and a narrative that positioned amphitheatre fare and the plays of the Blackfriars at opposite ends of a spectrum. But the performances that the company offered continued to draw patrons to the playhouse and recommend the company to Herbert and the court, and the Cockpit repertory went on to provide a stable foundation for Beeston's boy company after Queen Henrietta's Men were disbanded. How were revivals at the Cockpit sold and performed within the wider repertory and before the company's audience, and what kinds of theatrical experiences kept that audience '*throng[ing]*' in '*heapes*' to the playhouse, at least in Thomas Carew's imaginative perception?[1]

This chapter considers the practical and aesthetic challenges that the inherited Cockpit repertory posed for the company, and addresses some of the problems, demands, and opportunities that the staging requirements of plays written for the larger, open stages of the Red Bull and the Fortune might have presented to the actors and dramatists of Queen Henrietta's Men. For some time theatre historians considered amphitheatre plays unsuitable for performance in the indoor playhouses, as a result of their staging requirements and the refined sensibilities of the audience that is associated with the Cockpit. The Red Bull's reputation for 'Guns, Trumpets, [and] Drum', 'Squibs and Crackers' all suggested loud and boisterous theatrical effects that would not easily transfer to the closed and smaller spaces of the indoor theatres – at least not without revision.[2] Andrew Gurr once suggested, for instance, that the indoor playhouses favoured 'witplay' over 'swordplay', and that it was more common to 'present spectacles of costume rather than fireworks', which would have been both noxious and more dangerous indoors.[3] This is a view that is undergoing qualification as new research on the transfer of Globe plays to the Blackfriars continues; as Gurr has written more recently, the King's Men were accustomed to adapting to different venues, and while large battle scenes might have been scaled down, the play-texts of transferred revivals 'show little sign of much being done to the texts to facilitate the transfer'.[4] As this chapter explores, evidence relating to the ways in which revivals appear to have been integrated into the Cockpit repertory suggests that many of the traditions identified in the Cockpit's amphitheatre inheritance (including stage combat and the presentation of devils and gods, for instance) were retained and elaborated upon in performances on the Drury Lane stage.

The presentation of bloody spectacle offers an illustrative example, for this kind of fare has been associated with the tastes of amphitheatre audiences in the past – not only because of the amphitheatres' connection with the dramatic violence offered by staging depictions of war and target fighting, but also as a result of a conflation of the monetary wealth of an audience with a sense of cultural wealth and refined sensibility. This owes to a combination of factors, including the connection of violence with the visual, as opposed, in the narratives of early modern paratextual material, to the idea of the learned auditory. It is also a gendered distinction that might have been implied through that same seventeenth-century material – prologues such as that printed with Fletcher and Beaumont's *Rule a Wife, and Have a Wife*, which suggests that women spectators might hold their '*Fannes close*', possibly to shield their eyes, since a '*cruell Sceane did never Lady please*'; and the prologue printed with Shirley's *The Imposture*, which promised that ladies need not wrinkle their alabaster 'brow[s], no fright / Shall strike chast eares [...] No Innocence shall bleed in any scene.'[5] References to cruel scenes and bleeding innocence might have operated as conceits rather than referring straightforwardly to depictions of cruelty and violence, though as Gurr suggests, the latter prologue might indicate that the presence of respectable women in the hall-playhouses was seen by their authors as 'a firmly restraining influence'.[6] The printed prologue to Nabbes's *Hannibal and Scipio*, which reassures that 'Ladies [need not] fear the horrid sight: / And the more horrid noise of target fight' suggested to Gurr in his earlier work that 'gentry and their ladies [...] wanted neither battles nor noise, let alone blood'.[7] Richard Levin's research on women in the Shakespearean playhouses also suggested that the 'interests and feelings' of women came to be reflected in early modern repertories, and he traced, in particular, the repeated reference to women weeping in the audience, as a result of what he saw as a perceived female preference for 'pathetic plots and situations'.[8]

The use of bloody props offered plays across a range of dramatic genres texture and tonal variety, however, and violence and its effects might also, or in addition, have elicited such sympathetic emotional responses as those described in Levin's analysis.[9] Queen Henrietta's Men inherited a relatively large number of plays which feature varying degrees of violence and gore, from Ithamore's verbal description of the way that the slain Barnadine's 'brains drop out on's nose' in *The Jew of Malta*, to the enactment of the execution in Chettle's *Hoffman*, in which a 'crowne made flaming hot with fire' is placed on the titular character's temples.[10] The inherited repertory featured a number of other elaborate murders, including a complicated assassination in *The White Devil* and, in the same play, a prolonged poisoning.[11] In Heywood's *The Rape of Lucrece*, a revival which continued to be performed into the 1630s by the company, Queen Tullia treads on the dead body of her father and 'crimson[s]' her shoe 'with his vitall blood'.[12] Though the scene in which she rides over his body in her chariot is not staged, only described, the language itself is brutally graphic, as Brutus describes how Tullia's charioteer drove 'on, / And with his shod wheeles crush[ed] her Fathers bones', broke 'his craz'd scull' and 'dash[ed] his sparckled braines / Vpon the pavements' (B3r).

The performance of these revivals on the Cockpit stage attests to the continued currency of violence as a form of theatrical entertainment in the indoor playhouses, and instances of mutilation were also staged in newer plays, written specifically for this space and its audience. Dismembered body parts, limbs, and organs were displayed onstage, from the dismembered finger of *The Changeling*, a play inherited from Lady Elizabeth's Men at the Cockpit, to Annabella's dagger-skewered heart in *'Tis Pity She's a Whore*. The company had an opportunity to showcase its stock of body part properties in *The Bloody Banquet*, which features dismembered limbs and the 'flesh' and 'skull all bloody' which are served as part of a cannibalistic banquet.[13] A severed head appears to be brought onstage in Heywood's new play of 1630, *The Fair Maid of the West*, Part II, and one of the characters in Kirke's *The Seven Champions of Christendom* '*beates out his owne braines*'.[14] Thus Queen Henrietta's Men do not seem to have been disinclined, in their revivals or in their new plays, to stage scenes of violence that might have been confrontational or challenging. This kind of spectacle must be recognised as part of the vocabulary of entertainment, adding variety to the plays.[15] These moments drew on a rich theatrical tradition to exploit the characteristics of fare that the company had inherited, and to entertain the paying audience that it continued to attract.

The inheritance of a corpus of plays meant that, for Queen Henrietta's Men, some of the distinctive elements and characteristic features of the Cockpit repertory were determined before the company took to the stage. There are a few amphitheatre plays in the repertory that Queen Henrietta's Men were directly responsible for reviving at the Cockpit – *Hymen's Holiday*, for instance, which might have been originally performed at the Curtain.[16] But as it was the company's predecessors, and especially Queen Anne's Men under Beeston, who had overseen the original transfer of plays to the Cockpit, for the most part Queen Henrietta's Men inherited amphitheatre plays that already had a past history of performance in the indoor theatre. This history might have influenced both the company's approach to the repertory and the ways in which the audience responded to it. The companies that had occupied the theatre before left traces of their time there in the plays they left behind, and so Queen Anne's Men, Prince Charles's Men, and Lady Elizabeth's Men remained present in the theatre through their theatrical legacy. The performance of plays in revival is likely to have been layered and enriched by audience recollections of past performances, here and at other theatres, and the stage history of this drama. It is also likely to have influenced the way that some of the actors approached the plays – especially actors such as Perkins, who had performed some of the plays before at the Red Bull, and Sherlock and Turner, who had performed some at the Cockpit with Lady Elizabeth's Men. In William West's words, 'each performance unfolds already scored by previous performances'.[17]

The building itself might also have contributed to the ways in which Queen Henrietta's Men's performances were experienced by returning audience members. Sarah Dustagheer and Tiffany Stern have argued, independently, that its rival theatre, the Blackfriars, was 'haunted' in kind by its various pasts as the performance venue of the Children of the Queen's Revels and, before that, as a monastery and a court house.[18] These prior incarnations might have shadowed the performances of the King's Men through the collective, cultural memory of its audiences, and through material traces of the theatre's past lives that were inscribed in the architecture itself. The Cockpit had its own previous life as a cock-baiting ring, a site of violent entertainment; and Christian Billing has not only noted the theatre's association with the cockpit ring, but also the ways in which it might have been structurally reminiscent of the anatomy theatre.[19] In subtle ways, then, the venue's prior association with violent and old-fashioned blood sports might have inflected the aesthetic that Beeston and his company developed in the indoor playhouse in performance, which combined innovation with an appreciation of older Red Bull fare and an established theatrical past, even as it was being labelled 'rustic', 'antic', and 'musty' by its detractors. Equally, the building's former use might have influenced the audience's reception of that same theatrical fare, as first-hand memory or second-hand knowledge among audience members imbued violently staged moments with a certain resonance, underscoring experiences of spectatorship that might be shared in common between former audiences of the cock-fighting ring and those of the 1630s theatrical venue.

At the same time, the specific conditions of indoor playing provided circumstances that might have enhanced the performance of old plays upon a new stage, and on which dramatists and actors of Queen Henrietta's Men could draw in the enactment of new fare. Dustagheer has explored the particular kind of illumination offered by candlelight in the Blackfriars, and the effect that lighting had upon the spangled costumes and glistening jewellery of both audiences and actors, and the colours and designs used to decorate the auditorium: this all contributed to a 'dazzling visual aesthetic' within the indoor playhouse.[20] The 'distinct visual environment' offered by indoor playing, and the play of light that Dustagheer describes, might have lent its own rewards in the staging of particular scenes in the Cockpit repertory that feature the discovery space, for instance.[21] The detailed stage directions for some of these discoveries suggest that their ornate arrangement and preparation backstage might yield elaborate theatrical effects when revealed to the audience. In Shirley's *The Maid's Revenge* Signor Sharkino enters '*in his study furnished with glasses, viols, pictures of wax characters, wands, conjuring habit*', powders, and paintings.[22] The discovery in *The Jew of Malta* might have been similarly rich in presentational detail, when Barabas is revealed '*in his Counting-house, with heapes of gold before him*', or in *The City Gallant* (or *Greenes tu Quoques*) in the discovery of a shop.[23] These last two plays were performed originally at amphitheatres, but the display of shining piles of nuggets or coins, the curious miscellany of a shop front or counter, would have been well suited to display in the indoor playhouse, lit and accentuated by candles and lanterns. This chapter will endeavour to remain alert to the particular ways in which indoor performance might have altered, enriched, or diminished theatrical effects in some of the Cockpit plays, as it works towards an account of particular features of the repertory in performance.

The interpretation of stage directions is critical to this discussion, and the difficulties inherent in using this category of evidence must be foregrounded at the outset. While the discovery of Sharkino in his bedecked study conjures for the reader a scene intricate in detail, it does not follow that the language of the stage direction represents an accurate description of what audiences were presented with, or what they might have seen, perceived, or experienced. What can be legitimately inferred from a stage direction is highly contested, and whether stage directions can be considered reliable indicators of what happened onstage is a vexed matter. Plays were licensed for performance by Herbert in manuscript, and not as the printed texts from which we largely work and quote today.[24] Paul Werstine has explored the multiple possibilities of manuscript sources for printer's copy, while Mariko Ichikawa notes that authorial manuscripts might reflect 'the form of staging which the author expected or imagined as he wrote it, and not necessarily the form that actually took place on stage'.[25] Furthermore, plays could be subject to cuts when acted on stage, and were by their nature fragmentary and unstable in manuscript form as well as in performance.[26] In other instances, stage directions appear not to originate from either the dramatist or the theatre, but from the printing process and publication.[27]

It is also unclear, in the context of a print market in plays and the interests of the readerly consumer, whether stage directions are indeed directive, rather than descriptive, representative, or discursive prompts for that reader. Stage directions can reveal very little about the moment in performance; there are many ways to *Enter*, and taken alone stage directions might fail to acknowledge the language of costume and what it signified, in terms of locale and context, on the stage.[28] They might also be absent, and in some cases action or the presence of a property can be reasonably inferred from dialogue. When Roughman enters with a disembodied head in *The Fair Maid of the West*, Part II, there is no reference to the prop in any stage direction. But his words suggest that the prop is onstage and visible: 'I singled him [the Bandetties' Captain], / Fought with him hand to hand, and from his bloody shoulders / Lopt this head' (K1r). The analysis of stage directions cannot represent or reconstruct the rich experience of a play in performance, in which any particular moment might offer an opportunity for actors to embellish the action or offer their own particular reading of a moment, a reading that might differ from performance to performance.

Related to this concern is the problem of whether and how Queen Henrietta's Men, and their predecessors in the Cockpit, might have adjusted methods of staging when performing the plays that they inherited. Beeston paid Herbert for alterations to *Hymen's Holiday* when it was revived by Queen Henrietta's Men at the Cockpit, and it is unclear whether those revisions involved modifications to the play that would have facilitated its staging at the indoor theatre. But printings of other revivals from the period do not bear evidence of this kind of alteration. Some of the earlier plays were reprinted in the 1630s but, as Gurr observes with respect to early plays that transferred from the Globe to the Blackfriars, stage directions in the printed texts were not changed or revised to reflect changes that might have been made in performance. This does not mean that changes were not made, only that the printed texts fail to record them. The multiple publications of Heywood's *The Rape of Lucrece* might suggest that no substantial changes to stage directions were required in the transfer, for later printings of the play make incremental additions of songs which seem related to performance, while stage directions themselves remain unchanged.[29] In other instances, printed stage directions seem to have anticipated the practical difficulties of their enactment, with attention to the conditions of the playhouse in which the play might be performed.[30]

But even if printed stage directions were observed in performance throughout a play's life on various stages, and even if methods of staging and performance remained relatively consistent across amphitheatres and hall-playhouses, this is not to say that the transferred drama would remain 'the same play' in performance. Though the same text might have underpinned the performance of *The Rape of Lucrece* at both the Red Bull and the Cockpit, witnessing those performances would have amounted to very different experiences, as Martin White has explored in relation to the staging of *The Duchess of Malfi* at the Globe and the Blackfriars.[31] The different contexts in which a play was seen, the very different material sites in which it was performed, might have altered the substance of the play and its defining characteristics in ways that are difficult to imagine and articulate, and which are ultimately lost to us. In a similar manner, audiences might have responded very differently to what is ostensibly the 'same' effect from one day to the next.

But though the problems inherent to studying stage directions are myriad, in more cases than not the printed plays remain the only witness to what audiences might have been presented with when they visited the playhouses. For Sarah Dustagheer and Gillian Woods, the nature of stage directions and the status they claim as evidence offers a generative opportunity: 'complications of provenance and purpose are provocative starting points for investigation', and the stage directions themselves 'take us to the heart of *how* meaning is made in plays precisely because they foreground the dynamic between text and performance'.[32] As Alan Dessen and Leslie Thomson have noted, it seems significant that 'a host of playwrights in many theatres over many decades appear to be using the same language' in the formulation of stage directions.[33] The discussion that follows will concern itself as closely as possible with the specific language used in extant stage directions, while bearing in mind that the printed text might not necessarily represent a record of performance, and remaining attuned to the frailty of the evidence. Furthermore, the wider context of theatrical tradition, genre, and the ways in which plays were culturally inflected or historically situated forms part of the analysis and provides a broader frame of theatrical and cultural reference across which the repertory operated.

The account that follows is by no means exhaustive, but it aims to provide a sense of the repertory in all of its richness and, more concertedly, to establish the inventive ways in which the Cockpit dramatists were engaged in playful experimentation with features of the repertory that the company inherited. In particular, it reveals the ways in which the dramatists committed to a serious exploration of the theatrical possibilities that the integration of old and new dramatic styles could afford upon an indoor stage. This discussion is directly concerned with the dynamic between revivals and newly written plays in the 1630s, and is given over to unpicking the ways in which new plays written for the company might have been designed to sit alongside, complement, and in some instances distinguish themselves from the older fare that Queen Henrietta's Men offered. The repertory is broad and eclectic in nature, incorporating plays of many genres, composed by tens of dramatists, ranging across decades. For this reason the chapter is structured through a series of case studies that are focused around some of the repertory's staging requirements and features. Many of the dramatic features under consideration – dance, target fighting, 'squibs', and the staging of devils – belong in contemporary accounts to the traditions that came to be associated with the amphitheatres throughout the 1630s, as the prologue to Shirley's *The Doubtful Heir* underscored. They provide axes along which to read the repertory in performance, enabling a broad engagement with the repertory that remains meaningful and yields conclusions concerning the way in which this particular stock of plays was mobilised in performance.

The first section of the chapter focuses on the staging of combat and dance on the Cockpit stage, and the intertwining of tradition and experimentation that these theatrical opportunities afforded for the company, showcasing old styles against new. It establishes a reading of the dynamic interplay between revivals and newly written drama on the Cockpit stage, which underpins the remainder of the chapter. The second section explores the effects of different genres and theatrical modes on the repertory, and the impact of fashions in dramatic taste on performance on the Cockpit stage. As the discussion in Chapter 2 suggested, Beeston took the repertory in the direction of courtly fashions during the early 1630s in the commissioning of a set of plays that drew on interests associated with Queen Henrietta Maria. The analysis here explores the wider interplay of fashionable styles and ideas with dated drama, and the intermingling of effects and features belonging to particular genres within one repertory. The company's experimentation with the presentation of the supernatural offers several examples of the ways in which the interconnecting influences of theatrical genre and cultural context offered texture and tonal variety to the repertory, in the staging of classical gods, devils, and magic. The final section explores the means by which Queen Henrietta's Men experimented with light and shadow in the Cockpit, capitalising on the material conditions of performance in the playhouse.

While these case studies work to establish an understanding of the specific requirements that the repertory made of the actors of Queen Henrietta's Men, the prop store, and of the playhouse itself, they also demonstrate the work of the company in strengthening the dramatic characteristics of its repertory, and developing a style and aesthetic on the Cockpit stage. Rather than suppress or occlude characteristic features of amphitheatre drama, the discussion draws out some of the ways in which the Cockpit dramatists of the 1620s and 1630s worked with and exploited the staged spectacle of plays dating back to the early 1600s. It also draws attention to the centrality of theatrical experience, to a sense of the plays as performed, and the stimulation of the senses aroused by theatre for the audience's 'so many Ears, so many Eyes'. As Evelyn Tribble notes, Jonson's emphasis on words and poetry has encouraged the critical neglect of stage action and skilled display – dancing, duelling, and spectacular effect are too often 'relegated to ephemeral concessions to popular taste'. This chapter's focus on the potential impact, effects, and opportunities afforded by staged action recognises and gestures towards Tribble's deeper claim that 'reorienting our attention to skill display and to theatre as a form of entertainment, with as many affinities to sport as to literature, helps us to capture a fuller picture of the early modern stage'.[34]

'THE DANCE EXPRESSING A FIGHT': ARCHAISM AND ADAPTATION

Staging armed combat on the smaller indoor playhouse stages might have posed its challenges, particularly as the possibility of onstage spectators would have introduced problems in terms of ensuring the safety of paying customers.[35] But it appears that many plays revived by Queen Henrietta's Men contain the spectacle of sword fights, and it is likely that audiences at the Cockpit continued to enjoy plays punctuated by physical conflict into the 1630s. There are directions to '*fight*' in Beaumont's *The Knight of the Burning Pestle*, Marlowe's *The Jew of Malta*, and the first part of Heywood's *If You Know Not Me, You Know Nobody*. This relatively vague stage direction might be interpreted in a variety of ways, but sometimes the stage directions in printed plays provide more detail, narrating the particular outcome or theatrical effect that the fight should produce. *Cupid's Revenge* specifies a '*Fight here: the Prince gets his sword and gives it him.*[36] Variations on fights also appear in Dekker's *The Wonder of a Kingdom*, a play very tenuously connected with the Cockpit which features a *'thrust or two'*, and the *'bustle'* in *The Fair Maid of the West, Part I.*[37]

Fighting at barriers is featured in two revivals of Webster's plays on the Cockpit stage. This tradition of formal combat derived from the early to mid-sixteenth century, and was a form of martial exercise or tournament in which combatants fought each other on a ground across a barrier or palisade.[38] *The White Devil* calls for *'Charges and shouts: they fight at barriers; first single paires, then three to three'*, and *The Devil's Law-Case* specifies *'The Lists set up'* preceding a combat that might have *'continued to a good length'*.[39] Fighting at barriers might have held a particular resonance around 1611 and 1612, the time around which Webster wrote *The White Devil*, for two years prior to that Prince Henry's Barriers were staged: a martial combat which incorporated a masque by Ben Jonson. Inigo Jones had designed lavish sets and costumes for the barriers, while the masque itself was themed around Arthurian legend, featuring the Lady of the Lake and the magician Merlin, the awakening of Chivalry, and the glorification of ancient ideals of knighthood. This spectacular courtly event had a specific political function which positioned Prince Henry as a national champion and revived notions of militaristic valour; the masque went unpublished until 1616, but appears to have been a notable, and then memorable, event.[40] These moments in Webster's plays seem designed to evoke some of the gravitas and spectacle of Prince Henry's Barriers – particularly *The Devil's Law-Case*, which might have been written slightly later, after the masque's publication. Before the combat, Contarino enters *'in Friers habits, as having bin at the Bathanites, a Ceremony used afore these Combates'* (K3r). The reference to the 'Bathanites' remains obscure, but the direction emphasises the ritual nature of the combat, as do the *'Tuckets'* sounded by trumpets before the duel commences (L3r). These examples of ceremonial tournament called upon chivalric codes of honour and summoned an archaic ideal of knighthood to the stage, in a way that echoes the tournament held between Palamon and Arcite in Fletcher and Shakespeare's *Two Noble Kinsmen*, a retelling of Chaucer's 'The Knight's Tale' which was performed at the Blackfriars within the same few years, *c.* 1613–14. By the 1630s, at the time that Webster's plays were revived by Queen Henrietta's Men, the performance of chivalric valour appears to look back, again, to older narratives and traditions of chivalry that were already anachronistic at the time of the plays' original performance, reviving past theatrical convention and invoking an aesthetic on the Cockpit stage which celebrated and reappropriated mythic history and the layering of the cultural past.

The most demanding of the revivals to transfer to the Cockpit with respect to staging combat might have been Heywood's *The Rape of Lucrece*, which offers an especially war-torn final act on the page at least. Stage directions call for several representations of battle, and draw attention to the theatrical effects and outcomes that such violence was intended to have. An example includes the direction: '*Alarum, Enter in the fight Tarquin and Tullia flying, pursude by Brutus, and the Romans march with Drum and Colors.*'[41] The stage directions also describe the signs of physical exertion that the actors might exhibit throughout the battle: '*Alarum, a fierce fight with sword and target, then after pause and breathe*'; '*fight with single swords, and being deadly wounded and panting for breath, making a streak at each together with their gantlets they fall*' (L2r). Targetiers and pikemen are called for as the battle continues both onstage and off at various points in the action.

The play also calls for 'alarums' and drums, and these sound effects, or sennets and trumpets, are also used in revivals such as *Hoffman*, *The Rape of Lucrece*, and both parts of *If You Know Not Me, You Know Nobody*, as well as a new play printed in 1634, John Ford's *Perkin Warbeck*. It was once thought that the use of these instruments would have been deafening in the enclosed indoor theatres, but experiments in the Sam Wanamaker Playhouse have shown that 'loud percussion and wind instruments' are 'perfectly at home in the Playhouse [...] putting paid to the assumption that "drum and trumpet" musical styles were impossible in indoor theatres'.[42] Moving the action of these scenes from the amphitheatres to the Cockpit might also have been easily accomplished, though Marta Straznicky's work on the Red Bull repertory in print suggests that publications of some of the plays seem designed to recall or reconstruct the repertory in performance for readers, as stage directions seem 'unusually detailed and reader-oriented'.[43] It is possible that unaltered stage directions are a reflection of that publication strategy, the impulse to commemorate, recall, or embellish a spectacular performance on one stage that may have had little resemblance to the action enjoyed by the Cockpit audience watching the play in revival.

However, dramatists writing for Queen Henrietta's Men in the 1630s also recognised the theatrical interest and spectacle provided by the revivals in the Cockpit repertory, and contributed to the repertory with new plays concerned with battle and conflict. Davenport's *King John and Matilda* is one example, a tragedy that draws on archaic source material and contexts of civil unrest. The play is based on popular legend, and retells Anthony Munday's second Robin Hood play, *The Death of the Earl of Huntingdon*, written *c.* 1601. Two instances of combat take place, the first in the middle of a continuing battle. Though stage directions do not suggest a physical representation of battle in the way that Heywood appears to have envisaged, the drama is suffused with the threat of militarised violence. This is a tale of faction and revolt, captives of war and besieged castles, 'angry Lords' lifting 'Unnatu[r]all swords', confrontations on the battlements, and reports of an army twenty thousand strong 'thundering towards *Winsor*'.[44] The *'Charges'*, or calls to arms, which sound from backstage signal an ongoing battle that threatens to erupt on to the stage at any moment. In both its choice of subject matter and its staging, Davenport's new play for the Cockpit resonated with the archaic displays of war that Queen Henrietta's Men appear to have inherited in plays such as *The Rape of Lucrece*. This was a historical drama that summoned to the stage not only the popular legends at the centre of the play's narrative – the shades of Robin Hood and Maid Marian – but the memory of earlier traditions of theatre in the reimagining of Munday's Elizabethan play, and the resurrection of the same characters who had entertained audiences decades earlier at the Fortune playhouse. In this way, *King John and Matilda* appears to acknowledge the debt that 1630s drama owed to the earlier plays of the amphitheatres, and might be seen as something akin, perhaps, to a revival of popular theatrical material for a Caroline audience.

If Davenport's play kept the main battle offstage, other plays written for the Cockpit made more pointed use of old-fashioned, chivalric combat. Kirke's *The Seven Champions of Christendom* follows the adventures of St George and his band of *'arm'd and plum'd'* knights as they set out on a quest against all irreligious 'miscreants', 'blacke Inchantments', and 'witchcraft'.[45] Along the way members of their band travel through Trebizond, whose inhabitants live under the scourge of a great dragon; embark on a quest to bring back the severed head of a necromancer; and are almost consumed by a man-eating giant. Kirke's drama showcases a variety of mythic and supernatural characters; it also features several *'charges'*, *'Drums and Colours'*, and *'fights'*, and a climactic confrontation with Brandron the giant, in which the champions enter *'arm'd; weapons brought for* George', and take their turn to display their chivalric prowess: *'Each fight their severall Combates*: George *overcomes them all*: Brandron *stampes'* (L1r). James Shirley's romantic tragicomedy *The Arcadia*, written between 1630 and 1636, also drew on an archaic aesthetic. Shirley based his play on Philip Sidney's prose romance, notable for its own archaic appropriation as Sidney folded medieval lore and the traditions of Greek romance into his work. Shirley's play thus references a plurality of literary pasts when it stages a fight – *'some skirmish'* – and the entry of the King of Arcadia, wielding *'a two handed sword'* or broadsword.[46] As Evelyn Tribble has argued, rapiers and two-handed swords each claimed specific cultural meaning which drew into play constructions of nationhood and masculine identity. While rapiers were fashionable and expensive weapons from the Continent, two-handed swords claimed their own military lineage, and Tribble draws attention to the role played by an audience skilled in interpreting the representation of particular weapons and styles of combat on the stage with respect to the 'strongly held debates about the relationship of arms and identity' that played out in these scenes.[47] The King of Arcadia's entry is thus akin to the moment in *Romeo and Juliet* when old Capulet summons his longsword, a scene that Tribble sees as orchestrated to foreground the tension between different generations of both weapons and the bodies that wield them.[48]

The choice of specific weapons, styles of combat, and militaristic display in *The Seven Champions of Christendom* and *The Arcadia* seems likely to have created moments in performance that were culturally loaded and rich with meaning, twining associations of militaristic and theatrical tradition. Both plays were explicitly invested in the revival of older, archaic forms, and through the display of combat they inscribed this commitment within the drama far beyond plot level, bringing to the Cockpit stage a celebration not only of old styles and stories, but bodily performance. The inclusion of the plays in the Cockpit repertory has proved puzzling for some theatre historians, however. Bentley wrote that *The Seven Champions* is 'the sort of spectacular, naïve, and formless piece that one learns to associate with the Red Bull theatre'.[49] But the title-page of Kirke's play claimed performance by both the Red Bull and the Cockpit, and suggests that the play was meant for audiences at both the indoor playhouses and the amphitheatres, perhaps even at the same time.[50] For Alfred Harbage, *The Arcadia* was a problem play: he questioned Shirley's authorship, partly on the basis of the 'quaint facetiousness' and 'antique fun' that it exhibits. Though Harbage offered the internal evidence provided by the play as supplementary proof which cast doubt on Shirley's authorship, his view that the verse 'lacks James Shirley's melody and poetic imagery, [and] the characters are crudely drawn' bolstered his conclusion that the work was 'unworthy' of the 'ingenious' Shirley.[51] But the way that these two plays have been perceived in the past, as inferior and incongruous within either the Cockpit repertory or Shirley's dramatic output, does not recognise the extent to which they complement the revivals of the Cockpit repertory, and celebrate its dramatic history. These plays are not outliers, but can be seen as belonging in the repertory in a way that embraces their performance potential rather than denigrating or disowning it.

New plays also appropriated swordplay in the establishment of fresh fashions onstage – in Killigrew's *The Prisoners*, for instance, which contributed to a 1630s trend for tragicomic romance, and bears striking resemblances in parts to Shirley's *Arcadia*: both plays feature cross-dressing protagonists, the fulfilment of an oracle, and the miraculous reunion of long-lost family members in the concluding scenes. Killigrew's play features six swordfights, and in one stage direction Gallipus '*throwes his Sword at the King*'; later, a stage direction suggests that Pausanes throws his sword across the stage to another actor.[52] The choices that Thomas Nabbes made in the staging of *Hannibal and Scipio* suggest a very different approach, though. The prologue printed with this play was that which assured women in the audience that they need not fear 'horrid sight[s]' and the 'more horrid noise of target fight'. In contrast to the action suggested by extant stage directions in *The Rape of Lucrece*, the play represents the wars that provided the backdrop to the drama in the form of a masque. The soldiers are '*led in by their Captaines, distinguisht severally by their Armes and Ensignes* [... and] *put themselves into a figure like a battalia*'; after a song follows '*The dance expressing a fight*'.[53] Nabbes's innovative integration of dance and represented battle demonstrates the ways in which established staging conventions could be reimagined and embellished to very different dramatic effect, and in different contexts.

As Nabbes's appropriation of a dance '*expressing a fight*' suggests, dancing and duelling could have much in common in performance, and a very similar dynamic can be seen at play in evidence relating to the staging of dancing by Queen Henrietta's Men on the Cockpit stage, as old and newer theatrical traditions were showcased and intermingled in the repertory. The influence of courtly masques on the repertory in performance is discussed in further detail in the ensuing section, but it is worth noting that many of the new plays written especially for the company draw on the courtly spectacle of masques, either as part of the main dramatic narrative, or as inset pieces put on for the enjoyment of the characters onstage. Courtly dancing required technical rigour and was linked in the early modern imagination to the movement of the heavenly spheres, while the act of dancing itself was, as Tribble has explored, 'freighted with moral, social and ethical significance'.[54] It was not only the style of dance that reflected on those participating in it; the way in which the dancer held his or her body, the rhythmic harmony with which the dancer moved, and the relationship of the body to other bodies and to the ground could indicate moral and social status and identify the virtues of order and control.[55]

At the other end of the scale, dancing could be disruptive or rejuvenating, as in Shirley's *The Faithful Servant*, which stages a provocative masque-like sequence in which satyrs pursue nymphs across the stage and dance in a private garden filled with 'ravishing' music.[56] This particular sequence reflects the sexual and moral imbalance of Lodwick, the Duke's lascivious brother in the play, but within the larger plot it performs a restorative and transformative function, returning him to his wife and marriage. This dance also draws attention to the potential of masque sequences to add dramatic texture and tone, and to create mystical spaces or other worlds within the play, unbound by the conventions of the main plot and pulling fantastical creatures and classical characters into the same stage space.

Dances that evoked the organised chaos of the antimasque were similarly popular, in both old and new plays on the Cockpit stage. Among these is the presentation of various characters in Davenport's *A New Trick to Cheat the Devil*, in which a scrivener, knave, prodigal, beggar, puritan, whore, usurer ('*with money Bagges*'), and a devil enter one by one and dance '*a straine*'.[57] The dance of a selection of personified afflictions (including '*immodest Mirth*' and '*sicknesse*') in *The Seven Champions of Christendom* might have had visual similarities with the dance of Lust, pleasures, and furies in Shirley's new play *The Traitor*, while Middleton and Rowley's *The Changeling* features a dance of 'Madmen and Fools', and in 1634 Heywood staged a dance performed by '*Vulcan and his Cyclops*'.[58] John Ford also wrote two new plays for the Cockpit which include dances or masques. *Perkin Warbeck* features celebratory revels performed by '*Maskers*' dressed as '*Scotch Antickes, accordingly habited*', and '*wilde*', '*long hayred*' Irishmen, whereas *Love's Sacrifice* stages a murder in the midst of a dance.[59] The effect is described at some length in the stage direction: in the printed play-text, the masquers enter '*in an Anticke fashion*' and '*dance a little*', until eventually the women join hands and form a ring around Ferentes; '*at length they suddenly fall upon him, and stab him, he fals downe, and they run out at seuerall doores*'.[60]

Ford draws attention in both dances to antiquity, or the oddity of his dancers or dancing styles, for the term 'anticke' claimed a complementary double meaning: of olden times, but also, in the context of the stage direction in *Love's Sacrifice*, grotesque, incongruous, deliberately bizarre – as with Hamlet's 'anticke disposition'.[61] Queen Henrietta's Men exploited old-fashioned dancing in a number of other instances, including the village morris dance in *The Witch of Edmonton*. The performance of this morris in the wider context of the play has an instrumental role in exploring the 'social and interpersonal conflicts' that underpin the drama, as Roberta Barker has suggested, but at the same time Barker notes that by placing the morris 'at the very heart of its narrative', this play 'deals very self-consciously with its relationship to older performance forms'.[62] The figure of Delight in *The Sun's Darling* announces a morris by a 'company of rural fellows', as the figure of Spring worries that 'these sports' might be 'too rustick', while a troupe of country swains debate setting up a maypole in *The Seven Champions of Christendom* before being told to 'Lay by' their 'idle sports and vanities' (D3r).[63]

But alongside rustic or traditional dances, the theatrical event of the dance might also have offered Queen Henrietta's Men the opportunity to update older revivals on the Cockpit stage. A 'dance' could be essentially fluid by nature, and even when choreographed it was unfixed and change-able across time and from performance to performance. Tribble notes that a high level of skill was required by actors dancing on the stage, who needed to memorise multiple steps and complex sequences, but despite structured choreography, improvisation was also valued as a skill, as an 'embodied form of wit'.[64] Claire Hansen has also described dance as 'ephemeral, nonverbal, embodied, and culturally specific', and it is this sense of cultural specificity that is key to discussions of revival in perfor-mance, for that framework shifted over time.[65] It is possible that newer fashions in dancing could have been transposed on to traditional dances to which the stage direction might have referred, implicitly or otherwise, in older Elizabethan plays, providing a way of modernising the aesthetics of revivals. Such methods of transposition might either have been seamless or have appeared wildly incongruous in the context of a dated play or one that drew on archaic source material and contexts; and indeed part of the appeal of traditional or old-fashioned dancing seems to have resided in its recognition as old or self-proclaimedly rustic.

Some crossover between old and new traditions, and between rural celebration and the conventions of the courtly masque, seems likely to have occurred in Shirley's *Love Tricks* or *The School of Compliment*, originally written for Lady Elizabeth's Men at the Cockpit, in which dancing performed by shepherds and shepherdesses '*with garlands*' gives way to a '*maske of Satyres*'.[66] Similarly, in Shirley's later play *The Ball*, rural dancing appears to be appropriated in a fresh and fashionable context when, in the course of a dancing lesson taught by Monsieur Le Friske, a group of London ladies participates in '*a new Country Dance*'.[67] The structure of this play works to foreground dancing as an important social event, and Jean Howard has argued that the play's reference to dancing is essentially political in nature, as Le Friske functions as a 'reference to courtly fashions', but also as a figure through which the foreign dancing and masquing of Queen Henrietta Maria and her court was to be negoti-ated – in England and, more particularly, London.[68] The play also presents a number of opportunities for the actors to showcase (or send up) the latest trends in dancing.[69] In presenting a *new* country dance, *The Ball* thus 'refunction[s] popular practice', converting country dance into some-thing more metropolitan, original, and fresh.[70]

Dance offered Queen Henrietta's Men a means by which fresh innova-
tions in performance, gesture, and movement could be performed alongside
or within established narratives and familiar plots in revival, and it had
a cultural momentum of its own. Just as dance could enable shifts between
tone and genre, underscore and enable pivotal plot moments, and provide
alternative ways for actors to articulate and express staged emotions, it
might also have encouraged an experimental dynamic within theatrical
repertories and a means by which old and new traditions could be juxtaposed, reconciled, and freshly conceived.

A 'MESS OF MAD ELEMENTS': GENRE, MYTH, AND MAGIC

The echoes and inflections of courtly masques that resonated in the Cockpit
repertory are glimpsed not only in moments of dance, but also in the presentation of stylised and spectacular mythical gods on the stage. Heywood's
Love's Mistress staged Cupid's descent in the prologue for the play at the
Cockpit, and later in the action. It also offered the opportunity to stage
a host of diabolical characters from the classical underworld, including dancing cyclopes, Pluto (or Hades), Minos (portrayed with a coiled
tail by Dante Alighieri and then Michelangelo in preceding centuries),
Charon, and the many-headed Cerberus, who is given a speaking part.
While the composition of *Love's Mistress* in 1634 seems to have been
part of a focused effort to interest the company's namesake patron around
this time, in the wider context of the repertory and in performance on
the Cockpit stage it resonated with a number of masque-like sequences
and elements that ran through the repertory. These plays included older
revivals such as Beaumont and Fletcher's *Cupid's Revenge*, which John
Astington has suggested owed its original popularity in the Whitefriars
to a 'fascination with the staging and content of that particular Jacobean
phenomenon, the court masque'.[71] Astington suggests that the play was
partly responsible for a vogue at the indoor Blackfriars and Whitefriars
theatres after 1608 which drew on fashionable masque elements, and
it seems likely that *Cupid's Revenge* contributed in a similar way to
the Cockpit repertory in revival, for the masque's popularity at court
in the Caroline period did not dwindle. This play features two mono-
logues given by Cupid as he is described in stage directions as descending
over the stage (B2r, C2r) – a precedent, perhaps, for the descent of the
same character in *Love's Mistress*. Heywood's *The Escapes of Jupiter* – a
play with a less certain connection to the Cockpit repertory in performance – features at least one descent by Juno and Iris, another instance
in which the two characters appear 'in a Clowde aboue', and a moment

in which 'Iupiter discends / In his maiesty his thonder-bolt burning in his hande'.[72]

A small subset of 'late morality' plays are also to be found connected to the Cockpit repertory, all written for the theatre at various times. Middleton and Rowley's *The World Tossed at Tennis* is described on its title-page as a 'Courtly Masque' and was written for the Prince's Men to be performed in 1620. If it can be identified with the play named *The World* that was protected by William Beeston in 1639, then it is likely to have remained in the repertory of Queen Henrietta's Men. Ford and Dekker's 'Moral Masque' *The Sun's Darling* was written for Lady Elizabeth's Men at the Cockpit a few years later and was protected for performance by Beeston's Boys in 1639, and Nabbes's play *Microcosmus* might have been written and intended for Queen Henrietta's Men at the Cockpit, but is likely to have been performed later, at the Salisbury Court by Heton's Queen's Men.[73] Nevertheless, its possible composition for the Cockpit is suggestive, contributing to a small cluster of masque-like dramas written for Beeston's theatre. Each of these plays is modelled on an allegorical story-board and elucidates an *Everyman*-esque morality: *The Sun's Darling* tells the story of man's seasonal experience in the world, whereas *Microcosmus* details the seduction of man by sensuality, surrounded by the influence of the elements and their corresponding humours. While these are five-act plays, and do not resemble masques in terms of their form, structure, and social and commercial functions, they are highly emblematic pieces, and personify a raft of allegorical figures, including Time, Youth, and Spirit. *Microcosmus* also seems to specify the presentation of an arch, through which is seen 'a continuing perspective of ruines, which is drawne still before the other scenes whilst they are varied'; these other scenes include the elemental sphere, clouds that enable the descent of actors, an arbour, and a cave.[74] *The Sun's Darling* appears to have employed some kind of unusual stage effect, though it might have drawn on the resources of the audience's imagination rather than the ingenuity of the company. There is nothing unusual in the stage direction which suggests that the Sun '*takes his seat above*' (D3v), but shortly afterwards a direction reads: 'The Sun by degrees is clowded' (D4r). This might have been effected by the drawing of a curtain, or by another, more ambitious means involving a scenic device.[75] The prefatory material to *Love's Mistress* describes the kind of scenery and spectacle for which the court paid, but the use of specialised backdrops for commercial companies might have stretched resources too far: in the metatheatrical commentary of *The Arcadia*, Basilius humbly professes of an apparently undressed masque scene that 'our revells wants the state and glory / With which the Court delights [...] Our sceane is naturall' (B4v–C1r).

The costuming of the 'late moralities' is likely to have been visually striking, however. The prefatory material to *Microcosmus* dedicates three pages to a description of the 'Persons figur'd' and their costuming. Janus has 'two faces [and ...] a yellow robe, wrought with snakes', Nature wears a white robe covered with 'birds, beasts, fruits, flowers, clouds, starres', Fire wears a crown of flames, and Air has blue hair beneath a wreath of clouds. The play also presents the Humours, who are represented through costume choices that draw on the symbolism of colour and temperament: Choler is a fencer, clad in red (B1r–B2v). *The Sun's Darling* offers opportunity for the representation of the Seasons onstage, and the masque at the close of the play presents Earth, Air, Fire, and Water, and the four Humours. It is not unreasonable to assume that they would have been clad in the same costumes, or variations of them, as would have been used in *Microcosmos* if it had been performed at the Cockpit. Middleton and Rowley's 'masque', *The World Tossed at Tennis*, presents the nine worthies and the 'Five Starches' (White, Blue, Yellow, Green, and Red), who are '*all properly habited to expresse their affected colours*' (D2r).

But while these plays, and new additions to the repertory such as *Love's Mistress*, drew on elements of the courtly masque in a way that suggests tribute to the court, or (in Astington's terms) a 'fascination' with the genre, other plays in the repertory and beyond underscored the potential for ridicule inherent in such mythic or allegorical representation. The finale of Shirley's *The Ball* is discussed in more detail later in this book, but the play presents a bearded Cupid alongside an apparently absurd and misleading representation of a satyr.[76] Middleton had staged a similarly farcical scenario in *No Wit, No Help Like a Woman's* years prior to this at the Fortune, in which four men in the play take part in a masque of the elements. Sir Gilbert enters dressed as a personification of Fire, in a costume that anticipated Heywood's Apollo in *Love's Mistress*, with his 'yellow tresses' that shine 'Like curled flames' (B3r), and the crown of flames in *Microcosmus*: here, Sir Gilbert '*issues forth with Yellow-hair and Beard, intermingled with stroaks like wilde flames*'.[77] Mr Weatherwise '*comes down*' on to the stage '*hanging by a cloud*' when he enters as Air, while Mr Overdon's attempt to represent Earth involves wearing '*a number of little things like Trees, like a thick Grove upon his head*' (F7r). The sequence and its extensive stage directions reveal the detail in which these characters might have been costumed and the means by which various effects might be attained; each of the four winds has its face painted a different colour. But it also draws attention to the artifice of the piece. When the four winds blow at the end of their dance, they '*shove off*' the disguises of Earth, Air, Fire, and Water, to reveal the rejected suitors of the play's main action. This 'mess of mad Elements' is ended abruptly with shedding of costumes, and a disgruntled complaint made by Weatherwise about the cost of the entertainment: 'I ow money for the Clouds yet, I care not who knows it' (G1v, G1r). The performance of such plays on the London stage, and the metatheatrical commentary they offered, might have worked to collapse the boundaries and expectations of genre for playgoing audiences while drawing attention to the financial outlay that such entertainment demanded.

A similar effect might have been activated by the bringing together of different genres treating other forms of supernatural appearances on the Cockpit stage, particularly in the case of devils and witches. This was a broader circumstance which applied to all professional repertory companies as they filled a schedule of performance with plays of varied provenance and dramatic style, but the potential dramatic effect that it might have had on audiences comes into focus when particular examples from the Cockpit repertory are considered. Queen Henrietta's Men staged many devils, not only in number but also in kind. When the Devil entered on to the Cockpit stage in the Jacobean performances by Prince Charles's Men of *The World Tossed at Tennis*, the play's relationship to masquing traditions and costuming suggests that he could have been dressed according to convention, as the character appears on the play's title-page. The woodcut might represent a fictive imagining of the final scene and fail to correspond to stage practice, but it does suggest the detail that could go into this kind of costume: cloven hooves, webbed wings, claws.[78] Defined by a different set of generic expectations, the Devil takes on the shape of a talking dog in *The Witch of Edmonton*, written just a year or two later. In Davenport's *A New Trick to Cheat the Devil*, a number of devilish creatures present themselves onstage, only to be revealed later as mortal characters parading as satanic minions. A version of the Devil enters '*like a Gentleman, with glasse eyes*' (G1r) and initiates a satanic pact, but this bespectacled Beelzebub turns out to be the quite terrestrial Master Changeable, who has orchestrated an elaborate bewitching. In this play, the stage direction calls for devils to enter dancing 'with Fire wo[r]kes, and Crackers', and '*Thundering and howling*' (I1v–I2r) accompany Changeable's later entry disguised as Satan. Though it turns out that these devils are not actually emissaries from hell, Davenport drew on conventional tropes and effects to create the desired theatrical impact. The genre and narrative context of the play signalled to the audience that this was not a world in which 'real' devils belonged. But the Cockpit's staging of this play drew on the audience's intimacy with an established theatrical tradition, or at least with the way that tradition came to be described, in which 'shagge-hayr'd Deuills [ran] roaring ouer the Stage with Squibs in their mouthes' at the Fortune Theatre.[79] Queen Henrietta's Men might have staged a similar

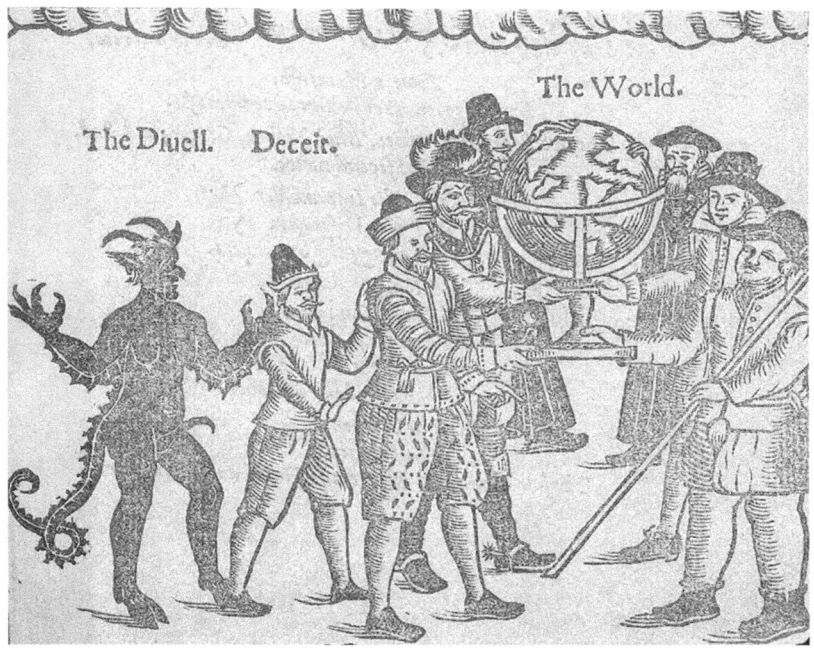

3   Title-page illustration from Thomas Middleton and William Rowley, *A Courtly Masque: The Device called, The World tost at Tennis* (London, 1620). Bodleian Libraries, University of Oxford, 2025. Weston Mal. 246 (4)

moment in *The Seven Champions* when a stage direction calls for '*Divels [who] run laughing over the stage*' (H1r). In Kirke's play, these creatures have a very different ontological status: they are not tricks or illusions, and take their place in an imaginative narrative rooted in fairytale and magic, and within a hierarchy of supernatural agents. Tarpax, a 'light wing'd' spirit of the Aire [...] prince of the grisly North' (B2r), forms part of this hierarchy, 'steele tipt pinions' on his wings (B2r), while the sorcerer of dark arts Ormandine enters '*with his spirits Canopy borne over his head*' (G1r). Later in the play the stage directions suggest that the audience might have experienced a representation of metamorphosis, when three 'swans' who '*turne*' into princesses shed their enchanted shapes (L3r).

The nature of witches and the status of the magic they performed were also juxtaposed in *The Seven Champions* and *The Witch of Edmonton*. Kirke's witch is surrounded by a host of familiars, rich in 'spels' and

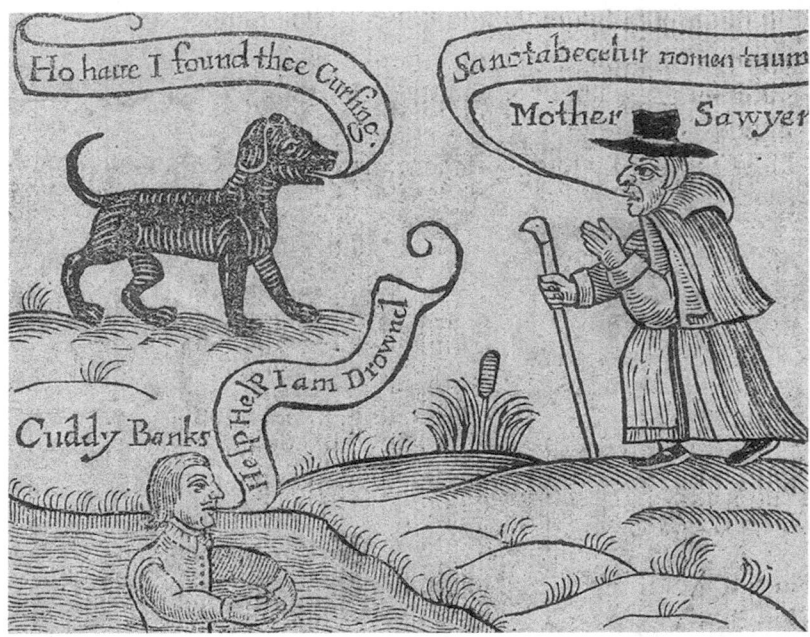

4   Title-page illustration from William Rowley, Thomas Dekker, and John Ford, *The Witch of Edmonton* (London, 1658). Bodleian Libraries, University of Oxford, 2025. Weston Mal. 158 (1)

'potent charmes', a murderess who commands the weather (B1v). The representation of this 'Dutchesse of *Witchcordia*' (B3r) stands in contrast to old Mother Sawyer, the 'witch' under whose 'curse' the villagers of rural Edmonton live. Sawyer describes herself as a 'poor, deform'd and ignorant' old woman, and bemoans her role in society as a scapegoat as she gathers sticks for her fire: 'where and by what Art learn'd? / What spells, what charms, or invocations?'[80] The play's title-page does not represent the staged action in the theatre, portraying as it does Cuddy Banks in a reedy pond, tussocks of grass sprouting by the water's edge. It may gesture towards one costuming possibility for Sawyer though, as a stooped, plainly clothed character.

The magic Mother Sawyer practises with the assistance of Tom, her devil-dog, is also of a very different nature to Calib's meteorological feats. She and Tom are responsible for Anne Ratcliffe's madness and suicide, but other than these her deeds seem full of petty spite. She bids Tom strike a horse lame and nip a 'sucking-childe', while the hound assures her that 'The Maid has been churning Butter nine hours; but it shall not come' (G2r). Bewitching cream in the dairy is also one of the mischiefs committed by 'that merry wanderer of the night' Puck in *A Midsummer Night's Dream*, as 'bootless' he makes 'the breathless housewife churn'.[81] The conclusion to each witch's storyline underscores, perhaps more than any other moment, the differences in genre at work within the plays. Calib is besieged by St George, and though her spirits hold him back he cleaves the rock she stands upon in two, with his newly acquired magic wand. She '*sinkes*', and is swallowed up into hell and its 'black inchanted vapours' (C2v). In contrast, Mother Sawyer is dragged away by her accusers and finally exits to the gallows. The character's real-life counterpart was hanged at Tyburn in 1621.

These contrasting representations of witchcraft and the supernatural can be linked more widely in the period to changing social, cultural, and theological attitudes towards superstitious belief, as observed by Keith Thomas. Towards the latter part of the seventeenth century, and for a variety of interlinked reasons, Thomas found that the number of prosecutions of witchcraft fell, the belief in Satan and devils as physical beings and in hell as a localised, non-symbolic place was in decline, and courts of law became increasingly sceptical of witchcraft claims or the possibility of proving the offence.[82] The intellectual shift towards scepticism appears to have been gradual and, Thomas argues, was not marked by any particularly noteworthy advance or event. In this respect Thomas described the shift in legal attitudes towards witchcraft, defined by the views of the 'educated classes who provided the judges, lawyers, Grand Jurymen and Petty Jurymen', as almost 'silent', but it was also being played out on the professional stage.[83]

In performance, differing cultural conceptions of witchcraft were pointed up and exacerbated by the repertory system, which folded plays of differing provenance into one corpus. At the same time, divergent portrayals of witchcraft and the supernatural, rooted in theological structures of belief and world-views, became manifest in aesthetic, visual, and performative terms, and they were knowingly crafted as such. Though Calib and Sawyer derive from contrasting cultural constructions of witches and divergent theatrical and generic influences, each play makes reference to and validates the other tradition. Calib's son asks her whether she was 'one of the Cats that drunke up the Millers Ale in *Lancashire* Wind-mills?' (B3r). This comment aligns Calib with the conception of witchcraft associated with old Mother Sawyer, transposing Kirke's witch from her mythical realm into provincial tales of remote and haunted English windmills. It also appears to refer to Brome and Heywood's play *The Late Lancashire Witches*, which at one point relates the tale of a miller harangued by demonic cats.[84] Like *The Witch of Edmonton*, Brome and Heywood's play was based on reported cases of witchcraft, and followed the highly publicised arrests and trials of the accused.[85] Kirke's reference to the bewitched windmill alludes not only to the more 'everyday' village witches explored in the narrative of *The Witch of Edmonton*, but also to the theatrical past and the history of performed witchcraft. At the same time, *The Witch of Edmonton* recognises the generic conventions attached to the representation of witchcraft, and reiterates them when Sawyer and the dog make their pact. He '*Sucks her arm*', and the same stage direction specifies '*thunder and lightning*' (D1r). This imports the folklore and spectacle deployed in *The Seven Champions* and plays of its genre: Kirke's first scene calls for thunder and lightning no fewer than eight times; Calib gives suck to Tarpax and, later, promises her spirits that she will 'ope Rivers of my blood to you, / And you shall drinke your fill' (C2v). This dramatic style provided the opportunity for Queen Henrietta's Men to experiment with the aurally fantastic, the visually extraordinary, and the sensational in performance, and connects Sawyer with a stage tradition steeped in extravagant effects, tropes, and devices. In this sense, the repertory was self-aware and self-reflexive. Queen Henrietta's Men negotiated between different traditions and configurations of the supernatural, and defined genres in opposition to each other. While representations of demonic magic in Jacobean theatre and culture may document a shift away from an emphasis on the 'factual' existence (or acceptance) of devilry towards more light-hearted, sceptical treatments, the staging of revivals and new plays in the same space in a schedule of performance worked to disrupt such a linear chronology.[86]

'BY THE HALFE LIGHT OF A LAMPE': SHADOW AND FIRE

The interaction of different theatrical styles, traditions, and genres fostered an environment in which familiar drama might be experienced afresh. But the specific environment of the Cockpit also lent itself to experimentation in the staging of plays of all ages, given the possibilities for contrasting levels of light that the indoor playhouse offered. Critics have reached varying conclusions concerning the illumination of the indoor playhouses, which could have been lit by natural daylight during afternoon performances, and by candlelight. Robert Graves found that the indoor playhouses for which evidence survives would have been lit largely by daylight and the sunshine falling through the windows, and argued that the assumption that the indoor playhouses would have been 'dim' is unsupported by the evidence.[87] But Martin White's research suggests that the case for darkness in the theatres is not so easily dismissed, and he draws on an evidence base that combines practice-based research using the Chamber of Demonstrations project at Bristol (a reconstruction of the stage and auditorium of the playhouse shown in the drawings now held at Worcester College, Oxford) with historical records relating to contemporary accounts of theatregoing and company expenditure on candles and lighting.[88] He suggests that available daylight is not likely to have illuminated the indoor playhouses as brightly as Graves thought, and that the evidence suggests that the playhouses were lit by far more candles than Graves had calculated. Both Graves and White agree that the relative lightness or darkness of a scene, and its contrast with what had come before or would come after, was key to the audience's perception of particular theatrical moments, and Graves accepts that indoor lighting was 'theoretically susceptible to more control than outdoor illumination'.[89] White suggests that productions at the reimagined Sam Wanamaker Playhouse have 'demonstrated that the operation and flexibility of the lighting are more user-friendly' than Graves supposed, and suggests that stage directions such as that in *Catiline* which reads '*A darkness comes over the place*' are not just suggestive to readers of that text, but are rather 'a precise description of how [that moment] was experienced by its audience when performed indoors'.[90] The King's Men only performed at the Blackfriars from September to April, using the Globe as the company's summer venue, and daylight would have been far reduced in the darker winter months. This circumstance does not apply to Queen Henrietta's Men at the Cockpit, who performed indoors all year round, but even in the lighter summer months it seems likely that the company would have wished to capitalise, as far as possible, on the control over lighting that being indoors offered, and the additional elements of theatrical experimentation that window shutters and candles could lend to the performances.

Evidence provided by stage directions relating to the representation of ghosts onstage offers an example of the ways that the company might have been working within, and thinking about, the space offered by the Cockpit and the theatrical effects it could deliver in terms of lighting and illumination. As with the examples of supernatural presences above, the repertory featured a number of different conceptions of ghostly visitation: those with independent agency, seemingly external to those who perceived them; ghosts that were figments of the imagination, products of diseased minds; and ghosts that turned out to be cases of mistaken identity, lost figures wandering through dark churchyards. In each case it seems likely that Queen Henrietta's Men drew on the particular conditions of production in the indoor Cockpit to create scenes of relative darkness and confusion.

Kirke's *The Seven Champions* calls for ghosts in the opening scenes who are accompanied by thunder and lightning and, extraordinarily for plays in the Cockpit repertory, these ghosts speak. Though such visual and aural cues might denote the diabolical nature of this supernatural appearance, other aspects of these ghosts' visit signal their benevolence: the stage direction for '*soft musicke*', for instance, and George's description of the ghosts as 'ayrie shapes' and 'sweet shadows' (C1v). The ghosts in other plays in the repertory remain silent, and appear to be conjured by the mind's eye, dependent on the psychology of those who observe them. In *The Witch of Edmonton* Frank lies in bed when '*the Spirit of* Susan *his second Wife comes to the Beds-side. He stares at it; and turning to the other side, it's there too*' (G4v). The revival of *The White Devil* staged several quiet ghosts. Francisco sees his sister Isabella's ghost after closing his eyes, 'And in a melancholique thought' he summons 'Her figure 'fore me' (G2r). The stage direction calls for the entry of Isabella's ghost, but Francisco only 'thinks' she stands before him, and the apparition seems to be dismissed when he shakes himself out of a reverie: 'remooue this obiect / Out of my braine with't' (G2v). The stage direction prompting the entry of Bracciano's melancholic ghost before Flamineo is particularly detailed in describing the ghost's appearance. But though the ghost throws earth over Flamineo, the vision fades in the next few lines: 'Hee's gone; and see, the scull and earth are vanisht' (L2r). Whether Bracciano's unspeaking ghost has its own agency outside of Flamineo's crisis of conscience is unclear. This 'terrible vision' seems more like something imagined, and does not seem to claim the same kind of materiality as the ghost of Alonso in Middleton and Rowley's *The Changeling*, another instance in which one of the dead returns to haunt the murderer. This ghost appears to De Flores in a dumb show, '*shewing*' De Flores '*the hand whose finger he had cut off*'.[91] When Alonso's ghost returns, De Flores dismisses it – ''Twas but a mist of conscience' – but Beatrice-Joanna sees it too, describing how 'it slides by' (H1v). This second testimony suggests that in the context of the play Alonso's ghost exists somehow independently of those who observe it – or is the product of a shared hallucination.[92]

It is very rare for stage directions to call for lights or the holding of candles alongside the entry of spectral characters. In the case of *The White Devil* this absence might be explained by the fact that the play was written for the Red Bull amphitheatre, upon whose daylit stage the use of candlelight is unlikely to have provided atmospheric effect. But lights and torches are often specified in amphitheatre plays in order to signal that the scene is taking place in an imagined night or darkness.[93] The absence of light might have been characteristic of ghostly scenes on stage. De Flores's cry, on the entry of Alonso's ghost, suggests the darkness of the appari- tion, though this might be a metaphorical and narrative darkness: 'Ha! What art thou that tak'st away the light / 'Twixt that starr and me' (H1v). And in *The White Devil*, the difficulty of making out what is happening onstage is anticipated by the dialogue. Flamineo's speech fills in for visual clues that the audience might miss: he reports that the ghost 'look'st sad', glosses the macabre prop carried by the spirit (a 'dead mans scull beneath the rootes of flowers'), and describes the ghost's actions as they occur: the stage direction says that '*The Ghost throws earth upon him*' while a bewildered Flamineo states what is obvious to the reader, but perhaps not to the audience of the play in performance: 'he throwes earth vpon mee' (L2r). While the play's original performance at the Red Bull might have made these actions visible and understood to an audience watching by daylight, the value of this explanatory dialogue might have increased once the play had transferred indoors, particularly if the company had chosen to experiment with light levels in this scene. White suggests that the lowering and raising of the chandeliers that hung over the stages of the indoor theatres provided 'variation in the light levels depending on [the chandeliers'] height above the stage', as a number of productions at the Sam Wanamaker Playhouse have also demonstrated.[94] This simple effect could be used by companies to introduce variations in tone and to provide innovative renderings of familiar scenes. As he suggests, it appears unlikely that dramatists and actors familiar with the effects provided by the chandeliers would not have been inclined to experiment with their more explicitly theatrical uses.[95]

There is evidence to suggest that James Shirley recognised the advan- tages of varying levels of lighting in 1633, when he revised Fletcher's *The Night-Walkers* for performance in the Cockpit. This play exhibits a preoc- cupation with light and its absence, and its revival by Queen Henrietta's Men might suggest in itself that the company was either experimenting with the conditions of candlelight at this time, or was already well practised in the staging of its effects. The comedy features a number of instances in which characters are mistaken for ghosts and devils. The dialogue and the narrative of the play suggest that the representation of varying levels of light was key to staging such confusions of judgement, and what can be inferred of the use of candles onstage suggests that light might have been carefully controlled. When Tom Lurcher and his 'boy' Snap meet at night to rob a house of plate, jewellery, and other riches, they devise an unconventional disguise to terrify unwelcome intruders: Snap dons a turban, a beard, and a long cloak and climbs on to Lurcher's shoulders to simulate an unnaturally tall devil. When the Nurse and Toby enter, the

Nurse instructs Toby to hold up his candle. She complains that the 'light burnes blewe' and asks Toby to snuff it (trim the wick), and then they glimpse the false giant, a 'Ghost', a fire-farting 'Devill', who is 'Steeple high' and 'sayles away'.[96] They leave, terrified, and shortly afterwards Lurcher asks: 'No light?'; and Snap replies: 'None left sir, / They are gone, and carried all the candles with 'em' (D2v). This, and Snap's assurance that he can find his way to the chest of riches 'Though it were ith' darke', suggests that the way of Lurcher and Snap is not lit and that they are not holding their own candles; the strange apparition of the devil is in shadow and this is why Toby and the Nurse do not perceive the monstrous shape at once. Even when they do, the dialogue suggests that the light is dim – Toby's wish that he 'had a ladder to behold it' (D2r) might refer not only to the height of the 'devil' but also the poor illumination of the scene. When Toby and the Nurse return, the logic of the dialogue continues to recognise the dramatic effect of darkness in this particular scene, as Newlove begs Wildbraine to 'put your candle out / For if I see the Spirit againe I dye fort': Wildbraine affirms that he has 'put the light out' (D3r–v). When Toby then enters, it is also in the (relative) dark: 'my light's out / And I grope up and downe like blind-man buffe / And breake my face, and breake my pate' (D3v). A farce of mistaken identity ensues, in which Wildbraine mistakes Toby for a 'hairie whore', and Toby mistakes Wildbraine for the house's now-infamous devil.

In performance the scene is likely to have been lit so that the audience could enjoy the confusion with which they were presented, but if the chandeliers had been raised the actors would have played on a dimmer stage, and been able to exploit these conditions in the narrative arc, punctuated by brief, candlelit illuminations. The murkiness that the scene at least evokes, if not stages, creates a number of tense and comical moments, but is also fundamental to the narrative of the play. When they next appear, Snap assures Lurcher that his Mistress is 'comming with a Candle', and agrees that 'plate is very heavie / To carry without light or helpe' (D4r). Under the confusion of darkness, they have mistakenly stolen a coffin containing the insensible body of Maria, rather than the chest full of treasure that they seek. They only realise their mistake when the Mistress holds up her light to illuminate the chest. On this discovery the trio set off in darkness to bury Maria's body, and encounter the Justice and his servant in the graveyard, jumping at shadows and wielding a single 'torch' – a hand-held light with the capacity, as White describes, to introduce 'a sudden burst of light on stage'.[97] In another trick, Snap hides behind Lurcher and utters a groaning sound, before frightening the servant into believing they have been apprehended by a ghostly bride and tricking the Justice into thinking he has conversed with the unseen shade of his dead wife. When Maria starts to rouse, Lurcher and Snap flee as she wakes to a 'Darkenesse', both metaphorical and literal, that 'spreads o're the world' (E3r). The nocturnal setting continues into the next scene, in which Hartlove appears wandering through the 'night, and all the evills the night covers, / The Goblins, Hagges, and the blacke spawne of darkenesse' (E4r). Meditating on spirits, he comes across Wildbraine, and the two almost fall into a fight when Maria stumbles upon them, guided by their voices in the gloom. They mistake Maria for her ghost, aided only by the light of Wildbraine's 'darke Lanthorne' (E4v) – a lighting instrument that became associated with clandestine behaviour.[98] Two further incidents turn on levels of lighting – one in which Toby is tricked into extinguishing his candle and Snap steals his clothes (and those of his company), and the other in which, 'by the halfe light of a lampe', two Furies enter with *'blacke tapers'* and Snap appears dressed *'like an Angell'* (H2r-v, H3r-v).

The play's obsession with light and darkness, and the way that it lent itself to performance in the enclosed space of the Cockpit, might have been characteristics that appealed to Shirley as a dramatist writing and revising for the venue. This was a play that mischievously drew on the capacity for confusion in dark spaces, and made explicit the power of the imagination in staging the supernatural. In performance, if hand-held lights were used to complement the variance in light levels that is implied by the dialogue and suggested by the stage directions, the play had the potential to recreate in the Cockpit something approximating the murky, eerie conditions that dominate the drama and that lead to confusion and superstitious terror – a hysterical belief in haunted houses and the walking, talking dead. In his analysis of lighting in the indoor theatres, Robert Graves made the astute point that early modern audience members would have found themselves 'in the dreary, dull light they saw every day in their homes, business, and inns', but the implied use of light and darkness in *The Night-Walkers* suggests that there was more meaning to be extracted from varying levels of illumination, and more extensive theatrical work to which it could be pressed.[99] *The Night-Walkers* at once exploited and demystified the staging of ghosts, delighting in the effects that play with light and dark lanterns could produce in narrative plots, but also, perhaps, in audience members as well.

If darkness in the theatre was a feature that the company exploited, there is some evidence to suggest that it might also have deployed brilliant displays of light. Fireworks had been popular on the outdoor stages, and the Red Bull in particular developed a tradition of spectacular pyrotechnics owing in part, as Eva Griffith has explored, to the tradition of sophisticated fireworks linked to the Danish court in which Queen Anne, the company's patron, had grown up.[100] The open-roofed amphitheatres have been thought of as the natural home for fireworks and similar effects, though the Globe's immolation in 1613, when, according to Edmond Howes, the 'negligent discharging of a peale of ordinance' during a production of *Henry VIII* set fire to the thatch and burned the playhouse down, shows that they too remained vulnerable to the dangers of fire.[101] Queen Henrietta's Men inherited a number of plays that, in their printed form, call for pyrotechnic display. Webster's *The White Devil* involves an intriguing dumb show preceding Isabella's murder, in which they poison the picture she is about to kiss; their alchemy suggests that perfumes were burned onstage as the perpetrators wear protective '*spectacles of glasse, which couer their eyes and noses*' (D4v). Lightning is invoked in *The Bloody Banquet*, which features a blazing star (G3v). Dekker's *Match Me In London*, a play performed by Lady Elizabeth's Men at the Cockpit and, possibly, by Queen Henrietta's Men later, calls for more thunder and lightning, created by rolling a cannon ball about the heavens or down a stepped trough (or 'thunder run'). In the outdoor theatres at least, lightning was represented through the use of swivels, rockets which ran along a guiding wire or mechanism.[102] Other early plays revived at the Cockpit gesture towards further uses of fire or bright light: in the second part of *If You Know Not Me, You Know Nobody*, another '*blazing starre*' is cued by the stage directions, which 'streakes' across the heavens.[103] It is possible that these aspects of performance were lost as the plays transferred from the amphitheatres to the hall-playhouses: characters might have responded to a comet unseen by the audience, for instance. But playwrights seem to have continued to write features inspired by the effects of fire into plays for the Cockpit after it first opened, with stage directions calling for lightning in Henry Shirley's *The Martyred Soldier* for Lady Elizabeth's Men, and *The Witch of Edmonton* for Prince Charles's Men, and the lighting of a handful of thatch acting as a test for witches in the latter. Heywood's *The Escapes of Jupiter*, which might have been written with performance at the Cockpit in mind, includes thunder and lightning, and a scene in which Jupiter immolates Semele in her bed, appearing to her with his thunderbolt 'burning in his hande'.[104]

Plays written specifically for Queen Henrietta's Men also seem to expect or invoke fire and pyrotechnics, which might indicate that these were manageable effects in the playhouse, to some degree at least. The continuation of fire-related effects also indicates that they were considered valuable or enriching to the repertory, for the kinds of theatrical tricks the company offered as part of its new fare were similar in nature to those it had inherited directly from the amphitheatre tradition. The printed play-text of Killigrew's *The Prisoners* suggests that one of the characters '*makes a fire upon the Stage*' that continues to burn there for most of the fifth act

(C3v). The 'devils' in *A New Trick to Cheat the Devil* dance accompanied by '*Fire wo[r]kes, and Crackers*' (I1v), and the spirits who take to the stage in *The Seven Champions of Christendom* are armed with '*fiery Clubs*' (G3v). The dramatists who wrote for Queen Henrietta's Men seem to have appreciated and at least hoped for these effects on the Cockpit stage, even if they were never realised in performance, and continued to write such effects into plays into the 1630s. If the Cockpit was suited to representing darkness on the stage, the effects it could bring about through the use of light might also have been recognised by dramatists, particularly given the effect of candlelight on the richly painted and reflective surfaces of the indoor theatres, and in interplay with the costumes of the actors and the 'decorated clothes and jewels of many in the audience'.[105]

CONCLUSION

This chapter has highlighted a few of the features of the Cockpit repertory in play, exploring the variety of drama and theatrical events in the repertory through which Queen Henrietta's Men appear to have attracted and entertained their audiences. It begins to open up possibilities for the extent to which new and old plays might have been performed together on the stage to create an amalgam of theatrical styles and traditions. Despite the negative associations around 1630s revivals, in which older plays were increasingly dismissed as 'musty' and 'stale', this analysis indicates the extent to which new plays for the indoor theatres appear to have drawn on and exploited the theatrical conventions of the amphitheatres, providing older plays with fresh currency and context when they were performed side by side. This was a repertory strategy that built the foundations of its success on the principles of continuity and variation. The use of older source material and modes of presentation in new plays written for the repertory affirmed the dated features of the Cockpit's revivals, but also worked to situate them more firmly within a rich dramatic and cultural history. What emerges is a continuum of tradition and innovation, and a repertory that came to be more than the sum of its parts. The strategy not only worked to create new spaces, both literal and metaphorical, for old drama, but also served to advertise it, generate interest in its styles and staging practices, and affirm its audience – both at the Cockpit and at the Red Bull, in which Beeston still held an interest.[106]

Attention to the staging requirements of the plays, as they are suggested by the extant play-texts, also gestures towards the important role that the actors played as originators, in the presentation of the repertory and the realisation of these plays in performance. The company's collaborative efforts and choices in fulfilling staging requirements, interpreting stage directions, and developing their own particular approach to the repertory would have been critical to its reception and continued currency in the market for plays.

The growing bifurcation of amphitheatre and hall-playhouse style that was reported in prefatory texts of the period does not appear to have corresponded to the practice of Queen Henrietta's Men, and is not reflected in the commitment of the company to revivals and to making the most of the styles of drama those plays had to offer. As the previous chapter suggested, this is not to say that Beeston's company was immune or oblivious to ambivalent attitudes towards revivals and the more negative associations gathering around Red Bull drama in particular, and the specific construction of the tastes of its patrons as dull and inferior. While the testimony of the printed play-texts suggests the extent to which the company embraced, augmented, and reappropriated older drama and some of the performance practices associated with the amphitheatre stage, the decision to do so required the labour and investment of its playwrights in ensuring this success. In this chapter, that labour and investment has been outlined in the extent to which dramatists drew on the conventions of older drama in the writing of new fare, but it was not always straightforward, and it involved – more than has been recognised – deliberate, self-conscious negotiation over the categories of audience preference, dramatic style, and historical provenance.

The next chapter moves on to explore Thomas Heywood's particular engagement with the repertory in this sense, as he worked to shape this corpus of plays and ensure both its coherence and the currency of its revivals. It reveals the ways in which he chose explicitly to address the narrative that sought to denigrate and devalue his amphitheatre work in revival at the Cockpit, and instil a renewed appreciation for old-fashioned drama and styles in the 1630s. This was an undertaking and a project that emerged not only in the formal content and design of the plays in performance – for Heywood updated his revivals and incorporated archaic material into new plays in the same way that this chapter on staging has already anticipated and outlined. The nature of his intervention into the continued success of the repertory was more sustained, and its reach deeper, written into dialogue, a narrative structure, and a metatheatrical debate that placed questions of theatrical taste and qualification at the heart of the repertory, and centre stage.

1 Thomas Carew, in William Davenant, *The Just Italian* (London, 1630), A3v–A4r.
2 J. C., *The Two Merry Milkmaids* (London, 1620), A2v; see the discussion on p. 105.

3 The use of fire was also dangerous outdoors; the Globe burned down in 1613 as a result of the use of cannon fire. For views on fireworks in the indoor spaces, see Andrew Gurr, 'Singing through the Chatter: Ford and Contemporary Theatrical Fashion', in *John Ford: Critical Re-visions*, ed. Michael Neill (Cambridge: Cambridge University Press, 1988), pp. 81–96 (p. 84); in the same discussion he suggests that Beeston transferred plays to the Cockpit which did not contain battles and duels, and 'left the battle plays to the amphitheatre company'. For 'spectacles of costume rather than fireworks', see Andrew Gurr, *The Shakespearean Stage, 1574–1642*, 3rd edn (Cambridge: Cambridge University Press, 1992), p. 15: 'indoors where the stages were much smaller and cluttered with fashion conscious gallants it was preferable to fence with words'. This discussion was revised in the fourth edition and these suggestions were omitted, though Gurr argues for a 'wealthier taste' at the indoor theatres, favouring wit and, among other features, 'more complex emotional patterns in romance and tragedy alike' (p. 27).

4 Andrew Gurr, 'The New Fashion for Indoor Plays', in *Moving Shakespeare Indoors: Performance and Repertoire in the Jacobean Playhouse*, ed. Andrew Gurr and Farah Karim-Cooper (Cambridge: Cambridge University Press, 2014), pp. 203–16 (p. 203). Gurr's fourth edition of *The Shakespearean Stage* (2009) also modifies the discussion of the differences between amphitheatre and hall-playhouse drama that is referenced above; see previous note.

5 Francis Beaumont and John Fletcher, *Rule a Wife, and Have a Wife* (London, 1640, prologue); James Shirley, *The Imposture* (1652), A4r.

6 Andrew Gurr, *The Shakespearean Stage, 1574–1642*, 4th edn (Cambridge: Cambridge University Press, 2009), p. 274.

7 Andrew Gurr, *The Shakespearian Playing Companies* (Oxford: Clarendon Press, 1996), p. 132.

8 Richard Levin, 'Women in the Renaissance Theatre Audience', *Shakespeare Quarterly*, 40 (1989), 165–74 (p. 171).

9 See Lucy Munro, '"They Eat Each Other's Arms": Stage Blood and Body Parts', in *Shakespeare's Theatres and the Effects of Performance*, ed. Farah Karim-Cooper and Tiffany Stern (London: Bloomsbury, 2013), pp. 73–93, on the conflicting emotions that might be aroused by the theatrical presentation of bloodied props.

10 Christopher Marlowe, *The Rich Jew of Malta* (London, 1633), G4v; Henry Chettle, *The Tragedy of Hoffman* (London, 1631), L2r. This scene can tread a thin line between the unspeakably terrible and the ridiculous, as the Malone Society's performance of the play in 2010 explored when its cast tried to solve the problem of how the red-hot crown is to be handled and safely picked up by those who administer its deadly effects. See Pete Kirwan's account on The Bardathon, https://drpeterkirwan.com/2010/09/26/the-tragedy-of-hoffman-malone-society-magdalen-college-oxford/ (accessed 30 June 2025).

11 John Webster, *The White Devil* (London, 1631). The first takes place during a competitive sport on a vaulting horse, in which Flamineo pitches the victim upon '*his necke*', '*wriths his necke about*' to check it is broken, and then folds the body '*double*' (D4v). Later in the play Brachiano's face is poisoned by an intoxicated helmet (J4v).

12 Thomas Heywood, *The Rape of Lucrece* (London, 1638), B2v.

13 'T. D.', *The Bloody Banquet* (London, 1639), G1v, G4v. *The Bloody Banquet* was protected by Beeston's Boys in 1639 and might well have been performed by Queen Henrietta's Men, though Bentley suggested that it might derive from Red Bull origins – a consideration based partly on the 'very crude and old-fashioned'

dramatic attributes that he perceived in the play. G. E. Bentley, *The Jacobean and Caroline Stage*, 7 vols (Oxford: Clarendon Press, 1941–68), III, p. 283.

14 Thomas Heywood, *The Fair Maid of the West*, Part II (London, 1631), K1r; John Kirke, *The Seven Champions of Christendom* (London, 1638), L1r.

15 As Martin White explores in his consideration of Renaissance drama with respect to the concept of the Grotesque in the arts, tragedy in particular might also present scenes that were highly comic or that juxtaposed shock with humour. Martin White, 'Poison in Jest: Some Comic (Ir)resolutions', in his *Renaissance Drama in Action* (London: Routledge, 1998), pp. 177–96.

16 Martin Wiggins, in association with Catherine Richardson, *British Drama, 1533–1642: A Catalogue* (Oxford: Oxford University Press, 2011–), #1651.

17 William N. West, 'Replaying Early Modern Performances', in *New Directions in Renaissance Drama and Performance Studies*, ed. Sarah Werner (Basingstoke: Palgrave Macmillan, 2010), pp. 30–50 (p. 35).

18 Sarah Dustagheer, *Shakespeare's Two Playhouses: Repertory and Theatre Space at the Globe and the Blackfriars, 1599–1613* (Cambridge: Cambridge University Press, 2017), pp. 139–63; Tiffany Stern, '"A ruinous monastery": The Second Blackfriars Playhouse as a Place of Nostalgia', in *Moving Shakespeare Indoors: Performance and Repertoire in the Jacobean Playhouse*, ed. Andrew Gurr and Farah Karim-Cooper (Cambridge: Cambridge University Press, 2014), pp. 97–114.

19 Christian Billing, 'Modelling the Anatomy Theatre and the Indoor Hall Theatre: Dissection on the Stages of Early Modern London', *Early Modern Literary Studies*, 13 (2004), http://purl.oclc.org/emls/si-13/billing (accessed 16 March 2018). The argument draws on the identification of the Worcester drawings with Inigo Jones's designs for the Cockpit theatre. This identification has now been disproved; see p. 18 n.31 of this book, and also Gordon Higgott's paper, 'Reassessing the Drawings for the Inigo Jones Theatre: A Restoration Project by John Webb?', https://www.bristol.ac.uk/drama/jacobean/research4.html (accessed 4 September 2023). However, Billing's more general points, which relate the shape of early modern cockpits to the architecture of anatomy theatres, are of relevance here, as Billing describes the way in which the physical similarities of a rounded indoor playhouse to the anatomy theatre may have 'created a new phenomenality of violence' connected with the increasingly popular practice of anatomy in the period, and 'demand from an educated and literary elite to see regular public anatomy demonstrations as entertainment' (para. 1, para. 4).

20 Sarah Dustagheer, 'Acoustic and Visual Practices Indoors', in *Moving Shakespeare Indoors: Performance and Repertoire in the Jacobean Playhouse*, ed. Andrew Gurr and Farah Karim-Cooper (Cambridge: Cambridge University Press, 2014), pp. 137–51 (pp. 144–6).

21 Dustagheer, 'Acoustic and Visual Practices Indoors', p. 137.

22 James Shirley, *The Maid's Revenge* (London, 1639), E3v.

23 Marlowe, *The Rich Jew of Malta*, B1v; John Cooke, *Greenes Tu Quoque* (London, 1614), B1r.

24 N. W. Bawcutt (ed.), *The Control and Censorship of Caroline Drama: The Records of Sir Henry Herbert, Master of the Revels 1623–73* (Oxford: Clarendon Press, 1996), pp. 41–2.

25 Paul Werstine, *Early Modern Playhouse Manuscripts and the Editing of Shakespeare* (Cambridge: Cambridge University Press, 2015); see Mariko Ichikawa, *The Shakespearean Stage Space* (Cambridge: Cambridge University Press, 2013), pp. 12–17, for a fuller summary of recent scholarship on the relationship between

manuscript and plays, printed plays, and plays in performance, and the ways in which this affects interpretative work around stage directions.

26 See Werstine, *Early Modern Playhouse Manuscripts*, pp. 148–99, for an account of the kinds of changes (and inconsistencies) that bookkeepers might introduce to playhouse texts as they were being prepared for performance. Importantly, Werstine finds that changes to stage directions were largely 'bibliographical' rather than 'functional', as Sarah Dustagheer and Gillian Woods summarise, but nevertheless Werstine suggests that bookkeepers' versions of stage directions 'can be less reliable as a guide to or record of who entered at a particular juncture in performance' than those provided by playwrights (p. 194). See Sarah Dustagheer and Gillian Woods (eds), *Stage Directions and Shakespearean Theatre* (London: Bloomsbury, 2018), p. 4.

27 John Jowett, 'Henry Chettle and the First Quarto of *Romeo and Juliet*', *The Papers of the Bibliographical Society of America*, 92 (1998), 53–74.

28 Alan Dessen, 'Stage Directions and the Theater Historian', in *The Oxford Handbook of Early Modern Theatre*, ed. Richard Dutton (Oxford: Oxford University Press, 2011), pp. 513–27 (p. 516).

29 See pp. 191–2.

30 One stage direction in Robert Greene's *Alphonsus, King of Aragon* reads: '*Exit Venus. Or if you can conueniently, let a chaire come downe from the top of the stage, and draw her up*' (London, 1599), I3r; Dessen, 'Stage Directions', p. 518.

31 Martin White, '"When Torchlight made an Artificial Noon": Light and Darkness in the Indoor Jacobean Theatre', in *Moving Shakespeare Indoors: Performance and Repertoire in the Jacobean Playhouse*, ed. Andrew Gurr and Farah Karim-Cooper (Cambridge: Cambridge University Press, 2014), pp. 115–36 (pp. 132–6).

32 Dustagheer and Woods (eds), *Stage Directions*, p. 6.

33 Alan C. Dessen and Leslie Thomson, *A Dictionary of Stage Directions in English Drama, 1580–1642* (Cambridge: Cambridge University Press, 1999), p. x; Dessen, 'Stage Directions', p. 515.

34 Evelyn Tribble, *Early Modern Actors and Shakespeare's Theatre* (London: Bloomsbury, 2017), p. 15.

35 In 1622 this appears to have been an issue at the amphitheatre playhouses too, when a feltmaker's apprentice was 'greevously wounded in the head' at the Red Bull by a weapon wielded in performance there: Andrew Gurr, *Playgoing in Shakespeare's London*, 3rd edn (Cambridge: Cambridge University Press, 2004), p. 232. A line of dialogue in Massinger's *The Roman Actor* suggests that swords used on stage were blunted, however, when Aesop refers to a prepared foyle, 'The point, and edge rebutted, when you act / To doe the murther.' Aesop continues, 'If you please to vse this / And lay aside your owne sword.' Philip Massinger, *The Roman Actor* (London, 1629), I1.

36 Francis Beaumont and John Fletcher, *Cupid's Revenge* (London, 1635), K2r.

37 Thomas Dekker, *The Wonder of a Kingdom* (London, 1636), B2v; Thomas Heywood, *The Fair Maid of the West*, Part I (London, 1631), B4r.

38 *The White Devil*, ed. John Russell Brown (London: Methuen, 1996), p. 12.

39 Webster, *The White Devil*, I4v; John Webster, *The Devil's Law-Case* (London, 1623), L3r.

40 Sir Charles Cornwallis recorded an account of the Barriers, and while John Chamberlain did not see them he wrote of the event in correspondence with Sir Ralph Winwood; Edmond Howe also added an account of them to John Stow's *Annales* in 1615. See C. H. Herford, Percy Simpson, and Evelyn Simpson (eds), *Ben Jonson, Volume 10: Play Commentary; Masque Commentary* (Oxford: Oxford

University Press, 1950), p. 513. Ben Jonson published *The Speeches at Prince Henries Barriers* in his *Works* of 1616.

41 Heywood, *The Rape of Lucrece*, 1638, I4v.

42 Farah Karim-Cooper and Will Tosh, 'The Indoor Performance Practice', in the programme to *'Tis Pity She's a Whore*, Sam Wanamaker Playhouse, 2014, p. 11.

43 Marta Straznicky, 'The Red Bull Repertory in Print, 1604–60', *Early Theatre*, 9.2 (2006), 144–56 (p. 151).

44 Robert Davenport, *King John and Matilda* (London, 1655), E4r–v, I2v.

45 Kirke, *The Seven Champions*, C4v, D1r.

46 James Shirley, *The Arcadia* (London, 1640), E2r.

47 Tribble, *Early Modern Actors*, pp. 82, 71.

48 Tribble, *Early Modern Actors*, p. 85.

49 Bentley, *Jacobean and Caroline Stage*, IV, p. 712.

50 See pp. 32, 253–4.

51 Alfred Harbage, 'The Authorship of the Dramatic "Arcadia"', *Modern Philology*, 35 (1938), 233–7 (p. 236). For further discussion and a counterargument, see pp. 212–19.

52 Thomas Killigrew, *The Prisoners* (London, 1640–41), B7r, B9r.

53 Thomas Nabbes, *Hannibal and Scipio* (London, 1637), I1v. Shirley's Cockpit play, *The Maid's Revenge*, was written almost a decade before *Hannibal and Scipio* and also features a '*maske of Souldiers*' (H3r).

54 Tribble, *Early Modern Actors*, pp. 101–2, 114.

55 See Tribble, *Early Modern Actors*, p. 114, and Jean E. Howard, 'Dancing Masters and the Production of Cosmopolitan Bodies in Caroline Town Comedy', in *Localizing Caroline Drama: Politics and Economics of the Early Modern English Stage, 1625–1642*, ed. Adam Zucker and Alan B. Farmer (Basingstoke: Palgrave Macmillan, 2006), pp. 183–211, who notes that country dancing was typically opposed to courtly dancing in that it 'emphasized rougher movements, groups of dancers rather than couples, and often bodies that bent parallel to the ground rather than being held elegantly erect' (p. 192).

56 James Shirley, *The Grateful Servant* (London, 1630), I2r–v.

57 Robert Davenport, *A New Trick to Cheat the Devil* (London, 1639), F4v.

58 Kirke, *The Seven Champions*, G4r; James Shirley, *The Traitor* (London, 1635), E4v, F1r; Thomas Middleton and William Rowley, *The Changeling* (London, 1653), G4v; Thomas Heywood, *Love's Mistress* (London, 1636), K1v.

59 John Ford, *The Chronicle History of Perkin Warbeck* (London, 1634), F2v.

60 John Ford, *Love's Sacrifice* (London, 1633), H1r–v.

61 *OED*, 'anticke in antic, adj. and n.'; 'anticke in antique, adj and n.', http://www.oed.com (accessed 6 February 2015).

62 Roberta Barker, '"An honest dog yet": Performing *The Witch of Edmonton*', *Early Theatre*, 12.2 (2009), 163–82 (pp. 169, 171).

63 John Ford and Thomas Dekker, *The Sun's Darling* (London, 1656), C1r–v.

64 Tribble, *Early Modern Actors*, p. 105.

65 Claire Hansen, 'The Complexity of Dance in Shakespeare's *A Midsummer Night's Dream*', *Early Modern Literary Studies*, 18 (2015), 5, https://extra.shu.ac.uk/emls/journal/index.php/emls/article/view/136 (accessed 4 September 2023).

66 James Shirley, *The School of Compliment* (London, 1631), L2r.

67 James Shirley, *The Ball* (London, 1639), C2v.

68 Howard, 'Dancing Masters', p. 184.

69 This was a play that was particularly, and pointedly, current: Henry Herbert censored it before the first performance since it 'impersonated divers members of the court'; Bawcutt (ed.), *Control and Censorship*, p. 177.

70 Howard, 'Dancing Masters', p. 192.

71 John Astington, 'The Popularity of Cupid's Revenge', *Studies in English Literature, 1500–1900*, 19 (1979), 215–27 (p. 225).

72 Thomas Heywood, *The Escapes of Jupiter*, ed. Henry D. Janzen, Malone Society Reprints (Oxford: Oxford University Press, 1978 [1976]), pp. 50, 52.

73 See Bentley, *Jacobean and Caroline Stage*, IV, pp. 937–8. It is likely that the play was written during the long plague closure in which Queen Henrietta's Men broke under Beeston's management. It was first performed at the Salisbury Court. Nabbes had written for both Queen Henrietta's Men and the Salisbury Court company prior to 1637. Wiggins (*British Drama*, #2543) gives 1636 as a best guess, however, placing this play with the King's Revels at Salisbury Court.

74 Thomas Nabbes, *Microcosmos* (London, 1637), B2r.

75 Martin Wiggins suggests the drawing of a curtain (*British Drama*, #2085).

76 See pp. 220–22.

77 Thomas Middleton, *No Wit, No Help Like a Woman's* (London, 1657), F6v.

78 But see David Nicol, 'The Title-Page of *The World Tossed at Tennis*: A Portrait of a Jacobean Playing Company?', *Notes and Queries*, 53.2 (2006), 158–9, who suggests that this woodcut may represent the original company onstage and in action.

79 John Melton, *Astrologaster* (London, 1620), p. 31.

80 John Ford, Thomas Dekker, and William Rowley, *The Witch of Edmonton* (London, 1658), C3r, C3v.

81 William Shakespeare, *A Midsummer Night's Dream*, in *The Oxford Shakespeare: The Complete Works*, ed. Stanley Wells and Gary Taylor (Oxford: Oxford University Press, 1988), 2.1.43, 37.

82 Keith Thomas, *Religion and the Decline of Magic* (London: Penguin, 1971), pp. 681–98.

83 Thomas, *Religion and the Decline of Magic*, p. 681.

84 Thomas Heywood and Richard Brome, *The Late Lancashire Witches* (London, 1634), D3v.

85 See Helen Ostovich's introduction to the play, on the *Richard Brome Online* edition: https://www.dhi.ac.uk/brome/viewOriginal.jsp?play=LW&type=CRIT (accessed 4 September 2023).

86 Barbara H. Traister, 'Magic and the Decline of Demons: A View of the Stage', in *Magical Transformations on the Early Modern English Stage*, ed. Lisa Hopkins and Helen Ostovich (Farnham: Ashgate, 2014), pp. 19–30.

87 Robert Graves, *Lighting the Shakespearean Stage, 1576–1642* (Carbondale: Southern Illinois University Press, 1999), pp. 125–57.

88 White, '"When Torchlight made an Artificial Noon"'.

89 White, '"When Torchlight made an Artificial Noon"', p. 118; Graves, *Lighting the Shakespearean Stage*, pp. 189, 197.

90 Martin White, 'By Indirections Find Directions Out: Unpicking Early Modern Stage Directions', in *Stage Directions and Shakespearean Theatre*, ed. Sarah Dustagheer and Gillian Woods (London: Bloomsbury, 2018), pp. 191–212 (p. 200).

91 Middleton and Rowley, *The Changeling*, F2r.

92 This may be possible within the logic of the play; for an illuminating account of the compulsive yet toxic relationship between Beatrice-Joanna and De Flores,

see Mary Floyd-Wilson's chapter on 'tragic antipathies' in the play, in her *Occult Knowledge, Science, and Gender on the Shakespearean Stage* (Cambridge: Cambridge University Press, 2013), pp. 91–109.

93 Both Romeo and Paris light their way to Juliet's tomb with torches, and this scene would have taken place in afternoon daylight upon an amphitheatre stage.

94 White, '"When Torchlight made an Artificial Noon"', p. 125.

95 White, '"When Torchlight made an Artificial Noon"', p. 125.

96 John Fletcher, *The Night-Walker*, rev. James Shirley (London, 1640), D2r.

97 White, '"When Torchlight made an Artificial Noon"', p. 127.

98 White, '"When Torchlight made an Artificial Noon"', p. 127.

99 Graves, *Lighting the Shakespearean Stage*, p. 195. Also in contrast to Graves's view, see Martin White's argument regarding the effects of light in the richly decorated theatres ('"When Torchlight made an Artificial Noon"', p. 129, and mentioned below).

100 Eva Griffith, *A Jacobean Company and its Playhouse: The Queen's Servants at the Red Bull Theatre (c. 1605–1619)* (Cambridge: Cambridge University Press, 2013), pp. 112–14.

101 *The Annales, or Generall Chronicle of England, begun first by maister Iohn Stow, and after him continued and augmented with matters forreyne, and domestique, anncient and moderne, vnto the ende of his present yeere 1614. By Edmond Howes* (London, 1615), p. 926, quoted in E. K. Chambers, *The Elizabethan Stage*, 4 vols (Oxford: Clarendon Press, 1923), II, p. 419.

102 Gwilym Jones, 'Storm Effects in Shakespeare', in *Shakespeare's Theatres and the Effects of Performance*, ed. Farah Karim-Cooper and Tiffany Stern (London: Bloomsbury, 2013), pp. 33–50 (pp. 35–7).

103 Thomas Heywood, *If You Know Not Me, You Know Nobody*, Part II (London, 1633), E2v.

104 Heywood, *Escapes of Jupiter*, ed. Janzen, pp. 52, 53.

105 White, '"When Torchlight made an Artificial Noon"', p. 129.

106 Griffith, *A Jacobean Company and its Playhouse*, pp. 69–70.

5
THOMAS HEYWOOD'S 'NOYSE AND SHOWS': RECONCILING THE RED BULL FARE

Thomas Heywood made the transfer from the Red Bull to the Cockpit with Christopher Beeston in 1616, and continued to write plays for the theatre throughout the next decade and during the occupancy of Queen Henrietta's Men. He was a self-proclaimed prolific writer, stating that he had a hand or '*at the least a maine finger*' in over two hundred and twenty works written over the period; he was also the second most prominent dramatist to contribute to and shape the Cockpit repertory.[1] Not only did he write new plays for the company, but many of his plays written originally for the Red Bull migrated with him to be revived by Queen Henrietta's Men into the 1630s, including *If You Know Not Me, You Know Nobody*, Parts I and II, *The Rape of Lucrece*, and Part I of *The Fair Maid of the West*. This circumstance meant that Heywood was obliged to revisit some of his oldest, earliest work decades later. In this chapter I focus on the specific ways in which this major dramatist worked to reconcile old drama with new fashions on the Cockpit stage, and create new aesthetic contexts for the Red Bull fare before audiences of the indoor playhouse. The discussion draws on the constructions of audience taste and theatrical traditions discussed in Chapter 3, and the appreciation of the breadth of repertory styles in play at the Cockpit developed in Chapter 4, to analyse the particular response of Heywood to the demands of the repertory. It suggests that Heywood not only sought to create continuity in staging across his drama for the Red Bull and the Cockpit, but in some cases worked actively to exaggerate or emphasise the 'old-fashioned' features of both new and old plays. At the same time, he was engaged in a strenuous renegotiation of dramatic currency and the expectations of particular audiences. In many ways, Heywood's cultural and theatrical agenda was pivotal to Beeston's project at the Cockpit, and the continued saleability of its repertory.

Yet Heywood's involvement in the repertory of Queen Henrietta's Men has been hitherto understated. This owes largely to his persistent association in criticism with older, outdoor-playhouse repertories, which has defined his capacity and reputation in criticism as a popular, 'amphitheatre' playwright.[2] Arthur Melville Clark described him as a 'journeyman-playwright *par excellence*', and suggested that 'Beaumont and Fletcher opposed the vulgar taste of the day and Jonson the unlettered, but of all the dramatists Heywood was the most compliant with the public'; he described Heywood's dramatic style in *Love's Mistress* as 'rather plebeian but wholly delightful'.[3] Heywood's early plays, such as the spectacular serialisation of *The Ages* and the standalone *The Rape of Lucrece*, have come to characterise his dramatic style – a style that is perceived as fundamentally and definitively opposed to the kinds of plays written for performance at the Cockpit. As we have seen in the last chapter, these styles and the dramatic features that defined them, including the use of fireworks and battle scenes, were in fact often revived and celebrated on the Cockpit stage. But in criticism, Heywood's interest in spectacle, in '*fire-workes all over the house*', remains linked to the outdoor venues for which he wrote in his early career.[4] Heywood, writing in his early to mid-sixties to satisfy the practical and aesthetic demands of the Cockpit as they have been construed, has become a peripheral figure in criticism of the 1630s and an unlikely representative of the repertory. He sits awkwardly at its edges, marooned by the apparently irreconcilable legacy of his theatrical past.

Heywood's difficult position in criticism is compounded by the often complicated history of his plays in print, the primary means by which repertories are now knowable. His ambivalence towards print was public and sustained. In the prefatory material to *The Rape of Lucrece* he articulated his resistance to the '*double sale*' of plays, '*first to the Stage, and after to the presse*'.[5] His address in the 1631 publication of *The Fair Maid of the West* stated that '*my Plaies have not beene exposed to the publike view of the world in numerous sheets, and a large volume; but singly (as thou seest) with great modesty, and small noise*'.[6] Yet Heywood's involvement with the quarto publication of his plays suggests that he considered publication to be a conspicuous dimension of his work. Elsewhere, he indicated that it had never been his ambition to be 'Volumniously read' through the publication of a collected works, but in 1632 he became preoccupied with publishing a collection of some of his works together.[7] Benedict Scott Robinson has attributed Heywood's 'marginal' role in 'our sense of the main currents of early modern drama' to 'the material forms in which [his plays] were produced', which did not include a Folio or collected works.[8] Robinson suggests that Heywood's publishing strategy and the privileging of performance over print was 'out of step with the publishing activities of his younger colleagues', while Nora Johnson has also argued for Heywood's individuality in the period as a playwright who 'relocate[d] the source of writerly authority' in theatrical and commercial performance rather than in opposition to it, and as a writer open to 'relax[ing] the strictures of learned decorum'.[9] Heywood's seemingly nonconformist approach has resisted the categories by which drama has been evaluated and classified. His perceived commitment to amphitheatre styles and 'popular' performance, over literary reputation and the newer fashions developing in the indoor playhouses, has affirmed his connections with an ageing Elizabethan era.

The attention bestowed on Heywood's earlier plays has also diminished recognition of the scale and impact of his work for the competitive Caroline repertory of Queen Henrietta's Men. Heywood is an important figure partly because his playwriting career spanned more than thirty years and a wide, almost comprehensive sweep of the London playhouses. His work straddles both amphitheatre and hall-playhouse traditions, and provides a powerful and illuminating example of the reappropriation of amphitheatre fare in process. As this chapter argues, his revivals and updated serialisations for Queen Henrietta's Men provide a bridge between drama written over spatial and temporal divides, and across the cultural gap that has been assumed to hold between plays of amphitheatre and hall-playhouse provenance. The need to return to Heywood's work in the context of Queen Henrietta's Men is imperative if the full extent of his contribution to the dynamics of 1630s drama is to be recognised.

In the discussion that follows, Heywood's engagement with the aesthetic and cultural discourse surrounding drama of the period moves him from the margins of critical accounts of the Cockpit repertory to its centre. As Heywood was aware, the strategy adopted in the revival of old drama at the Cockpit relied upon the continuity of taste among audiences divided by financial resources and time. The movement of plays between the amphitheatres and the hall-playhouses and their continued revival over the 1630s abjures any unproblematic distinction between what Bentley described as drama written for 'two different kinds of audiences frequenting two different kinds of theatres and demanding two different kinds of plays' – a distinction that he saw in place from 1625, with theatre audiences becoming increasingly divergent. In this reading theatre itself became a 'dual institution: one theatre for the court, the gentry, and the literate, another theatre for the vulgar masses'.[10] Yet though the act of revival works against such a division, Heywood seems to have become increasingly aware that the permeability of the boundaries between hall and amphitheatre drama required the careful renegotiation of his older plays within the Cockpit repertory. The complex, multifaceted discourse that was undergoing consolidation in the prologues and paratexts of the time, and that sought to establish distinctions between the theatres, their audiences and their tastes, worked to situate Heywood's Red Bull fare in an awkward position. For Heywood, it threatened discredit and devaluation. But this was a challenge that he chose to address directly and deliberately, in the negotiation of the emerging narrative that sought to separate and oppose his dramatic pursuits at the amphitheatres and at the Cockpit. Furthermore, Heywood's interest in the spectacularly theatrical, and the means and methods by which he attempted to bridge the widening critical gap between his plays for the Red Bull and the Cockpit, offers crucial insight into a very particular form of repertory management. This management was not administrative but rather creative, determined by Heywood's awareness of the professional need to celebrate the continued revival of old drama in the aesthetic climes of the 1630s.

The remainder of this chapter explores the different ways in which Heywood went about legitimising potentially outdated dramatic conventions on stage, through revival and revision, serialisation, and the composition of innovative repertory pieces that actively rehearsed and reshaped the debate over aesthetic value. It begins with an exploration of *The Escapes of Jupiter* – an elision and abridgement of his earlier *Ages* serialisation for the Red Bull, which appears to have been written with a Cockpit performance in mind – and then moves on to examine the cases of *If You Know Not Me, You Know Nobody* and its Caroline revival, and *The Fair Maid of the West*. The discussion provides a more in-depth analysis of the old-fashioned features of *The Rape of Lucrece*, which grew in popularity and prominence as the part of Valerius expanded over the 1630s. The final section of the chapter explores the cultural politics of *Love's Mistress*, Heywood's most explicit intervention into the debate over audience preference and the desirability of spectacular, so-called 'ignorant' conventions associated with 'dull' audiences.

SERIALISATION AND THE SYNTHESIS OF REPERTORY

The Escapes of Jupiter

In the prologue to *The Royal King and the Loyal Subject*, a play performed at the Cockpit between 1626 and the year of its publication in 1637, Heywood puts forward a case for the value of theatrically fantastic representations and for the importance of the past. Detailing his search for inspiration, a process requiring the stretching of '*Invention*' in order to furnish Chronicles that are otherwise 'barren growne', he writes that 'no History / We have left unrifled, our Pens have beene dipt / As well in opening each hid Manuscript'.[11] Heywood invokes a sense of 'high' and 'low' culture in his imaginative sweep of the earth and heavens, in which he has 'Div'd low as to the Center, and then reacht / Unto the *Primum mobile* above'. He ascribes equal priority to both the elevated and subterranean reaches of invention, parenthesising that 'Nor scapt things intermediate'. This metaphor of exploration as an analogy for playwriting works to legitimise the historical past and its possibilities. The threefold gathering of a classical past, theatrical history, and the real-time experience of seventeenth-century audiences is foregrounded most vividly in the prologue's opening, which claims that 'To give consent to this most curious Age / The gods themselves we have brought downe to the Stage, / And figur'd them in Planets, made even Hell / Deliver up the Furies' (A3r). Heywood connects past and present in the invocation of the physical embodiment of a classical and theatrical trope. But this prologue appears before a play conspicuously lacking in representations of mythological spectacle: some of these styles of representation 'live' still, he says, but some have been 'cast' away.

Four years prior to the publication of *The Royal King and the Loyal Subject*, the prologue accompanying Heywood's *The English Traveller* (1633) worked to justify the neglect of staging strategies associated with an earlier era of amphitheatre styles. Here, the speaker of the prologue warns the audience of Queen Henrietta's Men that it is '*A Strange Play you are like to have, for know, / We use no Drum, nor Trumpet, nor Dumbe show*' (he is quick to add that '*Yet these [are] all good, and still in frequent use / With our best* Poets').[12] The prologue's author attributes this '*defect*' to '*his selfe will*', in response to his perception of the market's oversaturation of '*so many*' plays '*in that kind*', rather than to an aesthetic judgement concerning its validity or appeal. Yet the uncertainty over the reception of the '*Strange Play*' is manifest, despite the prologue's notional conformity with the conception of a refined, witty, and learned Caroline drama that favours '*bare Lines*' over '*Song, Dance, Masque*' which can '*bumbaste out a Play*'.[13]

Heywood's *Ages* serialisation did not entrust theatrical success to 'bare Lines' alone. The series included *The Golden Age*, *The Silver Age*, and *The Brazen Age*, and treated classical, mythological material between 1611 and 1613 on the Red Bull stage. These are plays rich in extrovert display. Clark described them as 'gay comedies, rollicking farces, beautiful pastorals and masques, and blood-and-thunder tragedies, with a super-abundance of dumb-shows, spectacles, and machines'. He lists among their notable theatrical features 'descents from heaven and ascents from hell, metamorphoses, dumb-shows, battles and revels and hunting-scenes, elaborate and spectacular properties, fireworks and pageantry'.[14] This is the kind of spectacle that has become synonymous with the style of the open, older amphitheatres, but around a decade after the *Ages* plays were first performed Heywood appears to have recognised their potential appeal for the Cockpit audience. He began to prepare a manuscript text of *The Escapes of Jupiter*, a play which exists in that form alone. The drama reworks and condenses scenes from *The Silver Age* and *The Golden Age* into one play, and retains all of the spectacle of the original sources. This was an active reappropriation of the performance history of the Red Bull, and a decisive affirmation of the value that Heywood attached to it.

The Escapes of Jupiter has uncertain theatrical provenance; there is no clear evidence that it was ever acted. It seems to have been prepared with performance in mind, since one of the stage directions reads 'A song, iff you will'. Its relationship to Heywood's earlier amphitheatre drama led Clark and critics who followed him to associate the play exclusively with the Red Bull.[15] But the play was associated with the Cockpit, since Craven Ord's transcript of Henry Herbert's office-book entry states that, in 1623, this 'olde Playe' was licensed and 'taken from the Cockpitt upon the remove of some of the sharers' – likely to have been members of the Prince's Men, who had recently left the theatre.[16] The Escapes of Jupiter, or some version of the material, might well have been performed at the Cockpit prior to this date, then, embodying a popular repertory tradition that Heywood had been labouring to update, or make new, using scenes from his older and established Red Bull plays. Heywood's efforts to assimilate older drama into the Cockpit repertory appear to have taken the form of rewriting the Ages serialisation into a discrete, contained entertainment. Rather than edit or dumb down the spectacle of The Ages, it serves instead to condense and telescope the plays' dramatic effects and narrative. In this sense, The Escapes of Jupiter is a repertory piece of singular aesthetic concentration and focus, a bold testament to Heywood's investment in the continuing currency of amphitheatre fare.

If Heywood had intended The Escapes of Jupiter for performance at the Cockpit, this was also part of a strategy that he might have bolstered with the revival of The Iron Age. This two-part play continued the classical storytelling begun in the older Ages plays, this time relating the events of the Trojan War. It is unclear when The Iron Age plays were written. They were printed in 1632, and the note to the reader in the second part suggests they had 'beene long since Writ, and suited with the Time then', which suggests a much earlier date of composition than c. 1631.[17] But the plays' late publication in 1632 might suggest a renewed interest in this drama, and a revival of the plays in the Caroline era. Heywood's address to the reader in the first part notes that 'these were the Playes often (and not with the least applause,) Publickely Acted by two Companies, vppon one Stage at once, and haue at sundry times thronged three seuerall Theaters, with numerous and mighty Auditories'.[18] Joseph Quincy Adams suggested that the two companies to have performed these plays together were the Queen's Men at the Red Bull and the King's Men, since they presented The Silver Age and The Rape of Lucrece at court together in 1612.[19] The involvement of the King's Men was also suggested, to Adams, by the number of stages noted here: the Red Bull, home of the original

Silver Age and *The Rape of Lucrece,* and the two venues of the King's Men, the Globe and the Blackfriars.[20] But given that Beeston retained a share in the Red Bull, the other two public theatres in question could also have been the Cockpit theatre and the Curtain. E. K. Chambers also suggested the Curtain as a likelihood, but Eva Griffith's discovery of Beeston's interest in the site of the Curtain grounds the connection between the theatres more firmly.[21] The Curtain was also the venue to which the Prince's Men transferred following their occupancy of the Cockpit, though they had already moved to the Red Bull by August 1623 when they claimed *The Escapes of Jupiter* for their own use. If Beeston did choose to move plays around the theatres with which he was involved, as he appears to have moved acting troupes, the relationship between the Cockpit, Red Bull, and Curtain repertories was more complicated and permeable than has been recognised.[22] The stages of transition between companies and theatres that is evidenced by both *The Escapes of Jupiter* and *The Iron Age* might be indicative of this collaborative repertory process in action.

If You Know Not Me, You Know Nobody

Heywood was involved in the revival of other Red Bull plays around the same time – a two-part serialisation which relates parts of the story of Elizabeth I's reign, called *If You Know Not Me, You Know Nobody.* Serialisations were an important commercial phenomenon of Elizabethan theatre and, as such, of the early amphitheatre repertories.[23] These two plays, dating to between 1603 and 1605, have been thought representative of the 'old favourites' and 'Elect-Nation' plays that lauded 'the heydey of Elizabethan England' in Henslowe's day, characterised as 'Foxean' in their relentless Protestantism and choice of source material.[24] The abundance of editions of the plays that appeared in print from 1606 onwards has prompted claims for their 'box-office' success and 'enduring popularity'.[25] In terms of genre, the serial's quasi-historical focus aligns it with the English history plays, which reached the peak of their popularity in the professional repertory companies in the late 1590s but continued to be commercially successful beyond this moment.[26] The plays are also pointedly political, in that their glorification of Elizabeth I as a Protestant, divinely ordained monarch constitutes an oblique criticism of the reign of James I.[27] The staging of a queen not two years dead, and the proximity of the plays' performance to recent history, has worked to situate the serialisation within a specific cultural and theatrical moment.

The connection between *If You Know Not Me* and its original conditions of production has also been illustrated with reference to the plays' use of old-fashioned staging devices associated with the Elizabethan theatre. Part I employs several traditional processions of state and dumb shows: a symbolic mime reminiscent of morality plays, and a device which Michael

Dobson suggests would have appeared antiquated by around 1600, when it was incorporated by Shakespeare into *Hamlet*.[28] It features a clown figure – a stock character in early English drama, which has been convincingly linked to the Vice character of the morality plays – and angels materialise to overlay an allegorical, moralistic schema on the play's narrative events.[29] The staging of the 'blasing Starre' in Part II has a similar function, read as an omen within the play. Mark Bayer has related the play's design in these respects and others, including the attention to 'lower-class characters', to the inferred capacity of a Red Bull audience, describing how 'enhancing moments of spectacle, magnifying the role of lower-class characters, and focusing on the economic charity of Elizabeth towards her subjects' enabled Heywood to 'render the play intelligible and enhance its educative value for less educated audiences'.[30]

But the decision of Queen Henrietta's Men to revive both parts of the serialisation at the Cockpit suggests that these plays were not as bound to the moment of their original performance as has been assumed. A prologue to 'the Play of Queen Elizabeth as it was last revived at the Cockpit' was published in 1637 in Heywood's *Pleasant Dialogues and Dramas*, and is accompanied by an epilogue; both of these texts then appear in Nathanial Butter's 1639 edition of the first part. The second part, meanwhile, features evidence of dramatic revival through revisions made to the text which appear in the 1633 edition. This double revival signals the company's commitment to a duo of plays written thirty years previously, deemed by some to cater for the tastes of a Red Bull audience, and which pointedly invoke political and social nostalgia for the late queen and, through the act of revival, the drama and its themes of decades ago.

The new dramatic material that Heywood added to Part II, prior to its 1633 printing, includes the addition of an extra Chorus at the close of the play, and a new final scene. The effect of these revisions is to heighten the sense of gathering nostalgia around Elizabeth's reign and to affirm the play's relationship to the historical past by emphasising old or archaic features of performance. The liminal and old-fashioned Chorus figure illuminates the artifice of theatre through the exposition that he provides. This was a figure whom Heywood had retained in *The Escapes of Jupiter*, paying tribute to the origins of the device in ancient Greek drama: here, the character of Homer acts as the Chorus, interspersing the action with regular metatheatrical commentary. Heywood's Elizabethan Chorus in *If You Know Not Me* also embellishes the play's political commentary, however, and works – three decades after the drama was first written – to supplement the 'Foxean', anti-Catholic sentiments of the original. The Chorus draws attention to Elizabeth as 'strongly planted in her peoples heart' and 'vndaunted', while foregrounding Philip of Spain's 'stratagems, plots and designes / Both to the vtter ruine of our Land, / And our religion'; the closing scene centres on Francis Drake's return to English soil having defeated the Spanish Armada.[31] John Watkins has argued that the 'revised' character of Elizabeth I is conveyed here as 'bolder, more commanding, and more hostile', while Teresa Grant notes that the 'extra scenes make a huge difference to the way Elizabeth is perceived by the audience'.[32] She underscores the significance of the 1633 revival alongside the renewal of war with Roman Catholic Spain under the reign of Charles I.[33]

The design of these plays thus works to intermingle and inscribe political commentary with their formal presentation on the stage: Heywood sought here to anchor his amphitheatre drama on the indoor Caroline stage in a way that linked any political agenda he might have had with the ageing aesthetics of his serialisation. He recognised that part of the draw of the serialisation resided in its association with earlier styles of drama and a past cultural history, and worked to retroactively affirm the plays' relationships with their amphitheatre origins in an uncompromising assertion of the theatrical appeal of the traditional Chorus figure. Rather than revising or reworking the serial's theatrical features for a later audience by minimising or subsuming outdated presentational devices, these elements persist and are deliberately emphasised in the 1633 text.

The Fair Maid of the West

Heywood took a different approach when he came to revive *The Fair Maid of the West* with Queen Henrietta's Men in 1630. This play, too, was of old Red Bull stock, and also summons the spirit of Queen Elizabeth and her golden age – this time in her namesake Bess, a tavern-maid from Plymouth, who is both confused with the queen and inspired by her. Written between 1609 and 1611, this is a tale of seafaring adventure and piracy that features a dumb show and a Chorus. Instead of revising any part of the original drama for revival, Heywood went one step further to write a whole new play which would build on its former success and form a new serialisation: the earlier Part I was revived onstage alongside a brand new sequel, Part II. This strategy was more costly for the company, and entailed more risk than the revision of already old plays. The expenses of licensing fees had to be paid, the playwright needed to be paid (more than would be the case with revision for revival), and the company was required to source (or improvise) new properties and costumes.[34] Here, the 'cheap' option of revival turned into a more concerted project to build upon the foundations provided by the Red Bull repertory. The writing of a sequel represented a direct investment in the narrative and aesthetics of Part I, and constitutes Heywood's most concerted attempt to reframe one of his revivals for a 1630s audience.

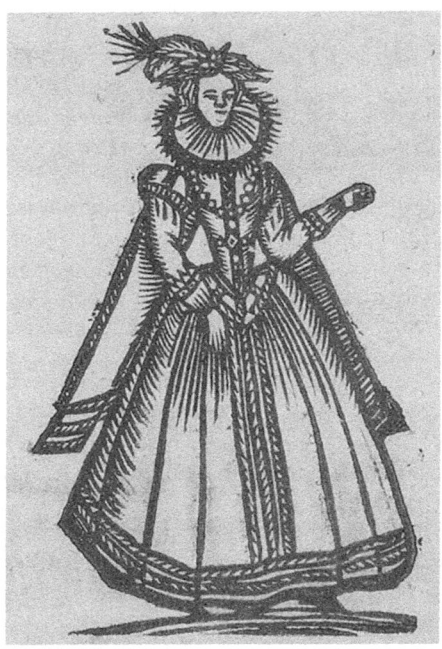

5   Title-page illustration from Thomas Heywood, *The Fair Maid of the West* (London, 1631). The Warden and Scholars of Winchester College

Heywood's sequel followed the original around twenty years after its first performance, and he chose to address the gap between composition and Caroline revival by appropriating and adapting newly fashionable genres to sit alongside the original play. In particular, Part II draws on the 1630s fashion for tragicomedy and the representation of heroic women that began to emerge over this period. In some ways the Jacobean original was an ideal candidate for revival under these terms, as dramatists and audiences began to place more emphasis on female agency and *femme forte*, in response to Queen Henrietta's powerful theatrical interventions in court drama and the creative endeavours of the courtier dramatists in their plays for the professional theatres.[35] Bess is a cross-dressing, sea-voyaging, virginal heroine with a distinctive voice on the early modern stage: the revival of this character in the 1630s, amid heroines who included the titular character of Shirley's *Rosania* and Evandra of Davenant's *Love and Honour*, was both timely and resourceful.[36]

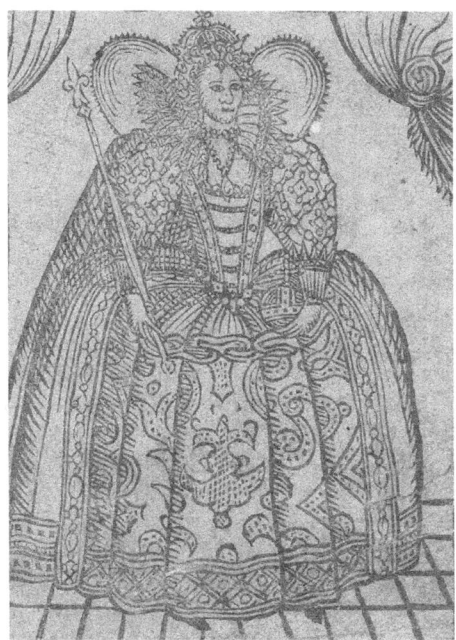

6   Title-page illustration from Thomas Heywood, *If You Know Not Me, You Know No Body* (London, 1633). Bodleian Libraries, University of Oxford, 2025. Weston Mal. 249 (3)

Heywood's experimentation with tragicomedy in the sequel similarly repositions the revival within a contemporary market for plays. Part II opens in a noticeably darker and more sinister vein, leaving the comic action of the first part behind as the action veers towards the bounds of tragedy. Soliloquies, the threat of sexual violence, and the dismembered head that is presented onstage are just some of the ways in which Heywood effects this transition in tone.[37] The scenes of rustic England in the first part are left behind for a foreboding foreign court, in which the lascivious Queen Tota broods, opening the play with a monologue that draws on the language and imagery of revenge tragedy:

> Can womanish ambition, heat of blood,
> Or height of birth brooke this, and not revenge?
> [...] I have a thousand projects in my braine,
> But can bring none to purpose.[38]

This contrasts starkly with the tone and action of Part I, which rehearses a comfortable formula of chastity tests which build towards final proof of Bess's standing as 'a Girle worth gold'.[39] The persistence of Mullisheg and Tota's mutually destructive behaviour in Part II poses a threat strong enough to Bess that she plans an elaborate bed-trick – a trope that has uncertain generic allegiances. Plays that employed the bed-trick in the middle of the first decade of the seventeenth century tended to be comedies, such as *All's Well That Ends Well* and *Measure for Measure*, but in 1622 Middleton had appropriated the device for tragic ends on the Cockpit stage in *The Changeling* – a play that remained in repertory alongside Heywood's new sequel.

Heywood's experimentation with genre in Part II granted the original Part I a fresh theatrical identity and a new lease of life upon the stage. But while Part II might suggest an impulse to revise and update a story for a 1630s audience, Heywood also ensured continuity in dramatic style by incorporating a Chorus and dumb show into his Caroline sequel, effectively 'backdating' the drama. The appearance of both of these more archaic features also occurs at a moment that enacts a decisive shift in the genre and dramatic style of the play, towards that of its much earlier prequel. Heywood effects a conspicuous return to seafaring adventure, in which Bess and her lover Spencer set sail only to be parted again at sea by marauding French pirates. A complicated romantic tryst takes place at court between the Duke of Florence and Bess, before Bess is publicly reconciled with Spencer. This is a moment at which the generic identity of the play becomes muddled again, as Spencer's life hangs in the balance throughout the play's final moments. Yet despite the play's threat to depart into tragedy, the second half of Part II ends as part-romance, part-comedy, in a finale characterised by discovery and reconciliation. In this respect the first half of Part II turns out to be incongruous in the context of the serialisation, veering experimentally away from comedic contexts that are established in Part I. The queasy tragicomic opening of the sequel is demarcated from the remainder of the narrative by the Chorus's entry on to the stage: his intervention heralds a crafted return to an older dramatic tradition. By reviving this traditional theatrical figure in his new play, Heywood worked to reaffirm the value of his earlier theatrical styles. At the same time this device worked to bind the serialisation more decisively, and cohesively, within the Cockpit repertory, linking the plays through the repetition of old dramatic traditions and a strong, shared aesthetic identity.

For Queen Henrietta's Men, the staggered serialisation of *The Fair Maid of the West* constituted an important repertory piece, in which Heywood's attempt to capitalise on Part I imbued it with a commercial value that extended beyond any potential that it had as a single play. The balancing act that Heywood performs here between exploiting new fashions and reaffirming the value of old traditions also provides an insight into his role in the development of the Cockpit repertory, while foregrounding some of the tensions inherent in that pursuit. Ensuring that new trends were incorporated into the repertory while retaining stage space for revivals that might otherwise become redundant was an important part of Heywood's work at the Cockpit.

CLOWNING IN THE COCKPIT: *THE RAPE OF LUCRECE*

Heywood's attempts to affirm the theatrical legitimacy of his revivals on the Cockpit stage through abridgement, revision, and delayed serialisation were decisive authorial steps that he made in the attempt to shape and govern the reception of Elizabethan and Jacobean drama on the Caroline stage. But *The Rape of Lucrece* offers a compelling example of the ways in which Red Bull drama could be adapted and transformed in revival through the collaborative efforts of the company and conditions of performance.

The Rape of Lucrece is likely to have passed from the Red Bull to the Cockpit in 1616, with both parts of *If You Know Not Me* and the first part of *The Fair Maid of the West*. The play has had a varied critical reception – Clark wrote that it 'was definitely a popular presentation of a classical plot for the Red Bull audience, to whom symmetry, restraint, form, and congruity were less intelligible than sentiment, tragical speeches, ribaldry, and the rest of the *olla podrida* of the plebeian theatres'.[40] But the inclusion of Heywood's *Lucrece* in the list of plays protected by the Lord Chamberlain for Beeston's Boys in 1639 suggests that it remained in the Cockpit repertory once Queen Anne's Men had left the premises, and continued to be a valuable repertory asset into the 1630s. This is also suggested by the play's multiple printings, which continually augmented the play with each new edition after 1608. As noted in the last chapter, the staging requirements of this particularly demanding play were unchanged as far as they are reflected by the stage directions in the printed texts. Instead, the changes that the text records took the form of musical contributions made by a visiting 'stranger' who took on the role of Publius Valerius in the play, and expanded it through the addition of new songs to the drama. The 1609 edition appends the first new song after the play, and foregrounds the incidental and impromptu nature of the additions by explaining that:

> Because we would not that any mans expectation should be deceiued in the ample printing of this booke. Lo (Gentle Reader) we haue inserted these few songs, which were added by the stranger that lately acted *Valerius* his part in forme following.[41]

The following edition of 1614 adds a 'Second Song', with no further emendation to the introductory material. After this date, the instability of the text escalates, as extra songs continue to appear in the text and are incorporated into the narrative. Four new songs appear in the 1630 edition, one of which also appears in Heywood's *Pleasant Dialogues and Dramas* (1637), and another in *A Challenge for Beauty* (1636). Five more emerge in the 1638 edition, the title-page of which states: 'The Copy revised, and sundry Songs before omitted, now inserted in their right places'.[42]

The continual addition of songs to the play embodies the theatrical process of improvisation and the organic development of performance while at the same time (paradoxically) fixing that process in print. Each text strives to represent a closed and authoritative version of the play 'lately acted', while simultaneously indicating the extent to which such closure and fixity could be indefinitely deferred. Whether any of these texts accurately represent a single performance of the play is highly doubtful, since old songs might have been substituted by new ones, verses dropped, or, as the 1638 title-page implies, simply 'omitted'. The staggered publication of the songs may suggest that their printing was prompted by performance, but whether or not the printed versions reflect even the sequence of the play in performance is also unclear; the collection of songs in the 1609 and 1614 editions in a kind of appendix at the end of the play-text suggests that these were songs that conspicuously resisted being consigned to 'their right places', though all of the texts are insistent on counting and cataloguing the songs that appear throughout the dialogue, referring to them in order as 'The first song', 'the second Song' up until 'The ninth song'. In the 1638 text, numbering the old songs is abandoned and priority is given to the new additions, drawing attention to their novelty by labelling them, for instance, 'The first new Song'.

Although the relationship between text and performance may be particularly difficult to unpick in this case, the performance of songs by a visiting actor was appropriate to the nature of Valerius's role in the play, which resonates with the traditional figure of the clown in early modern drama. For decades, clowns on the stage had offered theatrical interest by providing the real-time pleasures of improvisation, songs, and dance.[43] As Robert Weimann has argued, the role of the clown was also one that often failed to entirely subsume the personality of the actor, since like other characters on the early modern stage they ranged between the boundaries of the real world, in direct addresses to the audience, and the fictive world of the play.[44] The clown's traditionally low social status and his tendency to impromptu performance and audience interaction lent him an unpredictability, an openness and theatricality, that was potentially disruptive to the narrative time of the play. Bursting into song was just one manifestation of this kind of uncontainable event.

The role of Valerius had already been song-rich before the arrival of the visiting stranger at the Red Bull. Nora Johnson has suggested that Valerius's use of the festive mode of song offers the character a means of social commentary, and that the songs also function as emotional outlets for the play's unfolding events.[45] Valerius's early songs, which are present in the 1608 edition, do anchor his singing to the story's narrative framework: 'When Tarquin first in Court began, / And was approued King: / Some men for sodden ioy gan weepe, / And I for sorrow sing' (1608; C1v). This first melodious outburst is framed within an explicitly political context. Valerius's motivation for singing provokes rumours among his kinsmen, evidenced here by an extract of a conversation which takes place between Horatius and Colatinus:

> Whether it be that he is discontent
> Yet would not so appeare before the king
> Or whether in applause of these new Edicts.
> Which so distast the people, or what cause,
> I know not, but now hee's all musicall.
> Vnto the counsell chamber he goes singing,
> And whilest the king his wilfull edicts makes,
> In which nones tongue is powerfull saue the kings,
> Hee's in a corner, relishing strange aires. (1608; C1r–v)

There seems to be little more to say. The remainder of Valerius's songs in the 1608 edition are not accompanied by narrative exposition. And Valerius's songs become increasingly superfluous to narrative content as his role developed and was augmented over the course of the play's revival. As the influence and popularity of the 'stranger' grew, Valerius's role began to correspond more completely to the impromptu interventions of the traditional clown.[46] The increasingly extraneous nature of the songs also becomes more conspicuous as extra songs are added, and the narrative stream of this tragedy becomes further interpolated with bawdy and whimsical verse. The songs of the play are responsible for much of the critical distaste that has been directed at Heywood's retelling of this classical tragedy: Clark describes them as 'disgusting', 'inexcusable', and 'rubbish', part of 'the most shocking ribaldry and farce' to be found in the play; F. S. Boas suggested that Heywood's inclusion of the songs was a 'reprehensible concession to the taste of the audience at the Red Bull'.[47] Without committing to any kind of evaluative judgement, the accumulated narrative effect is clearly one of dispersion.

The interruption of narrative time by the numerous and spurious real-time performances of the singing actor recalls in particular the style of clowning developed by Richard Tarlton, who exploited the theatrical value inherent in improvisatory rhymes, extemporisation, and jokes.[48] By the 1630s this was a style of performance that had become long dated.[49] This was the same Tarlton, together with his successor Will Kempe, to whom one of Brome's characters in *The Antipodes* refers when he speaks of the 'dayes of *Tarlton* and *Kempe*, / Before the stage was purg'd from barbarisme'.[50] Wiles has suggested that after the 1590s, 'the clown was generally given a self-contained sub-plot and a smaller proportion of available stage time' than the character's predecessor, the Vice figure.[51] What we see in *The Rape of Lucrece* is the opposite of this phenomenon, as the role of Valerius is continually reinvigorated and develops into a larger and more conspicuous stage presence. It is likely that the visiting stranger was some kind of professional balladeer or peripatetic musician, a travelling tradesman in whose hands the role took on a life of its own. As the songs grew into the 1630s it seems unlikely that this same stranger would still have been intervening in the play on the Cockpit stage, but it is possible that giving the part to a travelling balladeer, or (more likely) continuing to embellish the singing part in performance, had become a tradition associated with Valerius's particular role. Transporting this kind of performance tradition into the Cockpit might have had a striking effect in the venue. We are accustomed to the nostalgic image of Tarlton raising raucous and spontaneous laughter from the amphitheatre audiences simply by peeping through a stage curtain, but the presence of this kind of personality in the indoor playhouses is a less familiar idea.

What is more extraordinary about Heywood's conception of Valerius and the way that his role was developed through revivals over the decades is the social standing of the character. For Valerius's role was not only increasingly prominent, it also became more and more socially charged, enacting an experiment with traditional clowning conventions that explicitly challenged the association of low, 'barbarous' theatre with the unrefined tastes of citizens. Clown figures on the early modern stage traditionally claimed a low social standing. But Publius Valerius was aristocratic, a member of Rome's ruling classes: as the title-page claims, he is a 'merry Lord among the Roman Peeres'. Despite his rank, Valerius's appropriation of clowning traditions still threatens to qualify his respectable status. The social decline that is effected by his perpetual singing is articulated by Collatinus, who states that:

> Conclusively hee's from a toward hopefull Gentleman,
> Transeshapt to a meere Ballater, none knowing
> Whence should proceed this transmutation. (1638, C1v)

Valerius's encounter with the named 'Clown' of the play nevertheless establishes a social hierarchy, in which the Clown begs 'My Lord Valerius' for a song and advice concerning 'how to choose a wench' (E2v–E3r). This is a scene that successfully points up the social divisions between the play's two clownish characters, while reaffirming Valerius's mastery of the theatrical tradition and its amusement value: he panders to the clown's requests, and indulges him (and us) in a bawdy digression.

It is through Valerius's social standing that Heywood articulates and enacts his wider defence of old-fashioned dramatic traditions. The 'transmutation' of a lord into a balladeer works to legitimise the pleasures brought to the stage by song and clowning, even while Valerius's peers speculate that his status sinks under the role. For Valerius is neither socially subservient nor rustic, though he is a 'friend of the people': Publius Valerius Poplicola, from *populus* (a people; the public) and *colo* (to cultivate; to tend). By ventriloquising traditionally 'low' forms of entertainment through his noble mouth, Valerius fulfils this function in explicitly theatrical terms. In this appropriation of the clowning tradition Heywood was not condescending to his audience at the Red Bull; rather, he was working to reposition simple theatrical pleasures as suitable and desirable entertainment for all, aristocrats and citizens alike; silken gulls and penny stinkards.[52]

For Heywood, this was a reworking of assumptions and social inflections that took root as early as 1607 or 1608, when *The Rape of Lucrece* was being written. But the character of Valerius became a vessel in which questions over older styles and traditions of drama converged, as the play moved on to the Cockpit stage and gained new cultural credence there. This case reveals how the collaborative powers of companies, dramatists, and actors could come together to enhance and maximise the performances and cultural politics of plays in repertory. As the role and prominence of Valerius grew into the Jacobean and Caroline eras, the contribution of Heywood's singing lord to the debate over high and low theatrical styles increased in direct proportion. And as Valerius's singing role was improvised and augmented over time, and its popularity multiplied as the decades wore on, Heywood's theatrical strategy was rewarded, and appreciation for the clown's songs on both the Red Bull and then the Cockpit stage was confirmed. In this sense, the company's investment in the clown figure through Valerius enabled it to address the aesthetic debate over desirable styles of drama through a character whose traditional function was to reach out beyond the world of the play, and help determine the preferences and responses of its audiences. In writing *The Rape of Lucrece*, Heywood sought to connect his drama with a musical tradition of clowning, innovate the role of the clown, and challenge assumptions of theatrical legitimacy and value all at once. It was the theatrical companies who performed the play that took their responsibility further – first Queen Anne's Men and then Queen Henrietta's – as they allowed and encouraged the character to grow in a way that embellished aspects of their theatrical identity.

IGNORANT ASSES: *LOVE'S MISTRESS*

Heywood's engagement with questions of audience taste and social status culminated in *Love's Mistress*, or 'The Queen's Masque'. This play is well known in theatre history because of its favourable reception before a royal audience in 1634 no fewer than three times in eight days, if its title-page is to be believed; it has become a landmark in the career of Queen Henrietta's Men. The play is representative of a perceived Caroline impulse among dramatists to connect their plays to courtly tastes, and is thought to demonstrate a concerted effort on the part of Heywood to ingratiate himself with the queen by writing in a new style of drama that drew on masque forms and appropriated source material that would appeal to her. But as this analysis will show, the play's popularity before Queen Henrietta Maria was not the sum of Heywood's accomplishment in *Love's Mistress*. This repertory piece performs a strenuous metatheatrical commentary on the value of the kinds of drama associated with the Red Bull and with Heywood's earlier citizen audiences, and presents a provocative aesthetic statement on behalf of Queen Henrietta's Men.

As the distinctions between old, amphitheatre-associated drama and new fashions sharpened further towards the mid-1630s, Heywood altered his approach and elected to challenge the debate by working it into the fabric of his newly written drama. In the extraordinary example that *Love's Mistress* provides, he used an innovative Choric framework to encompass the main action of the play, and transform a reflective commentary on theatrical style and presentation into something approaching active didacticism. Instructing the audience and guiding them through debates about aesthetic criteria, Heywood stages a radical intervention into audience-based judgements on dramatic traditions and makes his most cogent case for the continued currency of amphitheatre drama and its traditions on the indoor Caroline stage. He employs two classical characters to provide the Chorus through which this cultural agenda is articulated: Midas, who 'stands for ignorance' and is repeatedly ridiculed for his lack of artistic finesse and understanding, and Apuleius, who seeks in contrast to 'aduance / His Art', and refers to Midas as a dull and 'Mis-understanding foole'.[53] The Clown of the main plot functions as a mirror of Midas's cultural and aesthetic attitudes, and the relationship that is figured between the two is conceived as familial: Cupid calls the Clown a 'base *Midas* bastard' (E2v), and Apollo later refers to him as

Midas's 'squeaking sonne' (G2r). Midas's association with the idiotic is underscored when he enquires of an 'ignorant Asse' that enters onstage: 'What Reverend person's that of all the other? / I like him best.' He is answered drolly by Apuleius: 'That *Midas*, is thy brother, / A piece of mooving earth, illiterate, dull' (D1r–v).

The trope of the ass, so inextricably linked with Midas, is recurrent: ass's ears and costumes feature prominently as a visual motif that under-scores the distinction between rational, understanding man and the 'beast' whose 'dulnesse is increast' (B1r). It is Apuleius' task to enlighten Midas and, implicitly, the audience of the play from ignorance. His educative programme is made clear in the Introduction: 'Bee you the Judges, wee invite you all / Vnto this banquet Accademicall' (B2v) – and the audience's initial acceptance of the opposition between Apuleius and Midas is central to the success of Heywood's project. Between them, they ventriloquise the familiar narrative that 'The Vulgar are best pleas'd with noyse and showes' (K1v). Midas champions simple, clownish pleasures and begs Apuleius to 'let mee shew thee some of our fine sport, / Such as wee use heere in *Arcadia*', to which Apuleius acquiesces, commenting that 'Art some-times must give way to ignorance' (F1r). Later, Midas expresses a desire for 'some quaint device, / Some kick-shaw or other to keepe me waking': a triviality or 'worthless distraction' (K1r).[54] Apuleius obliges by ushering on to the stage the spectacular dance of Vulcan and the cyclopes, apolo-gising to the audience that 'by the leave of these spectators heere, / Ile suite mee to thy low capacitie' (K1r). The pleasure Midas takes in rustic comedy contrasts again with Apuleius' higher pursuits of poetry and art, but Heywood ultimately resists the legitimacy of this distinction. Midas's reference to 'some quaint device' calls to mind the use of stage apparatus or machinery for effects, such as that used in the prologue of *Love's Mistress* at its court performance: 'Cupid descending in a cloude' (A3r). The godly descent was a popular spectacle in court masques and on the Cockpit stage, yet Midas's account of the theatrical experience of listening to gods undermines any sense of reverence or awe that such a fantastic spectacle might produce in its audience. Midas has already complained:

> doe wee not daily see
> Every dull-witted Asse spit Poetrie:
> And for thy Scene, thou bring'st heere on the stage
> A young greene-sicknesse baggage to run after
> A little ape-fac'd boy thou tearm'st a god;
> Is not this most absur'd? (D1v)

Midas demands that the audience assess the effect from a practical per-spective, destabilising the wonder of what is before them.

Ben Jonson was also alert to the problems posed by stage descents, describing in the prologue to *Every Man In His Humour* 'the creaking throne' that was winched down over the stage in order to 'please' the 'boyes'.[55] His *Masque of Blackness* suffered a fate reminiscent of Midas's deconstructive analysis – the intended effect was of

> an artificial sea [that] was seen to shoot forth, as if it flowed to the land, raised with waves which seemed to move [...] two great sea-horses, as big as the life, put forth themselves, the one mounting aloft and writhing his head from the other, which seemed to sink forwards.

However, Sir Dudley Carleton witnessed the event and described instead 'a great Engine at the lower end of the Room, which had Motion, and in it were the Images of Sea-Horses [...] the Indecorum of it was, that there was all Fish and no water'.[56] Heywood thus figures the dramatic characteristics of courtly drama in contradictory terms. In one respect, he exploits its currency and markets the spectacle of *Love's Mistress* as a valuable commodity – the dedication advertises Inigo Jones's '*excellent Inventions* [... which appeared] *to the admiration of all the Spectators*' (A2v). He also ventriloquises its criticism through the dull and clownish Midas. And, in addition, he exposes it as a 'dull-witted' distraction that comes uncomfortably close to the 'noyse and showes' so despised by Apuleius.

Heywood continues to expose tensions at the heart of arguments that privileged courtly modes of drama over professional fare: the tastes of the elite over the commercial. The staging of entertainments that Apuleius publicly derides is a key strategy, as Heywood repeatedly indulges his audience with scenarios that actively oppose or undermine constructions of desirable taste with the onstage reality. Staging Apuleius' ridicule of rustic entertainment thus also creates the opportunity to experience its theatrical pleasure: even he admits of Midas's Arcadian dance that he is 'well pleased with your Pastorall mirth' (F1r). He later employs his own dance to educate Midas, in which '*a King and a Begger, a Young-man and an Old woman, a Leane man, a Fat woman*' enter and dance a round (H2r). The blurring of the boundaries here between low and 'ignorant' entertainment and educative 'art' destabilises any sharp distinction between the traditions at stake in the debate. The traditional function of the Chorus in *Love's Mistress* is manipulated and reworked here to operate as a site in which debates over taste and audience preference are rehearsed, and the theatrical appeal of Midas's brand of entertainment tested and affirmed. Lowly or rambunctious theatrical traditions become structurally inscribed within *Love's Mistress*, collapsing the category of 'art' and the traditions that it self-consciously claims to disown.

Furthermore, the debate reaches out of the Choric framework to interrupt the main action itself, when Midas is brought from the liminal range of the Chorus to act as an arbiter of taste in an adaptation of Pan and Apollo's musical contest. Pan's part is performed by the Clown, who delivers a verse of doggerel that delights in clunky rhyme and farce: '*Bee thou god, or bee thou man, / Thou art not like our Frying* Pan' (G1r). He is judged the winner by Midas, his 'father', but Apollo heaps scorn on the rustic and lowly song: 'Henceforth be all your rurall musicke such, / Made out of Tinkers, Pans, and Kettle-drummes' (G2r). In a familiar construal of responsibility over his audience's reception, he asserts that 'what's amisse / Is not in us, but in their ignorance'. But the staging of the contest, which is in itself a specific inflection of the debate over the legitimacy of theatrical traditions, reaffirms the pleasure that the Clown's song is able to provide in performance – a pleasure that is, in part, dependent on the construction of its rusticity. And the Clown and Midas escape the contest unharmed, in contrast to the fate of Marsyas. As Richard Rowland notes in his astute interpretation of this scene, Midas remembers 'poore *Marsias*' when he is summoned as judge to the competition: this was the upstart satyr who dared to challenge Apollo to his own musical contest, and 'for striving' with Apollo 'had his skin pull'd off' (F4r).[57] In Heywood's play, Apollo leaves the stage after bidding Midas's ears to lengthen, and wishing that 'all like thee' should 'Decay in knowledge' as they grow old, becoming 'twice Children' as they enter their elderly years (G2r).

The potential of Midas and Apuleius to expose tensions at the heart of arguments concerning spectacle and aesthetic judgements is central to Heywood's play: as the musical contest shows, their authority depends on the ways in which they are positioned in the drama as qualified arbiters of taste. Midas may be construed as 'dull' by his onstage companions, 'once of men, now King of beasts' (F4r), but it is his preferred styles of drama and entertainment that are authorised and validated in performance on the stage, and his judgement on which the outcome of the contest depends. Akin to the courtly Valerius in *The Rape of Lucrece*, King Midas's essentially 'royal' nature also complicates the classification of this character as 'low', in mischievous ways. Heywood's use of the ass's ears in costuming is also playful. The ass may be dull and beastly, but it is he who sports conspicuously outsized ears – perfect receptacles for hearing and for enabling the 'understanding auditory' that Webster had so desired in 1612. In this way, the ass's ears become a satirical manifestation of the prioritisation of learned poetry and the auditory over the delights of spectacle, the kickshaw and the quaint device. Furthermore, Rowland has drawn attention to the 'profound unreliability' of Apuleius as a narrator. This is a speaker who is contradictory, confused, and disingenuous all in his first few lines, 'sublimely unaware of the ambivalence that attends virtually his every utterance'.[58] The varying levels of authority that Heywood gives to Midas and Apuleius complicates their seemingly straightforward representation of two different traditions and viewpoints, then, so that what we are left with is a Choric framework that provides a staunch interrogation of the received cultural politics of aesthetics in the period.

The intellectual (or 'academic') 'banquet' of *Love's Mistress* ultimately resists an evaluative distinction between sophisticated and low tastes, between 'art' and the 'vulgar'. For Rowland, the play's 'confrontation between Apollo and Pan is a microcosmic version of the conflict between the new wave of court-sponsored dramatists and the older generation of playwrights who had earned their living [... on] the commercial stage'.[59] Bringing a wealth of critical perspectives and historical contexts to the table, Rowland explores how the figure of Apollo came to represent the 'ultimate arbiter of cultural taste' at the Caroline court; he reads the play as an attempt by Heywood to reclaim more irreverent cultures and arts from the tyranny of courtly aesthetics.[60] Here, I suggest that Heywood's energies are bound up to a lesser extent with the court itself, functioning primarily as an attempt to help legitimise the repertory of Queen Henrietta's Men, and the revivals that Heywood had contributed to it, in the face of emerging narratives that sought to delineate between amphitheatre styles and the new wit and poetry of the Caroline playhouses. These two approaches are not in conflict, or mutually exclusive: as I explored in Chapter 3, the role of the courtier playwrights in developing notions of aesthetic taste in the 1630s, and accelerating their cultural advancement, was an important factor in terms of the pressures that the dramatists of Queen Henrietta's Men faced. But the repertory-based reading presented here positions Heywood's struggle over the legitimacy of scorned and rustic theatrical traditions as directly related to the particular composition and provenance of the Cockpit repertory. Heywood's challenge to constructions of audience taste and social status, and his celebration of theatrical styles associated with clowns, swains, and the king of beasts, actively championed the visual and dynamic interest of the old Red Bull repertory in revival on the Cockpit stage. It also invited new dialogue on the strategy, interrupting the debate in the act of its representation.

Even in the assembly of *Love's Mistress* – a play that seems so particularly of its time – he appears to have drawn upon old source material from the Elizabethan stage. Several passages that appear in *Love's Mistress* had appeared before in *England's Parnassus*, an anthology of miscellaneous verse published by Robert Allot for the first time in 1600. The passages found in *Love's Mistress* have not always been attributed to Heywood, however, but instead to Thomas Dekker.[61] Dekker might well have written these verses. An entry in Henslowe's diary made on 14 May 1600 suggests that he had been collaborating with Chettle and Day on a play entitled 'the Gowlden asse cuped and siches', drawing on the same subject matter as the main plot of *Love's Mistress*. This entry records a payment made to Dekker, Chettle, and Day for the play, and appears to have been the third of this kind, presumably signalling its near-completion. Both E. K. Chambers and W. L. Halstead have suggested that Heywood might have acted in Dekker, Chettle, and Day's original play during his time as an actor at the Rose theatre.[62] Whether he did or not, *Love's Mistress* offers another example of the ways in which the dramatic legacy of the amphitheatres continued to be recycled and reappropriated on the Caroline stage. In this play, the pinnacle of Heywood's career as it is often presented, older work was once again to provide foundations for the new. For Heywood, the theatrical past was something that could not, and should not, be cast aside.

CONCLUSION

Love's Mistress made a complex intervention into debates over audience taste and the currency of old-fashioned spectacle on the 1630s stage. It enabled Heywood to articulate his investment in the styles of theatre that had been central to his work as a dramatist throughout his career. *The Escapes of Jupiter* provides an illuminating account of the dramatic continuity that might hold across the playhouse divide between amphitheatre and halls, while the revival of *If You Know Not Me* and the Caroline serialisation of *The Fair Maid of the West* capitalised on the ways in which old plays could be celebrated, and faced the challenges this posed. *The Rape of Lucrece*, and the company's commitment to the developing characteristics of Valerius in performance, enabled Queen Henrietta's Men to locate a new kind of value in their old repertory which drew directly, and with wildly spontaneous results, on an outdated tradition of clowning now associated with 'barbarism' on the 1630s stage. Through these performances Heywood expressed his allegiance to repertory staples that were threatened by the increasing bifurcation of the old open-air theatres and the new drama of the hall-playhouses – some of it issuing from the court. But in *Love's Mistress* he attempted to show how repertory need not be defined by the cultural and aesthetic associations attached to particular traditions, or their stereotypically low-ranking proponents. This was an effort to shape and control the critical reception of the repertory in the seventeenth century, and it required – through a series of social and theatrical transactions – a negotiation of the terms under which Heywood wrote for the Cockpit, and of the conditions under which the aesthetic criteria of the period were determined. Heywood was involved in an effort to erase, ridicule, or prove redundant demarcations between audience preference that were predicated on social standing – those judgements that linked traditional and popular spectacle with fools and ignorant dullards. In this sense, Heywood's drama and his contribution to the repertory of Queen Henrietta's Men was aesthetically progressive, and culturally and commercially meaningful in ways that have not been fully recognised.

This understanding of the nature of Heywood's work also provides an opportunity for a richly contextualised recalibration of the repertory in critical and historical terms. Many of the repertory's old revivals that have suffered from charges of theatrical irregularity or anomaly can be reclaimed for the repertory in a way that fully recognises their active aesthetic contribution to the company's wider commercial strategy. This applies to plays such as *The Bloody Banquet*, which appears in the 1639 list of protected plays for William Beeston as a drama of (presumably) lasting theatrical value. This type of spectacle, which extends to newer plays for the company including *The Seven Champions of Christendom*, can now be recognised as part of a challenging and commercially robust repertory which probed the boundaries of the aesthetic criteria adopted by both rivals and colleagues in the marketplace: the criteria voiced by Brome on the Blackfriars stage, for instance, with his description of the barbarous stage and rude forefathers of the past; and the negative association between the Red Bull and the Cockpit that Carew had encouraged in 1629. Heywood's attempt to bind old revivals and new plays together offers important context to an otherwise eclectic corpus of plays, recovering what seems to have been a part of the repertory's original identity and meaning.

Heywood's preoccupations were picked up and echoed in another revival on the Cockpit stage, which William Beeston was also to protect for his company in 1639. Francis Beaumont's *The Knight of the Burning Pestle* had already staged an extended metatheatrical exploration of the aesthetics of theatre and its suitability for consumption by different audiences around 1607, and conducted a satirical examination of dramatic types and their proponents. Like Midas in *Love's Mistress*, the definitively 'low' citizen couple and apprentice of *The Knight of the Burning Pestle* intervene in and reinterpret the action of the play according to their own preferences during the performance. *The Knight of the Burning Pestle* ridicules 'citizen' preferences, but only superficially. In a strategy similar to that used in *Love's Mistress*, the play's interest and success depend upon the celebration and performance of the styles and traditions deemed characteristic of undesirable or lowly drama. At one point in Beaumont's play, Heywood himself seems to be invoked in the construction of citizen tastes, when the grocer demands of the Prologue: 'why could not you be contented, as well as others, with the legend of *Whittington*, or the life & death of sir *Thomas Gresham?* with the building of the Royall Exchange' (B1r–v) – a theme that resonates conspicuously with the content of *If You Know Not Me, Part II*.[63] Beaumont's drama works to realign audience tastes with the buoyant theatrical tradition of the amphitheatres that this play repeatedly draws upon. But this objective was not achieved by the play's original company, the Children of the Queen's Revels. Its original audience in the early Jacobean years '*utterly rejected it*', '*for want of judgement, or not understanding the privy marke of* Ironie *about it*' (A2r). Perhaps it is not surprising that *The Knight of the Burning Pestle* only achieved theatrical recognition at the Cockpit, within its particular repertory, and in the theatrical climate of the 1630s. Its success alongside *Love's Mistress* renders this a highly provocative – and exciting – repertory combination.

Ben Jonson's *A Tale of a Tub* provides a further example of the cohesion in repertory and the mediation of aesthetic judgement that Heywood's efforts might have effected. Jonson wrote the play at the end of his career, and this is the only known instance in which he worked with Queen Henrietta's Men. The play is considered as something of an anomaly among the remainder of Jonson's theatrical canon. For one thing, its commercial success was dependent on the construction of old traditions as viable commodities on the Caroline stage. The prologue to 'our ridiculous play' emphasises the theatrical and cultural value of '*old Records,* [and] *antick Proverbs* [...] *countrey precedents, and old Wives Tales*'.[64] Anne Barton has suggested that through the use of 'an outmoded, clearly Elizabethan verse filled with archaic words and constructions', Jonson articulates a nostalgic affection for 'a long-ago world of rustic innocence'.[65] It is unclear how the play was received at the Cockpit, but at court beyond the bounds of Beeston's venue it was 'not likte'.[66] But though the language in which Jonson's play is couched draws attention to one construction of nostalgia on the Cockpit stage, Heywood's cultural agenda both demonstrates and affirms that there was nothing nostalgic or passive about the retention of archaic conventions in the repertory – not in the company's decision to stage new plays into which old conventions had been written, or its revival of old material. Repertory formation was an active, determined, and determining choice. Writing for Queen Henrietta's Men in the 1630s, Heywood exhibits an acute understanding and sensitivity to the kinds of choices and commitments that this repertory in particular required of him.

NOTES

1 Thomas Heywood, *The English Traveller* (London, 1633), A3r.
2 Kathleen E. McLuskie, *Dekker and Heywood* (Basingstoke: Macmillan, 1994), pp. 14–15, notes that Heywood's early work 'offers a paradigm of "popular" dramaturgy both in its location in the down-market amphitheatres of the Fortune and the Red Bull, and in its entertainment values'.
3 Arthur Melville Clark, *Thomas Heywood, Playwright and Miscellanist* (Oxford: Blackwell, 1931), pp. 208–9, 226.
4 Thomas Heywood, *The Silver Age* (London, 1613), K3r.
5 Thomas Heywood, *The Rape of Lucrece* (London, 1608), A2r.
6 Thomas Heywood, *The Fair Maid of the West* (London, 1631), A4r.
7 See Benedict Scott Robinson on the volume of works that Heywood intended to produce for an audience of readers 'not frequent in Poetry': 'Thomas Heywood and the Cultural Politics of Play Collections', *Studies in English Literature, 1500–1900*, 42 (2002), 361–80, esp. p. 374.
8 Robinson, 'Thomas Heywood', pp. 362–3.
9 Robinson, 'Thomas Heywood', pp. 365, 124. Nora Johnson terms Heywood's approach to the profession 'a radical departure' in a chapter titled 'Some zanie with his mimick action' in her *The Actor as Playwright in Early Modern Drama* (Cambridge: Cambridge University Press, 2003), pp. 122–51.
10 G. E. Bentley, *Shakespeare and His Theatre* (Lincoln, NE: University of Nebraska Press, 1964), pp. 106, 111.
11 Thomas Heywood, *The Royal King and the Loyal Subject* (London, 1637), A3r.
12 Heywood, *The English Traveller*, A3v.
13 See also, for comparison, pp. 123–4 on the prologue Heywood wrote for the 1633 court revival of Marlowe's *The Jew of Malta*, which reflects on the presentation of an old play at a time in which newer fashions may have been favoured.
14 Clark, *Thomas Heywood*, p. 222.
15 Clark, *Thomas Heywood*, pp. 88–9; see Thomas Heywood, *The Escapes of Jupiter*, ed. Henry D. Janzen, Malone Society Reprints (Oxford: Oxford University Press, 1978), p. ix.
16 N. W. Bawcutt (ed.), *The Control and Censorship of Caroline Drama: The Records of Sir Henry Herbert, Master of the Revels 1623–73* (Oxford: Clarendon Press, 1996), p. 143.
17 Thomas Heywood, *The Second Part of the Iron Age* (London, 1632), A4r.
18 Thomas Heywood, *The Iron Age* (London, 1632), A4v.
19 Joseph Quincy Adams, 'Shakespeare, Heywood, and the Classics', *Modern Language Notes*, 34 (1919), 336–9 (p. 338).
20 Adams, 'Shakespeare, Heywood', p. 339.
21 Eva Griffith, *A Jacobean Company and its Playhouse: The Queen's Servants at the Red Bull Theatre (c. 1605–1619)* (Cambridge: Cambridge University Press, 2013), p. 90.
22 See Eva Griffith, 'Christopher Beeston: His Property and Properties', in *The Oxford Handbook of Early Modern Theatre*, ed. Richard Dutton (Oxford: Oxford University Press, 2011), pp. 607–22 (p. 619), and also Chapter 1, p. 32.

23 Roslyn L. Knutson, *The Repertory of Shakespeare's Company, 1594–1613* (Fayetteville: University of Arkansas Press, 1991), pp. 50–3; Knutson notes that serials were an 'established feature' of repertory by 1592, and that the Admiral's Men regularly played serials after 1594–95 (p. 51); serialisation was also a feature of the history plays (p. 170).

24 Martin Butler, *Theatre and Crisis, 1632–42* (Cambridge: Cambridge University Press, 1984), pp. 200–1; Andrew Gurr, *Playgoing in Shakespeare's London*, 3rd edn (Cambridge: Cambridge University Press, 2004), p. 179; Andrew Gurr, *The Shakespearian Playing Companies* (Oxford: Clarendon Press, 1996), p. 321; see also Mark Bayer, 'Staging Foxe at the Fortune and the Red Bull', *Renaissance and Reformation*, 27 (2003), 61–94.

25 Teresa Grant, 'Drama Queen: Staging Elizabeth in *If You Know Not Me, You Know Nobody*', in *The Myth of Elizabeth*, ed. Susan Doran and Thomas S. Freeman (Basingstoke: Palgrave, 2003), pp. 120–42 (p. 121).

26 See Theodora A. Jankowski, 'Historicizing and Legitimating Capitalism: Thomas Heywood's *Edward IV* and *If You Know Not Me, You Know Nobody*', *Medieval and Renaissance Drama in England*, 7 (1995), 305–37 (p. 306).

27 John Watkins, *Representing Elizabeth in Stuart England* (Cambridge: Cambridge University Press, 2002), pp. 53–5; Grant, 'Drama Queen', pp. 129–37; Claire Jowitt, *Voyage Drama and Gender Politics, 1589–1642: Real and Imagined Worlds* (Manchester: Manchester University Press, 2003), pp. 26, 141–2.

28 Michael Dobson, 'Dumb Show', in *The Oxford Encyclopedia of Theatre and Performance*, ed. Dennis Kennedy, https://www.oxfordreference.com/view/10.1093/acref/9780198601746.001.0001/acref-9780198601746-e-1168 (accessed 23 October 2023). See also Marion Jones, 'Early Moral Plays and the Earliest Secular Drama' in *The Revels History of Drama in English, Volume I: Medieval Drama*, ed. A. C. Cawley et al. (London: Methuen, 1983), pp. 211–91 (pp. 238–42); Andrew Gurr notes that by 1600, 'dumb-shows that mimed a plot-story were seen by some of the more acid playwrights as laughably archaic' (*The Shakespearean Stage, 1574–1642*, 4th edn [Cambridge: Cambridge University Press, 2009], p. 234).

29 Robert Weimann, *Shakespeare and the Popular Tradition in the Theater*, ed. Robert Schwartz (Baltimore, MD: Johns Hopkins University Press, 1978); Robert Weimann and Douglas Bruster, *Shakespeare and the Power of Performance: Stage and Page in the Elizabethan Theatre* (Cambridge: Cambridge University Press, 2008), p. 77.

30 Bayer, 'Staging Foxe', p. 70.

31 Thomas Heywood, *If You Know Not Me, You Know Nobody*, Part II (London, 1633), I3v.

32 Watkins, *Representing Elizabeth*, p. 53; Grant, 'Drama Queen', p. 133.

33 Grant, 'Drama Queen', p. 134.

34 Knutson, *The Repertory of Shakespeare's Company*, pp. 34–7; see also Roslyn L. Knutson, 'Henslowe's Diary and the Economics of Play Revision for Revival, 1592–1603', *Theatre Research International*, 10 (1985), 1–17.

35 For *femme forte* and its popularity in the 1630s, see Rebecca A. Bailey, *Staging the Old Faith: Queen Henrietta Maria and the Theatre of Caroline England, 1625–1642* (Manchester: Manchester University Press, 2009), pp. 159–64.

36 See Eleanor Collins, 'Changing Fashions: Tragicomedy, Romance, and the Heroic Woman in the 1630s Hall-Playhouses', in *Moving Shakespeare Indoors: Performance and Repertoire in the Jacobean Playhouse*, ed. Andrew Gurr and Farah Karim-Cooper (Cambridge: Cambridge University Press, 2014), pp. 217–36, for more on these heroic female characters.

37 For a fuller account, see Eleanor Collins, 'From Court to Cockpit: *The Prisoners* and *Claricilla* in Repertory', in *Thomas Killigrew and the Seventeenth-Century English Stage: New Perspectives*, ed. Philip Major (Farnham: Ashgate, 2013), pp. 21–44.

38 Thomas Heywood, *The Fair Maid of the West*, Part II (London, 1631), B1r–v.

39 Thomas Heywood, *The Fair Maid of the West*, Part I (London, 1631), I4r.

40 Clark, *Thomas Heywood*, p. 220.

41 Thomas Heywood, *The Rape of Lucrece* (London, 1609), K2r.

42 Thomas Heywood, *The Rape of Lucrece* (London, 1638), A1r. All further quotations are from the 1638 edition unless indicated.

43 See David Wiles, *Shakespeare's Clown: Actor and Text in the Elizabethan Playhouse* (Cambridge: Cambridge University Press, 1987), pp. 11–42.

44 Weimann, *Shakespeare and the Popular Tradition*, pp. 215–23.

45 Johnson, *The Actor as Playwright*, pp. 145, 148.

46 As Wiles has noted with respect to clowning conventions, '[i]t is easier for the clown to separate himself from the main role and plot structure of the play if he remains distanced from the intrigues upon which the plot pivots' (*Shakespeare's Clown*, pp. 101–2).

47 Clark, *Thomas Heywood*, p. 219; F. S. Boas, *Thomas Heywood* (London: Williams and Norgate, 1950), p. 55.

48 Wiles, *Shakespeare's Clown*, pp. 14, 21–2. He describes Tarlton's relationship with the audience as 'interactive and competitive', and suggests that 'Tarlton's script existed only in order that he could destroy it' (p. 21). Tarlton's *Jests*, originally published in 1600, continued to be republished into the 1620s and 1630s; Andrew Crooke, one of the partnership that made up Shirley's primary publishers, was still republishing the book as late as 1638 to sell in St Paul's churchyard, which suggests continued public interest in the old traditions of the Elizabethan theatre.

49 Wiles suggests that, from the 1590s, '[a]s the relationship between player and spectator grew more impersonal, as a hunger for narrative was stimulated, Tarlton's techniques were superseded' (*Shakespeare's Clown*, p. 43).

50 Richard Brome, *The Antipodes* (London, 1640), D3v.

51 Wiles, *Shakespeare's Clown*, p. 43.

52 This was a concern that can be observed over the course of his writings in the 1630s and across genres, manifesting itself in *The Hierarchie of the Blessed Angells* (1635) and his last three pageants; see Richard Rowland, *Thomas Heywood's Theatre, 1599–1639: Locations, Translations, and Conflict* (Farnham: Ashgate, 2010), pp. 338–40, 360–9.

53 Thomas Heywood, *Love's Mistress* (London, 1636), M1v, M1r–v, D1v.

54 David Crystal and Ben Crystal, *Shakespeare's Words*, 2nd edn (London: Penguin, 2004), p. 251.

55 Ben Jonson, *Every Man In His Humour*, in *The Works of Benjamin Jonson* (London, 1616), A3r.

56 For discussion of Jonson's intention and the perception of his audience, see Stephen Orgel, 'The Poetics of Spectacle', *New Literary History*, 21 (1971), 367–89 (pp. 385–9).

57 Rowland, *Thomas Heywood's Theatre*, pp. 257–67.

58 Rowland, *Thomas Heywood's Theatre*, pp. 243, 245.

59 Rowland, *Thomas Heywood's Theatre*, p. 280.

60 Rowland, *Thomas Heywood's Theatre*, p. 289.

61 See Bentley, *Jacobean and Caroline Stage*, IV, p. 581.

62 W. L. Halstead, 'Dekker's *Cupid and Psyche* and Thomas Heywood', *English Literary History*, 11 (1944), 182–91 (p. 185).

63 Francis Beaumont, *The Knight of the Burning Pestle* (London, 1613), B1r–v.

64 Ben Jonson, *A Tale of a Tub*, in the *Works of Benjamin Jonson*, 2nd edn (London, 1640–41), p. 68.

65 Anne Barton, 'Harking Back to Elizabeth: Ben Jonson and Caroline Nostalgia', *English Literary History*, 48 (1981), 706–31 (pp. 725, 726).

66 Bawcutt (ed.), *Control and Censorship*, p. 186.

6

JAMES SHIRLEY, QUEEN'S MAN

Tracing the career of James Shirley has offered the most commonly chosen path through the repertory of Queen Henrietta's Men, and no account of the company would be complete without considering his contribution to its successes and reputation.[1] A considerable number of his plays from the repertory survive in print; at a conservative count, Shirley's output constitutes almost a third of the extant repertory. Based on the evidence as it survives today, no other dramatist contributed more to the company's quantitative stockpile of plays. Shirley's new plays not only made up a core component of the repertory, but have been thought to define the company's aesthetic and artistic direction as far as it is characterized by commissioned, contemporary works.[2] In critical accounts his plays have proved useful: his aesthetically streamlined, identifiably 'Caroline' corpus has brought a measure of cohesion to the repertory. He has also become an important historical figure in constructions of the trajectory of theatre history, as a definitively 'Caroline' dramatist. For decades the drama of this period was typified as exhausted and decadent, at once progressive in its anticipation of Restoration drama, and yet by turns highly derivative.[3] Shirley emerged in criticism as the leading playwright of the Caroline era, representing a high-water mark in a period of artistic decline; for Fredson Bowers, he was 'the one dramatist who was not thrown off balance by the demands of his age'.[4] This did not excuse him from charges of conventionality and contrivance, but these attitudes are now being revised in the wake of fresh critical interest in his plays – not least through the major new edition of his works that is underway.[5]

This chapter provides an account of Shirley's contribution to the Cockpit repertory and a re-evaluation of his work in light of the repertory in which it was originally performed. At the same time, it offers a portrait of Shirley as a fresh and engaged playwright, a dramatist working to forge new perspectives amid an already rich and animated repertory. For related to the old, critical consensus that Shirley's art was derivative is a lingering sense of the lateness of his writing, following, in narrative accounts, the innovative exuberance of the Elizabethan and Jacobean stage. Even while Shirley's originality is now recognised and celebrated, his 'belatedness' continues to haunt the critical reception of his works, while he is, perhaps at times inadvertently, portrayed as passive and 'inevitably nostalgic' in accounts which seek to rejuvenate him.[6] This chapter recognises the influences of the previous decades of drama upon his work, but offers an alternative account of Shirley's dramatic range and versatility as a playwright working both collaboratively and self-reflexively to develop the Cockpit repertory. It advocates a sense of Shirley as a spirited and experimental master of his craft, imbricated in the interplay of repertory and theatricality, and preoccupied with the arts of storytelling and performance.

QUEEN'S MAN FOR THE COMPANY

There is no doubt that Shirley was a valuable asset for Beeston and an important figurehead for Queen Henrietta's Men. When the Cockpit dramatists responded to Carew's insulting verse, it was through the prefatory material to Shirley's *The Faithful Servant*, published as *The Grateful Servant* in 1630.[7] This strategy served to position him at the centre of the debate over the Cockpit repertory and its commercial and artistic success. His fellow dramatists and company members claimed and celebrated him as a spokesperson and representative. In retrospect, this may seem inevitable given the prevailing narrative in theatre history of Shirley as a contracted playwright for the company, but the manoeuvre might have been a deliberate, collaborative, and commercial attempt on the part of Beeston to place him at the heart of matters. For despite this chapter's focus on Shirley's company role, it is also important to acknowledge, at the outset, that his commitment to Queen Henrietta's Men was not quite as unconditional, or definitive, as has sometimes been thought. The regularity of his dramatic output, as evidenced by the transcripts of Henry Herbert's office-book entries, tends to give the impression of an obedient and hard-working employee of Beeston. But he was simultaneously focused on pursuits and projects beyond Queen Henrietta's Men, and beyond the London stage, and between 1632 and 1639 was actively involved in the repertories of other playhouses and companies. In 1632 his play *The Changes; or, Love in a Maze* was licensed and then performed at either the Fortune or the Salisbury Court theatre, in the midst of his association with the Cockpit.[8] Shirley's independence of Queen Henrietta's Men is also suggested in one of Malone's notes on Herbert's 1635 records, which suggests that

> Shirley, who had the revisal of some of those pieces which were left imperfect by Fletcher [...] finding The New Inn unsuccessful, took the liberty to borrow a scene from it, which he inserted in Love's Pilgrimage, when that play was revived, or as Sir Henry Herbert calls it, *renewed,* in 1635.[9]

The New Inn was one of Jonson's plays, licensed in 1629 and performed by the King's Men, and Fletcher's plays are primarily associated with the King's Men in the 1620s and 1630s.[10] G. E. Bentley suggested that since 1635 fell in the midst of Shirley's allegiance to Queen Henrietta's Men, he 'would not have been working on plays which were the property of the King's company'.[11] The entry has been relatively neglected in critical accounts, and while Malone's transcript might be inaccurate or erroneous, the evidence as it survives presents the intriguing possibility that Shirley might have been working for the King's Men concurrently with Queen Henrietta's Men, and establishing professional contacts and networks with his contemporaries at the Blackfriars and Globe, which he would go on to exploit later in his career when he started writing more regularly for the King's Men. This may also suggest that the King's Men and Queen Henrietta's Men operated along more collaborative lines in the 1630s than is currently acknowledged – a conclusion that is more in tune with the operations of other 'rival' companies across the wider period.[12]

Shirley's theatrical pursuits outside the company also include his years spent abroad in Ireland from 1636 to 1640. His departure from London took place over the same period of plague that is blamed for the eventual breaking of the original Queen Henrietta's Men, though Shirley's connections with London continued to hold during his absence. The partnership of William Crooke and Andrew Cooke was responsible for the publication of the majority of the plays that Shirley wrote and revived for Queen Henrietta's Men, and some of these were published in London while he was in Ireland.[13] Furthermore, while Shirley was writing plays for Ogilby's Men in Dublin, a few of them may have migrated back to the London stage. It seems likely that *The Constant Maid* might have been written in Dublin, but it was performed, according to its 1661 title-page, by Queen Henrietta's Men at the Cockpit.[14] This indicates that Shirley may have been engaged in producing new fare for the Cockpit while being physically removed from the immediate conditions of its performance and reception. *The Politician* might also have been performed in Ireland: it remained unpublished until 1655, but was entered in the Stationers' Register by Humphrey Moseley at the same time as *The Gentleman of Venice*, a play of Irish provenance. The title-pages of both of these plays claim that they were performed by Her Majesty's Servants, though the later dating of these plays situates them with Heton's Queen's Men at Salisbury Court. It seems likely that two of Fletcher's plays were also performed in Ireland, since in 1646 Shirley's 'Prologue to Mr. *Fletchers* Play in IRELAND' was printed, which referred to 'another of Master *Fletcher's* Playes there'.[15] Making plays available for different stages in different places, and exploiting the advantages of simultaneous performance in Dublin and London, was a deliberate strategy, then, and both London and Dublin editions of Shirley's *The Opportunity* survive.[16]

Shirley's provision of *The Politician* and *The Gentleman of Venice* to Salisbury Court demonstrates further that he was not exclusively involved with Beeston's company while abroad. This move to write for a new theatre may demonstrate Shirley's opportunistic gain from a troupe in need of new fare, but it took place after the breaking of Beeston's Queen Henrietta's Men, the company with which Shirley had the longest association. *The Royal Master* was not published in connection with a London company, but it was licensed for the London stage in 1638, the year before *The Gentleman of Venice*. Christopher Beeston was still alive in April 1638, when the play was licensed, but he died in October of that year, leaving the business to his son William. Shirley's oldest associates, including Anthony Turner and William Sherlock – colleagues who had been at the Cockpit when Shirley wrote *Love Tricks* or *The School of Compliment* for Lady Elizabeth's Men – had now moved to Salisbury Court; Richard Perkins, who had taken major roles in Shirley's *The Wedding* and *The Lady of Pleasure*, had gone with them. The ties that had held the company together throughout the late 1620s and early 1630s had come at least partially undone, and the London companies' reshuffling – prompted partly by Herbert's interventions – meant that London's professional theatre would have looked very different to Shirley on his return, after a decade of relative stability with Christopher Beeston. Shirley did not return to the Cockpit to work with William Beeston; when he came back to London he started writing for the King's Men in the last two years before the closure of the theatres. This need not be seen as a defection or a desertion of the Cockpit. If Shirley had been working with the King's Men in 1629, it must have been a return for him, something of a continuation within a familiar professional environment.

While Shirley's commitment to Queen Henrietta's Men is evident but not unqualified, the same is true of his connection with the court. Shirley's critical reception and his importance to theatre history have been heavily bound up with the concerns of the court and his connection with Queen Henrietta Maria. In 1634 he was admitted to Gray's Inn, where he developed a circle of influential friends with literary interests.[17] Shirley had been formally educated, employed as the master of St Alban's grammar school, and was now negotiating the politics and friendships of some of the most influential courtiers and gentlemen of the country. At the same time, he was described as 'one of the valets to the chamber of Queen Henrietta's Men' – a servant to the queen herself – while during the course of his professional career he dedicated many of his plays to aristocratic and courtly recipients.[18] The allegiances that Shirley expressed through his writing and his dedications offer an important insight into the way that he was operating at court, and into his professional and personal life over this period.

The network of patronage that Shirley appears to have nurtured has certainly influenced the interpretation of his role as principal dramatist for Queen Henrietta's Men, and suggested to some scholars that his royal interests had political and artistic consequences for the repertory and the design of his plays: Ben Lucow wrote, for instance, that Shirley was 'devoted to England's Queen Henrietta Maria' and 'consistently produced a species of drama designed to glorify kingship'.[19] More recently, Rebecca Bailey's revealing book on the staging of Roman Catholic themes and ideas in Caroline drama has explored, in more nuance, the complex religious and political connections between Shirley's writing and the interests of the queen, and her faith in particular.[20] Shirley's composition of *The Gamester* for the company out of a plot devised by the king, the queen's gift of money to Beeston in 1630, and the degree to which Queen Henrietta's Men do appear to have been invested in the pursuit of royal favour over a particular period around 1633 to 1636, all contribute to the evidence linking Shirley and his professional endeavours with the court.[21] But consideration of Shirley's reworking of Sidney's *Arcadia*, in a play of the same name, demonstrates the ways in which less subtle readings of his connection with the court have occluded appreciation of his work as a repertory dramatist.

QUEEN'S MAN FOR THE COURT? *THE ARCADIA*

The Arcadia has occupied an awkward place in the Cockpit repertory, for a number of reasons. It is difficult to date, as one of only three of Shirley's plays for which licences have not been preserved, and it remained unpublished until 1640 – by which time the original Queen Henrietta's Men had broken. Thomas Nabbes's play *Covent Garden* contains a reference to 'Mopsa of the Arcadia', which might be a direct reference to the performance of this character in Shirley's play on the same stage; if this is the case, *The Arcadia* must have been in repertory at the Cockpit in the first half of the 1630s, since Nabbes's play dates between 1633 and 1634. Martin Wiggins dates *The Arcadia* to between 1630 and 1636, with a best guess of summer 1635.[22] Another possibility is that Henry Herbert passed an old play called *The Arcadia* to Beeston at the Cockpit, where it was later revised by Shirley and published under his name. In his edition of the office-book accounts, N. W. Bawcutt presents Edmond Malone's transcript of an entry dated 8 February 1624 as follows:

For the Kgs comp: an olde P. call: The honests [*sic*] mans fortune the original being lost was reallowed by me att M[r]. Taylors intreaty & on condition to give me a booke 8th. Feb: 1624.   The Arcadia[23]

The meaning of the entry is far from clear. Bawcutt describes how Malone wrote 'The Arcadia' in square brackets at the end of the entry, but in Chalmers's correspondent transcript the title is absent altogether. This might suggest that 'The Arcadia' was not part of the original entry.[24] Bawcutt believes that the addition is more likely to denote the enlarged 'booke' of Sidney's *Arcadia*, published in London in 1622 and 1623, than Shirley's play, though Herbert often referred to plays in their physical form as 'books'.[25] As we know, he also licensed an anonymous revival to Queen Henrietta's Men on 12 January 1632 'For allowing of an ould play, new written or forbisht by Mr. Biston'; and, in 1633, gave *Hymen's Holiday* to the Cockpit, where it might have been revised by one of the Beestons, or by Shirley, given the extent of his involvement with the company at that time.[26] There was a documented precedent for this method of play transmission and revival in the Cockpit repertory, and if the 'ould play' of the 1624 entry was an earlier version of *The Arcadia* and had previously belonged to the King's Men, then Shirley's revival provides one further instance of Herbert's contribution to the company's dramatic output. Given Wiggins's analysis of how the play fits into Shirley's writing commitments, and his observation that Beeston was investing in tragicomedies characterised by antiquated settings in the period, a composition date of the 1630s seems likely. But if further evidence should come to light which suggests that the play was indeed a revival by Shirley for the company, then such a creative undertaking constitutes, in any case, an intervention very similar in nature.

The play's reception in critical histories of the early modern stage has also been vexed. For Alfred Harbage, it exhibits a 'quaint facetiousness' and 'antique fun' which contributed to his doubts over Shirley's authorship.[27] Harbage suggested two alternative authorial candidates: John Kirke, 'whose single extant play, *The seven champions of Christendom*, is only slightly more crude than *The Arcadia*', and Heywood, considering that '[p]arts of *The Arcadia* suggest the manner of the later Heywood at his worst'.[28] Harbage was encouraged in this reading by an underlying conviction that the play does not accord with Shirley's practice or style:

The play [...] adheres sedulously to its literary original—a procedure quite foreign to the methods of the reminiscent but ingenious James Shirley [...] The verse lacks James Shirley's melody and poetic imagery, the characters are crudely drawn, the humor is naïve—the whole performance, putting it bluntly, is unworthy of [Shirley][29]

But other critics have seen *The Arcadia* as characterised by a strong impulse to align the repertory of Queen Henrietta's Men with the interests of the court. While for Harbage the anomalous qualities of *The Arcadia* located the play within a narrative of mis-ascribed authorship, Fleay located it instead within a band of royal taste. He suggested that Queen Henrietta Maria had acted in *The Arcadia*, and furthermore that the play was commissioned by the court and performed there in the Christmas season of 1632–33, during which the king's birthday fell.[30] Fleay believed that the play's 'peculiar character and careless workmanship look like writing "by command"'.[31] Robert Stanley Forsythe agreed, suggesting that 'Shirley was commissioned to produce' the play, based on 'the great interest in pastoral and pastoral-romantic drama at the court of Charles I'.[32]

There is no known evidence to suggest that the play was commissioned as part of a royal entertainment, or that the queen acted in it. But the play does belong to the genre of pastoral romance that was proving so popular at court with the queen. The 1630s saw a proliferation of plays that participated in this trend, including the King's Men's revival of Fletcher's *The Faithful Shepherdess*, which was patronised by Henrietta Maria and acted at court in 1634, and several dramas in which the queen herself performed at court, *The Shepherd's Paradise* among them. This was the trend on which Beeston and Queen Henrietta's Men attempted to capitalise between 1633 and 1636 with the production of a small quantity of revivals and new plays that fell into that genre, with the intent, it seems, of attracting royal interest.[33] *The Arcadia* thus made its own concerted contribution to the particular repertory approach that the company was taking over these few years; it might even have set the repertory on that path.[34]

The Arcadia made its own contribution, furthermore, to the development and refashioning of pastoral that was underway in the 1630s, as Lucy Munro has explored in her analysis of archaism and Stuart pastoral drama. Munro focuses on *The Faithful Shepherdess*, Milton's *Comus*, and Jonson's *The Sad Shepherd* to explore the role that archaic elements played in pastoral style, and the extent to which the genre, at once characterised as 'low, rustic [... and] determinedly old-fashioned' and also 'elevated, courtly, artificial, classical or continental in its derivation', was being reworked over this period in line with differing concerns and cultural and dramatic priorities.[35] Indeed, the old tendency exhibited by Harbage and Fleay to treat *The Arcadia* as derivative or bound slavishly to its source material, and the assumption that it was a royal commission composed in line with monarchical taste, occludes the creative impulse that Shirley brought to his adaptation. For while the play treats Sidney's old tale of the antics of disguised princes among shepherds, its representation of archaic source material seems to suggest that this play was a distinctly

Caroline repertory piece, written to appeal to a wide variety of playgoers, and designed to toy with the ideas of both storytelling and courtliness. In particular, the extent to which both courtly styles and rusticity are appropriated and worn by Shirley's characters runs as an undercurrent through the drama, mirroring the way that Shirley himself experiments with the trappings of innovation on the one hand, and the archaism of his source text on the other.

Musidorus, a prince disguised as a shepherd, is the agent of much of Shirley's experimentation. His dual status as aristocrat and undercover rustic allows Shirley to probe the extent to which style and register are strategically performed and selectively appropriated. When Musidorus first speaks in his rural disguise, his courtly origins threaten to betray him. Drawing on the neoplatonic language so popular at Henrietta Maria's court, he tells Mopsa, a shepherd's daughter, that 'neither pitty nor my prayers can soften' her marble heart, emphasising a few lines later 'the truth of my affection and with what / Religion it lookes upon your vertues'.[36] This focus on the spiritual purity of his courtship, intertwined as it is with religious piety, is reminiscent of the discourse constructed around idealised courtly love, while the object of his devotion is depicted as a source of wonder and fair nobility. He professes that 'one gracious word / From you would make me happie, let one beame / Shoot from your eye, and it will strike a spring / Into that frozen peece of earth, and make it / A bower for love to sport in' (B3v), and the invocation of eye beams suggests qualities of radiation and illumination, in this case life-giving, which are tied up with neoplatonic discourse.[37]

Elements of Musidorus's address can be found in the original source text, but Shirley rewrites and reimagines the speech in his telling – a choice that suggests an intentional recalibration of courtly discourse with the specifics of 1630s neoplatonic ideology. In contrast, Pamela's response to the speech is repeated verbatim from Sidney: she advises Mopsa that 'your Shepheard can speake well' (B4r). The princess Pamela is in fact the true object of Musidorus's desire, and the thrust of his speeches is directed, covertly, to her rather than Mopsa. Shirley's truncation of his source material gives Pamela's words a new specificity, however. In his dramatic adaptation, Pamela's appraisal is uttered in direct response to Musidorus's first amorous address, and as such refers unambiguously to his expertise in the language of courtly love. In Sidney's original, it is less certain whether Pamela refers to Musidorus's skills in courtship or gestures more generally to his narrative skill, as his amorous speeches and her seal of approval are divided by almost two thousand words of exposition in which Musidorus relates his tale to the women.[38] Shirley's omission of Musidorus's expository tale also works to align Pamela, swiftly and clearly, with courtly rhetoric and royal status, attuned as she is to his discourse.

In contrast, Mopsa replies that she finds his language 'queint' (B4r), a term which, when applied to speech or language, could mean ingeniously elaborate, refined, or affected, but also suggests cunning or skilful contrivance.[39] Again, the term appears in the source material but its proximity here to Musidorus's romantic overtures lends her comment a pointedness not found in the original, in which Mopsa might also or otherwise be referring to the artifice of his elaborate story. The disconnect between Mopsa's frank and forthright attitude and Musidorus's knowing hyperbole is underscored again when, in an exchange original to Shirley's adaptation, Musidorus proclaims that 'nature made / Your face the onely object of mans wonder', and in response Mopsa asks: 'Does my face looke like a flapiack [flapjack]?' (B4r).

Mopsa's rusticity is displayed not only in her verbal plainness and candour, but also in her dialect. When Pamela advises Mopsa to 'with some smiles encourage' the disguised Musidorus, Mopsa muses: 'Smoyles, let me alone to smoile' (B3v). Though the text presents 'smile' in three variant spellings within the space of nine words, the spelling 'smoile' had been associated before in literature of the period with country contexts and dialect.[40] When Mopsa ascends a tree on the promise that her wish to become queen will be granted, she cries 'up womee' four times, as she struggles to climb 'the right way' (E2v). Mopsa's dialect is not straightforwardly linked to a particular region, but Munro notes that regional 'versions of English were often assumed to preserve old words and forms of speech', so that even if Shirley does not appropriate archaic language, a regional accent might have been suggestive to audiences of old-fashioned speech and rustic stature.[41] Lexical informality is also a trait of Mopsa's mother Miso, who unleashes a flurry of colloquialisms prompted by the suggestion that her husband Dametas has been unfaithful: 'leaue your bogling and your trim tram tricks you must not flap me o'th mouth with fleering and with flams ...' (D3r). The rustic identifiers embedded in Mopsa's and Miso's utterances align them with a version of pastoral characterised as low, comic, humble, and plain, in contrast with Musidorus's elaborate speech.

When Mopsa describes Musidorus's speech as 'queint', the printed page of Shirley's play gives little sense of how far her recognition of his cunning might have been drawn out in performance. Whether the actor playing Mopsa chose to level an accusation or to play the comment as blithely ignorant, the suggestion of Musidorus's deceit could not be closer to the truth – especially where Mopsa and her family are concerned. True to source, Musidorus presents Mopsa with a jewel in the shape of a crab, which he describes as an emblem of his love, since it 'lookes another way / To that it moves' (B4r). Musidorus also exploits Mopsa's father Dametas, in a scene that works further to establish the rusticity of the shepherd family by underscoring Dametas's affinities with the earth and soil. Musidorus need only invoke a few practical details concerning his agricultural labour on the land to trick Dametas into thinking that he has discovered a fortune buried beneath a tree. Local detail relating to farming tools and bucolic life buoy him in his deception: he describes how he 'turne[d] up some turff with my mole-spade' and then 'digd till I came to a stone' (D2r), and the two men set about listing a brief inventory of earth-mining equipment to uncover the treasure: mattocks, shovels, hooks, ladders, spade, and pickaxes. This exchange, focused around agricultural work and land management, is designed to appeal to Dametas's sense of self, for beyond the promise of treasure he also recognises himself as 'Lord of the soyle' (D2r), a title that plays on Sidney's reference in the source material to Dametas's 'muddy mind'.[42] The reference is echoed later by the peasant rebels as the social hierarchy of Arcadia is reinforced: they will 'domineere like Lords of the soyle [...] we will live, we will eate and we will drinke' (F4r). This plainness, the focus on the earthly and the bodily rather than the spiritual, is contrasted with the elaborate expressions associated with the court, while Musidorus wears the accoutrements of either extreme lightly – when he puts on the language of courtly love to woo Pamela (which itself requires the feigning of affection to Mopsa), and in his dealings with Dametas. In both instances the performances that Musidorus undertakes might be heavily ironised when set in action on the stage, but either way this courtly representative is deceptive, moving one way while looking another – and, embodied in the theatre, always with an eye towards the playhouse audience that he entertains.

Musidorus can also be seen as something of a surrogate for Shirley, for like the playwright he is a wordsmith and the author of certain events. And Musidorus's bridging role between peasant life and high court culture stands in parallel with Shirley's intermingling of old source material overlaid with updates and embellishments. These were not only rhetorical, drawing on the neoplatonic language of Henrietta Maria's court, but inscribed within the physical realisation of the play on stage and the framing commentary surrounding it – particularly in relation to the scene at the close of Act 1, which presents a dance and revels. In Sidney's source material, the chapter that follows Musidorus's gift of a jewel to Pamela sees King Basilius and Queen Gynecia treat Zelmane to 'some sports prepared for her', which consist primarily of a heron and a gerfalcon in flight.[43] In Shirley's play, the falconry is replaced with song and dance, which seems to deliberately evoke courtly modes alongside the performance of the rustic and pastoral.

On the one hand, the entertainment is referred to variously as 'gambolls' (a festive holiday game or pastime, or playful leaping in dance), '*country sport*', and '*holyday / Shepheards Carroll Dance and play*' (B4v, C1r, C1v). Shepherds and rustics, including Mopsa, Miso, and the disguised Musidorus, take part in the festivities, and the earthy Dametas is 'the steward for this dayes mirth' (C1r); in his supervisory role he speaks in rhyming couplets to introduce the revels, which might have indicated to an audience a 'formal and old-fashioned' register.[44] Basilius also introduces the revels by apologising to the gathered ladies that 'our revells wants the state and glory / With which the Court delights might charme your senses / Our sceane is naturall' (B4v–C1r). While the statement might gesture towards the rustic, unadorned setting of the dance, it also suggests that this rusticity, a turn away from state and glory, is a deliberate and affected strategy with remedial and health-giving aims: it is meant to be 'A cure for times sicke feathers, and your mirth' (C1r).

On the other hand, the revels proceed to present Cupid, the '*Dandiprat that liv'd at Court*' (C1r). Cupid came to be of particular significance to Henrietta Maria, and in 1634 Heywood's *Love's Mistress* would draw on the myth of Cupid and Psyche, and present Cupid descending from the heavens in order to speak the prologue.[45] But Cupid already had a history of appearing in courtly masques, and though Dametas describes him as a '*wooddy god*' (of the woodland), the reference to him living at court might refer to the extent to which the god had been adopted by, and appropriated within, Caroline courtly circles and entertainments.[46] Courtly forms of dancing are also invoked, if not performed, when Dametas tells Musidorus that he 'shall have leave to shake your heeles, looke you be mannerly, and shew a cleane calf' (B4v). The dexterity and precision of movement implied by showing a 'cleane' calf suggests the kind of courtly dancing that demanded technical prowess and disciplined movement of the body, as opposed to the less refined conventions of a country dance. Yet it is Dametas who speaks these words, amid a flurry of nonsense. He mispronounces Zelmane's name as 'Lady *Salamandor*', and mixes up his verbs when he speaks of hearing the 'Dances and see[ing] the fine songs' (B4v). When they set out to the revels, he instructs Musidorus to 'Continue thy dutie *Dorus* and follow me with a reverence' (B4v) – a turn of phrase that could easily be heard as 'irreverance' in performance. Dametas's imagining of courtly conduct in the context of dance is therefore delivered in a comic vein, with little authority but great self-importance. He both sends up the conventions of courtly dancing in his misplaced instruction to a (disguised) prince, and sets up an expectation for this style of dancing which might or might not be delivered in the play, depending on how Queen Henrietta's Men chose to perform the scene.

Shirley thus draws on both rustic, rural traditions and their courtly counterparts to set up the scene, gesturing towards modes of Caroline courtly dancing at the same time as he refers back to the archaism of his source material in recognition of the popularity of pastoral at the Caroline court. The scene as printed does not straightforwardly advocate for archaism or innovation, but tangles the two in a way that seems distinctly of its moment, as a revival of old material for a new audience. Dametas's parodic and blasé summary of courtly dancing, Basilius's invocation of the state, glory, and courtly delights of typical court revels, and Cupid's presence on the stage work to disrupt and unsettle the archaic country context of the revels by gesturing to the pleasures that might lie beyond this rustic scene, and – if performed at court – to the expectations of an audience accustomed to such elaborate entertainments. At the same time, while Shirley adapts his source material in order to introduce the revels scene to his narrative telling of the *Arcadia*, the text suggests that he stops short of an indiscriminate importation of courtly or masque styles, emphasising through Basilius's words the wholesomeness of the 'naturall' scene and its curative potential. In Shirley's *Arcadia*, the court and its conventions are clearly acknowledged, but they are not unthinkingly idealised or appropriated. The ways in which Shirley adapted his source material show a creative and experimental repertory playwright at work, rather than a dramatist seeking the favour of the court alone.

Whether Shirley's *Arcadia* was a brand new piece, as seems more likely, or revived from an earlier work, its staging at the Cockpit in the 1630s would have aligned it with other new plays that would have accompanied it in repertory, including the revival of *Hymen's Holiday* and Heywood's *Love's Mistress*, both of which contain (or gesture towards) pastoral themes and draw upon classical source material. Midas's 'fine sport' in Heywood's play is, of course, characteristic of that 'use[d] heere in *Arcadia*' (F1r). The *Arcadia* claimed its own kind of logic in terms of the drama performed at the Cockpit theatre over these years, then; this 'crude' play, seen as something of an outlier, seems rather to have constituted an important and decisive development of the Cockpit repertory in recognition of the Caroline interest in pastoral. In this sense *The Arcadia* can certainly be counted among those plays performed as part of the company's efforts to attract interest from the court but, contrary to critical opinion of decades past, Shirley's adaptation suggests that this was neither a diligent retelling of source material nor a royal commission that straightforwardly celebrated Caroline courtly fashions and tastes. *The Arcadia*'s relation to its archaic origins, and to the contemporary contexts of courtly behaviours and preferences, are decidedly more involved and experimental.

Playful criticism of social artifice and courtly behaviours or pretensions is characteristic of Shirley's work when viewed in its wider context, and taking a broader perspective builds a more sustained account of Shirley's allegiances to his commercial audience at the playhouse. He had written on pastoral themes before, in *Love Tricks* for Lady Elizabeth's Men. The play stayed in the Cockpit repertory under Queen Henrietta's Men, and features a cross-dressing heroine who, horrified by her imminent wedding, runs away to the forest and dons '*Shepheards weedes*'.[47] The Arcadia that is represented by the forest of this play is a labyrinthine maze, a wilderness for those who lose their way (H4v). When Infortunio stumbles upon the 'school of complement', a finishing school that teaches its students how to speak and behave in accordance with courtly manners, he mistakes the place for hell and its students for the damned, and leaves to wander the woods in search of the Elysian Fields (F4v–G2v).

Shirley also wrote *The Ball* at around the same time that *The Arcadia* was in repertory at the Cockpit. The play is set in fashionable Caroline London society and as such is at a remove from Arcadia's carol dancing and broadswords. Instead of experimentation with source material, Shirley turns his attention here to subversions of courtly dramatic styles and masquing conventions to point towards the artifice of stately occasion and aristocratic behaviours. The play is structured around the theatrical pastime of dancing, and features a number of opportunities for different styles and fashions of dancing to be showcased. Some of the dancing seems likely to have consisted of fashionably updated traditional styles, such as the '*new Country Dance*' performed by a group of ladies in Monsieur Le Friske's dancing salon,[48] and the play's culmination at the long-anticipated ball stages the performance of a masque. Dressed for his part, Mr Barker enters '*like a Satyre Dancing*' – an effect that immediately prompts questions about what he is supposed to resemble (I3v). Freshwater introduces the spectacle as a 'Monster', though Lucina guesses correctly – 'What have we here a Satyre.' But Bostocke is confused: 'No, tis a dancing Beare' (I3v).

Courtly masques often presented manifestations of mythical creatures, and the Cockpit repertory contained a number of plays featuring satyrs, including two of Shirley's earlier offerings. A '*maske of Satyres*' (L2r) had appeared in *Love Tricks*, and in Shirley's *The Faithful Servant* '*Satyres rise and runne in*', pursue nymphs over the stage, and introduce Lodwick to a richly accoutred and mysterious woman who tells him that she is the Devil.[49] This moment, with its recorder music and the seemingly enchanted banquet, leads Lodwick to think that he can hear 'the motion of the Spheares', or else believe that he must be 'in Elisium' (I2r). It turns out that the set-up is an elaborate trick: there is no devil, and no real magic, though the otherworldly, mythical effect is convincing – at least within the narrative of the play. In *The Ball*, on the other hand, the effect of Barker dressed in a satyr's costume is clearly intended to be satirical. But if Barker were to have been wearing the same costumes used in *The Faithful Servant* and *Love Tricks*, his appearance is likely to have also evoked more sincere portrayals of mythical creatures on stage. This sending-up of masquing conventions – and, more generally, established theatrical practice – might well have extended to more subtle effects than costuming, for just as well-known songs and ballads travelled between plays and were performed in different theatrical contexts, dances or particular steps might have done the same. Barker's performance of particular movements associated with satyrs in other performances might have created kinetic mimics or echoes on the stage.

In similar style, the French dancing master Monsieur Le Friske takes on the role of Cupid in the masque that closes the play – 'A French *Cupid*', as Honoria observes (G3v). When Honoria points out that '*Cupid* is a childe, you have a beard Mounsieur' (G3v), Le Friske retorts (in his parodically French accent) that '*Venus* his moder have de mole, and *Cupid* / Her shild may have the blacke mussell [muzzle]' (G4r), and continues to defend the casting choice in the face of Honoria's concern that Monsieur Le Friske's bearded face does not correspond with reports that Cupid is 'faire' (G4r). The incongruity of a bearded Cupid draws attention to the fragility of theatrical illusion and the compromises forced by practical necessity: Le Friske's contribution to the ceremony of the masque, in which a '*golden Ball descends*' (I2v), must have tipped into the absurd. The spectacle of this 'stately' entertainment and, more broadly, the presentation of masquing conventions of courtly entertainments becomes a farce in Shirley's play, while the dancing master who shares his nationality with Queen Henrietta Maria is roundly satirised, and the representation of the courtly cherub Cupid rendered a joke.[50]

While *The Arcadia* strives to combine perceptions of rusticity and courtliness as part of its theatrical strategy for a 1630s audience, *The Ball* works to blur the boundaries of courtly artifice and its potential for absurdity in performance. Heywood may have invoked the image of the 'little ape-fac'd boy thou tearm'st a god' (D1v) to demystify courtly spectacle, but here Shirley's dramatic narrative exposes the mechanisms that lie behind the successes and staging conventions of early modern theatre to add extra layers of depth to his drama, so that, in *The Ball*, the result becomes disarmingly metatheatrical. While Heywood evoked masquing conventions in order to create new theatrical spaces and contexts for his older work, Shirley's artistic and creative responses to those conventions were quite different, as his transmutation of such traditions on the stage worked to expose the inherent risk of courtly spectacle and reveal its potential for failure. The protracted collapse of decorum in *The Ball*'s final act showcases the extent to which modes of 'courtly' performance and convention could quickly become interchangeable with comedic chaos under Shirley's direction. The courtly masque is not replicated or imitated here by Shirley – it is emptied of its traditional politicised meaning, and becomes a device through which Shirley can offer imaginative observation and commentary on the social conventions of fashionable London, and, in turn, on the expectations of his paying audience. The audience's willingness to invest in theatrical illusion plays as much of a role in the exposure of theatrical artifice and conventions as do the potential failures inherent in the realities of performance, and Shirley had adopted a similarly puckish approach in his revival of *The Night-Walkers*, when he reappropriated the Cockpit's established conventions in the staging of ghosts and manipulated conditions on stage to drive this plot, full of mistaken identity and trick hauntings, onwards.[51] For Shirley, it is almost as if the abundance of theatrical tropes and traditions made available over the history of early modern theatre – what might have seemed to approach oversaturation on the Cockpit stage, in its commingling of decades' worth of traditions and genres – led to the riotous collapse or unravelling of familiar convention, and the upending of expectation. But as both *The Ball* and *The Night-Walkers* emphasise, this was a circumstance that afforded its own distinctive theatrical pleasure in performance.

In the context of Shirley's theatrical strategy in *The Ball*, the witty, self-referential play between theatrical tradition on the one hand, and the experience and entertainment of the 1630s audience on the other, there should be little surprise that Shirley's retelling of the *Arcadia* sets its own agenda when it comes to its relation to the court and to courtly behaviour. While the courtly taste for pastoral may have been responsible for the inclusion of pastoral-inspired drama in the commercial repertories, Shirley's adaptation of his original source material demonstrates the same playful, experimental approach that is manifest elsewhere in his dramatic writing. *The Ball* makes fun of conventionalised stage spectacle and masquing traditions while paying tribute to their continued popularity, while his *Arcadia* gestures towards the characteristics, conventions, and tastes of the Caroline court but refrains from offering unqualified endorsement. The effect in *The Arcadia* may be subtler, but the impulse is similar. Though courtly behaviours and conventions provided resonant cultural and theatrical frameworks on which Shirley was free to draw, not even the interests of Charles and Henrietta Maria (perceived or actual) rendered these contexts exempt from subversion or ridicule. And in adapting the *Arcadia*, Shirley at once capitalised on the courtly taste for pastoral while writing well beyond that audience, for the repertory of Queen Henrietta's Men and the patrons of the playhouse.

THE BIRD IN A CAGE: 'MADE UP OF ALL PERFORMANCE'

Shirley's familiarity with theatrical and cultural history, alertness to the tastes and concerns of the court, adaptation of classical source material, and his mischievous exploration of staging conventions are all combined with provocative and compelling results in *The Bird in a Cage*. The play has long been read as a defence of Queen Henrietta Maria's performances at court – as a Queen Henrietta's Men's play that expressed public allegiance with the interests of their notional patron – and as such has held a central place in critical accounts of the repertory and of 1630s drama more widely. First printed in 1633, it carries a pointed satirical attack on its dedicatee, William Prynne. The prefatory material conveys Shirley's congratulations to Prynne on his '*happy* Retirement' – an involuntary circumstance on Prynne's part, brought about by his imprisonment.[52] Prynne was awaiting trial at the time that *The Bird in a Cage* was printed, following the publication of his anti-theatrical diatribe *Histriomastix*. This work contained passages that emphasised the impropriety of women acting on the stage, and was released for sale in London bookshops at the same time that Queen Henrietta Maria was immersed in rehearsal for Walter Montagu's *The Shepherd's Paradise*.[53]

The publication of *The Bird in a Cage* worked to configure the play as a statement of support on behalf of the queen, in a clear and clearly topical manoeuvre. But this packaging was a retrospective addition to an already completed and premiered play that had been in performance since its licensing earlier in the year under the name of *The Beauties*.[54] The play was retitled, in print at least, in what might have been an allusion to Prynne's newly caged condition. These alterations to the text seem to have been explicitly related to publication then, as Philip R. Rider has noted: 'Although Shirley's involvement in Prynne's troubles was purely tangential and after the fact, Cooke [the publisher] must surely have realised that a popular playwright's witty attack on a Puritan [...] would have had an immediate audience.'[55] Rider attributes the speed with which *The Bird in a Cage* was published, only two months after its licensing, to its topical currency.[56] It is worth bearing in mind here that although the play's publication followed hard on the heels of its initial staging, *The Bird in a Cage* in performance was – at least at first – distinct from its printed incarnation and independent of it.

But *The Bird in a Cage* is also thematically connected to the Prynne scandal, featuring a scene in which Princess Eugenia and her women stage their own performance of a play. Shirley's engagement in a meta-theatrical exploration of female performance at the same time as the queen's behaviour was drawing attention to the practice was certainly timely. In the introduction to their edition of the play, Hero Chalmers, Julie Sanders, and Sophie Tomlinson read the drama as 'empathetic to the notion of women and performance', and describe how Shirley can be seen to make 'careful attempts to maintain an air of decorum around the notion of the performing Queen'.[57] They take care to emphasise that its politics are not straightforward or unambiguous, but the importance of the play remains linked to its courtly connections. Shirley's role as a valet to Queen Henrietta, and the understanding of the politics of *The Bird in a Cage* as related to 'Shirley's relationship with the Cockpit and its specific connection to the queen's patronage', also contribute to the reading of the play.[58]

Queen Henrietta Maria's patronage of the company, as noted in Chapter 2, might certainly have contributed to Shirley's crafting of this play. At the same time, the Prynne trial has become an event around which narratives have been neatly organised, with appealing and intriguing results as far as the connection between the court and the theatre is evidenced. But as the following discussion explores, when the play is read in the context of the Cockpit repertory, and when Shirley's theatrical strategies are unravelled, the play seems as preoccupied with ideas surrounding the art and business of playing, and theatrical skill, as it does with female performance per se. This reading re-establishes the play as, first and foremost, a repertory piece for the Cockpit, and suggests that embracing it as such proffers a perspective that is as rewarding as those focused on Shirley's courtly allegiances. This is to give full recognition to another observation made by Sanders, Chalmers, and Tomlinson: that the play offers 'a sustained rumination on performance'; that it 'directly involves itself with themes of performance and pretence, seriousness and sports'.[59] This emphasis is similarly noted by the play's most recent editor, Clare McManus, who states that it offers 'a remarkable survey of early modern performance culture'.[60] *The Bird in a Cage* is interlaced with instances of playing and counterfeit: the women performing in the tower offer one strand of analysis, but in the art of performance they are joined by Philenzo, the prince disguised as a humorist; Bonamico, an artist trading in trickery and illusion; and Morello, a courtier who dons women's clothes. When these threads are woven together, it becomes clear that Shirley's engagement with theatrical and performance-related concerns throughout the play had its own resonance within the repertory of Queen Henrietta's Men, and addressed not only gender politics, but the nature of performance and the enactment of theatrical illusion on the professional stage. This reading works to resituate *The Bird in a Cage* as central to Shirley's engagement with the repertory, and to his role as one of the principal dramatists at the Cockpit.

From the outset, Shirley's play self-consciously gestures towards its author's familiarity with theatrical and cultural history, and foregrounds the different genres that this play draws upon. The action is set in an Italian court and steeped in a hybrid of fairytale and classical mythologies. Traditional and time-honoured values dominate the drama at its outset. The Duke has built a tower that he intends as a palace for his daughter Eugenia; at first it seems that this building will resemble a school or place of private study, in which Eugenia's 'mind shall be' its 'owne Commander', but this is a ruse through which Eugenia sees at once (B2r). The Duke's real concern is her chastity, and the building is nothing but 'a place to lay my Treasure in, / Safe from the Robber'. Until he finds a suitor to equal Eugenia's 'Birth and Vertues', she is to remain imprisoned in the tower, lest she 'mixe' her 'bloud' with any man beneath the station of a prince (B2r). Shirley's opening premise thus mirrors the beginnings of the story of Sidney's *Arcadia*; in Shirley's adaptation of the source, the King of Arcadia removes his daughters from 'the sight of the admiring world' in order to preserve their virginity, in response to a prophecy (quoted directly from Sidney) which suggests that his eldest daughter will be '*stolne*' and his youngest '*shall with natures blisse embrace*' an uncouth '*love*', while he himself will die (Shirley, *The Arcadia*, B1v).

The rich literary past with which Shirley infuses *The Bird in a Cage* continues to emerge in references to archaic stories and myths that had an important role in dramatic productions on the Cockpit stage. After the princess's imprisonment, Morello the courtier asserts with overstated grandiosity that 'Like orrand [errant] Knights our valiant wits must wrastle / To free our Ladyes from the inchanted Castle' (C2v). This references the dramatic genre to which *The Seven Champions of Christendom* belongs, with its '*arm'd and 'plum'd*' knights engaged in quests to liberate 'oppressed ladies', and more generally the chivalric displays of masculinity represented in plays including Webster's *The White Devil* and *The Devil's Law-Case*, and plays that drew on ideas of chivalry such as Jonson's *The New Inn* for the King's Men.[61] But while Shirley evokes these traditions on the stage, *The Bird in a Cage* works simultaneously to undermine their sincerity and gradually undo the generic characteristics of the drama. This occurs most obviously in Shirley's appropriation of the classical tale of Jupiter and Danae, which provides the subject matter for the play the women perform while imprisoned, and which contains its own potent prophecy concerning the procreation of daughters. The myth's narrative relevance to the storyline is recognised not only by Eugenia when she says that it 'comes neare our owne' (G4v), but also by the courtier Morello as he attempts to enter the forbidden building and invokes 'greate *Iupiter*, the patron of scapes' (E3r). Morello may draw on the famous exploits of a classical god, but his attempt to breach the tower by dressing in disguise as a woman is farcical and ridiculous. If Heywood's *The Escapes of Jupiter* had once been in performance at the Cockpit repertory and was still being staged at another theatre, then Shirley's playful parody here might poke fun at Heywood's dramatisation, providing purchase and recognition for the Cockpit's theatrical past while highlighting the histrionic potential of the drama.

The Bird in a Cage also abounds with references to other plays in performance on stages across London, and in doing so situates itself within a rich theatrical history. Characters in the play refer to 'the Play of the *Invisible Knight*' and 'That of the Ring too' (D3v). They point up the different genres of the plays – 'The one was Magick, and t'other an imposture' – calling to mind the options available to Shirley in the composition of this drama. Elsewhere, the King's Men's *Merchant of Venice* seems to be referenced, when Philenzo says that he 'heard a pound of flesh, a Iewes demand once' (E2r), and the plotline of *Romeo and Juliet* is evoked by the sleeping draught that mimics death.[62] Shirley weaves a self-referential web of stage traditions and well-known dramas, working to locate *The Bird in a Cage* within its context in a commercial repertory. He also keeps questions of genre, audience expectation, and accepted theatrical convention at the forefront of its spectators' minds.

This sense of metatheatricality is heightened when Shirley goes out of his way to deliberately foreground the artifice of staged trickery throughout the action of the enfolding drama. Bonamico's subplot works to expose the artfulness at the heart of all performance when, disguised as a ped-dling magician, he claims to have mastered the art of invisibility. When we first meet Bonamico we learn that his servant has been running 'about the City' and 'disperst' bills to advertise his master's feat, adorning 'every publike place' with a scroll intended to draw audiences to him (C2v) – an advertising strategy also deployed by professional London theatre com-panies.[63] Hoping that he will 'prosper, / In this beleeving Age', Bonamico catalogues the kinds of performances with which he will have to compete: juggling 'Mountibanks' among them, and the wonders advertised by trav-elling doctors who 'dawbe / Each Post' about the town 'with printed follyes' (C2v). When the disguised Philenzo meets Bonamico he suggests that the travelling trickster try another money-making gambit, advising him to 'Sticke your skin with feathers, and draw the rabble of the City for pence a peece to see a monstrous Bird brought from *Peru*' (C4r). Bonamico is dismayed that Philenzo seems to 'despise' his 'Art', but he is soon granted a new, more gullible audience in Dondolo and Grutti. These two relate the advertisement of the magical feat to their own experiences watching plays in the theatre, and warn Bonamico that they have seen tricks played onstage before, and 'are not so ignorant as wee seeme' (D3v); but Bonamico promises them the sight of strange and marvellous wonders: the vision of his 'head onely visible and hanging in the Ayre like a Comet', or 'one of [his] legs, hopping without a body' (D4r). Amazed and enthralled by the idea, Dondolo and Grutti make plans to profit from the trick by purchasing its secret and sending Bonamico 'into some other Province' to ensure their monopoly on its performance (D4v).

This kind of theatrical delight might well have been thought lucrative, for when Shirley summoned his peripatetic trickster on to the stage he also evoked a trade of travelling showmen who competed for the attentions of his audience beyond the doors of the theatres themselves, on the streets of London and in the provinces. Among the licences that Henry Herbert bestowed in his office as Master of the Revels are a great many for travelling shows and entertainments, including tumbling, dancing on the ropes, and the show of peculiar animals – 'a *strange fish*' and 'an outlandish creature, called a *Possum*' among them.[64] Philenzo's reference to the 'monstrous Bird brought from *Peru*' chimes with such spectacles, while suggesting that they could also be contrived and not entirely honest representations. Magic tricks seem to be implied by references in the transcripts of the office-book entries to 'slight of hand'.[65] Perhaps the closest to mystical entertainment was the 'showe in glass called the worlds wonder' that was licensed to be 'sett forthe' in London from 14 August 1623.[66] These shows were all part of the London audience's frame of reference when it came to theatrical entertainment – and some of the more physical shows and feats were staged in theatres themselves, including fencing prizes at the Red Bull, dancers on the ropes at the Fortune, and a Dutch vaulter's performance at the Globe and the Blackfriars.[67] They made up a part of the theatrical vocabulary and experience of the Cockpit audience, and the theatrical pleasure and excitement that they could generate should not be underestimated. We may lack many textual traces relating to these performances, but the transcripts of Herbert's office-book testify to the diversity of entertainments on offer, and their continued popularity into the 1630s. Bonamico's invisibility trick might have been an ambitious feat, but the kind of amazement it offered corresponded with the similarly curious and fantastic fare available across the wider theatrical landscape of London.

Disappointingly for the audience, however, Shirley's play exposes Bonamico as a fraudulent cheat. Bonamico's promise to walk invisible showing only his hand – 'euery line in't' (D4v) – turns out to involve the delivery of a letter in which his hand(writing) is presented before Dondolo and Grutti while its author is nowhere to be seen. The magic behind the theatrical trick is revealed as a cheap play on words, and its author identified as a 'decayd Artist' (F2v). But his skill in setting up the trick would not be lost on the audience: he is a master of his newly adopted trade. In a bid to entice Dondolo and Grutti, Bonamico and his servant Carlo disguise themselves as customers of the invisibility trick that they advertise, drawn to the 'signe of the invisible man' (D2v). Bonamico enters the house disguised, followed by Carlo, and then after re-entering in new disguises they pass over the stage once more and re-enter the house. Noting what they perceive to be a gathering audience, Grutti decides that 'this will bee a tricke worth our learning' (D3r). This elaborate charade may seem overdone, providing comic excess in the play, but Bonamico recognises that such attention to detail is worth it. He knows his bid for entertainment and profit might fail, a danger so recently brought home by Philenzo's condemnation of his peddling. As such he invests accordingly in manipulating the hopes and expectations of others.

What Bonamico does not recognise when Philenzo rejects his offer of a trick is that Philenzo is similarly enmeshed in his own performance of deception. Disguised as the money-driven 'humorist' Rolliardo, Philenzo 'talk'st very madly' in his role, and becomes known about the court as a 'wilde fellow' (F1r, B4r, B4v). Unwittingly, the Duke refers to him as 'the peece made vp of all performance' (E1r), and it may be that it is Philenzo's own putting on and off of character, reminiscent of Musidorus in some ways, that allows him to see through Bonamico's pretence: 'I see you my would be Invisible, fine Knave' (C4r). Similarly, Philenzo's position as a disguised outsider gives him the perspective required to call out the smaller, petty performances of the courtiers, or 'Court Mimicks' (D1v). Philenzo encourages Bonamico to 'distinguish men before you practise on 'em' (C4r), imparting wisdom learned from his own impersonation. If Bonamico had taken these pains, as he goes on to do in the deception of Dondolo and Grutti, he might have realised that he and Philenzo share the same desire not to be 'seen' for what they are. Indeed, though Bonamico is disguised as an itinerant trickster, his true profession is as an artist: he once 'made Properties, and grew poore for want of Pictures' (F2v). Though short of portrait commissions, he lived and worked in the world of representation, and he made and painted theatrical props and items used in performance such as the elaborate birdcage he makes for Philenzo later in the play. This work is professed a 'Master-piece' by the Duke (G3r), and described by Cassiana as 'one of the finest pieces of Pageantry that ere you saw [...] it mooves on wheeles' (H2v–H3r). The reference to pageantry, which links the birdcage to the pageantry of medieval drama and Lord Mayors' pageants, underscores Bonamico's theatrical credentials further.[68] When Philenzo inadvertently saves Bonamico from prison, Bonamico becomes, as his name suggests, his 'good friend'. But the logic of Shirley's drama suggests further that it is their mutual talent in the arts of representation that ultimately unites them: a shared commitment to sustained theatrical endeavour and craft.

In contrast, Morello's attempt at illusion and impersonation goes badly awry. When he enters 'like a Lady' in an attempt to breach Eugenia's tower, the pathetic 'magic' behind his transformation is effortlessly discovered in a series of farcical encounters. His comical prayer to Jupiter to 'assist my petticote, and at my returne, I will sacrifice my linnen-breeches to thee' paves the way for the absurdly humorous episode that ensues as he unwittingly self-sabotages his attempt at entry (E3r). Morello's performance is dire: he is woefully unprepared, having failed to appreciate the preparation and skill required for the delivery of a convincing performance. He has not even remembered to invent an alias for himself, and as he produces money in an attempt to bribe the guards (in a parody of the 'golden rain' in which Jupiter appeared to Danae in the original myth), he manages to expose his breeches before them. Suspecting him, they pretend that one among them is 'an abhominable Lecher [...] a very Satyre, he leapes all comes neare him' (E3v–E4r), and asks Morello ('Madam Thorne') to 'dispence with a private favour' to secure his passage (E4r). Morello worries that the lusty guard will 'ravish me, and discover all', but before his fear can be realised the guard 'throwes him downe, and discovers his Breeches' (E4r). They usher the 'sweet effeminate Signior' offstage (E4v).

The narrative does grant Morello the opportunity to learn from his overly hasty preparation for the role, however, as his punishment for attempting to gain entry to the tower is to 'weare the petticote for a Month' (G2r). Perenotto describes how, when given his sentence, Morello did not swoon, as was 'expected, [but] he grew fortifi'd, and most humbly besought the Duke' to allow him to take on the court jester's role for the term of humiliation, 'since hee could not shake off the Fooles Coat, that he might have that favourable pretence to keepe it on' (G2r). Morello thus gains immersion in a brand new persona, as it turns out that 'ever since, to the astonishment of the hearers, he is growne so iocund and ayrie, nay as if he had beene borne with a Song in's head' (G2r). An intriguing, inter-repertory relationship with another clown on the Cockpit stage adds further nuance to Morello's transformation, since the comic trajectory of Morello seems to parallel that of Heywood's Valerius from

The Rape of Lucrece, in its progression towards an increasingly and more explicitly clownish role. As Valerius is 'Transeshapt' from a 'hopefull Gentleman' to a 'meere Ballater' and becomes 'all musicall', the courtier Morello undergoes a similar metamorphosis.[69] He 'talkes everlasting Ballad, [and] no man laughes at him but hee lashes him in Rime worse then a Satyr' (G2r). When he enters '*like a Jeaster*' in his petticoat, the transformation is confirmed. Grutti's understated remark says it all: 'The case is alter'd with you' (G2r). Morello proceeds to sing at least one ballad (which is scripted), and another follows later. Shirley seems to be actively associating his singing courtier with Heywood's musical noble who took to the same stage. Though Morello's downturn in social status seems related, in unfortunate ways, to the wearing of women's clothes, it is clear that the costume he once wore in aid of a performance or a trick becomes a semi-permanent feature of his identity, definitive of his courtly standing and determinate of his relationships. Morello's 'fortifi'd' and humble commitment to the jester's role enables him to fully inhabit the clownish part, and to echo the performances of the talented visiting stranger who played Valerius. He comes to recognise that the accomplishment of a good performance has to be earned.

The women's staging of their play, *The New Prison*, further underscores the challenges associated with performance, even in play, and even in secluded privacy as here. Owing to the impromptu nature of the performance, Eugenia and her ladies are woefully underprepared – they may be 'perfect in the plot' (G4v), but certainly not in the execution. When Cassiana forgets her lines, she struggles to complete the rhyme of 'dreame' with 'beame, creame. / Helpe me *Katerina*, I can make no sense rime to't' (H1r). Mardona fumbles offstage – 'Must I enter already – h[e]m' (H1v), and the women joke about their 'Crabbed Language', and appalling rhyme (H2r). Eugenia's dreadful rhyming ('Was ever Father to his Childe / So unkind, it makes me wilde' [H1r]) also recalls, in its way, the kind of versification that we see in the Clown's farcical rhyming in the contest between Pan and Apollo that *Love's Mistress* stages. These amateur theatricals clearly foreground the most basic of practical problems in performance: the need for actors to know their parts.

But while the women may not be practised in the arts of performance, it is clear that they are well equipped when it comes to the theoretical understanding of theatrical entertainment, and the processes with which they must engage in order to realise their aims. Donella takes charge and instructs the women to 'referre yourselues to me for your parts' (F3v), and the women's collective experience as spectators of professional drama acquaints them well with the expectations of genre and stereotype when it comes to casting; when Cassiana proclaims that she will play a king,

Catherina observes that she will 'play a Tyrant brauely' (F3v). Donella notes that they will not be subject to the judgement thrown on professional players since they have no live audience, but only the figures portrayed in the hangings and tapestries that adorn the tower: 'our spectators cannot jeere vs' (F3v). When it comes to the performance itself, reference is made to the music that would usually introduce an act, and the convention of a spoken prologue is duly observed. The reliance of any theatrical performance upon the powers of imagination is also summoned, since Mardona lacks the facial hair that her role requires. The ladies are asked to imagine it, and to 'imagine our Scene exprest' (G4v), though later Mardona does attempt to enhance her performance by speaking 'through a Trunke' (or tube) when she delivers the king's part – presumably to make her voice deeper or create a booming echo effect (H1v). Though lacking the practical experience of performance, the women's collective knowledge of, and resourceful investment in, the conventions of professional playing is evident. They use their experience as spectators to realise the kinds of performances to which they aspire – a split perspective that is recognised by Kim Walker when she notes that the women 'slip in and out of their characters as they play actor and audience simultaneously'.[70] The improvisatory performance that they give is thus something quite different from the kind of performances in which Queen Henrietta Maria participated, which were well rehearsed and which involved weeks of memorising lines.[71] And so despite the obstacles that Eugenia and her women encounter, their performances are not demarcated in the play as necessarily inadequate or poor; rather, the sequence suggests that there is something inherent in the business of playing that Shirley recognises as difficult, an exposure to risk.

The performance of *The New Prison* is not, then, a failure in any sense, but can be seen as a knowing depiction of the demands of playing, providing wry comment on some of the everyday challenges that a repertory company such as Queen Henrietta's Men faced. Though Donella has already confirmed that they 'can receiue no disparagement' (F3v) since they lack any audience, the theme persists, pervading the women's amateur theatrics in the same way that the threat of censure attended the professional theatre.[72] Donella must 'speake the Prologue to our mixt audience of Silke and Cruell Gentlemen in the hangings', and Catherina urges her to make it a 'confident Prologue' (H1r). These words are tongue in cheek, poking fun at the fears of playwrights and repertory companies on the first staging of a new play, but they evoke again the risk of failure in theatrical entertainment: the '[Ju]dicious Hangings', those 'learned Criticks' who 'Hang Still', are ever-present (H1r). Shirley's affectionately comic scene also evokes actorly insecurity when Mardona and Fidelia hide behind the arras before their entry, prompting Cassiana to ask: 'Does not the Arras laugh at me? it shakes me thinks' (H1v). Donella's prologue draws on the same metaphors of palates and tastes as many in the period, appropriating the trope of preference in terms of diet but extracting it into pastiche: 'doe not looke for / Choyce dyet [...] let your Pallat / Expect at most then, but a Root or Sallat' (H1r).[73] The conventions of professional playing are made subject here to the women's mirth, but were matters of critical importance in the collaborative venture of professional playing. Shirley thus appears to make light of the mutual interests and concerns of Queen Henrietta's Men, while at the same time pointing up the real risks that the company faced in each performance of all of its plays, this one included.

Professional actors are also not spared comment. Allocating the parts, Donella warns her waiting cast: 'You will not be ambitious then, and quarrell About the parts, like your spruce Actor, that will not play out of the best Clothes' (G4v). Earlier, she had encouraged the women not to 'distrust your owne performance', for she 'ha knowne men ha bin insufficient, but women can play their parts' (F3v). She further suggests that the people in the hangings, the tapestries to which they perform, 'haue as much Iudgment, as some men that are but Clothes, at most, but walking pictures' (F3v). Though Donella may refer simply to overdressed male playgoers who invest more in dress than in wit, this comment might be thought to allude to those same 'insufficient' actors to whom she has just referred: men costumed for their roles, defined in character by their garments, set upon the stage to be observed as 'walking pictures' – those quarrelling 'spruce' actors. This critique of professional (male) performance and theatrical acuity is performed, of course, by the male actors of Queen Henrietta's Men: those very figures to whom the comments, in the abstract, might apply. But it is another example of the hazards of performance, this time on Beeston's professional stage.

Shirley's decision to use the staging of The New Prison as a commentary on the risks and challenges associated with convincing performance is thrown into sharper relief when compared with the representation of female performance in Jonson's The New Inn, first performed in 1629 at the Blackfriars. In Jonson's earlier play, Lady Frances Frampul and her chambermaid, Prudence, hold a court of love at the inn at which they lodge: a 'dayes sports deuised i'the Inne', over which Prudence resides as the 'Queene Regent of Loue'.[74] Both women carry out their roles with conviction, and Lady Frances's performance in the mock court is so convincing that it baffles many in attendance. Prudence observes of her mistress: 'Excellent actor! how she hits this passion!', but Latimer is less sure that this is a performance, asking 'But doe you thinke she playes?' (E5r). In the court's second hour of sitting, Lovel, charged with making the case for love, complains of

> the craft of crocodiles, womens piety,
> And practise of it, in this art of flattering,
> And fooling men [...]
> I haue lent my selfe out, for two howres,
> Thus to be baffuld by a Chambermaid,
> And the good Actor, her Lady (F7v–F8r)

The Lady's 'good' acting is such that even Prudence is confused. When Lady Frances confesses to being 'somewhat froward' in the course of the debate, she compares being forthright to putting on a visor, chiding Prudence: 'You'l let a Lady weare her masque, Pru.' (F8r). When Prudence protests that she finds it difficult to discern when her Lady puts on such a 'masque' or 'leaue[s] it off', Lady Frances evokes the gendered skill of intuition between women: 'You might ha' knowne that by my lookes, and language, / Had you beene or regardant, or obseruant. / One woman, reads anothers character, / Without the tedious trouble of deciphering' (F8r). It emerges that Lady Frances has indeed been won over by Lovel's arguments, though Prudence is amazed: 'I sweare, I thought you had dissembled, Madam' (F8v).

In Jonson's play the performance of women is skilfully executed, to the point that onlookers discover its seamless blending with genuine emotional affect in the case of Lady Frances. Like the tower in *The Bird in a Cage*, Jonson's inn provides 'a space of theatrical freeplay', which is key to the chambermaid's subversive but temporary social elevation as she takes on the part of sovereign.[75] Furthermore, as Sanders suggests, women's performance is associated more explicitly with aristocratic standing in the play, so that theatre 'is subtly being presented as an acceptable domain for women of rank', with the masquing tradition – and the performances of Queen Henrietta Maria – making its own contribution to the narrative.[76] It seems clear, in comparison, that Shirley's presentation of Eugenia's performance and that of her ladies was a choice and a strategy that knowingly departed from Jonson's theatrically gifted women. Within the wider framework of *The Bird in a Cage*, the difficulties that the women encounter in their own performances, however casual and playful they are, tie in to an engaged reflection on the nature of performance, and the effort and exertion it demands. As the plotlines of Philenzo, Bonamico, and Morello reveal, the credible personation of roles and parts requires sustained commitment, of the kind that Henrietta Maria herself exhibited in her weeks of rehearsal. The skilful perfection of a good performance does not come naturally or through intuition in *The Bird in a Cage*, but is hard won and demands perseverance.

It is likely that this seemed a truism for Shirley, a professional repertory playwright whose colleagues had dedicated their lives to acting and theatrical craft. This reading of the play and its emphasis on the skill, perseverance, and professionalism that must be invested in performance runs in parallel with Alison K. Deutermann's interpretation of the representation of literary craft and celebrity in *The Bird in a Cage*, and Shirley's emphasis on the creative labour that must be spent on the artifice of theatre.[77] Importantly, Deutermann's reading also emphasises Shirley's sustained engagement over the years with the developing traditions and conventions of theatrical performance, and the 'richly intertheatrical' nature of *The Bird in a Cage* as a contributing factor in the model of literary authorship which emerges from her reading of the play.[78] This is a play deeply invested in, and reflective of, the theatrical and literary circumstances of its production – a play that emphasises the achievements and dedication of the playwright and the actors who brought it to the stage, while artfully burying such a call for recognition and applause in the unfolding narrative of the drama, and in the lived enjoyment of the play by its audience in real-time performance.

Though I suggest here that the emphasis of the play rests on the accomplishment of consummate performance in the round, Shirley's inclusive approach towards female performance, and the warm representation of the women at play, remains noteworthy. Kim Walker's analysis of the play has emphasised the extent to which women in performance were carefully contained by the state, which served to 'authorize the female actor, [while] in the process recuperating her for patriarchy'.[79] Walker suggests that the female actor is licensed to speak and play only within a circumscribed space – both physical and cultural. In *The Bird in a Cage*, this arena is represented by the tower in which the women are imprisoned and where they act 'firmly in the private sphere'.[80] According to Walker's reading, *The Bird in a Cage* represents and advocates female performance, but only within the patriarchal social order; the play is thus neither radical, nor unconditional. But it is also important not to lose sight of the fact that in Shirley's world, female performance – in addition to female participation in theatrical enterprise as engaged and critical spectators – is part of the broader canvas of the theatrical scene, making up a rich picture of dramatic endeavour, and textured by the influences, borrowings, exchanges, and adaptations that characterised early modern professional drama. These metatheatrical features seethe through Shirley's drama, from intertheatrical references and the repurposing of source material to the representation of how characters fashion their own performances in life and in play, and they illuminate Caroline London's animated and enlivened theatrical culture. Though *The Bird in a Cage* has been read as an endorsement of Henrietta Maria's interests, and the text's prefatory apparatus has become instrumental in reading the drama's politics, this is a play concerned with theatricality and performance, with playwriting and acting and the world of the London stage itself. On this reading, the play is to be located explicitly within the context of the professional theatre, rather than in relation to the courtly circles that have previously defined it.

CONCLUSION

Attention to Shirley's drama for the Cockpit stage reveals the extent to which his work for the company required sustained engagement with the drama that had come before – in Beeston's venue but also across London more widely – which could be both self-reflexive and critical. When Shirley playfully ridiculed the serious, classical narratives (such as that of Jupiter and Danae) that provided the source material for plays such as *The Escapes of Jupiter* or *The Iron Age*, he was testing the boundaries of one of Heywood's chosen genres, looking for the moment when grandiose dramatic spectacle might give way to farce and hilarity. When he staged the capacity of the stately court masque to disintegrate on the entry of an incongruously bearded cupid in *The Ball*, he both destabilised and reanimated the curious collection of masque-like plays in the Cockpit repertory, including *The Sun's Darling*, *The World Tossed at Tennis*, and *Cupid's Revenge*. By the 1630s there was an incredible variety of dramatic traditions on stage, decades' worth of stocks of plays encompassing fashions from the Elizabethan history play to the revenge tragedy, Jacobean city comedies to Fletcherian tragicomedies. All of these genres and many more are expressed in one form or another in the Cockpit's amalgamated repertory. This abundance and the vibrant performance history on the stage to which it bears witness invited reflection on the development of genres, the meaning of theatrical performances, and their limits. As one of Beeston's leading dramatists at the Cockpit, augmenting the repertory incrementally and over a period of a decade, Shirley worked to negotiate the theatrical precedents that had come before, and find a path through them that afforded new contributions in both artistic and commercial terms.[81] This was a contribution that was not derivative in nature, but generative, undertaken in the same explorative and imaginative spirit as that seen at work in his adaptation of Elizabethan source material in *The Arcadia*.

Shirley's reach across the repertory is also worth emphasising, as he worked to provide fresh contexts for the multitude of dramatic traditions that had made a home on the Cockpit stage. In addition to reflecting on Heywood's classical reworkings and the masque-like plays of the repertory, the settings of his plays also drew on the quasi-historical folklore that came to be embodied in Cockpit revivals such as *George-a-Greene*, and that was newly invigorated by Queen Henrietta's Men in stagings of *King John and Matilda* and *The Seven Champions of Christendom*. Alongside his contemporary, John Ford, he exploited the tragic overtones of the repertory, building on the older styles found in Chettle's *Hoffman* and Middleton and Rowley's Jacobean *The Changeling*, to produce new tragedies in *The Traitor*, *The Maid's Revenge*, and *Love's Cruelty*. As we have seen, he encouraged – and may have introduced – new fashions on the Cockpit stage in the pastoral romance. And he also engaged directly with a new fashion in comedies in the 1630s, a new kind of drama concerned with Caroline London, its social life, and (sometimes) a 'place-realism' in the geographical detail that it offered.[82] Shirley's contribution to professional drama is indeed often characterised in terms of this sub-repertory of plays, which included *Hyde Park* and *The Lady of Pleasure* for Queen Henrietta's Men. Shirley proved himself a playwright able to move the repertory forwards and complicate its styles and characteristics, without denying the theatricality of older traditions or occluding the importance of the dramatic past. And his engagement with dated plays was hands-on and direct, in the revival of old drama on the company's behalf. In this respect, Shirley's role for the company accorded with the professional commitments of Heywood to Queen Henrietta's Men. Both dramatists were engaged in the provision of new fare for performance, while taking account of and accommodating the inheritance and continued accumulation of revivals.

Finally, Shirley's dramatic influence and legacy extended far beyond his immediate work for the company. The importance of Shirley's connection with Henry Herbert over the 1630s emerged in the discussion in Chapter 2 of the connection of the court with the company, as it is known that the relationship that held between Beeston, Shirley, and Herbert was to have a material impact on the repertory through the addition of new plays that arrived at the Cockpit through Herbert. This conduit for plays is likely to have affected the company's relationship to the court: those plays with which Herbert was directly involved, or commented on beyond his strictly professional role, all seem to have been performed there as far as the records reveal.[83] But, further to this, Shirley's commercial role for the company and his regular production of plays for the Cockpit became instrumental to Herbert's developing appreciations and his growing inter-est in the content of drama and its aesthetics. When Herbert censored *The Ball*, Beeston took it upon himself to punish Shirley, transferring the responsibility of censorship to himself. But this was also a manoeuvre that made Shirley accountable, and appears to have created the conditions under which Shirley was to be placed in a more immediate correspondence with Herbert, even if it might not have been direct. As noted in Chapter 2, when Shirley's comedy *The Young Admiral* provided Herbert with 'much delight and satisfaction in the readinge' the following July, he believed that Shirley would have access to read 'this approbation'.[84] And when he gave Shirley the plot for *The Gamester*, this appears to have approached (at the least) a direct transaction between the two men: Herbert says it was 'given him by mee'.[85]

The Young Admiral thus prompted a kind of aesthetic refinement and optimism in Herbert, who hoped that this new vein of dramaturgy might 'serve for a patterne to other poetts', who, when they 'heare and see his good success', would imitate his work.[86] It is unclear what exactly is meant by Shirley's 'good success', but in the context of the office-book this appears directly linked to Herbert's approval.[87] Herbert's response to Shirley's new play seems to have clarified his thoughts on the virtues of 'beneficial and cleanly' poetry – a development that might have given Herbert a renewed sense of engagement with professional drama, and with that the perception of a new dimension of control over it. Very few transcripts from Herbert's office-book which pass evaluative judgement on any of the plays survive prior to his comments on *The Young Admiral*,[88] but after this point the records as they have been preserved indicate a growing tendency on Herbert's part to offer critical comment on the drama or record its reception.[89] If the surviving transcripts reflect anything of Herbert's engagement with the drama, rather than the priorities and inter-ests of those who made them, Shirley's part in shaping Herbert's dramatic tastes and directing his attention to the merits of his own work and, by extension, to the Cockpit repertory is noteworthy. *The Young Admiral* seems to have helped to refine and crystallise Herbert's idea of what was desirable in early modern drama, and might actively have contributed to the criteria of aesthetic taste that were developing in the office of the Master of the Revels, at an explicitly supervisory and authoritative level. In theatre historical terms, Herbert's approval of *The Young Admiral* is a story that is well rehearsed, and centres Shirley within the company history; in that sense, Herbert's appraisal of Shirley has also come to govern historical accounts of the repertory, its critical reception and legacy. But Shirley's role might have been fundamental, in more ways than have been recognised, to the choices and decisions Herbert made in his professional role and, in that sense, to the wider development of Caroline drama over the period.

NOTES

1 See G. E. Bentley, 'The Theatres and the Actors', in *The Revels History of Drama in English, Volume IV: 1613–1660*, ed. Philip Edwards (London: Methuen, 1981), pp. 69–124 (p. 100); G. E. Bentley, *The Jacobean and Caroline Stage*, 7 vols (Oxford: Clarendon Press, 1941–68), I, pp. 226–30; Andrew Gurr, *The Shakespearian Playing Companies* (Oxford: Clarendon Press, 1996), pp. 152–4.

2 Bentley suggests, for instance, that '[i]t seems likely that the high repute of Queen Henrietta's company was due in part to the plays which James Shirley was writing for them' (*Jacobean and Caroline Stage*, I, p. 226).

3 Fredson Bowers writes that '[t]he age, in its literature as well as its mood, had lost its freshness and inspiration. The drama was becoming worn out.' Fredson Bowers, *Elizabethan Revenge Tragedy 1587–1642* (Princeton, NJ: Princeton University Press, 1966 [1940]), p. 217. Alfred Harbage suggests that '[i]t is Shirley to whom we must look as the chief harbinger of the Restoration tendency to seek the material of comedy among posturing members of polite society'. Alfred Harbage, *Cavalier Drama* (New York: Modern Language Association of America, 1936), p. 78. Richard Morton writes that 'Shirley's plays are doubtless conventional, but they are independent works of art, achieving their effects by their intrinsic qualities rather than by their position in literary history'. Richard Morton, 'Deception and Social Dislocation: An Aspect of James Shirley's Drama', *Renaissance Drama*, 9 (1966), 227–45 (p. 228). Shirley has also been charged with a lack of vitality; in relation to Shirley's *The Young Admiral*, a play so praised by Henry Herbert, Kathleen McLuskie writes that '[t]he satisfaction rather than the improvement of the quality seems to have been Shirley's chief professional aim and his rehearsal of the familiar ideology displays an almost parodic ease'. Kathleen McLuskie, 'The Plays and the Playwrights, 1613–42', in *The Revels History of Drama in English, Volume IV: 1613–1660*, ed. Philip Edwards et al. (London: Methuen, 1981), pp. 127–260 (p. 248). See also Barbara Ravelhofer's introduction to *James Shirley and Early Modern Theatre: New Critical Perspectives* (Abingdon: Routledge, 2017), and the description of Shirley as 'A Caroline Prospero [... who] made magic from the books of Webster, Sidney, Shakespeare, Middleton, Massinger, and so many others' (p. 4).

4 Bowers, *Elizabethan Revenge Tragedy*, p. 223.

5 *The Complete Works of James Shirley: An Edition in 10 Volumes*. The project's website can be accessed at http://community.dur.ac.uk/james.shirley/?page_id=152 (accessed 24 October 2023).

6 See Jeremy Lopez, 'Time for James Shirley', in *James Shirley and Early Modern Theatre: New Critical Perspectives*, ed. Barbara Ravelhofer (Abingdon: Routledge, 2017), who refers to Shirley as '[d]oggedly creative, inevitably nostalgic, ultimately a resigned witness to formerly inconceivable historical changes' (p. 19) and to Shirley's belatedness (p. 21); though Lopez also emphasises Shirley's originality and his ability to '[digest] antecedent drama not in order to recapitulate its work, but rather in order to make it disappear' (p. 25).

7 See pp. 125–30.

8 N. W. Bawcutt (ed.), *The Control and Censorship of Caroline Drama: The Records of Sir Henry Herbert, Master of the Revels 1623–73* (Oxford: Clarendon Press, 1996), p. 174; Martin Wiggins, in association with Catherine Richardson, *British Drama, 1533–1642: A Catalogue* (Oxford: Oxford University Press, 2011–), #2355.

9 Bawcutt (ed.), *Control and Censorship*, p. 194.

10 Bawcutt (ed.), *Control and Censorship*, p. 167; Wiggins, *British Drama*, #2263.

11 Bentley, *Jacobean and Caroline Stage*, III, p. 369.

12 The connections between the Red Bull, Cockpit, and Curtain in the 1630s have already been noted, but there are a number of instances concerning plays in the Cockpit repertory which point to boundaries between companies being more fluid, and less competitively defined, than some accounts would hold: for instance, the joint performance at court of *The Silver Age* by the King's and Queen's Men in 1612, and the ways in which plays moved in and out of the repertory to migrate to other companies; see pp. 32–3. More generally, Roslyn L. Knutson finds that the professional theatre industry was collaborative and cooperative in its pursuits and interests. Roslyn L. Knutson, *Playing Companies and Commerce in Shakespeare's Time* (Cambridge: Cambridge University Press, 2001).

13 Allan H. Stevenson, 'Shirley's Publishers: The Partnership of Crooke and Cooke', *The Library*, 4th series, 25 (1944–45), 140–61 (pp. 146–57).

14 See, however, A. P. Riemer's article, 'Shirley's Revisions and the Date of *The Constant Maid*', *Review of English Studies*, 17 (1966), 141–8, on the dating of *The Constant Maid*, which discusses the play's textual provenance and the implications of Stevenson's print-based argument for chronology, constructions of company, and the role of print for dramatists and companies.

15 Stevenson, 'Shirley's Publishers', pp. 149–50.

16 Stevenson, 'Shirley's Publishers', p. 157.

17 Sandra A. Burner, *James Shirley: A Study of Literary Coteries and Patronage in Seventeenth-Century England* (Lanham, MD: University Press of America, 1988), p. 48.

18 Included in his dedicatees are the Earl of Rutland, the Earl of Holland, Lord Lovelace (a Royalist nobleman, and one of the new courtier playwrights), Henry Osborne, George and Charles Porter, Captain Richard Owen, Walter Moyle, William Tresham, William Cavendish, William Gower, Sir Edward Bushel, and George Lord Berkeley. Shirley's interest in addressing his plays to potential patrons was more generally characteristic of dramatists' behaviour at the time: David M. Bergeron has noted the increase of dedications from the Elizabethan to the Caroline period, and suggests that '[i]nstead of ending such a practice when James put all companies under royal patronage, dramatists increasingly sought out noble patrons, at least on the basis of textual dedications'. David M. Bergeron, 'Patronage of Dramatists: The Case of Thomas Heywood', *English Literary Renaissance*, 18 (1988), 294–304 (pp. 298–9).

19 Ben Lucow, *James Shirley* (Boston: Twayne Publishers, 1981), pp. 15, 18–26.

20 Rebecca A. Bailey, *Staging the Old Faith: Queen Henrietta Maria and the Theatre of Caroline England, 1625–1642* (Manchester: Manchester University Press, 2009).

21 See pp. 74–84; 89–90.

22 Bentley, *Jacobean and Caroline Stage*, V, p. 1075; Wiggins, *British Drama*, #2481.

23 Bawcutt (ed.), *Control and Censorship*, p. 160.

24 Bentley has discussed the possibility that the passage is constituted of two separate entries, the second being a licence for a play called *The Arcadia* made on 8 February 1624, but eventually finds this unconvincing since the transcript fails to reflect the

usual organisation of Herbert's licence entries (*Jacobean and Caroline Stage*, V, pp. 1075–6).

25 Bawcutt (ed.), *Control and Censorship*, p. 160; see references to 'books' in transcripts of Herbert's records on, for example, pp. 180–3.

26 Bawcutt (ed.), *Control and Censorship*, pp. 174, 181. See also pp. 33 and 48 of this book.

27 Harbage suggested that the publishers misattributed the play to Shirley on publication as an attempt to pass off an old or anonymous play as Shirley's work, as had apparently occurred before in the case of *Look to the Lady*. Harbage's other explanation resided in the possibility that, in a moment of inspiration prompted by the convenience of shared names, Henry Shirley's name was substituted with James's in order to 'stimulate sales'. Alfred Harbage, 'The Authorship of the Dramatic "Arcadia"', *Modern Philology*, 35 (1938), 233–7 (pp. 235–6).

28 Harbage, 'Authorship', p. 237.

29 Harbage, 'Authorship', p. 236.

30 Discussed in Bentley, *Jacobean and Caroline Stage*, V, p. 1075; F. G. Fleay, 'Annals of the Careers of James and Henry Shirley', *Anglia: Journal of English Philology*, VIII (1885), 405–14 (pp. 406–7).

31 Fleay, 'Annals', p. 407.

32 Robert Stanley Forsythe, *The Relations of Shirley's Plays to the Elizabethan Drama* (New York: Columbia University Press, 1914), p. 268.

33 See pp. 74–84.

34 Depending on date of composition; see pp. 78–82.

35 Lucy Munro, *Archaic Style in English Literature, 1590–1674* (Cambridge: Cambridge University Press, 2013), p. 169.

36 James Shirley, *The Arcadia* (London, 1640), B3v, B4r.

37 See pp. 80–1.

38 See Philip Sidney, *The Countess of Pembroke's Arcadia*, ed. Maurice Evans (London: Penguin, 1977), pp. 227–33. This version of the *Arcadia*, Mary Herbert's 1593 'composite' with a bridging addition by William Alexander, comprises the *New Arcadia* with parts of the *Old Arcadia* added to its end, and it is the version to which Shirley would have had access, since the original *Arcadia* was unpublished before 1912 (see Maurice Evans's edition, pp. 10–14).

39 'quaint, adj., adv., and n.2.', *OED Online*, www.oed.com/view/Entry/155830 (accessed 5 July 2020).

40 'smile, v.', *OED Online*, www.oed.com/view/Entry/182597 (accessed 5 July 2020).

41 Munro, *Archaic Style*, p. 172.

42 Sidney, *The Countess of Pembroke's Arcadia*, p. 638.

43 Sidney, *The Countess of Pembroke's Arcadia*, pp. 235, 236.

44 See Munro, *Archaic Style*, p. 177, which focuses more explicitly on end-stopped rhyming couplets in *The Faithful Shepherdess*.

45 See p. 80.

46 Georg Rudolf Weckherlin began composing a masque between 1627 and 1630 which was intended for the queen's court and featured Cupid, though it is unclear whether it was completed and performed (Wiggins, *British Drama*, #2226). The character appears in Jonson's masque *Chloridia*, in which Queen Henrietta performed in 1631 (#2332), and Charles I performed (before the queen) in Jonson's *Love's Triumph Through Callipolis* in the same year (#2328) – this masque contained fifteen cupids. Cupid's popularity at court endured throughout the later 1630s. The character appeared in *Love's Welcome: The King and Queen's Entertainment*

at Bolsover, performed in 1634 as William Cavendish's entertainment for his royal audience, though unpublished until 1640–41 (#2439); in a pastoral court masque in which Queen Henrietta Maria performed in 1633 (#2398); in Shirley's masque, *The Triumph of Beauty*, performed before 1646 (best guess 1634) (#2435); and in William Davenant's *The Triumphs of the Prince D'Amour*, a masque performed before court at Middle Temple in 1636 and published in the same year (#2532). Beaumont and Fletcher's *Cupid's Revenge* was performed at court by Beeston's Boys in 1637.

47 James Shirley, *The School of Compliment* (London, 1631), E2r.

48 James Shirley, *The Ball* (London, 1639), C2v.

49 See pp. 154–5. James Shirley, *The Grateful Servant* (London, 1630), I2r.

50 See also Jean Howard, 'Dancing Masters and the Production of Cosmopolitan Bodies in Caroline Town Comedy', in *Localizing Caroline Drama: Politics and Economics of the Early Modern English Stage, 1625–1642*, ed. Adam Zucker and Alan B. Farmer (Basingstoke: Palgrave Macmillan, 2006), pp. 183–211, esp. pp. 190–1, 195 on the representation of 'Frenchness' in *The Ball*.

51 See pp. 164–71.

52 James Shirley, *The Bird in a Cage* (London, 1633), A2r.

53 Fleay suggested that it was *The Arcadia* in which the queen was preparing to perform, rather than *The Shepherd's Paradise*; Bentley, *Jacobean and Caroline Stage*, V, p. 1075; see also the discussion in *Three Seventeenth-Century Plays on Women and Performance*, ed. Hero Chalmers, Julie Sanders, and Sophie Tomlinson (Manchester: Manchester University Press, 2006), pp. 23–4.

54 Bawcutt (ed.), *Control and Censorship*, p. 178.

55 Philip R. Rider, 'The Concurrent Printing of Shirley's *The Wittie Fair One* and *The Bird in a Cage*', *Papers of the Bibliographical Society of America*, 71 (1977), 328–33 (p. 333).

56 Rider, 'Concurrent Printing', p. 333.

57 *Three Seventeenth-Century Plays on Women*, pp. 29, 28.

58 *Three Seventeenth-Century Plays on Women*, p. 25.

59 *Three Seventeenth-Century Plays on Women*, pp. 30, 25.

60 *The Bird in a Cage*, ed. Clare McManus, in *The Routledge Anthology of Early Modern Drama*, ed. Jeremy Lopez (Abingdon: Routledge, 2020), p. 1079.

61 John Kirke, *The Seven Champions of Christendom* (London, 1638), C4v, D1r.

62 See also Clare McManus's introduction to her edition of *The Bird in a Cage*, which lists several other plays that are drawn on in the course of the drama (p. 1079).

63 See Tiffany Stern, '"On each Wall and Corner Poast": Playbills, Title-pages, and Advertising in Early Modern London', *English Literary Renaissance*, 36 (2006), 57–89, on the advertisements hung on posts around London, which included bills for theatres.

64 Bawcutt (ed.), *Control and Censorship*, pp. 145, 161, 175, 212.

65 Bawcutt (ed.), *Control and Censorship*, pp. 145, 176, 212.

66 Bawcutt (ed.), *Control and Censorship*, p. 142.

67 Bawcutt (ed.), *Control and Censorship*, pp. 139, 140, 161, 212.

68 See *Three Seventeenth-Century Plays on Women*, p. 246, n. 174.

69 Thomas Heywood, *The Rape of Lucrece* (London, 1638), C1v.

70 Kim Walker, 'New Prison: Representing the Female Actor in Shirley's *The Bird in a Cage* (1633)', *English Literary Renaissance*, 21 (1991), 385–400 (p. 400).

71 Also noted in *Three Seventeenth-Century Plays on Women*, p. 242, n. 62.

72 See pp. 110–12.

73 See p. 114.

74 Ben Jonson, *The New Inn* (London, 1631), B8r, E2r.

75 Julie Sanders, '"A Woman Write a Play!"': Jonsonian Strategies and the Dramatic Writings of Margaret Cavendish; or, did the Duchess Feel the Anxiety of Influence', in *Readings in Renaissance Women's Drama*, ed. S. P. Cerasano and Marion Wynne-Davies (London: Routledge, 1998), pp. 293–305 (p. 301); see also Julie Sanders, '"The Day's Sports Devised in the Inn": Jonson's *The New Inn* and Theatrical Politics', *Modern Language Review*, 91 (1996), 545–60 (pp. 546–8).

76 Sanders, '"A Woman Write a Play!"', p. 301.

77 Allison K. Deutermann, 'Literary Celebrity and Theatrical Culture in Shirley's *Bird in a Cage*', in *Historical Affects and the Early Modern Theater*, ed. Ronda Arab, Michelle Dowd, and Adam Zucker (Abingdon: Routledge, 2015), pp. 54–65.

78 Deutermann, 'Literary Celebrity', p. 63.

79 Walker, 'New Prison', p. 395.

80 Walker, 'New Prison', p. 395.

81 Deutermann explores this in 'Literary Celebrity', and Jeremy Lopez notes that Shirley's writing can be seen to demonstrate 'accumulated layers of theatrical convention'; he might be thought to have accomplished a 'nearly complete internalisation of the drama that had preceded him' ('Time for James Shirley', pp. 25, 21).

82 See Theodore Miles, 'Place-Realism in a Group of Caroline Plays', *Review of English Studies*, 18 (1942), 428–40.

83 *The Young Admiral*, *The Gamester*, *The Night-Walkers*, and *Hymen's Holiday*; Bawcutt (ed.), *Control and Censorship*, pp. 184–5, 187.

84 Bawcutt (ed.), *Control and Censorship*, p. 180.

85 Bawcutt (ed.), *Control and Censorship*, p. 187.

86 Bawcutt (ed.), *Control and Censorship*, p. 180. See also pp. 75–6 of this book.

87 Bawcutt (ed.), *Control and Censorship*, p. 184 .

88 A notable exception is Herbert's marginal comment on *More Dissemblers Besides Women* in 1624, which specified that it was 'The worst play that ere I saw'; Bawcutt (ed.), *Control and Censorship*, p. 148.

89 Not only do the transcripts record whether plays were 'likt' or not at court, as noted in Chapter 2, but Herbert noted, for instance, that the masque presented by the Inns of Court contained a show that 'was glorious', and that the king's masque, performed shortly afterwards, was 'the noblest masque of my time to this day, [with] the best poetrye, best scenes, and the best habitts'; Bawcutt (ed.), *Control and Censorship*, p. 187.

CODA

Queen Henrietta's Men were disbanded in 1636. Their last mention in the transcripts of Henry Herbert's records refers to a February performance of *The Knight of the Burning Pestle* at court in 1636, and then, two weeks later, the licensing of Glapthorne's *Love's Trial, or The Hollander.*[1] The theatres were closed for plague in May. By mid-February 1637 their successors, Beeston's Boys, had already performed at court at least two plays previously performed by Queen Henrietta's Men.[2] When the theatres reopened at the end of that month, it was this company, which Beeston had been 'commanded to make', that would occupy the Cockpit until the closure of the theatres in 1642.

The disappearance of the first Queen Henrietta's Men from the London stage seems to have been unrelated to the success and aesthetic legitimacy of their repertory. The Cockpit repertory continued to be performed by Beeston's Boys, and had an important role to play in early modern professional theatre until 1642. In 1639 the Lord Chamberlain protected the rights of Beeston's Boys in forty-five of its plays, which included a large proportion of revivals that had already been old in 1625 when Queen Henrietta's Men inherited them.

In this way the rich variety of dramatic tradition contained within the repertory was retained at the Cockpit. As the theatre's repertory had done for Queen Henrietta's Men, it now formed the basis of success for the new Beeston troupe. But if the repertory was not immediately relocated, it was provided with new context and a new life in performance by Beeston's Boys. The company's large proportion of boy players would impact significantly on the plays' dramatic effects and resonances in performance. The performance by boys of roles such as Apuleius and Midas in *Love's Mistress*, and of Morello in *The Bird in a Cage*, might have radically altered the cultural politics and theatrical effect of these plays on the Cockpit stage. The potential for sending up, comic insincerity, or youthful candour might have resulted in a churlish, adolescent Midas, sulky and capricious in his preferences, or a more tragic rendering of Morello as a court innocent, a mocked and more pathetic Malvolio-like character with whom audiences could sympathise, in contrast with the ridiculous and overblown buffoon we can otherwise imagine. These were performance choices that were also available to Queen Henrietta's Men, of course, but the new company might have chosen to define these established roles in contrast to the performances given by Queen Henrietta's Men, reinterpreting and rebranding the repertory through its continued revivals. So although Christopher Beeston kept the repertory, it seems he was 'commanded' to try and achieve something new with it; an endeavour that his son, William, would bear beyond Christopher's death in 1638.

Beeston's Boys was a different kind of company; its formation was, in some sense, officially instructed, its presence at court required. The repertory did not provide the only continuity at the theatre, for many of the adult actors from Queen Henrietta's Men remained there to join Beeston's new 'young' company. Their familiarity with the repertory of Queen Henrietta's Men must have been extremely valuable for the new company. But enormous changes had taken place. It is unclear how voluntary the departure of Anthony Turner, William Sherlock, John Sumner, and Richard Perkins was when they left for the Salisbury Court theatre, for Herbert suggests that he 'disposed of' them there, and 'joynd them with the best of that company'.[3] Four of Beeston's original Queen's players left to join the King's Men.[4] Heywood wrote two plays for the King's Men in 1634, and then withdrew from the professional activities of the London stage. Shirley departed to Ireland while maintaining his connection with Queen Henrietta's Men in London, though when he returned his future work in theatre was to be defined by its context in the repertory of the King's Men.

Parts of the repertory continued to be performed on the Restoration stage, and one play was performed at the Red Bull during the Interregnum itself while the theatres were officially closed.[5] A great proportion of it faded from history, in terms of its public performance and theatrical use. Some plays were lost. The repertory was split up, but a number of the plays retain their appeal and importance today, in contemporary revivals; in this sense, the repertory continues to prove its portability. This book has demonstrated the importance of Queen Henrietta's Men to the interpretation and dynamics of the repertory, portable and changeable by nature though it was, as it was performed in the particular conditions of the 1630s: material, commercial, and aesthetic. It recognises the achievement of one of the most important companies in early modern theatre history, under whose collaborative efforts the extraordinarily diverse and eclectic Cockpit repertory became most visible, and offered the most serious and sustained challenge to its competitors.

At the same time, it is clear that particular individuals linked to the company were responsible for major developments in its career, and in very different capacities. Christopher Beeston was, of course, instrumental in the formation and management of the company, and emerges here as a figure deeply rooted in, and sensitive to, the professional environment of the early modern theatre. This was an environment that was not only commercial but also collegial and, to a certain extent, familial, and Beeston's awareness of the complex and subtle connections that continued to underpin early modern theatre into the 1630s was key to his responsive and intuitive management of the company over a decade. Henry Herbert is another presence who permeates the story of Queen Henrietta's Men, and the mutually affirming relationships that he held with Beeston and with James Shirley make clear that he had a particular interest in the workings of this company, its creative output, and its artistic direction and aspirations. And with respect to the playwrights, we have seen how seriously both Shirley and Thomas Heywood took their roles as dramatists for the company, and the lengths to which they went to shore up and legitimise a repertory that was in danger of appearing outdated and confusingly multifarious in contemporary descriptions of repertory identity – but without downplaying those very features that contributed to its theatrical appeal and its characteristically miscellaneous nature.

More broadly, this account of Queen Henrietta's Men has tried to demonstrate the shifting nature of repertory and the extent to which plays came to mean or signify differently across temporal and spatial divides – a feature that Beeston, Herbert, Heywood, and Shirley were required to negotiate each in their own ways. In the same way that Elizabethan Red Bull plays were reactivated in revival alongside new drama of the 1630s, those plays written under Beeston's management at the Cockpit, designed at the time to make a specific contribution to Beeston's repertory, would also become untethered from their original conditions of production once staged by other companies and in other locations. And these temporal and spatial divides and boundaries – between categories such as amphitheatre and hall-playhouse, old and new, courtly and commercial – may also not be what they seem, rooted as they often are in early modern commentary on the London theatre industry, or constructed in historical retellings or in the narratives of theatre history that hold or that are emerging today. In fact, the early modern playing scene and the repertory system itself has been shown, time after time, to depend on the collapsibility of these categories, and it is more helpful to see repertory composition and identity as an extension of performance itself: fluid, flexible, to some extent indeterminate and transient. To do this we need to look more closely at the plays themselves, rather than the ways in which they have been artfully packaged as early modern texts by printers, publishers, or their authors; and we need to account for and openly recognise each play's specific performance history on a case-by-case basis, rather than leaning on the ways in which they have been handed down to us in written accounts of theatre history, from the early modern period to today.

NOTES

1 N. W. Bawcutt (ed.), *The Control and Censorship of Caroline Drama: The Records of Sir Henry Herbert, Master of the Revels 1623–73* (Oxford: Clarendon Press, 1996), p. 198.

2 Bawcutt (ed.), *Control and Censorship*, p. 200.

3 Bawcutt (ed.), *Control and Censorship*, p. 201.

4 Michael Bowyer, William Robbins, William Allen, and Hugh Clark.

5 Fletcher's *Wit without Money* was performed at the Red Bull during the Interregnum itself (Martin Wiggins, in association with Catherine Richardson, *British Drama, 1533–1642: A Catalogue* [Oxford: Oxford University Press, 2011–], #1758), and constitutes an important example of the theatre's continued presence in London over this time. In 1672 the play was performed by the Restoration's King's Company, as a debut in their new theatre. A large proportion of the plays performed by Queen Henrietta's Men were also revived in the Restoration, either by the King's Company in London or further afield. John Ford's *'Tis Pity She's a Whore* was seen in Norwich by 1662, for instance (G. E. Bentley, *The Jacobean and Caroline Stage*, 7 vols [Oxford: Clarendon Press, 1941–68], III, p. 462); Daborne's *The Poor Man's Comfort* was performed in Oxford in 1661 (ibid., III, p. 192). Heywood's *Love's Mistress* was revived at Salisbury Court in 1660 (ibid., IV, pp. 579–80), and *The Fair Maid of the West* was performed in London and Norwich in 1662 (ibid., IV, pp. 569–70). The majority of Shirley's plays for Queen Henrietta's Men continued to be performed into the Restoration.

APPENDIX A
THE REPERTORY OF QUEEN HENRIETTA'S
MEN

The entries below give details about all of the plays that are likely to have belonged to Beeston's Cockpit repertory during the time of Queen Henrietta's Men's tenure at the theatre. These entries should be read in conjunction with this brief headnote, which explains the different kinds of evidence considered below. Date of composition and licensing information, where known, is given, including the company to which the play was licensed. Date spans in which a play was composed or premiered follow Martin Wiggins's *British Drama, 1533–1642: A Catalogue* or, if unavailable at the time of writing in the *Catalogue*, Bentley's *The Jacobean and Caroline Stage*. The catalogue number of each play in Wiggins's *Catalogue* is given at the end of each entry where applicable. The date of first publication is also given, alongside claims concerning company and theatre that are printed on the title-page.

In 1639 William Beeston, Christopher Beeston's son and the manager of Beeston's Boys at that time, petitioned the Lord Chamberlain to protect a list of plays for the performance of Beeston's Boys at the Cockpit alone, and the Lord Chamberlain issued an edict to that effect. The document confirms that Beeston retained plays formerly owned by companies that had performed in his theatre, since remnants of the repertories of all the Cockpit companies prior to Beeston's Boys appear in the list. Tracing the provenance of the plays in the list establishes a relatively secure repertory route, by which plays travelled with Queen Anne's Men to the Cockpit to remain there after the company broke in 1619; troupes that performed subsequently in the theatre also left behind new drama that they had premiered under Beeston's management. Since this migratory pattern is strong, a play's inclusion in the 1639 list can, on a case-by-case basis, constitute evidence of its having been performed by Queen Henrietta's Men if it is dated to within the timeframe of the operation of the company, or if the play is known to have been performed by a previous company managed by Beeston at the Cockpit.

Plays that seem to have a marginal connection to Queen Henrietta's Men at the Cockpit appear in a secondary list at the foot of the appendix; readers may expect to see some consideration made for these plays, but there is insufficient evidence to support any confident claim that they belonged to the repertory.

Beaumont, Francis. *The Knight of the Burning Pestle.* Date: 1607. First published in 1613. The play was originally performed by the Children of the Queen's Revels at the Blackfriars, but the 1635 edition title-page gives the acting company as Her Majesty's Servants at the private house in Drury Lane (the Cockpit), and Queen Henrietta's Men performed the play at St James's Palace in 1636. Wiggins #1562.

Beaumont, Francis, and John Fletcher. *Cupid's Revenge.* Date: between 1606 and 1611. First published in 1615. The play was originally performed by the Children of the Queen's Revels, and was later revived and performed at court by Lady Elizabeth's Men in 1624. Beeston's Boys then performed the play at court in 1637 and it is included in the list of plays protected for that company in 1639. It is likely that the play would have been performed in the interim by Queen Henrietta's Men, as a repertory piece retained by Christopher Beeston at the Cockpit. Wiggins #1533.

Chapman, George (revised by James Shirley). *Chabot, Admiral of France.* Date: between 1611 and 1634; revised version licensed for performance on 29 April 1635. First published in 1639. The entry for the play in the Stationers' Register, made in 1638, refers to Shirley as author (presumably due to his role in revising the work). The 1639 title-page claims performance by Her Majesty's Servants at the private house in Drury Lane (the Cockpit). The play was included in the list of plays protected in 1639 for performance by Beeston's Boys at the Cockpit. Wiggins #1676.

Chettle, Henry. *Hoffman* (published as *The Tragedy of Hoffman*). Date: 1603. First published in 1631; the title-page claims performance at the Phoenix (Cockpit) in Drury Lane. In 1631 Queen Henrietta's Men were performing at the theatre. Wiggins #1384.

Cooke, John. *The City Gallant* (published as *Greene's Tu Quoque, or The City Gallant*). Date: 1611. First published in 1614; the title-page claims performance by the Queen's Majesty's Servants, who were at that time Queen Anne's Men, in residence at the Red Bull. Records also evidence performance of the play at court by Queen Anne's Men in 1611 and 1612, and then, in 1625, by Lady Elizabeth's Men. In *c.* 1636–37 the play was performed in Dublin, but prior to this it might have continued in repertory on the Cockpit stage during the tenure of Queen Henrietta's Men, following the breaking of Lady Elizabeth's Men and given Beeston's retention of some of the earlier company's repertory at the Cockpit. Wiggins #1649.

Daborne, Robert. *The Poor Man's Comfort.* Date: between 1615 and 1617. First published in 1655; the title-page asserts performance at the Cockpit in Drury Lane. The play might have been revived by Queen Henrietta's Men and/or Beeston's Boys. Wiggins #1796.

Davenport, Robert. *The City Nightcap.* Date: 1624; licensed on 14 October 1624 for performance at the Cockpit. The play appears to have been retained by Beeston after first performance there by Lady Elizabeth's Men, for when it was first published in 1661 its title-page asserted performance at the Phoenix (Cockpit) in Drury Lane by Her Majesty's Servants. It was then included in the list of plays protected in 1639 for performance by Beeston's Boys at the Cockpit. Wiggins #2139.

Davenport, Robert. *King John and Matilda.* Date: between 1628 and 1634. First published in 1655; the title-page asserts performance by Her Majesty's Servants at the Cockpit in Drury Lane and the cast-list printed within names actors of Queen Henrietta's Men. The play was included in the list of plays protected in 1639 for performance by Beeston's Boys at the Cockpit. Wiggins #2238.

Davenport, Robert. *A New Trick to Cheat the Devil.* Date: between 1624 and 1634. First published in 1639. The play was included in the list of plays protected in 1639 for performance by Beeston's Boys at the Cockpit. Wiggins finds a composition date of 1626–27 a 'strong possibility', making first performance by Queen Henrietta's Men likely; if the play was written before then, performance by Lady Elizabeth's Men at the Cockpit would be congruent with the play's retention in the Cockpit repertory through to 1639. Wiggins #2198.

Dekker, Thomas, and Thomas Middleton. *The Bloody Banquet.* Date: between 1605 and 1613 (?). First published in 1639. Included in the list of plays protected in 1639 for performance by Beeston's Boys at the Cockpit. Since the play was composed well before the 1630s it might have passed to Beeston's Boys as part of the existing Cockpit repertory, as did so many of the boy company's plays. Wiggins #1624.

Dekker, Thomas, and Thomas Middleton. *The Patient Man and the Honest Whore* (published as *The Honest Whore*). Date: 1604. First published in 1604. Originally performed by the Prince's Men at the Fortune, but the 1635 printing of the quarto refers to performance by Her Majesty's Servants on its title-page. This may indicate a revival by Queen Henrietta's Men since some of the plays performed by the Prince's Men remained at the Cockpit following their departure from that theatre. Wiggins #1431.

Dekker, Thomas, John Ford, Thomas Middleton, and William Rowley. *The Spanish Gypsy.* Date: 1623; licensed for performance by Lady Elizabeth's Men on 9 July 1623. First published in 1653. The title-page refers to performance at both the private house in Drury Lane (the Cockpit) and then Salisbury Court. The play was performed at court on 5 November 1623 by Lady Elizabeth's Men; it was later included in the list of plays protected in 1639 for performance by Beeston's Boys at the Cockpit. Given the play's performance by Lady Elizabeth's Men and Beeston's Boys at the Cockpit, it is likely that Queen Henrietta's Men also performed it at the same venue in the interim, though the indication that it might also have been performed at Salisbury Court does complicate matters, since a second theatre is involved. Wiggins #2049.

Fletcher, John (revised by James Shirley). *The Night-Walkers* (published as *The Night-Walker*). Date: between 1613 and 1616, revised 1633; the revised version was licensed for performance by Queen Henrietta's Men on 11 May 1633. First published in 1640; the title-page claims performance by Her Majesty's Servants at the private house in Drury Lane (the Cockpit). The play was performed at Court by Queen Henrietta's Men on 30 January 1634. It was included in the list of plays protected in 1639 for performance by Beeston's Boys at the Cockpit. Wiggins #1772.

Fletcher, John. *Wit without Money.* Date: between 1614 and 1615. First published in 1639–40. It seems likely that Lady Elizabeth's Men performed the play first, and the 1639–40 edition of the play gives Her Majesty's Servants at the private house in Drury Lane (the Cockpit) as the acting company and venue. The play was then performed at court by Beeston's Boys in 1637, and was included in the list of plays protected in 1639 for performance by Beeston's Boys at the Cockpit. Wiggins #1758.

Ford, John. *The Fancies* (published as *The Fancies, Chaste and Noble*). Date: between 1635 and 1636. First published in 1638; the title-page gives the Queen's Majesty's Servants at the Phoenix (Cockpit) in Drury Lane as the company and venue. Wiggins #2528.

Ford, John. *Love's Sacrifice.* Date: between 1626 and 1633. First published in 1633; the title-page gives the Queen's Majesty's Servants at the Phoenix

(Cockpit) in Drury Lane as the company and venue. The play was included in the list of plays protected in 1639 for performance by Beeston's Boys at the Cockpit. Wiggins #2360.

Ford, John. *Perkin Warbeck* (published as *The Chronicle History of Perkin Warbeck*). Date: between 1625 and 1634. First published in 1634; the title-page gives the Queen's Majesty's Servants at the Phoenix (Cockpit) in Drury Lane as the company and venue. Wiggins #2399.

Ford, John. *'Tis Pity She's a Whore*. Date: between 1621 and 1631. First published in 1633; the title-page gives the Queen's Majesty's Servants at the Phoenix (Cockpit) in Drury Lane as the company and venue. The play was included in the list of plays protected in 1639 for performance by Beeston's Boys at the Cockpit. Wiggins. #2329.

Ford, John, and Thomas Dekker. *The Sun's Darling*. Date: 1624; licensed on 3 March 1624 for the Cockpit company (Lady Elizabeth's Men at that time). First published in 1656; the title-page asserts performance by Their Majesties' Servants (Beeston's Boys) at the Cockpit and by the same company at court. The play was included in the list of plays protected in 1639 for their performance. In the years between performance by Lady Elizabeth's Men and by Beeston's Boys at the Cockpit, it is possible (indeed likely, given Beeston's retention of plays performed at the Cockpit) that Queen Henrietta's Men also performed the play as part of the playhouse's repertory. Wiggins #2085.

Ford, John, Thomas Dekker, and William Rowley. *The Witch of Edmonton*. Date: 1621. The play was first performed by the Prince's Men at the Cockpit but was revived *c.* 1635 at the same playhouse by Queen Henrietta's Men; a new prologue was written to mark the occasion and printed in the first edition (1658); this, along with an epilogue, is signed by members of Queen Henrietta's Men. Wiggins #1992; Bentley III, pp. 269–72.

Glapthorne, Henry. *Love's Trial, or The Hollander* (published as *The Hollander*). Date: 1636; licensed for performance by the Queen's Company (Queen Henrietta's Men) on 12 March 1636. First published in 1640. The play seems to have passed to Beeston's Boys; the title-page claims performance by Their Majesties' Servants at the Cockpit in Drury Lane. Wiggins #2536.

Heminges, William. *The Fatal Contract*. Date: between 1629 and 1638. First published in 1653; the title-page claims performance by Her Majesty's

Servants. Wiggins believes 1633 is a convincing date for the play, based on an internal allusion aligning it with *The Shepherds' Paradise*. This would place the play with Queen Henrietta's Men at the Cockpit, rather than with the later company of the same name at Salisbury Court. Wiggins #2412.

Heywood, Thomas. *The English Traveller.* Date: between 1623 and 1624. First published in 1633; the title-page gives Her Majesty's Servants at the Cockpit in Drury Lane as the acting company and venue. The play was presumably first performed by Lady Elizabeth's Men at the Cockpit and then retained by Beeston at the playhouse. Wiggins #2098.

Heywood, Thomas. *The Fair Maid of the West,* **Part I and Part II.** Date of Part I: between 1609 and 1611; originally performed by Queen Anne's Men at the Red Bull. Part II was composed between 1621 and 1631 for Queen Henrietta's Men, and Wiggins finds a date of 1630 most likely. Both plays were first published in 1631 and the title-page gives the Queen's Majesty's Comedians as the acting company; the edition also provides a list of roles and the actors of Queen Henrietta's Men who took those parts. In 1630–31 the two plays, one a revival and the other new, were performed with a special epilogue at court. Wiggins #1607 and #2320.

Heywood, Thomas. *If You Know Not Me, You Know Nobody,* **Part I and Part II.** Date (both parts): between 1603 and 1605; originally performed by Queen Anne's Men, probably at the Curtain or Boar's Head. Part I was first published in 1605, and Part II in 1606. A 1639 edition of Part I included a new prologue and epilogue that had appeared two years earlier in Heywood's *Pleasant Dialogues and Dramas*; this prologue was to 'the Play of Queen Elizabeth as it was last revived at the Cockpit'. A revised version of Part II was then published in 1633. The two plays might have been revived together at the Cockpit by Queen Henrietta's Men, having moved to the playhouse with Queen Anne's Men. Wiggins is cautious with respect to inferring the revival of Part II alongside its prequel. Wiggins #1427 and #1433.

Heywood, Thomas. *Love's Mistress.* Date: 1634. First published in 1636; the edition gives the Queen's Comedians at the Phoenix (Cockpit) in Drury Lane as the acting company and venue, and refers to the company's performances of the play at court. The play was included in the list of plays protected in 1639 for performance by Beeston's Boys at the Cockpit. Wiggins #2451.

Heywood, Thomas. *A Maidenhead Well Lost.* Date: between 1625 and 1634. First published in 1634; the title-page names Her Majesty's Servants at the Cockpit in Drury Lane as the acting company and venue. Wiggins #2289.

Heywood, Thomas. *The Rape of Lucrece.* Date: between 1607 and 1608. First published in 1608. Performed originally by Queen Anne's Men at the Red Bull, and performed at Greenwich Palace by the King's Men and Queen Anne's Men in 1612. The play was revived by 1628 by Queen Henrietta's Men at the Cockpit. It was included in the list of plays protected in 1639 for performance by Beeston's Boys at the Cockpit. New songs appear in the 1630 edition and then again in the 1638 edition, which may also suggest that the play was being revived and actively updated to include new musical interludes during these years. Wiggins #1558.

Heywood, Thomas. *The Royal King and the Loyal Subject.* Date: between 1605 and 1618. First published in 1637; the title-page claims performance by the Queen's Majesty's Servants. At the time of printing the Queen's Servants were Queen Henrietta's Men. Wiggins #1504.

Heywood, Thomas, and William Rowley. *Fortune by Land and Sea.* Date: between 1607 and 1609, or between 1619 and 1626. First published in 1655; the title-page claims performance by the Queen's Servants. Wiggins favours a date of 1623, which places the original performance with Lady Elizabeth's Men: the Queen's Servants of the title-page would then refer to Queen Henrietta's Men, who would inherit the play, rather than to the earlier Queen Anne's as has previously been suggested. Wiggins #2069.

Jonson, Ben. *A Tale of a Tub.* Date: 1633; licensed for performance on 7 May 1633. First published in 1640–41. Performed at court by Queen Henrietta's Men on 14 January 1634. Wiggins #2403.

Killigrew, Thomas. *The Prisoners.* Date: between 1632 and 1635. First published in 1640–41. Wiggins's 'best guess' for the date of composition is 1635, based on the date of the source material's publication and Killigrew's departure from England; the title-page claims performance by Her Majesty's Servants at the Phoenix (Cockpit) in Drury Lane, which is consistent with this dating (for *Claracilla*, see below under 'Plays of Doubtful or Uncertain Attribution'). Wiggins #2487.

Kirke, John. *The Seven Champions of Christendom.* Date: between 1625 and 1634. First published in 1638. The title-page claims that the play was acted at both the Cockpit and the Red Bull; the Cockpit performance would have been given by either Queen Henrietta's Men or by their successors at the theatre, Beeston's Boys; Wiggins's 'best guess' is 1634 due to the play's topical allusions, including one to the Lancashire Witches, interest in which was revived in 1633–34 due to the later Pendle witch trials over that period. The King's Men staged their play, *The Late Lancashire Witches*, at the Globe in 1634. A date of 1634 for *The Seven Champions of Christendom* would therefore place the play with Queen Henrietta's Men. Wiggins #2432.

Marlowe, Christopher. *The Jew of Malta* (published as *The Rich Jew of Malta*). Date: between 1589 and 1590. First published in 1633, with a dedication by Thomas Heywood. The play was originally performed by Lord Strange's Men at the Rose; the 1633 title-page claims performance by Her Majesty's Servants at the Cockpit. A new prologue in the edition also names Richard Perkins, a company member of Queen Henrietta's Men in the 1630s, as the actor playing Barabas at the Cockpit. The company performed the play at court between 1630 and 1633. Wiggins #828.

Marmion, Shackerley. *The Antiquary.* Date: between 1634 and 1636. First published in 1641; the title-page claims performance by Her Majesty's Servants at the Cockpit. Wiggins #2458.

Massinger, Philip. *The Noble Bondman* (published as *The Bondman*). Date: 1623; licensed for performance 3 December 1623. First published in 1624. The title-page names Lady Elizabeth's Servants at the Cockpit in Drury Lane as the company and venue. The play was performed at court by the same company on 27 December 1623. The play is included in the list of plays protected in 1639 for performance by Beeston's Boys at the Cockpit. It is likely therefore to have remained at the Cockpit between the tenures of Lady Elizabeth's Men and Beeston's Boys, and so to have made up part of the repertory performed in the interim by Queen Henrietta's Men. Wiggins #2074.

Massinger, Philip. *The Great Duke* (published as *The Great Duke of Florence*). Date: 1627; licensed for performance by the Queen's Servants on 5 July 1627. First published in 1636. The title-page claims performance by Her Majesty's Servants at the Phoenix (Cockpit) in Drury Lane; the play is also included in the list of plays protected in 1639 for performance by Beeston's Boys at the Cockpit. Wiggins #2214.

Massinger, Philip. *The Maid of Honour.* Date: 1630. First published in 1632; the title-page claims performance by the Queen's Majesty's Servants at the Phoenix (Cockpit) in Drury Lane. Performed at the Cockpit in 1630, as evidenced by the prologue written for the play and transcribed into a manuscript miscellany. The play is included in the list of plays protected in 1639 for performance by Beeston's Boys at the Cockpit. Wiggins #2291.

Massinger, Philip. *A New Way to Pay Old Debts.* Date: between 1626 and 1632. First published in 1633; the title-page claims performance by the Queen's Majesty's Servants at the Phoenix (Cockpit) in Drury Lane. The play is included in the list of plays protected in 1639 for performance by Beeston's Boys at the Cockpit. Wiggins #2180.

Massinger, Philip. *The Renegado.* Date: 1624; licensed for performance on 17 April 1624, for the Cockpit company, who were Lady Elizabeth's Men at that time. First published in 1630; the title-page gives the Queen's Majesty's Servants at the private playhouse in Drury Lane (the Cockpit) as the company and venue, and also features a list of actors that names members of Queen Henrietta's Men. The play is included in the list of plays protected in 1639 for performance by Beeston's Boys at the Cockpit. Wiggins #2090.

Middleton, Thomas, and William Rowley. *The Changeling.* Date: 1622; licensed for performance by Lady Elizabeth's Men on 7 May 1622. The company was performing at the Cockpit at this time. First published in 1653. The title-page claims that the play was performed at the private house in Drury Lane (the Cockpit) and at Salisbury Court. Lady Elizabeth's Men performed the play at court on 4 January 1624 and it was seen in London in 1635 by John Greene, as evidenced by the diary he kept. William Robbins, of Beeston's Queen Henrietta's Men, might have played the role of the Changeling, according to an anonymous pamphlet published in 1648 (*A Key to the Cabinet of the Parliament*). The play was also included in the list of plays protected in 1639 for performance by Beeston's Boys at the Cockpit, though the title-page would suggest that it had been performed prior to that by Heton's Queen Henrietta's Men at Salisbury Court. Bentley suggests that such a performance by the new Queen's Men might in part have prompted William Beeston to protect the list of plays for his company (*Jacobean and Caroline Stage*, IV, p. 863). Wiggins #2010.

Middleton, Thomas, and William Rowley. *A Fair Quarrel.* Date: between 1612 and 1617. First published in 1617; the title-page claims performance by the Prince's Servants (Prince Charles's Men). By around 1620 the play was probably at the Cockpit, as were Prince Charles's Men: at this time it appears in a list compiled at the Revels Office of other plays performed by Prince Charles's Men. The play was also included in the list of plays protected in 1639 for performance by Beeston's Boys at the Cockpit. It is likely to have remained at the Cockpit in the interim and to have been performed there by Queen Henrietta's Men. Wiggins #1798.

Middleton, Thomas, and William Rowley. *The World Tossed at Tennis.* Date: 1620; designed for performance at court in that year. First published in 1620; the title-page claims performance by the Prince's Servants (Prince Charles's Men). The entry in the Stationers' Register refers to performance at 'the Prince's Arms', an unidentified/uncertain venue, but the company's usual venue at this time was the Cockpit. A play titled *The World* was included in the list of plays protected in 1639 for performance by Beeston's Boys at the Cockpit, and so it might have been retained in the Cockpit repertory from the 1620s through to 1639 (and beyond). Wiggins finds it more likely that *The World* refers to an entirely distinct drama. Wiggins #1931 and #2133.

Nabbes, Thomas. *Covent Garden.* Date: between 1633 and 1634. First published in 1638; the title-page claims performance by the Queen's Majesty's Servants and gives the year of first performance as 1632; however, Wiggins finds this erroneous and argues for 1634 as the likeliest date of first performance. The title-page's attempt at chronological specificity in terms of first performance would suggest that the Queen's Majesty's Servants to which it refers was the active troupe in that period (early 1630s) – Beeston's Queen Henrietta's Men at the Cockpit – as opposed to Heton's Queen Henrietta's Men who were playing at Salisbury Court in 1638 when the play first published. Wiggins #2424.

Nabbes, Thomas. *Hannibal and Scipio.* Date: 1635. First published in 1637; the title-page gives the year of first performance and claims performance by the Queen's Majesty's Servants at their private house in Drury Lane (the Cockpit). A cast-list, naming members of Queen Henrietta's Men at the Cockpit, is also included in the edition. Wiggins #2480.

Rowley, William. *All's Lost by Lust.* Date: between 1619 and 1620. First published in 1633. The title-page claims performance by both Lady Elizabeth's Servants and, 'lately', by Her Majesty's Servants at the Phoenix (Cockpit) in Drury Lane. The play was probably at the Cockpit by 1620, as were Prince Charles's Men: at this time it appears in a list compiled at the Revels Office of other plays performed by Prince Charles's Men. It appears that, having become part of the Cockpit repertory, it was then performed by Lady Elizabeth's Men followed by Queen Henrietta's Men, as the title-page suggests. Following this the play was performed by Beeston's Boys, since it was included in the list of plays protected in 1639 for performance by that company at the Cockpit. Wiggins #1895.

Rowley, William. *Hymen's Holiday* [Lost]. Date: between 1607 and 1612. First performed by the Duke of York's Men in 1612; in 1633 it was performed by Queen Henrietta's Men at the Cockpit, and Sir Henry Herbert received a gratuity from Beeston for the performance. It was then performed by Queen Henrietta's Men at the Cockpit-in-Court on 16 December 1633. The play was included in the list of plays protected in 1639 for performance by Beeston's Boys at the Cockpit, under its alternative name, *Cupid's Vagaries*. No version of the text is known to survive in either manuscript or print form. Herbert licensed 'alterations' to the play in August 1633. Wiggins #1651.

Rutter, Joseph. *The Shepherds' Holiday.* Date: between 1629 and 1635. First published in 1635; the title-page claims performance by the Queen's Servants. Wiggins #2402.

Shirley, Henry. *The Martyred Soldier.* Date: between 1622 and 1623. First published in 1638. Performed by Lady Elizabeth's Men at the Cockpit, as evidenced by transcripts of Henry Herbert's office-book; the play seems to have then been, at least temporarily, transferred by Herbert to the Fortune for performance by Palsgrave's Men, at the request of Richard Gunnell. The 1638 title-page claims performance by the Queen's Majesty's Servants at the private house in Drury Lane (the Cockpit) and at 'other publicke Theaters'. Wiggins #2030.

Shirley, James. *The Arcadia.* Date: between 1630 and 1636. First published in 1640; the title-page claims performance by Her Majesty's Servants at the Phoenix (Cockpit) in Drury Lane. It is possible that the play was a revival in the 1630s rather than an original play newly written for the Cockpit, but the evidence for this is muddled and not at all conclusive. See pp. 212–3 for a fuller discussion. Wiggins #2481.

Shirley, James. *The Ball.* Date: 1632; licensed for performance on 16 November 1632. Shortly afterwards, Beeston sought to make amends with Henry Herbert over material found to be offensive and/or too topical in the play. First published in 1639; the title-page claims performance by Her Majesty's Servants at the private house in Drury Lane (the Cockpit). Wiggins #2389.

Shirley, James. *The Bird in a Cage* (also known as *The Beauties*). Date: 1633; licensed for performance on 21 January 1633. First published in 1633; the title-page states that the play was performed at the Phoenix (Cockpit) in Drury Lane, the venue of Queen Henrietta's Men at this time. Wiggins #2396.

Shirley, James. *The Constant Maid.* Date: between (?)1636 and 1640. First published in 1640; the title-page of the 1661 edition claims performance by Her Majesty's Servants at the Phoenix (Cockpit) in Drury Lane. It is possible, however, that the play was written by Shirley for staging in Dublin while he was working at Ogilby's Theatre, and that, as Bentley observes, the later title-page, published over two decades later, might not be accurate. Bentley, *Jacobean and Caroline Stage*, V, pp. 1095–6.

Shirley, James. *The Coronation.* Date: 1635; licensed for performance on 6 February 1635. First published in 1640; the title-page claims performance by Her Majesty's Servants at the private house in Drury Lane (the Cockpit). The play was included in the list of plays protected in 1639 for performance by Beeston's Boys at the Cockpit. Wiggins #2464.

Shirley, James. *The Duke's Mistress.* Date: 1636; licensed for performance on 18 January 1636. Date of first publication: 1638; the title-page claims performance by Her Majesty's Servants at the private house in Drury Lane (the Cockpit). Performed at court by the company in February 1636. Wiggins #2526.

Shirley, James. *The Example.* Date: 1634; licensed for performance on 24 June 1634. First published in 1637; the title-page claims performance by Her Majesty's Servants at the private house in Drury Lane (the Cockpit). The play was included in the list of plays protected in 1639 for performance by Beeston's Boys at the Cockpit. Wiggins #2437.

Shirley, James. *The Gamester.* Date: 1633; licensed for performance on 11 November 1633, after King Charles's plot for the play was given by Henry Herbert to James Shirley. First published in 1637; the title-page claims performance by Her Majesty's Servants at the private house in Drury Lane (the Cockpit). Performed at court on 6 February 1634. Wiggins #2418.

Shirley, James. *The Faithful Servant* (published as *The Grateful Servant*). Date: 1629; licensed for performance on 3 November 1629. First published in 1630; the title-page claims performance by Her Majesty's Servants at the private house in Drury Lane (the Cockpit). The play was included in the list of plays protected in 1639 for performance by Beeston's Boys at the Cockpit. Wiggins #2287.

Shirley, James. *The Duke* (published as *The Humorous Courtier*). Date: 1631; licensed for performance on 17 May 1631. First published in 1640; the title-page claims performance at the private house in Drury Lane (the Cockpit), the venue of Beeston's Queen Henrietta's Men at the time that the play was licensed. Wiggins #2339.

Shirley, James. *Hyde Park.* Date: 1632; licensed for performance on 20 April 1632. First published in 1637; the title-page claims performance by Her Majesty's Servants at the private house in Drury Lane (the Cockpit). Performed at Middle Temple on 1 November 1632. The play was included in the list of plays protected in 1639 for performance by Beeston's Boys at the Cockpit. Wiggins #2367.

Shirley, James. *The Lady of Pleasure.* Date: 1635; licensed for performance on 15 October 1635, and seen at the Cockpit on 5 or 6 November 1635 by a group of playgoers. First published in 1637; the title-page claims performance by Her Majesty's Servants at the private house in Drury Lane (the Cockpit). The play was included in the list of plays protected in 1639 for performance by Beeston's Boys at the Cockpit. Wiggins #2515.

Shirley, James. *Love's Cruelty.* Date: 1631; licensed for performance on 14 November 1631. First published in 1640; the title-page claims performance by Her Majesty's Servants at the private house in Drury Lane (the Cockpit). The play was included in the list of plays protected in 1639 for performance by Beeston's Boys at the Cockpit. Wiggins #2349.

Shirley, James. *Love Tricks* (published as *The School of Compliment*). Date: 1625; licensed for performance on 11 February 1625, for the Cockpit company (Lady Elizabeth's Men at this time). First published in 1631; the title-page claims performance by Her Majesty's Servants at the private house in Drury Lane (the Cockpit). The play was included in the list of plays protected in 1639 for performance by Beeston's Boys at the Cockpit. Wiggins #2158.

Shirley, James. *The Maid's Revenge.* Date: 1626; licensed for performance on 9 February 1626. First published in 1639; the title-page claims performance by Her Majesty's Servants at the private house in Drury Lane (the Cockpit). The play was included in the list of plays protected in 1639 for performance by Beeston's Boys at the Cockpit. Wiggins #2173.

Shirley, James. *The Opportunity.* Date: 1634; licensed for performance on 29 November 1634. First published in 1640; the title-page claims performance by Her Majesty's Servants at the private house in Drury Lane (the Cockpit). The play was included in the list of plays protected in 1639 for performance by Beeston's Boys at the Cockpit. Wiggins #2455.

Shirley, James. *The Traitor.* Date: 1631; licensed for performance on 4 May 1631. First published in 1635; the title-page claims performance by Her Majesty's Servants. The play was included in the list of plays protected in 1639 for performance by Beeston's Boys at the Cockpit. Wiggins #2337.

Shirley, James. *The Wedding.* Date: between 1626 and 1629. First published in 1629; the title-page claims performance by Her Majesty's Servants at the Phoenix (the Cockpit) in Drury Lane, and the edition includes a cast-list naming members of Queen Henrietta's Men. The play was included in the list of plays protected in 1639 for performance by Beeston's Boys at the Cockpit. Wiggins #2184.

Shirley, James. *The Witty Fair One.* Date: 1628; licensed for performance on 3 October 1628. First published in 1633; the title-page claims performance by Her Majesty's Servants at the private house in Drury Lane (the Cockpit). The play was included in the list of plays protected in 1639 for performance by Beeston's Boys at the Cockpit. Wiggins #2251.

Shirley, James. *The Young Admiral.* Date: 1633; licensed for performance on 3 July 1633. First published in 1637; the title-page claims performance by Her Majesty's Servants at the private house in Drury Lane (the Cockpit). Performed at St James's Palace on 19 November 1633. The play was included in the list of plays protected in 1639 for performance by Beeston's Boys at the Cockpit. Wiggins #2410.

Webster, John. *The White Devil.* Date: between 1611 and 1612. First published in 1612; the title-page claims performance by the Queen's Majesty's Servants (who were Queen Anne's Men at this time). The 1631 edition's title-page claims performance by the Queen's Majesty's Servants at the Phoenix (the Cockpit) in Drury Lane, so it appears likely that the play was retained at the Cockpit after Queen Anne's Men left, to be performed by later companies including Queen Henrietta's Men. Wiggins #1689.

Webster, John, and Thomas Heywood. *Appius and Virginia.* Date: between 1625 and 1634. First published in 1654. The play was included in the list of plays protected in 1639 for performance by Beeston's Boys at the Cockpit. Since its composition is dated to the period during which Queen Henrietta's Men were performing at the Cockpit it is likely that the play was performed by them and then retained at the Cockpit beyond the company's years of operation. Wiggins #2186.

PLAYS OF DOUBTFUL OR UNCERTAIN ATTRIBUTION

Carlell, Lodowick. *The Fool Would be a Favourite.* Date: uncertain; between 1625 and 1642? First published in 1657. A joint title-page (shared with *Osman, the Great Turk*) asserts performance by the Queen's Majesty's Servants, though as Bentley observes this may be inaccurate since *Osman* was licensed for performance by the King's Men and Carlell's other plays were performed by the King's Men. It is possible that the play migrated to the Cockpit repertory following performance by the King's Men, but there is no clear evidence. Bentley, *Jacobean and Caroline Stage*, III, pp. 117–18.

Carlell, Lodowick. *Osman, the Great Turk.* Date: 1622; licensed for performance by the King's Players on 6 September 1622. First published in 1657. A joint title-page (shared with *The Fool Would be a Favourite*) asserts performance by the Queen's Majesty's Servants. The company attribution made on the title-page may not be accurate since the play was licensed for performance by the King's Men. But, as above, it is possible that *Osman* migrated to the Cockpit repertory following first performance by the King's Men. Wiggins #2022.

Dekker, Thomas. *Match Me in London.* Date: between 1621 and 1622; licensed for performance in 1621–22, and then relicensed on 21 August 1623 for Lady Elizabeth's Men at the Cockpit. First published in 1631; the title-page asserts performance at the [Red] Bull and then the Phoenix (the Cockpit) in Drury Lane. At the time of publication, Queen Henrietta's Men were in occupancy at the Cockpit. The play might have been retained in the Cockpit repertory beyond the breaking of Lady Elizabeth's Men, as others were, but there is no firm evidence to support this. Wiggins #1997.

Dekker, Thomas. *The Second Part of The Honest Whore.* Date: between 1604 and 1608. First published in 1630. Originally performed by the Prince's Men at the Fortune. After 1635, copies of the quarto of the play were bound together with its sequel, *The Patient Man and the Honest*

Whore; see entry on p. 249–50. The two plays might have travelled together to the Cockpit to be revived as a serialisation, though this is very conjectural: there is no independent evidence for the performance of the second part by Queen Henrietta's Men. Wiggins #1459.

Dekker, Thomas. *The Welsh Ambassador.* Date: between 1622 and 1624. The unpublished manuscript of the play is written in the same scribal hand as *The Parliament of Love*, a play performed by Lady Elizabeth's Men, and the two manuscripts were stored together. There is no firm evidence to suggest that either play was retained in the Cockpit repertory, however, despite this migratory path being well established. Wiggins #2041. See entry for Massinger, *The Parliament of Love*, below.

Dekker, Thomas. *The Wonder of a Kingdom.* Date: between 1619 and 1631. First published in 1636. Evidence linking this play to the repertory of Queen Henrietta's Men is very scant; it shares a prologue (in print) with Rowley's *All's Lost by Lust* which 'might suggest that both plays were owned by the same company'; Wiggins #2017. *All's Lost* (see entry above) was performed by Prince Charles's Men and Lady Elizabeth's Men before 1625, so even if *The Wonder of a Kingdom* was performed at the Cockpit it might not have been by Queen Henrietta's Men, and the play is not included in the list of plays protected in 1639 for performance by Beeston's Boys.

Fletcher, John. *Father's Own Son* (published as *Monsieur Thomas*). Date: between 1613 and 1619. First published in 1639. The play was included in the list of plays protected in 1639 for performance by Beeston's Boys at the Cockpit. It is possible the play was revived as part of the Cockpit repertory prior to this date, but there is no firm evidence to support this. The 1639 title-page claims performance at the Blackfriars, but this ascription appears to be inaccurate. Wiggins #1788.

Glapthorne, Henry. *Argalus and Parthenia.* Date: between 1632 and 1638. First published in 1639; the title-page claims performance at the private house in Drury Lane (the Cockpit) by Their Majesties' Servants, and at court. It is possible the play was written earlier, for Queen Henrietta's Men, and then passed to Beeston's later company, but there is no firm evidence. Bentley, *Jacobean and Caroline Stage*, IV, pp. 479–81.

Glapthorne, Henry. *The Lady's Privilege.* Date: between 1632 and 1640. First published in 1640; the title-page claims performance at the Cockpit in Drury Lane and at court by Their Majesties' Servants (Beeston's boys).

It is possible the play was written earlier, for Queen Henrietta's Men, and then passed to Beeston's later company (as was the case with Glapthorne's *The Hollander*), but there is no independent evidence in support of this. Bentley, *Jacobean and Caroline Stage*, IV, pp. 485–7.

Greene, Robert. *George-a-Greene.* Date: between 1587 and 1592. First published in 1599. The play is included in the list of plays protected in 1639 for performance by Beeston's Boys at the Cockpit. It is not known whether the play became part of the Cockpit repertory prior to this date. Wiggins #893.

Heywood, Thomas. *The Escapes of Jupiter.* Date: 1623 or earlier; the manuscript play is an adaptation of scenes from *The Golden Age* and *The Silver Age* and was licensed on 26 August 1623, once Henry Herbert had ascertained that the occupants of the Cockpit were content for the play to be performed elsewhere. It is unclear whether the play was ever performed, though Wiggins suggests that it would have been staged as licensed by Prince Charles's Men at the Red Bull. It appears likely, given the evidence, that the play was not performed by Queen Henrietta's Men at the Cockpit since it left the venue in 1623, but I suggest that Heywood might have worked on *The Escapes* with a Cockpit performance in mind. Wiggins #1637 and #1645.

Killigrew, Thomas. *Claracilla.* Date: between 1636 and 1639; licensed for performance in 1639. First published in 1641. The title-page claims performance by Her Majesty's Servants at the Phoenix in Drury Lane (the Cockpit), but if the play was not licensed until 1639 this must be incorrect: the later Queen's Men would have been performing at Salisbury Court by this time. Wiggins #2529.

Massinger, Philip. *The Parliament of Love.* Date: 1624; licensed for performance at the Cockpit on 3 November 1624. The company performing at the Cockpit at that time was Lady Elizabeth's Men. The play was not published and there is no direct evidence that it stayed in the Cockpit repertory following the departure of Lady Elizabeth's Men – though, since Massinger's other Cockpit plays of this period did, this is a possibility. Wiggins #2144.

Nabbes, Thomas. *Microcosmus.* Date: between 1629 and 1637. First published in 1637. The title-page claims performance at Salisbury Court; Wiggins dates the likely first performance as 1636 prior to the closure of the theatres, and this would make the original players the King's Revels company at Salisbury Court. Nabbes had been writing for Queen Henrietta's Men at the Cockpit in the previous few years though (see entries above), so it is possible that the drama was originally written for that company. Wiggins #2543.

Nabbes, Thomas. *Tottenham Court.* Date: between 1633 and 1634. First published in 1638; the title-page gives the year of first performance as 1633 and the playhouse as Salisbury Court. In 1639 the quarto was reissued with a cancel title-page, which named the Queen's Men as the acting company. It is very likely that this refers to Heton's Queen's Men, however, who were playing at Salisbury Court in 1639. There is no evidence that the play was performed at the Cockpit prior to 1638, though Nabbes did write two other plays for Beeston between 1633 and 1635. Wiggins #2405.

Webster, John. *The Devil's Law-Case.* Date: between 1617 and 1619. First published in 1623; the title-page claims performance by Her Majesty's Servants (this refers to Queen Anne's Men in 1623). The play might have followed the same repertory route as Webster's *The White Devil*, which was performed originally by Queen Anne's Men and then retained at the Cockpit to be performed later by Queen Henrietta's Men, but there is no evidence to suggest this. Wiggins #1875.

APPENDIX B
EVIDENCE FOR SPECIFIC COURT
PERFORMANCES GIVEN BY QUEEN
HENRIETTA'S MEN

1629/30: ten performances

A warrannt for payment of 100^{li} vnto the Queenes players for 10 playes by them Acted at Court betweene October & Febr. 1629 signed ye 5th of Iulie. 1630./

MSC II.3, p. 352

1630/31: sixteen performances

A warrant for payment of 170^{li}. vnto Mr Christopher Beeston for him-selfe & the rest of the Queenes Players for sixteene Playes by them Acted betweene the 10th of October & the 20th of Februarie. 1631. May 25 1631.

M^d his Lo^p added (aboue the ordinary Allowance of 10^{li} for euery play) 10^{li} more in consideration of their Charge in Attending at Hampton Court where they Acted three playes.

MSC II.3, p. 355

1631/32: nine performances

A Warraunt for payment of 100^{li} vnto Christopher Beeston for 9 playes at 10^{li} a piece for 8 of them & 20^{li} for one Acted at Hampton Court in consideration of their trauaile & charge. in October &c. 1631. Dec. 5. 1632.

MSC II.3, p. 359

1632/33: fourteen performances

A Warraunt for paym^t of 240^{li} vnto the Queenes Players for 14 playes by them Acted. their bill signed by Sr Henry Herbert. eod. [*27 Oct. 1633*]

MSC II.3, p. 361

1633/34: at least seven performances

On tusday the 19th of November, being the king's birth-day, The Young Admirall was acted at St. James by the queen's players, and likt by the K. and Queen.

Bawcutt (ed.), *Control and Censorship*, p. 184

On Monday night the 16 of December, 1633, at Whitehall was acted before the King and Queen, Hymens Holliday or Cupids Fegarys, an ould play of Rowleys. Likte.

Bawcutt (ed.), *Control and Censorship*, p. 185

A warrant for paym^t of 70^li vnto Christopher Beeston for himselfe & the rest of the Queenes Players for playes Acted by them in Anno 1633 signed Dec. 31. 1634

MSC II.3, p. 374

and see also:

To Christopher Beeston for himself and the rest of his Company the Qeeenes ma^te Comedians for vij Plaies by them acted before the king and Queenes ma^tie in the yeare 1633 by warrant dated the xxij^th of december 1634

MSC VI, p. 84

The Tale of the Tub was acted on tusday night at Court, the 14 Janua. 1633, by the Queenes players, and not likte.

Bawcutt (ed.), *Control and Censorship*, p. 186

The Night-Walkers was acted on thursday night the 30 Janu. 1633 at Court, before the King and Queen. Likt as a merry play. Made by Fletcher.

Bawcutt (ed.), *Control and Censorship*, p. 187

On thursday night the 6 of Febru. 1633, The Gamester was acted at Court, made by Sherley, out of a plot of the king's, given him by mee; and well likte. The king sayd it was the best play he had seen for seven years.

Bawcutt (ed.), *Control and Censorship*, p. 187

1634/35: *at least eight performances*

A Warr^t for payment of 90^li vnto M^r. Chr̃er Bieston for 8 Playes Acted by ye Queenes Players at Court in Anno 1634 whereof one at Hampton Court. March 24 1635.

MSC II.3, p. 378.

Her *Majestie* Inviting the *King* to *Denmarke House*, in the *Strand*, upon His Birth-day, being *November* the 19. This Play (bearing from that time) the Title of the *Queenes Masque*, was againe presented before Him.

Thomas Heywood, prologue to a royal performance of *Love's Mistress* (1634; published 1636)

1635/36: *at least nine performances*

A Warrant for ye payment of 150^li vnto Mr Christopher Bieston for Playes Acted by the Queenes servants (vizt) fower at Hampton Court for xx^li ꝑ play in Anno 1635 5 at Whitehall in ye same yeere and two Playes Acted by the new Company. May 10. 1637

MSC II.3, p. 383.

The Dukes Mistres played at St. James the 22 of Feb. 1635. Made by Sherley.

Bawcutt (ed.), *Control and Censorship*, p. 197

The 28 Feb. The Knight of the Burning Pestle playd by the Q. men at St. James.

Bawcutt (ed.), *Control and Censorship*, p. 198

BIBLIOGRAPHY

EARLY PUBLISHED WORKS AND MANUSCRIPTS

Beaumont, Francis, *The Knight of the Burning Pestle* (London, 1613, 1635)
Beaumont, Francis, and John Fletcher, *Cupid's Revenge* (London, 1635)
— *Fifty Comedies and Tragedies* (London, 1679)
— *Rule a Wife, and Have a Wife* (London, 1640)
Bride-oake, R., 'Upon Mr. *Randolph's Poem, collected and published after his death*', in *Poems, with the Muses Looking Glass and Amyntas* (London, 1638)
Brome, Richard, *The Antipodes* (London, 1640)
Chettle, Henry, *The Tragedy of Hoffman* (London, 1631)
Comenius, *Orbis Sensualium Pictus* (London, 1659)
Cooke, John, *Greenes Tu Quoque, or The City Gallant* (London, 1614)
Daborne, Robert, *A Christian Turned Turk* (London, 1612)
Davenant, William, *The Just Italian* (London, 1630)
— *The Unfortunate Lovers* (London, 1643)
Davenport, Robert, *King John and Matilda* (London, 1655)
— *A New Trick to Cheat the Devil* (London, 1639)
Day, John, *The Isle of Gulls* (London, 1606)
Dekker, Thomas, *The Gull's Hornbook* (London, 1609)
— *If This Be Not a Good Play, the Devil Is In It* (London, 1612)
— *News from Hell* (London, 1606)
— *The Raven's Almanac* (London, 1609)
— *The Seven Deadly Sins of London* (London, 1606)
— *The Wonder of a Kingdom* (London, 1636)
Drayton, Michael, *Poems* (London, 1606)
Duppa, Brian (ed.), *Jonsonus Virbius* (London, 1638)
Fennor, William, *Fennors Descriptions, or a True Relation of Certaine and Diuers Speeches* (London, 1616)
Fletcher, John, *The Night-Walker*, revised by James Shirley (London, 1640)
Florio, John, *Florio, His First Fruits* (London, 1578)
Ford, John, *The Chronicle History of Perkin Warbeck* (London, 1634)
— *Love's Sacrifice* (London, 1633)
— *'Tis Pity She's a Whore* (London, 1633)
Ford, John, and Thomas Dekker, *The Sun's Darling* (London, 1656)
Ford, John, Thomas Dekker, and William Rowley, *The Witch of Edmonton* (London, 1658)

Gayton, Edmund, *Pleasant Notes upon Don Quixot* (London, 1654)
Glapthorne, Henry, *The Lady's Privilege* (London, 1640)
Goffe, Thomas, *The Careless Shepherdess* (London, 1656)
Greene, Robert, *Alphonsus, King of Aragon* (London, 1599)
Guilpin, Everard, *Skialetheia* (London, 1598)
Heath, John, *Two Centuries of Epigrams* (London, 1610)
Heywood, Thomas, *The Brazen Age* (London, 1613)
— *The English Traveller* (London, 1633)
— *The Fair Maid of the West*, Part I and Part II (London, 1631)
— *If You Know Not Me, You Know Nobody*, Part I (London, 1605)
— *If You Know Not Me, You Know Nobody*, Part II (1633)
— *The Iron Age* (London, 1632)
— *Love's Mistress* (London, 1636)
— *Pleasant Dialogues and Dramas* (London, 1637)
— *The Rape of Lucrece* (London, 1608, 1609, 1614, 1630, 1638)
— *The Royal King and the Loyal Subject* (London, 1637)
— *The Second Part of the Iron Age* (London, 1632)
Heywood, Thomas, and Richard Brome, *The Late Lancashire Witches* (London, 1634)
Howard, Edward, *The Six Days' Adventure* (London, 1671)
'J. C.', *The Two Merry Milkmaids* (London, 1620)
Jonson, Ben, *Every Man In His Humour*, in *The Works of Benjamin Jonson* (London, 1616)
— *Every Man Out of His Humour* (London, 1600)
— *The Faithful Shepherdess* (London, 1609)
— *The Magnetic Lady*, in *The Works of Ben Jonson* (London, 1640–41)
— *The Masque of Blackness* (London, 1616)
— *The Masque of Queens* (London, 1609)
— *The New Inn* (London, 1631)
— *The Staple of News* (London, 1631)
— *A Tale of a Tub*, in *The Works of Benjamin Jonson* (London, 1640–41)
Killigrew, Thomas, *The Prisoners* (London, 1640–41)
Kirke, John, *The Seven Champions of Christendom* (London, 1638)
Lenton, Francis, *The Young Gallant's Whirligig* (London, 1629)
Marlowe, Christopher, *The Rich Jew of Malta* (London, 1633)
Marston, John, *Jack Drum's Entertainment* (London, 1601)
Massinger, Philip, *The Roman Actor* (London, 1629)
Melton, John, *Astrologaster* (London, 1620)
Middleton, Thomas, and William Rowley, *The Changeling* (London, 1653)
— *Father Hubbard's Tale* (London, 1604)
— *No Wit, No Help Like a Woman's* (London, 1657)
— *The World Tossed at Tennis* (London, 1620)
Nabbes, Thomas, *Hannibal and Scipio* (1637)
— *Microcosmos* (London, 1637)
Prynne, William, *Histriomastix: The Player's Scourge, or Actor's Tragedy* (London, 1632)

Randolph, Thomas, *Poems, with the Muses Looking Glass and Amyntas* (London, 1638)

Rutter, Joseph, *The Shepherds' Holiday* (London, 1635)

Shakespeare, William, *Poems* (London, 1640)

Shirley, Henry, *The Martyred Soldier* (London, 1638)

Shirley, James, *The Arcadia* (London, 1640)

— *The Ball* (London, 1639)

— *The Bird in a Cage* (London, 1633)

— *The Doubtful Heir* (London, 1653)

— *The Duke's Mistress* (London, 1638)

— *The Gamester* (London, 1637)

— *The Grateful Servant* (London, 1630)

— *The Imposture* (London, 1652)

— *The Maid's Revenge* (London, 1639)

— *The School of Compliment* (London, 1631)

— *The Traitor* (London, 1635)

— *The Wedding* (London, 1629)

Stow, John, *Annales, or a Generall Chronicle of England, continued and augmented by Edmund Howes* (London, 1631)

Tatham, John, *The Fancies Theater* (London, 1640)

Taylor, John, *The Praise, Antiquity, and Commodity of Beggery, Beggers and Begging* (London, 1621)

'T.D.', *The Bloody Banquet* (London, 1639)

Turner, William, *A Dish of Lenten Stuff* (London, 1613)

Webster, John, *The Devil's Law-Case* (London, 1623)

— *The White Devil* (London, 1612, 1631)

Wither, George, *Abuses Stript and Whipt* (London, 1613)

Wright, James, *Historia Histrionica* (London, 1699)

TRANSCRIPTS AND EDITIONS

Acts of the Privy Council, ed. J. R. Dasent, 32 vols (London: His Majesty's Stationery Office, 1890–1907)

Bawcutt, N. W. (ed.), *The Control and Censorship of Caroline Drama: The Records of Sir Henry Herbert, Master of the Revels 1623–73* (Oxford: Clarendon Press, 1996)

Brome, Richard, *Richard Brome Online* edition, https://www.dhi.ac.uk/brome/viewEssay.jsp?file=EC_SALISBURY (accessed 29 April 2025)

A Complete Collection of State Trials and Proceedings for High Treason and Other Crimes and Misdemeanours from the Earliest Period to the Year 1783, compiled by T. B. Howell, 33 vols (London, 1816–28)

Diary and Correspondence of Samuel Pepys, the Diary deciphered by J. Smith, with a Life and Notes by Richard Lord Braybrooke, 6 vols (London, 1875–79)

Documents Relating to the Office of the Revels in the Time of Queen Elizabeth, ed. Albert Feuillerat (Louvain, 1908)

Foakes, R. A. (ed.), *Henslowe's Diary*, 2nd edn (Cambridge: Cambridge University Press, 2002)

Ford, John, *'Tis Pity She's a Whore*, ed. Martin Wiggins, New Mermaids Series (London: A. & C. Black, 2003)

Heywood, Thomas, *The Escapes of Jupiter*, ed. Henry D. Janzen, Malone Society Reprints (Oxford: Oxford University Press, 1978 [1976])

Letter of John Chamberlain to Dudley Carleton, 8 March 1617, transcribed in *The Letters of John Chamberlain*, ed. Norman Egbert McClure, 2 vols (Philadelphia: The American Philosophical Society, 1939), II, pp. 59–60

Letter of Edward Sherbourne, 8 March 1617, transcribed by J. O. Halliwell-Phillipps in the *Fortune* scrapbook, and reproduced by G. E. Bentley in *The Jacobean and Caroline Stage*, 7 vols (Oxford: Clarendon Press, 1941–68), VI, p. 54

'A letter to the Lord Major and Aldermen of London, and Commissioners of Oyer and Terminer in the citty of London and countye of Midlesex', 5 March 1617, transcribed in *Acts of the Privy Council of England, 1616–1617* (London: His Majesty's Stationery Office, 1927)

Malone Society Collections, I.1, Malone Society Reprints (Oxford: Oxford University Press, 1907)

Malone Society Collections, I.3, Malone Society Reprints (Oxford: Oxford University Press, 1910)

Malone Society Collections, II.3, Malone Society Reprints (Oxford: Oxford University Press, 1931)

Malone Society Collections, VI, Malone Society Reprints (Oxford: Oxford University Press, 1962)

Malone Society Collections, X, Malone Society Reprints (Oxford: Oxford University Press, 1975)

Malone Society Collections, XIII, Malone Society Reprints (Oxford: Oxford University Press, 1986)

Middlesex Sessions Rolls: 1622, in *Middlesex County Records: Volume 2, 1603–25*, ed. John Cordy Jeaffreson (London, 1887)

A Pepysian Garland, ed. Hyder E. Rollins (Cambridge, MA: Harvard University Press, 1922)

Records of Early English Drama, Coventry, ed. R. W. Ingram (Toronto: University of Toronto Press, 1981)

Records of Early English Drama, Norwich, ed. David Galloway (Toronto: University of Toronto Press, 1984)

Reports of the Historical Manuscripts Commission, XII, Part 10 (London: Her Majesty's Stationery Office, 1891)

Shakespeare, William, *The Oxford Shakespeare: The Complete Works*, ed. Stanley Wells and Gary Taylor (Oxford: Oxford University Press, 1988)

Shirley, James, *The Bird in a Cage*, ed. Clare McManus, in *The Routledge Anthology of Early Modern Drama*, ed. Jeremy Lopez (Abingdon: Routledge, 2020)

Sidney, Philip, *The Countess of Pembroke's Arcadia*, ed. Maurice Evans (London: Penguin, 1977)

Three Seventeenth-Century Plays on Women and Performance, ed. Hero Chalmers, Julie Sanders, and Sophie Tomlinson (Manchester: Manchester University Press, 2006)

Webster, John, *The Duchess of Malfi and Other Plays*, ed. René Weis, Oxford World's Classics (Oxford: Oxford University Press, 1996)

— *The White Devil*, ed. John Russell Brown (London: Methuen, 1996)

SECONDARY SOURCES

Adams, Joseph Quincy, 'Shakespeare, Heywood, and the Classics', *Modern Language Notes*, 34 (1919), 336–9

Archer, Ian, 'The City of London and the Theatre', in *The Oxford Handbook of Early Modern Theatre*, ed. Richard Dutton (Oxford: Oxford University Press, 2011), pp. 396–412

Astington, John H., 'Court Theatre', in *The Oxford Handbook of Early Modern Theatre*, ed. Richard Dutton (Oxford: Oxford University Press, 2011), pp. 307–22

— *English Court Theatre, 1558–1642* (Cambridge: Cambridge University Press, 1999)

— 'Playing the Man: Acting at the Red Bull and the Fortune', *Early Theatre*, 9.2 (2006), 130–43

— 'The Popularity of *Cupid's Revenge*', *Studies in English Literature, 1500–1900*, 19 (1979), 215–27

Bailey, Rebecca A., *Staging the Old Faith: Queen Henrietta Maria and the Theatre of Caroline England, 1625–1642* (Manchester: Manchester University Press, 2009)

Barker, Roberta, '"An honest dog yet": Performing *The Witch of Edmonton*', *Early Theatre*, 12.2 (2009), 163–82

Barroll, J. Leeds, 'Drama and the Court', in *The Revels History of Drama in English, Volume III: 1576–1613*, ed. Clifford Leech et al. (London: Methuen, 1975), pp. 1–27

— *Politics, Plague, and Shakespeare's Theater: The Stuart Years* (Ithaca, NY: Cornell University Press, 1991)

Barton, Anne, 'Harking Back to Elizabeth: Ben Jonson and Caroline Nostalgia', *English Literary History*, 48 (1981), 706–31

Bayer, Mark, 'Staging Foxe at the Fortune and the Red Bull', *Renaissance and Reformation*, 27 (2003), 61–94

Beal, Peter, 'Massinger at Bay: Unpublished Verses in a War of the Theatres', *The Yearbook of English Studies*, 10 (1980), 190–203

Benbow, Mark R., 'Dutton and Goffe versus Broughton: A Disputed Contract for Plays in the 1570s', *REED Newsletter*, 6.2 (1981), 3–9

Bentley, G. E., *The Jacobean and Caroline Stage*, 7 vols (Oxford: Clarendon Press, 1941–68)

— *Shakespeare and His Theatre* (Lincoln, NE: University of Nebraska Press, 1964)

— 'The Theatres and the Actors', in *The Revels History of Drama in English, Volume IV: 1613–1660*, ed. Philip Edwards (London: Methuen, 1981), pp. 69–124

Berger, Thomas L., and Sonia Massai (eds), *Paratexts in English Printed Drama to 1642* (Cambridge: Cambridge University Press, 2014)

Bergeron, David M., 'Patronage of Dramatists: The Case of Thomas Heywood', *English Literary Renaissance*, 18 (1988), 294–304

Berry, Herbert, 'The Globe Bewitched and *El Hombre Fiel*', *Medieval and Renaissance Drama in England*, 1 (1984), 211–30

Billing, Christian, 'Modelling the Anatomy Theatre and the Indoor Hall Theatre: Dissection on the Stages of Early Modern London', *Early Modern Literary Studies*, 13 (2004), http://purl.oclc.org/emls/si-13/billing (accessed 17 March 2025)

Bly, Mary, *Queer Virgins and Virgin Queans on the Early Modern Stage* (Oxford: Oxford University Press, 2000)

Boas, F. S., *Thomas Heywood* (London: Williams and Norgate, 1950)

Bowers, Fredson, *Elizabethan Revenge Tragedy, 1587–1642* (Princeton, NJ: Princeton University Press, 1966 [1940])

Britland, Karen, *Drama at the Courts of Queen Henrietta Maria* (Cambridge: Cambridge University Press, 2006)

Brooks, Douglas A., *From Playhouse to Printing House: Drama and Authorship in Early Modern England* (Cambridge: Cambridge University Press, 2000)

Bruster, Douglas, and Robert Weimann, *Prologues to Shakespeare's Theatre: Performance and Liminality in Early Modern Drama* (Abingdon: Routledge, 2004)

Burner, Sandra A., *James Shirley: A Study of Literary Coteries and Patronage in Seventeenth-Century England* (Lanham, MD: University Press of America, 1988)

Butler, Martin, 'Adult and Boy Playing Companies 1625–1642', in *The Oxford Handbook of Early Modern Theatre*, ed. Richard Dutton (Oxford: Oxford University Press, 2011), pp. 104–19

— 'Exeunt Fighting: Poets, Players, and Impresarios at the Caroline Hall Theaters', in *Localizing Caroline Drama: Politics and Economics of the Early Modern Stage, 1625–1642*, ed. Adam Zucker and Alan B. Farmer (Basingstoke: Palgrave Macmillan, 2006), pp. 97–128

— 'Royal Slaves? The Stuart Court and the Theatres', *Renaissance Drama Newsletter*, Supplement 2 (1984), 1–23

— 'Stuart Politics in Jonson's "Tale of a Tub"', *Modern Language Review*, 85.1 (1990), 12–28

— *Theatre and Crisis, 1632–1642* (Cambridge: Cambridge University Press, 1984)

Cerasano, Susan, 'The "Business" of Shareholding, the Fortune Playhouses, and Francis Grace's Will', *Medieval and Renaissance Drama in England*, II (1985), 231–51

Chambers, E. K., *The Elizabethan Stage*, 4 vols (Oxford: Clarendon Press, 1923)

Clark, Arthur Melville, *Thomas Heywood, Playwright and Miscellanist* (Oxford: Blackwell, 1931)

Clark, Ira, *Professional Playwrights: Massinger, Ford, Shirley, and Brome* (Lexington: University of Kentucky Press, 1992)

Collins, Eleanor, 'Changing Fashions: Tragicomedy, Romance, and the Heroic Woman in the 1630s Hall-Playhouses', in *Moving Shakespeare Indoors: Performance and Repertoire in the Jacobean Playhouse*, ed. Andrew Gurr and Farah Karim-Cooper (Cambridge: Cambridge University Press, 2014), pp. 217–36

— 'From Court to Cockpit: The Prisoners and Claricilla in Repertory', in *Thomas Killigrew and the Seventeenth-Century English Stage: New Perspectives*, ed. Philip Major (Farnham: Ashgate, 2013), pp. 21–44

— 'Ghosts in the Archive: Edmond Malone, Craven Ord, and the Missing Texts of Henry Herbert's "office-book"', *Critical Quarterly*, 55 (2013), 30–41.

— 'Repertory and Riot: The Relocation of Plays from the Red Bull to the Cockpit Stage', *Early Theatre*, 13.2 (2010), 132–49

— 'Richard Brome's Contract and the Relationship of Dramatist to Company in the Early Modern Period', *Early Theatre*, 10 (2007), 116–28

— 'Richard Brome and the Salisbury Court Contract', *Richard Brome Online*, https://www.dhi.ac.uk/brome/viewEssay.jsp?file=EC_SALISBURY (accessed 29 April 2025)

Craig, D. H. (ed.), *Ben Jonson: The Critical Heritage* (Abingdon: Routledge, 2010)

Craik, George L., Charles MacFarlane, and Hans Claude Hamilton, *The Pictorial History of England*, 8 vols (London, 1838–49)

Crystal, David, and Ben Crystal, *Shakespeare's Words*, 2nd edn (London: Penguin, 2004)

Cunningham, Peter, *Shakespeare Society's Papers*, 4 vols (London: Shakespeare Society, 1844–49)

Dawson, Lesel, '"New Sects of Love": Neoplatonism and Constructions of Gender in Davenant's *The Temple of Love* and *The Platonick Lovers*', *Early Modern Literary Studies*, 8.1 (2002), 4.1–36, https://extra.shu.ac.uk/emls/o8-1/dawsnew.htm (accessed 29 April 2025)

Dessen, Alan, 'Stage Directions and the Theater Historian', in *The Oxford Handbook of Early Modern Theatre*, ed. Richard Dutton (Oxford: Oxford University Press, 2011), pp. 513–27

Dessen, Alan, and Leslie Thomson, *A Dictionary of Stage Directions in English Drama, 1580–1642* (Cambridge: Cambridge University Press, 1999)

Deutermann, Allison K., 'Literary Celebrity and Theatrical Culture in Shirley's *Bird in a Cage*', in *Historical Affects and the Early Modern Theater*, ed. Ronda Arab, Michelle Dowd, and Adam Zucker (Abingdon: Routledge, 2015), pp. 54–65

Doelman, James, *The Epigram in England, 1590–1640* (Manchester: Manchester University Press, 2017)

Dustagheer, Sarah, 'Acoustic and Visual Practices Indoors', in *Moving Shakespeare Indoors: Performance and Repertoire in the Jacobean Playhouse*, ed. Andrew Gurr and Farah Karim-Cooper (Cambridge: Cambridge University Press, 2014), pp. 137–51

— *Shakespeare's Two Playhouses: Repertory and Theatre Space at the Globe and the Blackfriars, 1599–1613* (Cambridge: Cambridge University Press, 2017)

— 'To Glisten in a Playhouse: Cosmetic Beauty Indoors', in *Moving Shakespeare Indoors: Performance and Repertoire in the Jacobean Playhouse*, ed. Andrew Gurr and Farah Karim-Cooper (Cambridge: Cambridge University Press, 2014), pp. 184–200

Dustagheer, Sarah, and Gillian Woods (eds), *Stage Directions and Shakespearean Theatre* (London: Bloomsbury, 2018)

Dutton, Richard, *Mastering the Revels: The Regulation and Censorship of English Renaissance Drama* (London: Macmillan, 1991)

— (ed.), *The Oxford Handbook of Early Modern Theatre* (Oxford: Oxford University Press, 2011)

— *Shakespeare: Court Dramatist* (Oxford: Oxford University Press, 2016)

Egan, Gabriel, 'Hearing or Seeing a Play? Evidence of Early Modern Theatrical Terminology', https://www.dora.dmu.ac.uk/bitstream/handle/2086/7053/GEgan_Hearing_or_Saying_2001.pdf?sequence=1 (accessed 27 March 2025)

Erne, Lukas, *Shakespeare and the Book Trade* (Cambridge: Cambridge University Press, 2013)

Farmer, Alan B., and Zachary Lesser, 'Canons and Classics: Publishing Drama in Caroline England', in *Localizing Caroline Drama: Politics and Economics of the Early Modern English Stage, 1625–1642*, ed. Adam Zucker and Alan B. Farmer (Basingstoke: Palgrave Macmillan, 2006), pp. 17–41

— 'Vile Arts: The Marketing of English Printed Drama, 1512–1660', *Research Opportunities in Renaissance Drama*, 39 (2000), 77–165

Fleay, F. G., 'Annals of the Careers of James and Henry Shirley', *Anglia: Journal of English Philology*, VIII (1885), 405–14

Floyd-Wilson, Mary, *Occult Knowledge, Science, and Gender on the Shakespearean Stage* (Cambridge: Cambridge University Press, 2013)

Forsythe, Robert Stanley, *The Relations of Shirley's Plays to the Elizabethan Drama* (New York: Columbia University Press, 1914)

Freehafer, John, 'Leonard Digges, Ben Jonson, and the Beginning of Shakespeare Idolatry', *Shakespeare Quarterly*, 21 (1970), 63–75

Gossett, Suzanne (ed.), *Thomas Middleton in Context* (Cambridge: Cambridge University Press, 2011)

Gough, Melinda J., 'Courtly *Comédiantes*: Henrietta Maria and Amateur Women's Stage Plays in France and England', in *Women Players in England, 1500–1660: Beyond the All-Male Stage*, ed. Pamela Allen Brown and Peter Parolin (Aldershot: Ashgate, 2005), pp. 193–215

— '"Not as Myself": The Queen's Voice in *Tempe Restored*', *Modern Philology*, 101 (2003), 48–67

Grant, Teresa, 'Drama Queen: Staging Elizabeth in *If You Know Not Me, You Know Nobody*', in *The Myth of Elizabeth*, ed. Susan Doran and Thomas S. Freeman (Basingstoke: Palgrave, 2003), pp. 120–42

Greenfield, Jon, and Peter McCurdy, 'Practical Evidence for a Reimagined Indoor Jacobean Theatre', in *Moving Shakespeare Indoors: Performance and Repertoire in the Jacobean Playhouse*, ed. Andrew Gurr and Farah Karim-Cooper (Cambridge: Cambridge University Press, 2014), pp. 32–64

Greg, W. W., 'The Escapes of Jupiter', in *Collected Papers*, ed. J. C. Maxwell (Oxford: Clarendon Press, 1966), pp. 156–83

Graves, Robert, *Lighting the Shakespearean Stage, 1576–1642* (Carbondale: Southern Illinois University Press, 1999)

Griffith, Eva, 'Christopher Beeston: His Property and Properties', in *The Oxford Handbook of Early Modern Theatre*, ed. Richard Dutton (Oxford: Oxford University Press, 2011), pp. 607–22

— *A Jacobean Company and its Playhouse: The Queen's Servants at the Red Bull Theatre (c. 1605–1619)* (Cambridge: Cambridge University Press, 2013)

Gurr, Andrew, 'The New Fashion for Indoor Plays', in *Moving Shakespeare Indoors: Performance and Repertoire in the Jacobean Playhouse*, ed. Andrew Gurr and Farah Karim-Cooper (Cambridge: Cambridge University Press, 2014), pp. 203–16

— *Playgoing in Shakespeare's London*, 3rd edn (Cambridge: Cambridge University Press, 2004)

— *The Shakespeare Company, 1594–1642* (Cambridge: Cambridge University Press, 2004)

— *Shakespeare's Opposites: The Admiral's Company, 1594–1625* (Cambridge: Cambridge University Press, 2009)

— *The Shakespearean Stage, 1574–1642*, 3rd edn (Cambridge: Cambridge University Press, 1992)

— *The Shakespearean Stage, 1574–1642*, 4th edn (Cambridge: Cambridge University Press, 2009)

— *The Shakespearian Playing Companies* (Oxford: Clarendon Press, 1996)

— 'Singing through the Chatter: Ford and Contemporary Theatrical Fashion', in *John Ford: Critical Re-visions*, ed. Michael Neill (Cambridge: Cambridge University Press, 1988), pp. 81–96

— 'Three Reluctant Patrons and Early Shakespeare', *Shakespeare Quarterly*, 44 (1993), 159–74

Gurr, Andrew, and Farah Karim-Cooper (eds), *Moving Shakespeare Indoors: Performance and Repertoire in the Jacobean Playhouse* (Cambridge: Cambridge University Press, 2014)

Haaker, Ann, 'The Plague, the Theatre, and the Poet', *Renaissance Drama*, n.s. 1 (1968), 283–306

Hackel, Heidi Brayman, 'Popular Literacy and Society', in *The Oxford History of Popular Print Culture, Volume 1: Cheap Print in Britain and Ireland to 1660*, ed. Joad Raymond (Oxford: Oxford University Press, 2011), pp. 88–100

Halstead, W. L., 'Dekker's *Cupid and Psyche* and Thomas Heywood', *English Literary History*, 11 (1944), 182–91

Hansen, Claire, 'The Complexity of Dance in Shakespeare's *A Midsummer Night's Dream*', *Early Modern Literary Studies*, 18 (2015), https://extra.shu.ac.uk/emls/journal/indexphp/emls/article/view/136.html (accessed 29 April 2025)

Harbage, Alfred, 'The Authorship of the Dramatic "Arcadia"', *Modern Philology*, 35 (1938), 233–7
— *Cavalier Drama* (New York: Modern Language Association of America, 1936)
Herford, C. H., Percy Simpson, and Evelyn Simpson (eds), *Ben Jonson, Volume 10: Play Commentary; Masque Commentary* (Oxford: Oxford University Press, 1950)
Higgott, Gordon, 'Reassessing the Drawings for the Inigo Jones Theatre: A Restoration Project by John Webb?', paper based on a lecture given at Shakespeare's Globe, 13 February 2005, The Chamber of Demonstrations, https://www.bristol.ac.uk/drama/jacobean/research4.html (accessed 27 March 2025)
Hirschfeld, Heather, 'Collaborating Across Generations: Thomas Heywood, Richard Brome, and the Production of *The Late Lancashire Witches*', *Journal of Medieval and Early Modern Studies*, 30 (2000), 339–74
Howard, Jean E., 'Dancing Masters and the Production of Cosmopolitan Bodies in Caroline Town Comedy', in *Localizing Caroline Drama: Politics and Economics of the Early Modern Stage, 1625–1642*, ed. Adam Zucker and Alan B. Farmer (Basingstoke: Palgrave Macmillan, 2006), pp. 183–211
Ichikawa, Mariko, *The Shakespearean Stage Space* (Cambridge: Cambridge University Press, 2013)
Jankowski, Theodora A., 'Historicizing and Legitimating Capitalism: Thomas Heywood's *Edward IV* and *If You Know Not Me, You Know Nobody*', *Medieval and Renaissance Drama in England*, 7 (1995), 305–37
Jenner, Mark, 'London', in *The Oxford History of Popular Print Culture, Volume 1: Cheap Print in Britain and Ireland to 1660*, ed. Joad Raymond (Oxford: Oxford University Press, 2011), pp. 294–307
Johnson, Nora, *The Actor as Playwright in Early Modern Drama* (Cambridge: Cambridge University Press, 2003)
Jones, Gwilym, 'Storm Effects in Shakespeare', in *Shakespeare's Theatres and the Effects of Performance*, ed. Farah Karim-Cooper and Tiffany Stern (London: Bloomsbury, 2013), pp. 33–50
Jones, Marion, 'Early Moral Plays and the Earliest Secular Drama' in *The Revels History of Drama in English, Volume I: Medieval Drama*, ed. A. C. Cawley et al. (London: Methuen, 1983), pp. 211–91
Jones, Oliver, 'Documentary Evidence for an Indoor Jacobean Theatre', in *Moving Shakespeare Indoors: Performance and Repertoire in the Jacobean Playhouse*, ed. Andrew Gurr and Farah Karim-Cooper (Cambridge: Cambridge University Press, 2014), pp. 65–78
Jowett, John, 'Henry Chettle and the First Quarto of *Romeo and Juliet*', *The Papers of the Bibliographical Society of America*, 92 (1998), 53–74
Jowitt, Claire, *Voyage Drama and Gender Politics, 1589–1642: Real and Imagined Worlds* (Manchester: Manchester University Press, 2003)
Keenan, Siobhan, *Acting Companies and their Plays in Shakespeare's London* (London: Bloomsbury, 2014)
Keilen, Sean, 'Jonson', in *The Oxford History of Classical Reception in English Literature, Volume 2: 1558–1660*, ed. Patrick Cheney and Philip Hardie (Oxford: Oxford University Press, 2015), pp. 621–40

Kingsley-Smith, Jane, *Cupid in Early Modern Literature and Culture* (Cambridge: Cambridge University Press, 2010)

Kirwan, Peter, '*The Tragedy of Hoffman* @ Magdalen College, Oxford', The Bardathon, http://blogs.warwick.ac.uk/pkirwan/entry/the_tragedy_of/ (accessed 30 August 2020)

Knutson, Roslyn Lander, 'The Adult Companies and the Dynamics of Commerce', in *Thomas Middleton in Context*, ed. Suzanne Gossett (Cambridge: Cambridge University Press, 2011), pp. 168–76

— 'Henslowe's Diary and the Economics of Play Revision for Revival, 1592–1603', *Theatre Research International*, 10 (1985), 1–17

— *Playing Companies and Commerce in Shakespeare's Time* (Cambridge: Cambridge University Press, 2001)

— *The Repertory of Shakespeare's Company, 1594–1613* (Fayetteville: University of Arkansas Press, 1991)

Lazarus, Micah, 'Aristotelian Criticism in Sixteenth-Century England', in *Oxford Handbooks Online* (Oxford: Oxford University Press, 2016), DOI: 10.1093/oxfordhb/9780199935338.013.148

Lesser, Zachary, *Renaissance Drama and the Politics of Publication: Readings in the English Book Trade* (Cambridge: Cambridge University Press, 2004)

— 'Walter Burre's *The Knight of the Burning Pestle*', *English Literary Renaissance*, 29 (1999), 22–43

Levin, Richard, 'Women in the Renaissance Theatre Audience', *Shakespeare Quarterly*, 40 1989), 165–74

Lopez, Jeremy, 'Time for James Shirley', in *James Shirley and Early Modern Theatre: New Critical Perspectives*, ed. Barbara Ravelhofer (Abingdon: Routledge, 2017), pp. 17–31

Lucow, Ben, *James Shirley* (Boston: Twayne Publishers, 1981)

The Map of Early Modern London, ed. Janelle Jenstad (Victoria, BC: University of Victoria), http://mapoflondon.uvic.ca/COCK5.htm (accessed 4 September 2023)

Martin, Peter, *Edmond Malone, Shakespearean Scholar: A Literary Biography* (Cambridge: Cambridge University Press, 1995)

Matusiak, Christopher M., 'The Beestons and the Art of Theatrical Management in Seventeenth-Century London', unpublished PhD thesis, University of Toronto, 2009

McInnis, David, and Mathew Steggle, *Lost Plays in Shakespeare's England* (Basingstoke: Palgrave Macmillan, 2014)

McLuskie, K. E., *Dekker and Heywood* (Basingstoke: Macmillan, 1994)

— 'Figuring the Consumer for Early Modern Drama', in *Rematerialising Shakespeare: Authority and Representation on the Early Modern Stage*, ed. Bryan Reynolds and William N. West (Basingstoke: Palgrave Macmillan, 2005), pp. 186–206

— 'Politics and Aesthetic Pleasure in 1630s Theater', in *Localizing Caroline Drama: Politics and Economics of the Early Modern Stage, 1625–1642*, ed. Adam Zucker and Alan B. Farmer (Basingstoke: Palgrave Macmillan, 2006), pp. 43–68

— 'The Plays and the Playwrights: 1613–42', in *The Revels History of Drama in English, Volume IV: 1613–1660*, ed. Philip Edwards et al. (London: Methuen, 1981), pp. 127–260

McLuskie, K. E., and Rebecca Rogers, 'Who Invested in Early Modern Theatre?', *Research Opportunities in Renaissance Drama*, XLI (2002), 29–61

McMillin, Scott, and Sally Beth Maclean, *The Queen's Men and their Plays* (Cambridge: Cambridge University Press, 1998)

Miles, Theodore, 'Place-Realism in a Group of Caroline Plays', *Review of English Studies*, 18 (1942), 428–40

Morrah, Patrick, *Restoration England* (London: Constable, 1979)

Morton, Richard, 'Deception and Social Dislocation: An Aspect of James Shirley's Drama', *Renaissance Drama*, 9 (1966), 227–45

Munro, Lucy, *Archaic Style in English Literature, 1590–1674* (Cambridge: Cambridge University Press, 2013)

— *Children of the Queen's Revels: A Jacobean Theatre Repertory* (Cambridge: Cambridge University Press, 2005)

— 'The Queen and the Cockpit: Henrietta Maria's Theatrical Patronage Revisited', *Shakespeare Bulletin*, 37.1 (2019), 25–45

— '"They Eat Each Other's Arms": Stage Blood and Body Parts', in *Shakespeare's Theatres and the Effects of Performance*, ed. Farah Karim-Cooper and Tiffany Stern (London: Bloomsbury, 2013), pp. 73–93

Nicol, David, 'The Title-Page of *The World Tossed at Tennis*: A Portrait of a Jacobean Playing Company?', *Notes and Queries*, 53.2 (2006), 158–9

O'Connell, Michael, *The Idolatrous Eye: Iconoclasm and Theater in Early Modern England* (New York: Oxford University Press, 2000)

Orgel, Stephen, 'The Poetics of Spectacle', *New Literary History*, 21 (1971), 367–89

Oxford Dictionary of National Biography, https://www.oxforddnb.com

Palfrey, Simon, and Tiffany Stern, *Shakespeare in Parts* (Oxford: Oxford University Press, 2007)

Payne, Deborah C., 'Patronage and the Dramatic Marketplace under Charles I and II', *Yearbook of English Studies*, 21 (1991), 137–52

Peacey, Jason, 'Pamphlets', in *The Oxford History of Popular Print Culture, Volume 1: Cheap Print in Britain and Ireland to 1660*, ed. Joad Raymond (Oxford: Oxford University Press, 2011), pp. 453–70

Price, Eoin, *'Public' and 'Private' Playhouses in Renaissance England: The Politics of Publication* (Basingstoke: Palgrave Macmillan, 2015)

Rappaport, Steve, *Worlds Within Worlds: Structures of Life in Sixteenth-Century London* (Cambridge: Cambridge University Press, 1989)

Ravelhofer, Barbara (ed.), *James Shirley and Early Modern Theatre: New Critical Perspectives* (Abingdon: Routledge, 2017)

Reynolds, G. F., *The Staging of Elizabethan Plays at the Red Bull Theater, 1605–1625* (New York: Modern Language Association of America, 1940)

Rider, Philip P., 'The Concurrent Printing of Shirley's *The Wittie Fair One* and *The Bird in a Cage*', *Papers of the Bibliographical Society of America*, 71 (1977), 328–33

Riemer, A. P., 'Shirley's Revisions and the Date of *The Constant Maid*', *Review of English Studies*, 17 (1966), 141–8

Robinson, Benedict Scott, 'Thomas Heywood and the Cultural Politics of Play Collections', *Studies in English Literature, 1500–1900*, 42 (2002), 361–80

Rowland, Richard, *Thomas Heywood's Theatre, 1599–1639: Locations, Translations, and Conflict* (Farnham: Ashgate, 2010)

Ryner, Bradley D., 'Narratives of Value in Richard Brome's Dispute with the Salisbury Court', *Early Theatre*, 23.2 (2020), 79–94

Sager, Jenny, *The Aesthetics of Spectacle in Early Modern Drama and Modern Cinema: Robert Greene's Theatre of Attractions* (Basingstoke: Palgrave Macmillan, 2013)

Salkeld, Duncan, 'Literary Traces in Bridewell and Bethlem, 1602–1624', *The Review of English Studies*, 56 (2005), 379–85

Sanders, Julie, '"The Day's Sports Devised in the Inn": Jonson's *The New Inn* and Theatrical Politics', *Modern Language Review*, 91 (1996), 545–60

— '"A Woman Write a Play!": Jonsonian Strategies and the Dramatic Writings of Margaret Cavendish; or, did the Duchess Feel the Anxiety of Influence', in *Readings in Renaissance Women's Drama*, ed. S. P. Cerasano and Marion Wynne-Davies (London: Routledge, 1998), pp. 293–305

Schneider, Brian, *The Framing Text in Early Modern English Drama: 'Whining' Prologues and 'Armed' Epilogues* (Abingdon: Routledge, 2011)

Shady, Raymond C., 'The Stage History of Heywood's *Love's Mistress*', *Theatre Survey*, 18 (1997), 86–95

Sisson, Charles J., *The Boar's Head Theatre: An Inn-yard Theatre of the Elizabethan Age* (London: Routledge and Kegan Paul, 1972)

— 'Notes on Early Stuart Stage History', *The Modern Language Review*, 37 (1942), 25–36

— 'The Red Bull Company and the Importunate Widow', *Shakespeare Survey*, 7 (1954), 57–68

Slack, Paul, *The Impact of Plague in Tudor and Stuart England* (Oxford: Oxford University Press, 1985)

Smith, Helen, and Louise Wilson (eds), *Renaissance Paratexts* (Cambridge: Cambridge University Press, 2011)

Smith, Simon, 'Acting Amiss: Towards a History of Actorly Craft and Playhouse Judgement', *Shakespeare Quarterly*, 70 (2017), 188–99

Steggle, Matthew, *Richard Brome: Place and Politics on the Caroline Stage* (Manchester: Manchester University Press, 2004)

— *Wars of the Theatres: The Poetics of Personation in the Age of Jonson* (Victoria, BC: University of Victoria Department of English, 1998)

Stern, Tiffany, *Documents of Performance in Early Modern England* (Cambridge: Cambridge University Press, 2009)

— '"On each Wall and Corner Poast": Playbills, Title-pages, and Advertising in Early Modern London', *English Literary Renaissance*, 36 (2006), 57–89

— '"A ruinous monastery": The Second Blackfriars Playhouse as a Place of Nostalgia', in *Moving Shakespeare Indoors: Performance and Repertoire* in the Jacobean Playhouse, ed. Andrew Gurr and Farah Karim-Cooper (Cambridge: Cambridge University Press, 2014), pp. 97–114

— 'A Small-Beer Health to his Second Day: Playwrights, Prologues, and First Performances in the Early Modern Theater', Studies in Philology, 101 (2004), 172–99

Stevenson, Allan H., 'Shirley's Publishers: The Partnership of Crooke and Cooke', The Library, 4ᵗʰ series, 25 (1944–45), 140–61

Straznicky, Marta, 'The Red Bull Repertory in Print, 1604–60', Early Theatre, 9.2 (2006), 144–56

Thomas, Keith, Religion and the Decline of Magic (London: Penguin, 1971)

Traister, Barbara H., 'Magic and the Decline of Demons: A View of the Stage', in Magical Transformations on the Early Modern English Stage, ed. Lisa Hopkins and Helen Ostovich (Farnham: Ashgate, 2014), pp. 19–30

Tribble, Evelyn, Early Modern Actors and Shakespeare's Theatre (London: Bloomsbury, 2017)

Walker, Kim, 'New Prison: Representing the Female Actor in Shirley's The Bird in a Cage (1633)', English Literary Renaissance, 21 (1991), 385–400

Wallace, C. W., 'Three London Theatres of Shakespeare's Time', Nebraska University Studies, IX (1909), 287–342

Wallace, Joseph, 'Wandering Eyes: Jonson's Catiline and the Problem of Sight', Renaissance Drama, 41 (2013), 85–106

Watkins, John, Representing Elizabeth in Stuart England (Cambridge: Cambridge University Press, 2002)

Weimann, Robert, Shakespeare and the Popular Tradition in the Theater, ed. Robert Schwartz (Baltimore, MD: Johns Hopkins University Press, 1978)

Weimann, Robert and Douglas Bruster, Shakespeare and the Power of Performance: Stage and Page in the Elizabethan Theatre (Cambridge: Cambridge University Press, 2008)

Werstine, Paul, Early Modern Playhouse Manuscripts and the Editing of Shakespeare (Cambridge: Cambridge University Press, 2015)

West, William N., 'Replaying Early Modern Performances', in New Directions in Renaissance Drama and Performance Studies, ed. Sarah Werner (Basingstoke: Palgrave Macmillan, 2010), pp. 30–50

White, Martin, 'By Indirections Find Directions Out: Unpicking Early Modern Stage Directions', in Stage Directions and Shakespearean Theatre, ed. Sarah Dustagheer and Gillian Woods (London: Bloomsbury, 2018), pp. 191–212

— Renaissance Drama in Action (London: Routledge, 1998)

— '"When Torchlight made an Artificial Noon": Light and Darkness in the Indoor Jacobean Theatre', in Moving Shakespeare Indoors: Performance and Repertoire in the Jacobean Playhouse, ed. Andrew Gurr and Farah Karim-Cooper (Cambridge: Cambridge University Press, 2014), pp. 115–36

Wickham, Glynne, Early English Stages, 1300–1660, 3 vols (London: Routledge, 1959–81)

Wickham, Glynne, Herbert Berry, and William Ingram (eds), English Professional Theatre, 1530–1660 (Cambridge: Cambridge University Press, 2000)

Wiggins, Martin, in association with Catherine Richardson, *British Drama,*
  1533–1642: A Catalogue (Oxford: Oxford University Press, 2011–)
Wiles, David, *Shakespeare's Clown: Actor and Text in the Elizabethan Playhouse*
  (Cambridge: Cambridge University Press, 1987)
Wood, Christopher S., and Alexander Nagel, *Anachronic Renaissance* (New
  York: Zone Books, 2010)
Woods, Penelope, 'Shakespeare's Globe Audiences: Old and New', in *The*
  Cambridge Guide to the Worlds of Shakespeare, Vol. 2: 'The World's
  Shakespeare, 1660 to the Present', ed. Bruce R. Smith and Katherine Rowe
  (Cambridge: Cambridge University Press, 2016), pp. 1538–44
Zucker, Adam, and Alan B. Farmer (eds), *Localizing Caroline Drama: Politics*
  and Economics of the Early Modern Stage, 1625–1642 (Basingstoke: Palgrave
  Macmillan, 2006)

INDEX

EU authorised representative for GPSR:
Easy Access System Europe, Mustamäe tee 50,
10621 Tallinn, Estonia
gpsr.requests@easproject.com

www.ingramcontent.com/pod-product-compliance
Lightning Source LLC
LaVergne TN
LVHW011708060226
831107LV00004B/158